Under Fire

Under Fire

Essex and the
Second World War
1939–1945

by Paul Rusiecki

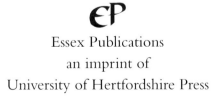

Essex Publications
an imprint of
University of Hertfordshire Press

First published in Great Britain in 2015 by
Essex Publications
an imprint of
University of Hertfordshire Press
College Lane
Hatfield
Hertfordshire
AL10 9AB

British Library Cataloguing in Publication Data
A catalogue record for this book is available from the
British Library

ISBN 978–1–909291–28–7

Design by Arthouse Publishing Solutions Ltd
Printed in Great Britain by Charlesworth Press

For my children, Marcus Paul and Helen Elizabeth
and my grandson, Samuel James

Publication has been made possible by a
generous grant from the Essex branch of the
Historical Association (www.history.org.uk)

Contents

List of illustrations   viii

Select abbreviations   xi

Acknowledgements   xiii

Introduction   1

1   War, Phoney War and disaster   8

2   Nightmares come true: the Blitz   35

3   Fortress Essex   64

4   Popular protest   127

5   Second front   142

6   Carrying on   177

7   Criminals, conchies and clergymen   215

8   Doodlebugs, rockets and victory   254

Bibliography   289

Index   300

Illustrations

Maps

1   Essex during the Second World War   *xii*
2   Essex and the Continent   *2*
3   Group 7   *36*
4   Map showing where V-1/V-2s landed in the
     Chelmsford ARP area 1944–5   *267*

Figures

1.1   St Angela's school, evacuated to Cornwall (Newham
       Heritage & Archives)   *13*
1.2   The 'Searchlight Café', on the beach on Mersea Island
       (Mersea Museum/Keith Lee)   *23*
1.3   Signposts placed in a field as obstructions against enemy
       gliders (Imperial War Museum)   *24*
1.4   Clacton evacuees (Essex Record Office)   *29*
1.5   Mortar section of the 18th Battalion of the Essex Home
       Guard (Mersea Museum/Ron Green)   *32*
2.1   Devastation caused by German minelaying aircraft in
       Clacton, 1940 (Paul Rusiecki)   *37*
2.2   Downed Luftwaffe pilot at Shoeburyness railway station,
       1940 (Essex Record Office)   *39*
2.3   Waker air-raid shelter in Dagenham (London Borough of
       Barking & Dagenham Archives and Local Studies Centre)   *40*
2.4   'Gilman's Dare Devils' (Newham Heritage & Archives)   *43*
2.5a Extracts from the Blitz diary of William Riddiford (Part 1)
       (London Borough of Barking & Dagenham Archives
       and Local Studies Centre)   *48*

2.5b Extracts from the Blitz diary of William Riddiford (Part 2)
(London Borough of Barking & Dagenham Archives
and Local Studies Centre)   48

2.6   South Hallsville School after the disaster of September 1940
(Newham Heritage & Archives)   55

3.1   Road barriers at Woodford Wells (Imperial War Museum)   68

3.2   George VI watching Essex Home Guard training (Essex
Record Office)   70

3.3   Colchester Wings for Victory Week, 1943 (Essex Society for
Archaeology & History)   71

3.4   Launch of minesweeper J537 at Wivenhoe (Mersea Museum/
Leo Michael Smith)   79

3.5   An anti-aircraft gun on the Crittall's factory (BRNTM
2012.1089.6, Braintree District Museum Trust)   81

3.6   Female wardens at an incident post in Waltham Holy Cross
(Waltham Abbey Historical Society)   90

3.7   Mary Page, Women's Land Army (BRNTM 2014.869.2,
Braintree District Museum Trust)   96

3.8   Women's Land Army volunteers on a tractor (Mersea
Museum/David Green)   96

3.9   Advertisement for rat control measure (Essex
Farmers' Journal)   112

4.1   Tom Driberg (Maldon Constituency Labour Party)   129

4.2   Driberg's campaign leaflet on Tobruk (Maldon Constituency
Labour Party)   135

5.1   US servicemen and children of Lindsell Primary School, near
Dunmow (Essex Record Office)   155

5.2   The Hoffmann ball-bearing factory at Chelmsford, 1940
(Essex Record Office)   164

6.1   Secondary school evacuees in Hatfield Peverel classroom
(Essex Record Office)   184

6.2   Evacuee certificate (BRNTM 2010.237, Braintree District
Museum Trust)   186

6.3   Radio listeners in a pub in Springfield, near Chelmsford
(Imperial War Museum)   196

6.4   Colchester Repertory Company's production of *French without
tears*, 1940 (Essex Record Office)   201

7.1 Diagram outlining the investigation of a molasses theft in
     Holehaven, 1941   *220*
7.2 Conscientious objectors undergoing training (Imperial
     War Museum)   *234*
8.1 Prefabs at Dagenham (Barking and Dagenham Archive and
     Local Studies Centre)   *258*
8.2 Female wardens digging out an incendiary bomb
     (Waltham Abbey Historical Society)   *261*
8.3 Railway damage by a V-1 at Stratford (Newham
     Heritage & Archives)   *266*
8.4 Smoke from a V-1 explosion in Sewardstone (Waltham
     Abbey Historical Society)   *269*
8.5 Devastation caused by a V-2 in Waltham Holy Cross
     (Waltham Abbey Historical Society)   *274*
8.6 The rescue of Mrs K. Peck, Waltham Holy Cross
     (Waltham Abbey Historical Society)   *275*
8.7 Effigy of Hitler on a VE Day bonfire (Essex
     Police Museum)   *282*
8.8 VE Day bonfire lit (Essex Police Museum)   *283*
8.9 Witham VE Day parade (BRNTM NEG 4240, Braintree
     District Museum Trust)   *284*

Select abbreviations

AA	anti-aircraft
AEU	Amalgamated Engineering Union
ARP	air-raid precautions
ATS	Auxiliary Territorial Service
BA	*Burnham Advertiser*
BEF	British Expeditionary Force
BT	*Billericay Times*
BUF	British Union of Fascists
CBC	Colchester Borough Council
CDC	Chelmsford Diocesan Chronicle
CEPS	Church of England Primary School
ChBC	Chelmsford Borough Council
CLSL	Colchester Local Studies Library
CPS	County Primary School
EC	*Essex Chronicle*
ECC	Essex County Council
ECS	*Essex County Standard*
ECT	*Essex County Telegraph*
EFCPA	Essex Farmers' and Country People's Association
EFJ	*Essex Farmers' Journal*
EJSC	Essex Joint Standing Committee
ENSA	Entertainment National Service Association
ERO	Essex Record Office
EWAC	Essex War Agricultural Committee
IWM	Imperial War Museum
LDV	Local Defence Volunteers
LNER	London and North Eastern Railway
MOA	Mass Observation Archive
NFU	National Farmers' Union
PCC	Parochial Church Council
RCS	Roman Catholic School
RDC	Rural District Council

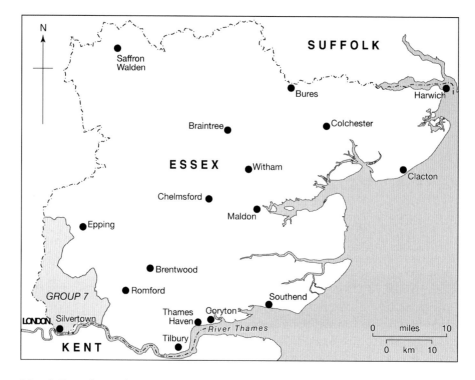

Map 1. Essex during the Second World War.

SE	*Stratford Express*
SSt	*Southend Standard*
ST	*Southend Times*
TNA	The National Archives
UDC	Urban District Council
USAAF	United States Army Air Force
UXB	unexploded bomb
VCH	*Victoria County History of Essex*
WLA	Women's Land Army
WT	*Woodford Times*
WVS	Women's Voluntary Service

Acknowledgements

Many people have helped to bring this book to fruition. First and foremost I would like to thank my friend Dr Chris Thornton. He gave up a considerable amount of his own time and work to read the entire typescript and, as chairman of the Essex Publications editorial panel, made many helpful suggestions which have undoubtedly improved this work. It was he, too, who first suggested that the University of Hertfordshire Press might be interested in publishing my work. His contribution has been invaluable. I should also like to thank the other members of the editorial panel, Shirley Durgan, Dr Herbert Eiden and Dr Jane Pearson.

Jane Housham guided the book through all the pitfalls of publishing once UH Press took the project on board. Her wise advice and calm encouragement have been a great source of comfort and inspiration to me.

I owe particular thanks to Shirley Durgan, one of the editorial panel and Chairman of the Essex branch of the Historical Association, and the rest of the branch committee, for their support and encouragement, and for a generous financial grant which both enabled me to obtain images from the Imperial War Museum and funded the cost of the book's launch at the Essex Record Office.

As ever, I owe a huge debt to the staff of the Essex Record Office, who, over the years I have spent researching this book, have invariably been helpful, knowledgeable and kind. The archivists made it possible for me to have access to materials which I would not otherwise have been able to use. The staff at the libraries at Colchester, Chelmsford, Southend and Stratford have helped in so many ways. I am grateful to the staff at the Mass Observation Archive, the National Archives and the Imperial War Museum for their helpfulness and courtesy, and to both the trustees of the Imperial War Museum and the individual copyright holders for allowing me access to the collections of papers held by the Museum and for permission to publish extracts from them. While every effort has been made to locate the owners of copyright material, in some cases this has not proved possible.

Cath D'Alton used her marvellous computer skills to produce all the wonderful maps and the police investigation chart. I will be eternally grateful to Chris Thornton and also Neil Wiffen of the Essex Record Office for pointing me in her direction when I was in need of an excellent cartographer.

As with my book on Essex and the Great War, it was a great joy that my son Marcus worked alongside me on some of the key research at the Imperial War Museum's Department of Documents, the Essex Record Office and Southend Central Library, where my wife Julie also joined us. Julie also had the dubious pleasure of spending four nights in wintry Brighton as we did research at the Mass Observation Archive at the University of Sussex. Although a historian, the twentieth century is far from her favourite period and this was undoubtedly above and beyond the call of marital duty.

The family of Eric Rudsdale have very kindly allowed me to reproduce extracts from his journals. David Bloomfield very generously loaned me a copy of his unpublished typescript on his family's transport business. Janet Grove was kind enough to send me a copy of the book of her father's air-raid precautions (ARP) diary and, subsequently, supplied me with the negatives of the illustrations in it for me to use. Jean Nightingale allowed me to use a letter written by her mother Mabel Jervis, while Pat Lewis let me use the diary of her mother, Evelyn Jessie Grubb, née Potter. Pat was also helpful in arranging for me to interview her mother, Patricia Clayden and Arthur Atterbury about their wartime experiences.

Last of all my thanks go to my wife Julie, who has endured my perennial obsession with two world wars with patience, forbearance and much love. To her I owe everything.

Introduction

The last year of peace

By the autumn of 1938 the people of Essex had become accustomed to thinking that a new war was looming. The aggressions of Japan and Italy, the Spanish Civil War and Hitler's violations of the Treaty of Versailles had made the world a more unstable place. In September 1938, as a result of Hitler's demands on the Czech Sudetenland, a new European conflict loomed. 'How can anybody blame the Sudeten Germans for wishing to rejoin their fellow countrymen?' wrote the curator of Colchester Castle, Eric Rudsdale.[1] His opinion was shared by many people in Essex. The *Essex Chronicle*, which had consistently supported appeasement, felt that Czechoslovakia was not worth fighting for. Its view was that territorial concessions to Germany would not warrant 'the loss of a single British soldier or the desolation of a single British home'.[2] Therefore, the Munich agreement was celebrated throughout Essex. W.S. Deavin of Burnham wrote a poem praising Chamberlain as an international hero:

> For all your services to mankind and peace,
> For all our feelings of intense relief,
> For all your bold initiative and sense,
> For all that helped us in our dire suspense,
> We thank you, sir.[3]

The *Chronicle* noted that Chamberlain's policy 'cannot be called glorious or magnificent, but it is at least wise and prudent'.[4] However, these feelings were not shared by everyone. One correspondent of the *Burnham Advertiser* wrote, 'On Sunday I was in church trying to be thankful for something or other. I thought I was expected to thank God my skin had been kept safe from

---

1   ERO D/DU 888/20, journal, 10 September 1938.
2   EC 18 March 1938.
3   BA 8 October 1938.
4   EC 30 September 1938.

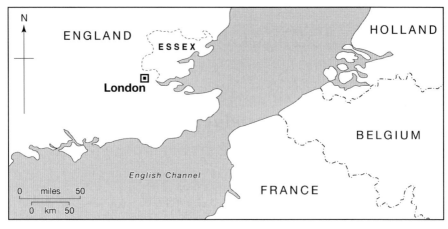

Map 2. Essex and the Continent

suffering and from hardships as a result of enormous sacrifice by the Czechs ...
I wanted to be sick.'[5]

In March 1939, only six months after he had annexed the Sudetenland,
Hitler's troops marched into Prague and destroyed the Czech state. It was clear
that he had fooled Chamberlain and that his word could not be trusted. Those
Essex residents who had opposed the Munich settlement felt vindicated. W.J.
Hughes of Colchester raged:

> Will they listen now – the people who would not believe when we
> told them months, years ago the things that are happening in Europe
> today ... What do we others see now? This. That the fight against us
> has long ago begun ... It may not be too late yet to prevent the almost
> inevitable.[6]

Chelmsford's Conservative MP, Jack Macnamara, lamented that:

> 'Some of us have seen this coming along for a long time ... It is
> Germany's wish to dominate and she will not be satisfied until she can
> dominate, not merely a neighbouring state, but far, far wider.'[7]

Hitler now made demands on Poland, and Chamberlain guaranteed that
country's territorial integrity. In the summer of 1939 war grew closer and
preparations for war, started but immediately abandoned after Munich, went

5   BA 8 October 1938.
6   ECS 25 March 1939.
7   EC 24 March 1939.

2

on apace. Those wishing to avoid war, even by making further concessions to Hitler, maintained the position they had adopted over the Sudetenland. The *Chronicle* asserted that 'The Germans have some sort of a case, and it is not practical politics to refuse to consider an adversary's partly reasonable claim through fear that it may be followed by demands wholly unreasonable.'[8] Even the *Essex County Telegraph*, which had opposed appeasement, urged an eleventh hour diplomatic solution which offered 'security for posterity'.[9]

Germany's invasion of Poland destroyed all hopes of security. Blackout regulations came into force. The *Essex County Telegraph* urged its readers to 'Pray and Stand Fast'.[10] At Romford Girls' School the staff listened to the news bulletins all through Friday 1 September. A young pupil teacher noted that 'Everyone was terribly grave and most eyes were on the ceiling.'[11] On Saturday the Essex crime novelist Margery Allingham spent the day placing three hundredweight of old books against her downstairs windows as air-raid protection. She recalled how she strolled in her garden mulling over her thoughts:

> This time everything has been thought over so much that there was not that muddle of ideas which is excitement's staple ingredient, and you could see your section of civilisation, the bit that you had helped to build for better or worse, cracking and splitting and crumbling as the shell hit it.[12]

Not knowing of the Government's ultimatum to Germany on the previous day, she and many others went to bed that night fearing the worst.

Essex voices and the war

Just as the extracts above illustrate the thoughts of Essex people on the eve of the outbreak of war, this book attempts to convey something of the experiences of Essex people on the Home Front during the Second World War. Its writing has been made possible by the enormous range of source material that is now available to the historian. Much of this body of evidence was produced by residents of the county, and a major aim of the book has been to place the authentic voices of those who lived through the conflict at the very heart of the account.

---

8   EC 5 May 1939.
9   ECT 17 June 1939.
10   ECT 2 September 1939.
11   Quoted in D. Sheridan, *Wartime women: a mass-observation anthology: the experiences of women at war* (London, 1990), p. 51.
12   M. Allingham, *The oaken heart* (London, 1941), p. 74.

The diaries, journals and letters of Essex residents provide invaluable insights into the opinions of a variety of individuals. The journals of Eric Rudsdale,[13] for example, express opinions that are often at variance with popular opinion, such as his opposition to the Allied bombing of Germany or his distaste for the influx of foreign servicemen. On the other hand, the diaries of Ernest Edwards,[14] written in 1940–41, are profoundly patriotic and jingoistic, and unwaveringly optimistic about the prospects of victory. Those of Joan Wright,[15] a young farm labourer, reveal something of the hidden side of the war, as she writes about her dangerous liaisons with Italian prisoners of war. Even a solitary letter can be helpful. That of Lucy Weald,[16] the wife of the stationmaster at Chelmsford, provides a glimpse of the hectic activity over the weekend that war was declared.

The terrible ordeal of the county at the hands of the Luftwaffe meant that the Blitz and later raids were paramount in people's wartime recollections. In this respect Essex is fortunate to have many well-written and thorough accounts of the impact of German bombing, often written by leading Civil Defence officials. These accounts were invariably written as a tribute to local citizens who had been affected by bombing raids, both victims and survivors. One example will suffice to convey these authors' aims. Glyn Richards' *Ordeal in Romford* (1945) was intended to record the borough's trials as a 'front-line town' and 'to produce good from evil'. Richards added that 'This publication will have been justified if it serves but to commemorate the 143 civilians (the majority of them women and children) who lost their lives as a result of the enemy's indiscriminate attacks upon our home town.' These books are excellent accounts of German air attacks, although the social impact of the war was generally not part of their authors' agenda.

Not all wartime publications focused exclusively on air raids. In *The oaken heart* (1941), Margery Allingham's wonderful account of the early years of the war, her village, Tolleshunt D'Arcy, was disguised as the fictitious village of Auburn. Her book is superbly reflective about the events and emotions of these years and provides the best contemporary account of life in Essex in wartime. Hervey Benham's *Essex at war* (1946), although not as elegant or thoughtful as Allingham's work, provides an account of life in north Essex that was probably based on information printed in the *Essex County Standard*, which he owned.

To corroborate these accounts the historian can rely on a vast range of materials produced by the Civil Defence services, most of which are found in the Essex Record Office. They range from reports written on the morning

13   ERO D/DU 888; there are several volumes of his journals.
14   ERO S3150.
15   ERO A12799.
16   ERO T/B 416/1.

after raids to hand-written communications produced at the very height of an attack, detailing developments on an almost minute-by-minute basis. Although they are very practical documents, and were certainly not produced with future historians in mind, they do portray life during that ordeal in ways that are intensely vivid and, at times, remarkably moving.

We can also draw on unofficial sources produced by eyewitnesses. Doreen Idle's book *War over West Ham*, published in 1943, was based upon her own experiences as an investigative reporter in the London borough of West Ham in 1941–42. She was a first-class observer and commentator and she saw at first-hand both the administrative chaos in the aftermath of the Blitz and the borough's struggle to rebuild its social and economic life. The journalist Ritchie Calder experienced the horrors of the first days of the Blitz in the area and, in his book *The lesson of London* (1941), he described his desperate attempt to prevent the worst disaster that took place in Essex during the war, that at South Hallsville School, from happening.

A group of sources without which this book would have been very hard to write is Essex's newspapers. Their pages are packed full of the minutiae of everyday life during the war, from air raids to farming, from social activities in towns and villages to the huge variety of jobs done by women. Some, such as the Liberal *Essex County Telegraph* and the Conservative *Essex Chronicle*, provided a weekly editorial outlining the owners' views on key domestic and foreign issues. The former, with its nonconformist viewpoint, referred to Hitler throughout the war as the 'Anti-Christ' and advocated pursuing the war with unremitting ruthlessness. Nevertheless, in spite of their political differences, their views coincided on a whole range of wartime issues such as the Beveridge Report in 1942. Their letters pages, moreover, are extremely helpful in revealing how Essex residents responded to both local and national controversies, as well as allowing the historian to monitor people's views on practically every aspect of the war. When used with care and in conjunction with other unofficial sources they allow the historian to flesh out wartime life in a very personal manner. The very depth of material forces the historian to be selective, and a mere fraction of what was discovered has been included in this book.

The Essex Sound Archive at the Essex Record Office contains recordings of the memories of people who lived in Essex during the war. They complement many other sources, including official records, by outlining what the person recalled of their experiences, often in great detail. Most of the recordings were made half a century after the war and for that reason any factual claims made do have to be verified by checking contemporary records.

The Mass Observation Archive at the University of Sussex also contains a wealth of contemporary information, including much that is relevant to Essex.

The diaries, boxes of material and directive replies (replies to questionnaires which were sent out to their respondents) are particularly helpful as they shed light on people's attitudes on a range of topics, such as Americans and other nationalities, evacuation, food shortages and sexual behaviour during wartime, to name but a few. The Imperial War Museum contains the correspondence of people who experienced the war in Essex. They included Moyra Charlton, who, as a member of the Auxiliary Territorial Service (ATS), was evacuated from France and subsequently recalled her thoughts as she faced the possibility of invasion. Mrs J.L. Stevens, a Land Army girl, provides us with an account of the problems of farm labouring. The firemen T.H. Pointer and F.W. Hurd gallantly fought the Blitz in Metropolitan Essex. All have left us with their written memories, some produced at the time.

The secondary works used to write this book are too many to mention in this brief survey. They include Angus Calder's ground-breaking national study *The people's war* (1969) and the comprehensive account by Juliet Gardiner, *Wartime: Britain 1939–1945*. There are no detailed accounts of the war encompassing the whole county, but, on the other hand, hardly a village or town in Essex does not possess a book devoted to the war, or one which has at least a chapter on it. These often include the testimonies of participants. One of the most recently published is Jacqueline Cooper's admirable *Clavering at war 1939–45* (2012). Similarly, many books and articles have shed light on individual aspects of the county's experience of war. P. Finch's *Warmen courageous: the story of the Essex Home Guard* details the story of the county's Home Guard from its inception to its disbandment. Marjorie Geere's *Reminiscences of a Land Girl in Witham* is a lively account of the joys and hardships experienced by these women. J. Foynes' *Under the white ensign: Brightlingsea and the sea war 1939–1945* outlines the contribution made by this small port to the war effort. G. Godwin's *Marconi 1939–45: a war record* and Hilary St George Saunders' *Ford at war* are insightful studies of these industrial giants' part in the county's war effort. Both are immensely detailed on the production side of the war, although the latter is also helpful for anyone wishing to learn about the company's workforce. One of the county's most flamboyant figures during the war, Tom Driberg MP, wrote a warts-and-all autobiography, *Ruling passions*, which is very useful on the Maldon by-election. Even modest sporting organisations recorded their experience of war, as in, for instance, J. Wise's *The story of the Blackwater Sailing Club* and K. Warden and M. Williams' *Chelmsford Golf Club 1893–1993*. The struggle facing women who sought to make a full contribution to the war effort is explained in J. Wilkinson's excellent article 'Women at war: the provision of childcare in Second World War Chelmsford'.

Another major aim of this book has been to produce a synthesis of contemporary and later material in order to produce an in-depth account of

Essex during the Second World War. In this endeavour all these types of source have been helpful in some way. The author is also particularly indebted to those who pointed the way to further lines of enquiry and subsequent discoveries. Much material has been included and much omitted, but the endnotes and bibliography will point the reader towards any part of the county's war that they may be interested in.

1

War, Phoney War and disaster

The declaration of war

On Sunday 3 September the BBC announced that the prime minister, Neville Chamberlain, would broadcast to the nation at 11.15am. With no sign of Hitler halting his invasion of Poland two days earlier, few people could have been under any illusions about what Chamberlain would say. In Essex, as throughout the country, families gathered around their wireless sets at home or arranged communal gatherings.[1] Barbara Kaye, of Takeley Street, unable to bear the tension, went to the village hall. She found it half filled with rows of chairs facing the platform, on which had been placed a portable wireless on a card table.[2] At Rayleigh, the rector, A.C. Souter, set up a wireless on the chancel steps and interrupted the service to switch it on when Chamberlain's broadcast began.[3] The Rev. John Muir Elliott recalled how, at Westcliff, he and his congregation braced themselves for the final minutes of peace:

> Accordingly we installed a wireless set in Church, and began our service at 11 o'clock, we gave ourselves first to Penitence and Confession, then to Thanksgiving for all God's past mercies, and then to awaiting the soul-stirring pronouncement in calm readiness for whatever it might be.[4]

Two young girls in Grays attended Mass and heard the siren when they came out:

> A man comes by on a bike, 'Get home, quick, there's a war on … Hurry up home and get into your air raid shelter!' It scared the living daylights out of us. Poor Joan, she was three and a half, and we were dragging her along the road, feet hardly touching the ground.[5]

---

1 See J. Gardiner, *Wartime: Britain 1939–1945* (London, 2004) pp. 2–6, and V. Nicholson, *Millions like us: women's lives in war and peace 1939–49* (London, 2011), pp. 16–21.
2 B. Kaye, *The company we kept* (London, 1986), p. 61.
3 EC 8 September 1939.
4 ERO D/P 557/28/4, parish news bulletin, October 1939.
5 ERO SA 1/455/1, BBC Radio Essex broadcast, 'Essex at War, Christmas Under Fire', 1989.

At Stubbers, near South Ockenden, Pamela Russell went off to church with her Sunday school charges as usual:

> About halfway through the service an anxious parent rushed in and withdrew its children, but we sang lustily on. I collected a car-load and knowing war must be declared, was for hurrying home, we then heard the wailing of the 'all clear' raid signal and realised that in the throes of hymn singing and organ grinding we had missed the first air raid warning![6]

Lucy Weald, the wife of Chelmsford's stationmaster, listened to the broadcast in her husband's office during a break from working with evacuees: 'I felt very sorry for poor Mr Chamberlain,' she wrote to her daughter. 'I thought he sounded so depressed and miserable.' She did, however, experience a feeling of relief: 'Well, darling, we have at least finished with that wretched feeling of suspense, and know what we have to face … We are all right and have done all we can to get ready.'[7] Barbara Kaye was similarly affected. She later wrote that 'it was moving to listen to his confession of failure … and impossible not to feel sympathy for him'.[8] Margery Allingham, the well-known crime writer, felt that Chamberlain sounded like 'the family solicitor, so kindly and so very upset …'. After the broadcast she took refuge in her garden. Half expecting to see the Luftwaffe appearing over the horizon, she felt a 'breathless feeling of mingled relief and intolerable grief'. Her fear, like that of millions of others, was eased by the assurance that she was not alone: 'I said I wasn't frightened … and that three-quarters of the families in England were saying and thinking the same sort of thing the same moment …. We were all in it together, anyway.'[9] Nearby in the same village was the Dawson family, who had cycled into Tolleshunt D'Arcy only two days before on holiday. Mr Dawson recalled that on that Sunday morning they were strolling through its quiet streets. As 11 o'clock approached they were allowed to enter a cottage to listen to the Prime Minister's speech. After the broadcast they were struck by the peaceful nature of the village scene outside, which was complemented by the quiet resignation with which the family greeted the news.[10]

This mixture of relief and stoicism was typical of the way in which the broadcast affected people all over the country. Sybil Olive, a left-wing political activist, was at an open-air meeting near the West Ham Docks. She recalled

---

6   ERO D/DRu C5, letter from Pamela Russell, 4 September 1939.
7   ERO T/B 416/1, letter from Molly Weald to her daughter, 3 September 1939.
8   Kaye, *The company we kept*, pp. 62–3.
9   M. Allingham, *The oaken heart* (London, 1941), pp. 82–3.
10   University of Essex, Margery Allingham Papers, Box 21, Letter J. W. Dawson to M. Allingham, 14 August 1943.

'there was a feeling of inevitability about the feeling one had, and fright, and well, it's come, that's it'.[11] Not everyone was anxious to hear the broadcast. At Holland-on-Sea a group of young people was playing tennis on the Hereford Road tennis courts that morning. The caretaker called them over to listen to the wireless, and at that point they abandoned their game and dispersed.[12] Eric Rudsdale, assistant curator at Colchester Castle, could not bear to listen and went for a ride on his bike. It was a warm day, many houses along the Mile End Road had their windows open and, hearing Chamberlain's broadcast, he just had to stop: 'A man saw me from his window and called out, "It's come, matey!"' After that Rudsdale went rowing on the pond at Bourne Mill, reflecting bitterly on where things had gone wrong since the last war:

> Twenty five years rolled back – the last war, 'the war to end all wars', they told us there could never be another – and we believed it. Think of the millions of lives lost in the last war, all wasted. Think of the misery now of relatives, who have believed that their dear ones died 'to save civilisation.' Now they want another million to die. What rubbish! What rotten, sinful rubbish![13]

Chamberlain's broadcast had scarcely ended when an air-raid warning sounded over London and Essex. It turned out to be a false alarm but was terrifying enough. In the south of the county a man, with the help of his neighbour, had been digging an air-raid shelter in his garden for their two families. On 3 September it was six inches deep in water and had no roof. Nevertheless, when the siren sounded both families jumped in it. The neighbour, a veteran of the Great War, thought he smelled gas and they frantically put on their respirators. The daughter of one of them wrote: 'We stood there, feet and ankles wet, clothes covered in mud and mask visors all steamed up – cold, terrified and waiting for the end.'[14] At Colchester the town's post office stayed open all night to issue travel warrants to servicemen who had been recalled to the colours.[15] Buses were commandeered in order to ferry men back to their units. Trains, buses and boats bringing evacuees into the town rolled into their destinations throughout the day. Hervey Benham, the Colchester newspaper proprietor, recalled watching a long line of cars streaming back from the coast along the town's bypass, many of them with bedding fastened to the back. Just as

---

11   ERO SA 24/1457/1, recording of Sybil Olive.
12   R. Kennell, *The story of Holland-on-Sea during the Second World War* (author, 2003), p. 5.
13   ERO D/DU 888/22, Journal of Eric Rudsdale, 3 September 1939.
14   Federation of Essex Women's Institutes, *Essex within living memory* (Newbury, 1995), p. 209.
15   ECT 9 September 1939.

in 1914, they were holidaymakers who had decided that discretion was the better part of valour and were cutting short their holidays.[16]

That night, for the first time in over twenty years, the county was engulfed in the dark gloom of the blackout, a gloom eased only by a harvest moon. At about 3.30am there was a further air-raid warning over much of Essex. At Colchester, bugles sounded out from the barracks and people claimed that planes could be heard high above. The girls of Tottenham High School, who had arrived at their evacuation destination at Saffron Walden only a few hours earlier, were roused from their beds when the siren blared out. One pupil, Edna Brownjohn, recalled the terror of that night:

> We were all shivering from cold and fear, for we did not know what was going to happen to us, and I think we all imagined horrible deaths …. The aeroplanes, too, droned unceasingly above us, and altogether it was very ghostly and unreal. The trees around us played havoc with our imagination as a branch struck us as resembling an aged hand of gnarled and careworn fingers, or a man's pointed features.[17]

The first civilian deaths of the war were caused by the air-raid siren. It proved too much for 77-year-old Emily Bone, of Upminster, who succumbed to the shock of the siren and died.[18] A 26-year-old man at Southend was also unfortunate. Injured in a road accident on the first night of the blackout, he died six days later.[19] These were the first of thousands of Essex residents who would – albeit, in these cases, indirectly – lose their lives in this terrible conflict.

The first evacuation

Faced by the possibility of air raids, the government had decided that, in the event of war, vulnerable groups – schoolchildren together with their teachers, mothers with young children, pregnant women, the elderly and the disabled – would be evacuated from areas liable to air attack and taken to places deemed to be safe. In reality the vast majority of those evacuated were children, removed as whole schools where possible, and they were the first concern of the government.[20] The country was divided into evacuation, neutral and reception areas. Evacuation areas were urban areas which, by virtue of their size and industrial importance, were considered prime targets for enemy air

---

16   H. Benham, *Essex at war* (Colchester, 1946), p.15.
17   ERO D/DU 1712/1, Tottenham High School evacuation magazine, May 1940, p. 37.
18   EC 8 September 1939.
19   EC 8 and 15 September 1939.
20   ECC minute, 1 March 1938.

raids. Neutral areas were recognised as potential targets but less obviously so than evacuation areas. However, as air raids on them were a possibility they were deemed unsuitable to receive evacuees, but neither were people to be evacuated from them. Reception areas, usually villages and rural towns, were those places to which evacuees were transported because they were considered relatively safe.

After the Munich Agreement in 1938 the hurried evacuation arrangements of that time were replaced by more detailed plans. The evacuation plans for Greater London included Metropolitan Essex, from where 124,000 schoolchildren out of almost 800,000 who were to be dispersed from the capital were allocated to reception areas elsewhere in the county.[21] However, there was an irony in a county with a North Sea coastline, that was therefore exposed to invasion as well as being at risk of air raids aimed at nearby London, containing both evacuation and reception areas. Typical arrangements were similar to those at Burnham and Clacton, where a reception officer, an assistant reception officer and billeting officers and helpers had been appointed to receive the influx of evacuees. Anticipating problems with the allocation of evacuees, billeting tribunals were set up.[22] On 31 August the Ministry of Health ordered local authorities to implement evacuation plans and the whole business was set in motion. Germany's invasion of Poland the next day seemed to justify its decision.

The teaching staff of many Essex schools had already anticipated the worst. Many returned early from their holiday or were recalled to those schools that were to act as assembly points. The head teacher at West Mersea County Primary School (CPS) returned from holiday on 25 August and resumed duties. Four days later all the staff had returned.[23] Not everyone seems to have been as aware as the West Mersea staff, as an entry in the logbook of Layer de la Haye Church of England (C of E) CPS makes clear: 'Hearing on the wireless that the evacuation of schoolchildren was commencing today, Miss Barrett, Miss Rice and I reported at the school which was open in case it was needed.'[24]

The south of Essex, comprising the large metropolitan area adjacent to the capital, contained the county's evacuation areas. From West Ham 32,000 people were evacuated, the last of the four priority batches departing on 4 September. A total of 15,570 people was evacuated from East Ham and 6,000 schoolchildren left Leyton, accompanied by virtually all the borough's teaching staff. They were mainly allocated to villages around Epping, although some were sent to the West Country. Other Leyton children found themselves deep

---

21   ECS 2 September 1939.
22   BA 9 September 1939; ERO D/UCt M1/39, Clacton Urban District Council, Evacuation Scheme, 7 September 1939.
23   ERO D/P 452/4, West Mersea CPS logbook, 25, 29 August, 1 September 1939.
24   ERO T/P 417/4–5, Layer de la Haye Church of England CPS, logbook, 1 September 1939.

Figure 1.1. St Angela's Roman Catholic school evacuated – whole school photograph taken after the whole school was evacuated to Cornwall. (Newham Heritage & Archives)

in the Essex countryside. On 1 September 167 pupils arrived at Felsted, and two days later they were joined by 51 teachers and children from Noel Park School, Wood Green.[25] At Brightlingsea almost 900 children and 36 teachers and helpers arrived from Bow and West Ham.[26] The first batch of evacuees arrived at Colchester St Botolph's station on 1 September and from St John's Green CPS they were dispersed all over the district.[27] The schoolchildren of Wanstead and Woodford were scattered over a wide area, including Saffron Walden, Chelmsford, Rochford, Maldon and Danbury: 1,352 children were evacuated, together with 996 mothers with children under five years old and 83 pregnant women.[28]

The majority of evacuated people travelled by train, which made the main line through the county incredibly busy. At Colchester, with some 14,000 children expected in just four days en route to their various destinations, the railway timetable was tight. Some 4,000 children a day arrived at St Botolph's station, four trainloads on each of the first three days (Friday, Saturday and Sunday), and two on Monday 4 September. Each child was given rations for 48 hours.[29] It was equally hectic at Chelmsford. Lucy Weald, the stationmaster's wife, wrote to her daughter Molly in Edinburgh to say:

25   ERO E/ML 181/4, Felsted CPS logbook, 4 September 1939.
26   ERO T/P 457/11, Colne High School, Brightlingsea, logbooks, 1, 2, 3 September 1939.
27   ERO T/P 464/1–3, St John's Green CPS, logbook, 1 September 1939.
28   S. Tiquet, *It happened here: the story of civil defence in Wanstead and Woodford 1939–45* (Wanstead, 1947), p. 22.
29   N. Jacobs, *The sunshine coast: bygone Clacton, Walton, Frinton and District* (Lowestoft, 1986), p. 57.

The trains (children's) have been going through about every quarter of an hour, so you can guess what a business it has been. Daddy has an inspector to help. We have had thousands of children through the station, and also through the town on their way to villages outside. Those coming in by train were marched through to the bus station and given rations before being sent on by bus. I believe a lot are still in Chelmsford. I went to help yesterday and again this morning. The bus station is an ideal place for the job, and the men have been very kind. They collected amongst themselves, and bought a lot of lemonade syrup and fruit for the children. It is heart-breaking to see the mothers and babies. One poor woman I helped yesterday had three children, the youngest not yet two years old, and they generally have various cases, carriers etc; she had a canvas pack on her back. It is surprising how cheerful and good on the whole the children are.[30]

One of the teachers arriving at Chelmsford said, '[w]e didn't know where we were going. First of all that was the most important part for the children. They kept going up to the bus drivers and asking where they were going …'.[31] It would be many hours before most of them got their answer.

The Phoney War

During the first eight months of the conflict, the so-called 'Phoney War', there was little land action following the fall of Poland. The *Telegraph* referred to 'this strangest of wars – this war of boredom and waiting for many'.[32] In common with the rest of Britain, Essex experienced nothing remotely hostile. Nevertheless, Essex people were affected by what did occur. The Royal Navy was engaged with its German counterpart almost as soon as war began. Kenneth Ainger of Colchester was a seaman on HMS *Ajax* when she took part in the Battle of the River Plate against the German pocket battleship *Graf Spee*.[33] The sinking of the *Graf Spee* was not the end of the story for some merchant seamen, who had been picked up by the warship when their vessels had been sunk and transferred to the German supply ship *Altmark*. The *Altmark* was intercepted off Norway by a British destroyer, HMS *Cossack*, on 17 February 1940. The ship was boarded and 299 British prisoners were set free. They included John Bammant of Dovercourt and eighteen-year-old Bernard Ward from Romford. An Essex man serving aboard the *Cossack*, Kenneth Fulton, was one of the

30   ERO T/B 416/1, Molly Weald, letter, 3 September 1939.
31   ERO SA 1/455/1, 'Christmas Under Fire.'
32   ECT 9 December 1939.
33   ECS 17 February 1940.

boarding party, and he brought home with him a German seaman's cap as a souvenir.[34]

Other reminders of the war had a sobering impact. The Germans began laying mines in the seas around the south-east coast to disrupt trade, demoralise the Merchant Navy and hamper the Royal Navy's activities. On 22 November 1939 aircraft dropped magnetic mines near Southend pier, two of which were found lying in the mud at low water near Shoeburyness. Two naval officers from HMS *Vernon* worked on the mines as they lay there, disarming them, and as a result the Admiralty soon understood how they worked.[35] However, coastal waters remained hazardous. In November 1939 fourteen survivors from the Dutch liner *Simon Bolivar*, which had hit a mine, were taken to Essex County Hospital, as were four survivors of the collier *Torchbearer*. Pamela Russell, an Essex resident, knew one of the casualties of the latter, Charles Keith, who suffered severe spinal injuries. He survived the chilly water and was very ill for a time in Harwich Hospital. In February 1940 she noted that he was recovering, 'but he will walk like a robot to the end of his days'.[36] In what was to become a frequent occurrence along the east coast, the body of an unidentified sailor was washed ashore at Bradwell on 30 January 1940. The coroner's verdict was that he had come from a ship that had been mined.[37]

Conscription, which had been introduced somewhat half-heartedly in the summer of 1939, was extended to cover men up to the age of 41. Distribution of forms in Colchester began on 24 September and 54 enumerators were hired to carry out the work.[38] At the end of October the first men called up, those aged between twenty and 22, registered there. The *Essex County Standard* noted with pride that, out of almost 1,000 men, only four from Colchester and sixteen from the wider area registered themselves as conscientious objectors.[39]

The new blackout regulations concerned everyone and had to be thorough. ARP wardens watched out for windows which were not blacked out or revealed just a chink of light, and became intensely unpopular as a result. Lucy Weald described how 'Frank and Daddy fixed a piece of that thick card-board over the coal-house window, and today Frank and I have pasted strips of brown paper all over the door cracks, keyhole, etc.',[40] while Joyce Nightingale of Leytonstone wrote that 'You would be annoyed, May, if you could see the streets now. On a moonless night it's as black as pitch – I don't know about Chadwell Heath, but the wardens here are very particular, and not a glimmer

34   EC 23 February 1940.
35   A.P. Herbert, *The battle of the Thames: the war story of Southend pier* (London, 1947), p.1.
36   ERO D/DRu C5, letter, 18 February 1940.
37   EC 9 February 1940.
38   ECS 30 September 1939.
39   ECS 28 October 1939.
40   ERO T/B 416/1, letter, 3 September 1939.

of light is allowed.'[41] Accidents and fatalities in the blackout became a regular feature of wartime life. Between December 1938 and December 1939 there was a 56 per cent increase in deaths nationally from road accidents. Of the 78 deaths in East Anglia during that period, 49 of them occurred during the blackout. The number of injuries was even greater. Most of those affected were thought to be people over 50.[42] Pedestrians were advised to 'walk left', facing the traffic, although the pitch-black environment meant that there were also many hazards on pavements. 'I am very nearly blind at night,' wrote Eric Rudsdale, 'and make my way through the streets full of jostling soldiers at considerable peril.'[43] At Brightlingsea so many people were bumping into lamp posts that they were painted with so-called 'detector paint'.[44] Rural areas, many of which had never had any form of street lighting, nevertheless had their own problems. For instance, Harlow Parish Council had white warning patches attached to trees as well as lamp posts, posts and footpath signs.[45]

Many organisations were compelled to reschedule their events in order to hold them before the blackout came into force. The Church of England was particularly affected, as the huge windows in its parish churches were rarely susceptible of being blacked out, which often rendered the later celebration of evensong impossible between autumn and late spring. Consequently most churches held evensong in the afternoon.[46] At Emmanuel Church, Forest Gate, its Harvest Festival, which was to have been celebrated as an evening service, was rescheduled for 5pm, and Sunday evening services were put back to 3pm[47]

As the months progressed and the threatened air raids did not materialise, thousands of evacuees from all over the country began to drift home from the county's reception areas. By early December the number of evacuees at Braintree had almost halved.[48] At Chelmsford the fall-off was even greater: in September there had been 2,543 evacuees in the town, 1,437 of them schoolchildren, but by early May the total number had declined to 610.[49]

A degree of relaxation became apparent. Nevertheless, some people who had supported the necessity for war saw no reason to change their minds. Anglican clergy in particular tended to have a straightforward view of the war as a righteous crusade. In a letter to the *Guardian* Canon Gerald Rendall of Dedham was critical of what he saw as the lukewarm approach to the war

---

41   Letter, 30 October 1939, quoted by permission of Jean Nightingale.
42   EC 2 February 1940.
43   ERO D/DU 888/22, journal, 3 December 1939.
44   ECS 21 October 1939.
45   ERO T/A 524/4, Harlow Parish Council minutes 1928–44, minute, 1 November 1939.
46   E.S. Turner, *The phoney war on the home front* (London, 1961), pp. 62–3.
47   ERO D/P/592/29/4, Emmanuel Church, Forest Gate, PCC minute, 4 September 1939, Register of Services, 3 September 1939.
48   ECS 21 October, 8 December 1939, 17 February 1940.
49   ChBC minutes, 12 September 1939, 14 May 1940.

which sections of the media had adopted. To him the future of civilisation was at stake:

> Week by week in your columns, as in the broadcast homilies … we are regaled with half-hearted compunctions on the morality of meeting force with force, with academic exegesis of disputed texts, with Quixotic assertions of contributory guilt, or with encomiums on the fine consistency of the Conscientious Objector.[50]

C.H. Ridsdale, the Bishop of Colchester, spoke of a crusade against 'arrogant and diabolical forces' and enemies 'drunk with domination'.[51] Many lay people agreed. The author Margery Allingham spoke of Hitler's aims as 'the most gigantic and most naïvely mistaken project since Lucifer got himself kicked out of heaven'. She regarded the war against the Germans as 'a simple battle for the continued existence of man as a civilized animal in the generation after next'.[52]

However, the easing of the atmosphere of crisis also assisted those who had opposed the war all along. With Britain's immediate survival no longer apparently at stake these individuals continued to voice their opinions. The belief that a modern war would annihilate civilisation was still a strongly held one. J.A. Thom of Langham wrote that, even if the war was won, 'the prize will be bitter-sweet, and the lofty ideals will never be attained'. He predicted the westward spread of Bolshevism, the Empire endangered, post-war economic chaos, increasing unemployment and 'serious rioting and lawlessness'.[53] Thomas Wisbey of West Bergholt felt that the war would leave the world stuck in its old ways:

> The rich man will still suffer from a disease which makes him try to double his riches and also makes him forget his fellow humans who have very little. The middleman will also suffer, as now, from the disease which makes him take what he can from both rich and poor; and the poor man will also be suffering from the disease which makes him envious of all who are better off than he.[54]

A frequent complaint during the Phoney War concerned the government's failure to give the country a clear statement of war aims, and the result was that people felt that there was a lack of leadership, a sense of drift at the top. The

50   Quoted in ECS 4 November 1939.
51   ECS 27 April 1939.
52   Allingham, *Oaken heart*, pp. 144–5.
53   ECS 11 November 1939.
54   ECS 20 January 1940.

national press led the call for such a statement, as, in Essex, did the *Chronicle*.[55] However, not everyone blamed the government for the slackness of the time. A Colchester councillor warned people against 'self-complacency': 'We think we can win this war on twopence a week,' he said, 'but I am afraid we shall have a fairly rude awakening.'[56] That rude awakening was waiting just around the corner.

Defeat and deliverance

The Phoney War ended on 9 April 1940, when the Germans invaded Denmark and Norway. Moyra Charlton, from Great Canfield, who was serving with the ATS in France, felt that vulnerable neutral countries should have resisted the Nazis: 'If only they had stood together then', she wrote.[57] The fiasco of the Norwegian campaign, culminating in the evacuation of British troops, resulted in the fall of Chamberlain and the appointment of Winston Churchill as prime minister. Dissatisfaction with the government reverberated locally, too. Ernest Edwards, the Southend diarist, wrote, 'All this to us seems very mystifying – first we are told that all is well in Norway … and now we learn that our force has had to leave the area. The prestige of the Government has had a severe blow.' The next day he wrote, 'But we must be told, we do not like setbacks glossed over by nice talk and technical phrases.'[58] Such 'nice talk' availed little now and, over the next six weeks, the British Expeditionary Force's (BEF's) disastrous campaign in Belgium and France, culminating in the evacuation from Dunkirk, and the collapse of France itself, left England fighting the war alone and eastern and southern counties such as Essex facing the possibility of a German invasion.

On 10 May, the day that Churchill replaced Chamberlain, the Germans had struck again, invading France and the Low Countries. Eric Rudsdale wrote, 'I see nothing cheering in seeing the war coming nearer and nearer to Essex.'[59] Margery Allingham recalled how her windows rattled faintly in their frames, just as they had done when she was a child during the Great War and the guns on the Western Front could be heard in Essex.[60] People were able to follow these events closely in the newspapers and on the radio, and the BEF's predicament was not lost on Essex people. On 18 May the *Standard* noted that Britain was pitted against 'a formidable, ferocious and unscrupulous foe'.[61] The *Chronicle* commented that 'the enemy has an

55 ECS 3 November 1939; Turner, *Phoney war*, p. 185.
56 ECS 24 February 1939.
57 Imperial War Museum Deparment of Documents, 1031, Moyra Charlton diary, vol. 3, 9 April 1940.
58 ERO S 3150, diary of Ernest Edwards, 3, 4 May 1940.
59 ERO D/DU 888/23, journal, 10 May 1940.
60 Allingham, *Oaken heart*, p. 162.
61 ECS 17 May 1940.

enormous mechanical equipment', an early reference to its Blitzkrieg tactics that magnified its supposed superiority in equipment.[62]

Suspicions of French weaknesses also began to creep into people's discussions. For instance, the *Billericay Times* snarled that 'Our credulity as a nation, in the uprightness of our neighbours, is partly our undoing; for that we are to blame.' Similarly, 'It is obvious ... that the French army is very badly beaten,' wrote Rudsdale on 22 May. 'There is great consternation everywhere.'[63] Evelyn Jessie Grubb, a young mother in Metropolitan Essex, was just as gloomy when she confided to her diary on 24 May: 'Germans in Boulogne. Grave state of affairs. I can't settle to work in the house.'[64] In view of the gravity of the situation in France George VI authorised a National Day of Prayer on 26 May. The vicar of Emmanuel Church, Forest Gate, wrote 'Church crowded – tip-up chairs used – extra chairs and benches put in, but still some people reported that they were unable to get in. Probably about 800 people.'[65] Belgium surrendered on 28 May and the Belgian king, Leopold, was widely reviled throughout Britain.[66] The *Standard* condemned King Leopold for 'assisting the enemy and betraying his helpers by an act of treachery and cowardice unparalleled in history.' He personally was described as 'dishonourable and contemptible' and was compared unfavourably to his father, King Albert, who had stood up to the Kaiser in 1914. The hostility to Leopold was intensified by the awareness that Belgium's surrender had further imperilled the already hazardous predicament of the BEF.[67]

Small boats from Essex coastal towns were involved in Operation Dynamo, in which the BEF and thousands of French troops were evacuated from Dunkirk. Arthur Joscelyne and his brother Harold from Southend ended up on a sailing barge, *The Shannon*. From Ramsgate they crossed the Channel, meeting fishing boats full of Dutch and Belgian refugees heading in the opposite direction. They were open boats, only eighteen feet long, and completely crowded, so that only the remarkably calm sea saved their occupants from disaster. The barge's speed was slow, about four knots, so that they sailed through the night, with the sound of gunfire getting louder. 'We had lost all sense of time,' he later wrote, 'living in a timeless capsule of fear and apprehension until at last night closed in and we continued under a starlit sky with a phosphorus wake all around us.' At dawn the gunfire was much louder, there was a thick mist, the sea was oily with flotsam in it and there was a great deal of smoke around. After

---

62   EC 18 May 1940.

63   ERO D/DU 888/23, journal, 19, 21, 22 May 1940.

64   Diary of Evelyn Jessie Grubb, 24 May 1940.

65   ERO D/P 592/1/52, Emmanuel Church, Forest Gate, register of services, 26 May 1940.

66   M. Gillies, *Waiting for Hitler: voices from Britain on the brink of invasion* (London, 2006), p. 63; A. Calder, *The myth of the Blitz* (London, 1991), p. 93.

67   ECS 1 June 1940.

working off the beaches the barges, now fully laden with soldiers, recrossed the Channel in equally perilous circumstances and eventually reached Ramsgate, disgorging their human cargo. To preserve secrecy about the operation they were given orders to stay aboard near one of the Godwin Light Ships, where they remained all night before being allowed to return to Southend.[68]

Dunkirk may have been a defeat but it stirred people. Churchill's description of it as 'a miracle of deliverance' and the famous Dunkirk Postscript, broadcast by the writer J.B. Priestley, contributed to a sense of national pride and achievement. 'The whole nation is thrilled with pride,' wrote the *Chronicle*, although it warned that 'the natural pride in such a glorious achievement must not make us lose our sense of proportion, though; or cause us to forget the testing time ahead'.[69] In this it echoed Churchill's assertion that wars were not won by evacuations. However, these sober appraisals went unheeded and the evacuation quickly assumed the status of a divine deliverance. Leonard Stokes, vicar of St Alban, Westcliff, wrote: '[w]e firmly believe that the prayers of the nation were in this way answered by God.'[70]

After Dunkirk the situation on the Continent deteriorated rapidly. When Mussolini declared war on Britain on 10 June Rudsdale was saddened: 'A terrible tragedy that it should be Italy,' he wrote; 'now I shall never see the wonders of Rome, Pompeia, Naples.'[71] Others, too, felt great poignancy at Italy's entry on the side of Hitler. The Bishop of Chelmsford lamented:

> But the tragedy is that the gentle and kindly Italian race, who love beauty and music and all arts, and who have so wonderfully enriched the whole world with their talents should have had their minds so twisted and distorted that they have turned away from the beautiful to the hideous.[72]

Nevertheless, it was the news that France had requested an armistice on 16 June that was regarded as the greatest calamity of the war. 'You will have shared all our anguish as one little country after another collapsed,' wrote Pamela Russell to her American friend in Massachussetts. She continued:

> Then that darkest saddest day when France threw in her hand. One had foreseen it coming and yet when it came one was utterly appalled for us, and desolated – La belle France and that she should come to this,

---

68   ERO TS 315, A. Joscelyne, 'Dunkirk Recollections' (1980).
69   EC 31 May 1940.
70   ERO D/P 535/28/34, St Alban, Westcliff, parish magazine, July 1940.
71   ERO D/DU 888/23, journal, 10, 14 June 1940.
72   CDC July 1940.

so soon....There was an extraordinary hush over the land on that sad day, the housewives stood about the shop doors with empty baskets and even the pea-pickers seemed to stand about in a trance.[73]

Woolf Jacobs was training with his army unit at Clacton when his lance-corporal said to them, '"Lads, I've got some news for you. France has turned it in" and we all thought it was the end then ... came as a bit of a shock when we were told that.'[74] 'Can you beat it, France over-run in five weeks,' exclaimed Herbert Maxwell Scott. Disbelief was uppermost in his thoughts:

> The German Army is undoubtedly very fit, very well organised and the co-operation between Air, Tank, Infantry and Supply is magnificent, but that is no reason why we and France should not have been as good, and they don't seem to have used anything that we could not have foreseen![75]

This military disaster gave rise to a defiant mood later described as 'the spirit of 1940' or 'the Dunkirk spirit'. The fall of France came as a relief to many, as there were now no allies to appease. 'In fact being "Alone" has considerably bucked us up,' wrote Herbert Maxwell Scott on 22 June.[76] Pamela Russell felt that people's morale had actually risen: 'everyone serene and confident, though we now stand almost alone,' she wrote.[77] Moyra Charlton, evacuated from France and back at her home in Great Canfield, said,

> Home again, unbelievably lovely and the garden a haven of peace. Paris has fallen and France has asked Hitler for peace terms, so we are left alone to champion the cause of truth and beauty, and all that makes life worth living. It makes one dread the endless future and the menacing present, but really we must be proud that we are the ones who are to uphold this centuries-old England in her terrible and glorious hour.[78]

One Essex resident wrote:

> Don't think that we are downhearted. We are not ... The task of defeating the abominable German is going to be harder than we thought. But defeat him in the end we shall ... we shall exact a toll that

---

73 ERO D/DRu C5, letter, 22 June 1940.
74 ERO SA 16/760/1, interview with Woolf Jacobs.
75 S. Maxwell Scott, *Pa's wartime letters and this and that* (2010), p. 35.
76 Scott, *Pa's wartime letters*, p. 37.
77 ERO D/DRu C5, letter, 22 June 1940.
78 IWM 1031, 19 June 1940.

will make the mothers of Germany regret most bitterly the days when they brought men-children into the world.'[79]

The Colchester newspaper proprietor Hervey Benham wrote that,

With Dunkirk, that turning point in history, Colchester, in common with the rest of the country, rolled up its shirt sleeves, shook off its easy torpor and got down to work. The days of 'can't somebody find us something to do to help in this war?' came abruptly to an end.[80]

Invasion expected

Britain anticipated a German invasion in the summer of 1940 and Essex seemed a good deal more vulnerable than most English counties. The *Essex County Telegraph* told its readers, 'Those who used to say that the war was distant and unreal now have proof that actual invasion is closer to this dear land than it has been for nearly a thousand years. The war is real, active, and on our doorstep.'[81] That doorstep was lapped by the waters of the North Sea and to the east was the enemy. Perhaps understandably, Essex people saw their county as a tempting target, with its broad estuaries, its navigable rivers, its absence of significant topographical obstructions and its proximity to London.

Its geographical position meant that Essex became part of a coastal defence system which stretched from the Wash to the Isle of Wight. Behind the coastal defence line along the Essex shoreline three defensive lines – the eastern Command Line, the General Headquarters (GHQ) Line and the Outer London Defence Line – all ran through parts of the county. Coastal areas, especially those with tempting sandy beaches, were now off-limits to all but residents and a curfew order was enforced along the rural part of the Essex coastline. A seven-mile stretch from Leigh-on-Sea to Shoeburyness was closed. On Clacton seafront barbed wire and anti-tank blocks or 'pimples' were positioned as anti-tank obstacles.[82] At Southend there were 1,804 of these blocks along the seafront. Along miles of beaches anti-invasion tubular metal scaffolding, ten feet high and strengthened with a barrier of barbed wire, was erected to obstruct enemy landing craft, and mines were planted in the sand. All rivers were mined across their estuaries. A strict security regime was imposed in which the coastal region of Norfolk, Suffolk and Essex was classed as a defence area and from 10 July only residents and officially

79   R.J. Thompson, *Battle over Essex* (Chelmsford, 1946), pp. 24–6.
80   Benham, *Essex at war*, p. 23.
81   ECT 1 June 1940.
82   ERO Box Z11B, G. Elcoat, 'Invasion preparations on the Essex Coast 1940–41' (1960).

Figure 1.2. The 'Searchlight Café'. This café, sited on the beach on Mersea Island, was aptly named, as it had a searchlight in its structure. (Mersea Museum/Keith Lee)

authorised vehicles were permitted access. Holidaying and day tripping were banned for the duration. Harwich once more became a key naval base, with 22 destroyers and a heavy cruiser based there.[83] The town was protected by the Essex Regiment using the Beacon Hill and Redoubt forts and the quay was cordoned off with barriers and barbed wire.[84]

Throughout the county concrete pillboxes designed to halt the advance of tanks and infantry were erected. They were armed with Lewis guns or two- and then six-pounder anti-tank guns. A café on the beach on Mersea Island had a searchlight placed in it. Part of the village of Wix on the Harwich Road had barbed wire entanglements three rolls high, and portable road barriers were placed on every road leading into the village.[85] To tackle any enemy forces attempting to sail up the Thames the defences of the Coalhouse Fort were strengthened further by the installation of remote-controlled searchlights. The fort was protected by large guns, barbed wire, trenches and mortar positions, and the river there was mined.[86] Clacton pier was breached so that the enemy could not use it to land troops and supplies.[87] Abberton reservoir, near Colchester, was

83   R. Douglas Brown, *East Anglia 1940* (Lavenham, 1981), p. 96.
84   P.J. Cone, *Harwich and Dovercourt in the twentieth century* (Harwich, 2004), p. 179.
85   D. Budds, *Wix at war* (2002), p. 17.
86   V.T.C. Smith, *Coalhouse Fort, and the artillery defences* (Southend, 1985), pp. 26–7.
87   Kennell, *Holland-On-Sea*, p. 7; Jacobs, *Sunshine coast*, pp. 58–9.

Figure 1.3. These signposts were first removed from roadsides to prevent them being used by the enemy, and were then placed in this field as obstructions against enemy gliders. (Imperial War Museum)

mined to prevent enemy seaplanes from landing on it.[88] Signposts were taken down to deny enemy invaders easy information.

Essex residents anticipated the worst. 'Now we are alone,' wrote Evelyn Jessie Grubb, on 25 June, 'Invasion expected.'[89] On 1 June the Mayor of Colchester warned that 'It is quite certain that people are getting fidgety and we in responsible positions must do all we can to exercise a steadying influence.'[90] One observer noted that morale in Romford was low and had not been helped by the appearance of a demoralised group of soldiers fresh from Dunkirk.[91] Moyra Charlton was finding it hard to cope: 'One way or another I spent most of the evening in tears,' she wrote. 'The threat of this German invasion that may wipe out our home, Canny, the granary, the roses, this old house that has stood for five hundred years – it's still almost unbelievable.'[92] Official reports certainly suggested that nerves were taut, especially along the Essex coastline. People were unnerved by the evacuations that summer, by the partial demolition of Clacton pier and by the cessation of normality represented by the premature end of the holiday season. Reports suggested nervousness elsewhere, too. A talk on gas attacks by Sir John Anderson was said to have caused alarm in Chelmsford, and at West Ham it was alleged that fear of air raids had produced much reduced attendances at clubs and social centres.[93] At Romford, Local Defence Volunteers (LDV) sentries were so anxious about fifth-columnists that they opened fire on a car. The driver's exhaust had backfired and he had not heard their order to stop. Four people in the car were killed.[94]

Defeatist talk was now a criminal offence but, nevertheless, there was certainly a good deal of rumour circulating in 1940.[95] The *Essex County Telegraph* described defeatists as '[l]ong-faced nincompoops who go about moaning over our prospects and saying to all and sundry, "We can't win"'.[96] One person wrote to the newspaper to say:

> The defeatists in our midst are few and far between, but, such as they are, they can do much harm to the morale of our people, particularly of the womenfolk, who will have enough to do without listening to the lugubrious outpourings and jeremiads of such spunkless defeatists.[97]

88   Benham, *Essex at war*, p. 22.
89   Diary of Evelyn Jessie Grubb, 25 June 1940.
90   ECS 22 June 1940.
91   MOA TC23/10/M, Air Raid material, Romford, 25 June 1940.
92   IWM 1031, 23 June 1940.
93   P. Addison and J. Craig (eds), *Listening to Britain: home intelligence reports on Britain's finest hour, May to September 1940* (London, 2010), pp. 27, 61, 78, 110, 141, 290.
94   Gardiner, *Wartime*, p. 241.
95   Gillies, *Waiting for Hitler*, pp. 161–5. For the formation of the LDV, see below pp. 31–33.
96   ECT 29 June 1940.
97   ECT 29 June 1940.

A letter to the *Billericay Times* urged everyone to inform the authorities of anyone who held or had held Fascist views, 'or have expressed in conversation, views favourable to German aims or leaders. In this way investigation may be made into the records of such persons, and a number of potential enemies of this country in time of danger put out of harm's way.' The letter noted that 'Some of them may have committed no greater sin than being "cranks", but that must not excuse them.'[98] A clerk from Grays heard a middle-aged woman express approval of the arrest of Blackshirts, but she also ventured to say that she half-expected the king and queen to be linked to them.[99] One wonders whether the person at Leigh-on-Sea who was overheard asking whether the country would be worse off if Hitler came or the man who asserted that the government had backed a loser when they declared war on Germany would have been classed as cranks, defeatists or fifth-columnists.[100] Just being a foreigner aroused suspicion. When the well-known American radio broadcaster Ed Murrow stopped at an Essex pub, his accent marked him out as a fifth-columnist as far as locals were concerned.[101]

However, thoughts of invasion could take a more positive line. Margery Allingham recalled, perhaps a little tongue in cheek, that 'As far as I could hear each private castle was to be held to the last, each sacred doorstep to be a Thermopylae.'[102] Pamela Russell rejected the worst. In an impassioned letter to her American friend she asserted that

> It is impossible to believe in ultimate defeat when so much is at stake and though I don't believe it is possible as we are now to defeat Germany yet I am convinced that … if only we can hold out long enough, and if we can get enough material help from America, even if we don't get fighting men. I think we can put up a really good show for a long time.[103]

Rayleigh Council breathed defiance into a letter it wrote to Churchill, as the man who now embodied Britain's determination to fight on: 'Ask of us what you will; direct and command us in any way you think necessary, and we shall not fail you; but surrender – never!'[104]

The fear of Nazi parachutists also embedded itself in the nation's imagination that summer, particularly after their successful airborne actions in the Low

---

98   BT 8 June 1940.
99   MOA Diarist 5414, 10 July 1940.
100   MOA Diarist 5416, 30 June, 4 July 1940.
101   Gillies, *Waiting for Hitler*, p. 163.
102   Allingham, *Oaken heart*, p.164.
103   ERO D/DRu C5, letter 22 June 1940.
104   BT 6 July 1940.

Countries.[105] Stanley Wilson, a county councillor from Saffron Walden, wrote that:

> This is a very real danger … . The whole population should keep a look-out for them. Large fields should have obstructions put across them so that it is difficult for planes to land. Beware of strangers. Spies and parachutists often dress up in British battle dress, just like our own soldiers. They may even pretend to be British officers and give you orders, and they may talk perfect English. Don't answer questions about aerodromes, movement of troops, etc. but refer questions to the police.[106]

In the fields around Thurrock scaffolding poles were placed in threes, linked by cables.[107] In June 1940 Essex County Council urged farmers to block fields with farm carts, old lorries, cars and hayricks.[108] The County Surveyor concluded that the best form of obstruction was a revetment made from wattle hurdle, six feet long and four feet high, filled with earth. He urged people to '[m]ake a wattle once a day. This will keep our foe away.' Ironically the invasion threat resuscitated, albeit temporarily, the threatened rural craft of hurdlemaking. Aided by experts, some 400 volunteers and 30 schools made 5,000 hurdles that summer.[109]

The possibility of a combined airborne and seaborne invasion was taken very seriously. One experienced officer advised the Home Guard that

> [i]f the Germans attempt invasion of this country … their troops will fully realise that they are embarking on a desperate venture, and will leave nothing undone, however ruthless or treacherous, to win the day … you must expect any form of cunning, trickery, or treacherous action … The only answer is to adopt the following battle slogan … 'Destroy every German, landing or when landing, whenever met'.[110]

Individuals made their own preparations for an enemy landing. Margery Allingham hid the manuscript that she had been working on for six months in a biscuit tin.[111] A friend of the Essex journalist R.J. Thompson noted 'I have opened an account for emergencies with a bank in Wales, sent documents and

---

105 Gillies, *Waiting for Hitler*, pp. 222–4.
106 EC 12 July 1940.
107 R. Reynolds and J. Catton, *Thurrock goes to war* (Wickford, 1997), p. 28.
108 ECS 13 July 1940.
109 ECS 20 July, 3 August 1940; ECC 26 July, 2 August 1940; Essex CC minute, 1 October 1940.
110 ERO D/DS 505/1/20, typescript, 'If Invasion Comes', no author, 1940.
111 Allingham, *Oaken heart*, pp. 163, 185.

the best of my old silver down to my father-in-law's. The family pictures and furniture will have to take their chances with their owner, however.'[112] Simon Bensusan planned to bury his brandy and wine in a rabbit hole on a nearby hillside.[113] Other preparations had a darker side. One woman living near the Essex coast was determined to save her four-year-old daughter from the enemy. To this end she put aside a bottle of 100 aspirins, saying that, 'If the Germans came, we'd have dissolved them in some milk and given them to her to drink … That's how real it was.'[114]

Shortly after the outbreak of war the Master of the Rolls and the British Records Association appealed to owners and custodians of historical documents to ensure their safety by placing them in official repositories. This was designed to prevent their destruction in air raids and protect them from government-inspired paper clearances and waste paper drives; much valuable material had been lost in this way in the previous war. Much Essex material of historic value, including Colchester Borough Council's large collection of manorial records, was deposited in the newly established Essex Record Office as a result of this policy. During the summer a ton of the latter's most valuable documents were relocated to a place of safety in rural Wales, although huge numbers of materials continued to pour in well into 1944.[115]

The police also removed all the small arms in Chelmsford Museum and other items 'likely to be of use to undesirable persons' and placed them in storage. All historical maps of potential value to the enemy were also put away.[116]

The second phase of evacuation

Most parts of the country experienced only one evacuation, in September 1939, when schoolchildren were removed from London and industrial centres. The experience of Essex, Norfolk and Suffolk was somewhat different, because the possibility that coastal towns could become a battleground in the event of invasion led to further evacuations. Parents were urged to evacuate all schoolchildren in the coastal area who had not left or who had returned home. All evacuees who had been sent to coastal areas at the start of the war were now moved to the West Country and the Midlands. On 2 June 1,168 schoolchildren left Harwich and 1,300 left Clacton.[117] About 4,000 schoolchildren were evacuated from Southend.[118] A third and fourth evacuation of children and

---

112 Thompson, *Battle over Essex*, p. 27.
113 S.L. Bensusan, *Fireside papers* (London, 1946) p.117.
114 Quoted in Nicholson, *Millions like us*, p. 62.
115 ECC minutes, 21 May, 2 July, 1 October 1940; *Essex Review* July 1943, pp. 100–103, January 1944, pp. 56–9.
116 ChBC minutes, 8 July 1940.
117 ERO D/B 4M1/1, Harwich Borough Council minutes, 11 July 1940; ECS 29 June 1940.
118 SSt 6 June 1940.

Figure 1.4. Evacuated Clacton schoolchildren milling around as they await the trains to take them to the Midlands in June 1940, following the fall of France. (Essex Record Office)

vulnerable adults took place from Southend on 27 June and 10 September.[119] Southend General Hospital's allocation of civilian patients was now so small that five sisters and 24 nurses were moved to Black Notley Hospital near Braintree. The matron, a Miss Syer, wrote, 'We didn't feel very cheerful and some of us wondered if we would ever return, but we made the best of it; after all, it was "total war" and we couldn't pick and choose.'[120] Others ended up much further afield. On 23 August 1940 25 Colchester schoolchildren, including Doreen, Beryl and Basil Moles, arrived as evacuees in Saskatchewan, Canada, after a journey of 5,000 miles. More than 3,000 people turned out to greet them. Fifteen Colchester schoolchildren, including Dennis and Trevor Burrell, reached the other side of the world in Tasmania.[121] Not everyone was anxious to send their children this far away. Herbert and Eileen Scott, who lived in Widdington, near Saffron Walden, turned down offers from friends in

119   ERO D/DS 270/8, Southend Borough Council, Evacuation of Civil Population, 27 June 1940.
120   P. Finch, *Voluntary hospitals of Southend-on-Sea 1887–1948* (Southend, 1948), p. 68.
121   ECS 14, 28 September 1940, 4 January, 1 February 1941.

Canada and America to take in their children on the grounds that 'it is no time for people of our class to set a bad example!'[122]

At Southend the authorities urged everyone not engaged in essential work to leave. A local journalist recalled that 'Officialdom was at its worst and there is no doubt that hundreds who left Southend either misunderstood or were made to misunderstand the evacuation instructions.'[123] On 22 June a 59-year-old nurse at Leigh-on-Sea was told by one woman that the warning had had the desired effect and about half the population had left, with the rest staying on at their own risk.[124] In spite of official pressure only 62 per cent of the town's schoolchildren were registered for evacuation and the *Southend Standard* estimated that there were still 3,000–4,000 children of school age remaining.[125] The new evacuations meant, however, that Southend's population plummeted. Southend's Chief Constable estimated that, of the population of 135,000, some 80,000 left in June 1940.[126] The nurse at Leigh found that the only people hanging around enjoying the good weather were soldiers.[127] In mid-August a visitor came away with a similar impression, noting that

> two shop girls sat down for about half an hour, and a young man with a book and a packet of sandwiches occupied a seat for a little while, otherwise I was the only person thus idling time away…. It was all very pathetic – in a way – to see such an empty shell of a place.[128]

John Pritchard, the pastor of Leigh-on-Sea baptist church, wrote, 'Busy tradesmen found themselves standing at ease, healthy churches opening their doors to skeleton congregations.'[129] At Clacton a visiting journalist wrote, 'It is sad to drive along the deserted front. Here and there an empty car park, shops all boarded up, theatres closed, and restaurants deserted. You can go down whole streets of boarded up villas without meeting a soul.'[130]

The seaside resorts of Essex were not the only ones affected by the new evacuations. In September 1939 only about 35 per cent of eligible schoolchildren in the London Region had been evacuated.[131] As a result there were in the summer of 1940 still about 24,000 schoolchildren in West Ham, many having returned in the previous few months, although 6,000 were evacuated on 13–14

122 Maxwell Scott, *Pa's wartime letters*, pp. 35, 41, 43.
123 A.P. Goodale, *Southchurch: the history of a parish* (Southend, n.d.), p. 40.
124 MOA Diarist 5416, 30 June 1940.
125 SSt 6 June 1940.
126 ST 20 June 1945.
127 MOA Diarist 5416, 26, 30 June, 1 July 1940.
128 BT 17 August 1940.
129 ERO D/NB 11/5/84, Leigh-on-Sea Baptist Church, *The Outlook*, August 1940.
130 Quoted in Douglas Brown, *East Anglia 1940*, p. 129.
131 R. Titmuss, *Problems of social policy* (London, 1976), p. 104.

June. At Barking registrations in June 1940 amounted to only about twelve per cent of the normal school population, and even when this tripled, to over 3,000, this still left 6,000 children unregistered. Essex's metropolitan boroughs also faced unforeseen problems. While schoolchildren were moved out, adults moved in. Against official advice, many people moved from the coastal areas to outer London, perhaps to stay with family and friends. For instance, at East Ham the number of ration books issued in July was 112,000, which was 10,000 more than had been in circulation in January.[132]

The formation of the Home Guard

In the early days of the war some government officials, such as Winston Churchill, urged the creation of a half-a-million-strong home defence force as a supplementary organisation in the event of an invasion. In Essex some men over the age of conscription joined the self-styled 'League of Frontiersman', which provided rudimentary military training, and the organisation eventually came to the attention of the government. Similar unofficial groups were formed throughout the country, although the lack of activity during the Phoney War dampened the enthusiasm of some who enlisted.[133] An article in the *Daily Mirror* in March 1940 described the men as 'The County of Essex Volunteer Corps'. According to the article the volunteers, aided by the Territorial Association and officer training corps, guarded crops, road junctions, railway stations and bridges. They wore ordinary clothes with special armlets. In March 1940 the Bishop of Chelmsford called for the formation of a 'town guard' for the town made up of men aged 40 to 60.[134]

During the Battle of France, as German forces reached the Channel coast and as fears of invasion, particularly by parachutists, grew, there were growing calls in the press and from private individuals for the creation of a home defence force. The government, anxious to avoid the unofficial arming of civilians, and to prevent them developing into *francs-tireurs* in the event of an invasion, pre-empted any such move by creating the Local Defence Volunteers (LDV).[135]

The LDV was formed after an appeal by the Home Secretary, Sir Anthony Eden, in his broadcast on 14 May. He called on men between the ages of seventeen and 65 to enrol in a new organisation called the Local Defence Volunteers. Volunteers would receive uniforms and be trained and armed to supplement the regular army. The name Local Defence Volunteers was

---

132 SE 7, 14 June, 12 July 1940.
133 S.P. MacKenzie, *The Home Guard: a military and political history* (Oxford, 1995), pp. 19–20.
134 P. Finch, *Warmen courageous: the story of the Essex home guard* (Southend, 1951), pp. 7–8; ECT 18 May 1940; CDC March 1940.
135 MacKenzie, *Home Guard*, pp. 20–31.

F. W. STRAW   9 St. John's Street   COLCHESTER

Figure 1.5. The first Dad's Army. Mortar section of the 18th Battalion of the Essex Home Guard. The photograph confirms that some of the men who stepped forward were quite elderly. (Mersea Museum/Ron Green)

soon abandoned, however, and replaced by the term Home Guard. Col. Sir Edward Ruggles-Brise was appointed as County Commander of the Essex Home Guard. He had had a distinguished military and public career and was a natural choice for the role. During the Great War he had served with the Essex Yeomanry, and he had been MP for the Maldon Division since 1924.[136] Men considered to be capable of assuming leadership roles, invariably former army officers, were appointed to command local companies.[137]

Eden's broadcast produced a nationwide response as men stampeded to enrol. Major R.G. Garrod, who was eventually to be in charge of the Rayleigh Company, wrote about those first few shambolic days:

Immediately after Mr Eden's appeal on the radio … I phoned the local Police Station and asked whether an LDV unit would be formed in

136   Finch, *Warmen*, p. 10.
137   For instance, Major Guy Gold was in charge of the Braintree Company: Finch, *Warmen*, p. 160.

Rayleigh. I was told that it would and that my name was already down on the list! I visited the Police Station the following morning and was duly sworn in and told to await further instructions.

Two days later he was called to the police station, 'and found I was the last of a dozen fellows all scrambling for some ghastly denim suits – none of which were ever intended for normal-sized men – and the most ridiculous fore and aft hats that were all boys' sizes'.[138] At Brentwood the local ARP men supervised enrolment. The first volunteers began arriving just minutes after Eden's broadcast and the flood was such that enrolments continued for several days. F. W. Alderton, the clerk to the ARP organisation, recalled that:

One of my chief impressions at the time was the diversity of the people who came in. Old men, veterans of the Boer War some of them, young lads still at school, City clerks, professional men, workmen, some could not write well enough to complete the form, some even were cripples. Many were ex-officers of the '14–'18 war. Every one of them was keen and eager to get in; one could feel the enthusiasm of men who up to then had, so to say, been shut outside, owing to being over age – or for some reason or other, and suddenly found the door open.[139]

The leadership of the Home Guard projected confidence. Speaking at a parade at Romford in August, one officer said,

We can be perfectly sure – as sure as that we are assembled here this afternoon – that we shall not only maintain our own freedom, but we will also restore freedom to those who are down-trodden under the heel of Hitlerism. We shall not rest until that day comes.[140]

The disastrous events of the summer of 1940 left Britain facing its enemies alone. Because of its geographical position between the North Sea and London, Essex was now a front-line county, facing the possibility of seaborne and airborne invasion and an enemy bombing campaign. Defences were hastily erected along the coast and over much of the county. Residents had to face the possibility that the coastline might become a battlefield; the evacuation of children and adults was renewed and government regulations meant that the coastal fringe was almost entirely isolated from its interior. For these reasons Essex's experience of war in 1940 was rather more strained than that of many

138   Finch, *Warmen*, p. 52.
139   Finch, *Warmen*, p. 182.
140   Finch, *Warmen*, p. 45, 2 August 1940.

parts of England, particularly inland counties. There was an underlying sense of unease among residents and it remained to be seen how they would contend with the German onslaught when it eventually arrived.

Nightmares come true: the Blitz

Skirmishes

In 1940, as summer drifted into autumn, Essex, like other parts of the eastern and southern counties, was confronted by two possible calamities. Firstly, it faced the possibility of invasion and, secondly, as in the Great War, its proximity to London meant that it would be in the front line of any German air offensive. The government recognised that London would be a certain target for the enemy and with this in mind it had divided Outer London into nine groups for ARP purposes. Metropolitan Essex became Group 7, consisting of the boroughs and urban districts of Barking, Chigwell, Chingford, Dagenham, East Ham, Ilford, Leyton, Walthamstow, Waltham Holy Cross, Wanstead, Woodford and West Ham. The rest of the county, referred to officially as 'Extra-Metropolitan Essex', was part of the Eastern Civil Defence Region.[1] Certain areas in it were designated as 'especially vulnerable': the area around the oil refineries on the north bank of the Thames, the areas adjacent to Group 7 and the port of Harwich. For both civil defence purposes and anti-invasion preparations, the county was under the supervision of Sir Will Spens, Master of Corpus Christi College, Cambridge, and the Regional Commissioner for the East of England.[2]

The increased likelihood of air attacks meant that the subject of school shelters assumed enhanced significance. The county council's original plans anticipated that in evacuation areas schools would be shut and no shelters would be required. As reception areas were largely rural, there was no incentive to provide shelters there either. The problem was the provision of school shelters in neutral areas, where most children had remained and where schools stayed open. It was to these areas that the county council allocated £40,000 for shelters. However, the three-fold evacuation division of the county could not be kept watertight and the clamour for school protection in some towns in reception areas, mainly on the coast, and at some large schools, led to a

---

1   Essex County Council, *A report of the ARP committee on the organisation and administration of the civil defence services with a brief account of the operations in which they were engaged 1939–45* (Chelmsford, 1947), p. 7.
2   ERO C/W 2/3/2, Group 7 War Diary Operational Report 1939–45.

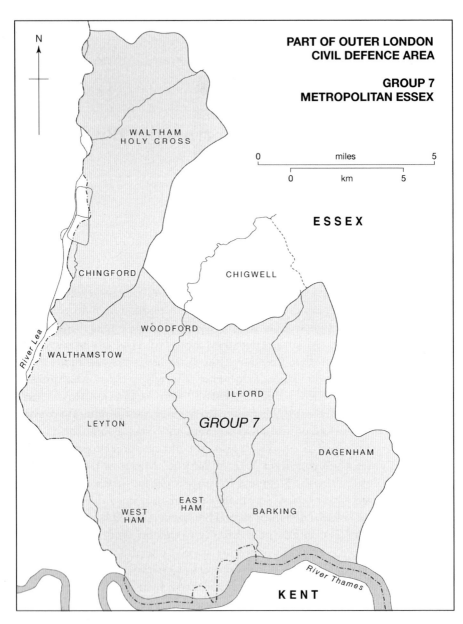

Map 3. Group 7

Figure 2.1. The devastation caused by the German minelaying aircraft in Victoria Road, Clacton, 30 April 1940. (Paul Rusiecki)

supplementary sum of £40,000 being allocated.[3] The situation was further complicated by the limited response to evacuation in the south of the county. A county council report noted that in late 1939 there were still over 1,600 secondary, 600 technical and about 25,000 elementary school pupils still there.[4]

In November 1939 the government authorised the reopening of secondary schools in evacuation areas provided that the buildings were considered to be secure. Six Essex metropolitan secondary schools met the official criteria and were reopened, catering for 1,636 pupils. However, 80 per cent of elementary schools in Essex failed to meet the Board's wartime requirements.[5] The county council and, in many cases, head teachers and governors kept them closed until shelters were provided but, given the shortage of labour and materials, this led to lengthy delays. In the meantime, tutorial and correspondence courses were organised in the children's family homes. Chelmsford Borough Council, for example, adopted a so-called 'Scattering Scheme'. Those children living nearest the school were to be sent home as soon as the siren went. If there were public shelters near the school and the number of children sent home was quite small then the remaining children were to be taken to the shelter by their teachers. School staff opposed this as reckless, however, and the council began to provide shelters in spite of the cost.[6] Nevertheless, the issue of school shelters remained unresolved in many parts of the county when German air activity began. At Burnham local children had attended school for the previous nine months but the lack of shelters now

---

3   ECC minute, 3 October 1939.
4   ECC, 5 December 1939, Report of a Special Committee regarding the Re-Opening of Schools in Evacuation Areas.
5   ECC, 5 December 1939, Report of a Special Committee regarding the Re-Opening of Schools in Evacuation Areas.
6   ChBC minutes, 21 July, 10 October 1939.

led some parents to keep them at home.[7] Parents of children at the Victoria Girls and Infants' Schools in Chelmsford expressed concern because of their proximity to the railway and local factories, and because of the general structure of the buildings. Recognising the legitimacy of parental concerns, the borough council ordered both schools to be closed and the pupils transferred.[8]

The threat from the skies suddenly came home to Essex on 30 April, when a Heinkel bomber which had been carrying two mines was hit by anti-aircraft fire over Harwich and crashed in a residential area in Clacton. One of its mines exploded. The crew of four died, as did two civilians – the first civilian deaths of the war on the mainland. A total of 156 people were injured, 34 seriously.[9] The county then had a three-month reprieve before serious air attacks began. Although the skies over Essex were not the central focus of the Battle of Britain, there were numerous dogfights overhead. James Hough, the headmaster of Brentwood School, recalled: '[W]e had about half a dozen battles round and above Brentwood, twice in particular the air seemed full of them as one looked up, far too many to count and it all seems over in a short time as they leave us and draw nearer to the coast.'[10] During August 1940 the appearance of German aircraft became more frequent and the novelty of the experience was conveyed by an excitable *Essex Chronicle* reporter:

> Then we had the thrill of our lives – coming in from the sea was a huge squadron of German bombers, in very exact formation, a leader in front, with the others in set echelon fashion strung out behind. We counted thirty-four quite easily, and it was really a fine sight, desperate in its fearsomeness. The menfolk cheered defiantly, the ladies rushed up banks and on to higher land to get a better view, while boys climbed trees, yelling with excitement. It was a cheering demonstration of the irrepressible high spirits of English folk when faced with danger.[11]

On 26 August Eric Rudsdale saw a large-scale dogfight above Colchester. 'We have all heard this sound so often on films that it really seems quite natural,' he noted, 'and one tends to forget that this is real, and that you are watching young men go down to a particularly unpleasant death.'[12] Essex newspapers now carried pictures and silhouettes of German aircraft – troop-carrying gliders as well as fighters and bombers – to encourage people to learn to recognise enemy aircraft.[13]

7   BA 31 August 1940.
8   ChBC minutes, 11 June 1940.
9   ECC Report of ARP Committee, Essex County Council minutes 1939–45.
10   ERO D/DBg 80/30, James Hough letter, 25 November 1940.
11   EC 23 August 1940.
12   EC 26 August 1940.
13   ST 26 June 1940.

Figure 2.2. A downed Luftwaffe pilot under arrest at Shoeburyness railway station in August 1940, at the height of the Battle of Britain. (Essex Record Office)

German air activity over Group 7 developed in the form of armed reconnaissance raids by day and night, and only about 120 high explosive bombs were dropped between the end of July and the end of August. Nevertheless, the number of 'alerts' – the term used to describe the period between the sirens sounding and the 'all-clear' being given – was increasing. The first very long night alert, from 9.27pm to 3.37am, occurred on the night of 26/27 August 1940. It was to be the first of dozens of alerts which went on night after night, lasting ten, eleven or twelve hours at a time, and which was such a distinctive feature of the Blitz. However, in early September the Luftwaffe changed its tactics and launched a sustained attack on the oil refineries around Tilbury, on the north bank of the Thames.[14] These attacks, at Thameshaven, Coryton and Shellhaven, created blazes which were almost impossible to extinguish and

---

14   The next section is based on ERO C/W 2/3/2, Group 7 Operation report.

Figure 2.3. The modernistic Waker air-raid shelter in Dagenham. (London Borough of Barking & Dagenham Archives and Local Studies Centre)

fire brigades were brought from the Midlands to fight them.[15] Casualties were light but the German tactics were recognised by the civil defence authorities as extremely ominous. On 6 September Group 7 received the following message:

> In future please report at once … serious fires caused by enemy bombing which may act as guide to enemy aircraft and invite further attack on the same night and one hour before sunset any such fires which are still burning as the result of earlier attack.[16]

In August and September 1940 Essex was the county which bore the brunt of the growing German air offensive. Its residents, particularly along the coast and in the metropolitan area, were becoming accustomed to frequent alerts and very long periods of overnight residence in shelters. As they emerged they must have been surprised that comparatively little damage had been done and few people hurt. From 31 August to 7 September only 81 people were killed and 236 hospitalised with serious injuries in Group 7.[17] People began to take these things in their stride. On 6 September the Civil Defence authorities in Ilford, Leyton and Walthamstow, for instance, reported that 'Morale of population excellent'.[18] That morale, however, was about to be tested to its limit.

On 24 August 1940 German bombers dropped several bombs on London and Churchill ordered retaliatory attacks on Berlin. Hitler was enraged and authorised a massive bombing campaign against London, promising to raze it to the ground. The date set for this campaign to begin was 7 September,

15   ERO C/W 1/6/1, Operational Summaries, Extra-Metropolitan Essex, 1–8 September 1940.
16   ERO C/W 2/4/1, Group 7 general file, 6 September 1940.
17   ERO C/W 1/5/11, Group 7 Situation reports 27 July–29 September 1940; 2, 7 September 1940.
18   ERO C/W 1/5/11, Group 7 Situation reports, 6 September 1940.

a day since referred to as 'Black Saturday'.[19] It was a decision which was to transform the experience of war for the population of Essex. In mid-afternoon 348 bombers and 617 fighters took off from their bases in occupied France. The vast armada of German aircraft, twenty miles wide and occupying 800 square miles of sky, headed for the London docks. The few RAF squadrons available to challenge them were overwhelmed by the sheer number of enemy aircraft and the bombers flew on facing minimal effective opposition.

The sirens of Group 7 sounded at 4.43pm. T.H. Pointer, an ARP warden stationed at the Royal Victoria Docks, was not unduly alarmed:

> Strolling to the door with a cup of tea in my hand I looked around and up for a sight of them. Gunfire could now be heard and at last almost overhead could be seen over fifty aircraft at a rather low altitude with gunfire bursting in front and around them.[20]

Bryan Forbes, who was later to become an accomplished actor and film director, was thirteen years old at the time. That afternoon he was watching *Gaslight* in the Odeon Theatre at Forest Gate. The performance was brought to an abrupt end and, as he stepped outside, he and the rest of the cinema audience watched spellbound as the German air armada flew overhead.[21]

The Luftwaffe's target was the London docks, but several boroughs in Metropolitan Essex were near the river and, as bomb-aiming was not an exact science, every one of them was hit. Silvertown, a working-class district of West Ham comprising terraced streets crammed together adjacent to the docks, was surrounded by chemical and gas works, petrol stores, factories, timber yards and workshops. The whole area was a lethal tinder-box awaiting the Luftwaffe's spark. High explosive bombs, incendiaries and crude oil bombs crashed down for an hour and a half. The first bombs fell on the Ford works at Dagenham. A few minutes later St Mary's Hospital in Stratford received a direct hit, demolishing the nurses' quarters. Silvertown itself, with its population of some 13,000, was pulverised. By 7.48pm only two factories were left intact.[22] Nearby, T.H. Pointer ran for cover. 'This time we could hear the whine as the bombs were falling,' he wrote, 'and they ripped across towards us so I knelt and put my head on the floor and my hands on my neck.' The force of the explosions rocked his shelter like a cradle. He emerged in the pauses between enemy formations flying over, but the situation deteriorated:

---

19   J. Gardiner, *The Blitz: the British under attack* (London, 2010), p. 5.
20   IWM 3957, Private Papers of T. H. Pointer.
21   Quoted in P. Stansky, *The first day of the Blitz* (Yale, 2007), p. 36.
22   ERO C/W 2/1/10A, Group 7 raid messages, 7–9 September 1940.

It was worse than before and I got lower and lower on the floor until I layed [sic] on my stomache [sic]. The gunfire could not be heard above the noise of the explosion of bombs and I thought I would be lucky to survive such a raid.[23]

Something of the desperate situation in the area can be glimpsed in these short raid messages, sent by civil defence workers in West Ham:

8.07   Please send help. Incident. 100 people shocked in air raid shelter under docks in Oriental Rd. There is fire. Rendezvous Silvertown Way. Guide will be sent. Proceed with caution. No knowledge of raid damage.

8.27   Silvertown is a raging inferno. Send all cars and ambulances possible. Depot Superintendent at Drew Road [School] reports … 200 people in the playground. Have sent all help available.

9.12   Can't contact Albert Dock hospital.

10.11   25 UXBs.

10.16   ARP HQ hit but carrying on.

10.45   Arrangements made [to] take casualties from Silvertown to North Woolwich Pier. Number to be removed unknown.

11.45   Damage and UXB at Temple Mills [railway marshalling yard]

11.48   UXB now exploded.

11.54   DAB [delayed action bomb] at West Ham Generating Station.

00.25   Beckton Gasworks alight.

02.10   Reference message as to two Rescue parties standing by … Much regret it is impossible I am informed to get in or out of Silvertown as all roads … are blocked.

03.31   Ten coaches required to go to Holbrook Rd School, Plaistow, to transfer people to Stock St School because of UXB at Holbrook School.[24]

All over the area water mains were smashed and supplies were polluted by sewage. Both sides of the river were ablaze for miles and the waves of heat which hit the faces of the firemen made them gasp for breath. The low tide made it even harder to get water from the Thames and fire brigades had to improvise by erecting static canvas water tanks filled from water tankers.[25] Damage to electric cables was so severe that civil defence personnel worked using candles in jam jars; similarly, the damage to telephone lines meant using

---

23   IWM 3957.
24   ERO C/W 2/1/10A, Group 7 raid messages, 7–8 September 1940.
25   ERO C/W 2/3/2, Group 7 War Diary: Operational Report 1939–45, 8 September 1940.

Figure 2.4. 'Gilman's Dare Devils'. The boy messengers of the borough of West Ham, who defied the blitz in 1940–41. (Newham Heritage & Archives)

young lads as messengers. In West Ham they were known as 'Gilman's Dare Devils', after the councillor in charge of them. These boys risked their lives every time they went outside:

> One lad named Mick by his pals, great tall lad, his hair always dishevelled, face dirty, knew no fear … he came into the centre, reported and then stated that he had been blown off his machine by the explosion of a bomb, into a crater in the blackness and stunned. When he came to, he cycled back as hard as he could to the centre, pleased and proud that he had achieved another task, ready to go out again.[26]

The massive amount of glass from broken windows in West Ham hampered civil defence vehicles and an appeal was made for ten mechanical sweepers, although only six arrived.[27] The fire brigades of Dagenham, Barking, and East and West Ham had all called for aid and by 8.00pm more than 500 fire engines had arrived from other areas. A journalist on the *Stratford Express* watched helplessly as the raid unfolded: 'I stood at the door of my house miles from the scene of devastation, and there stretched before my eyes an ocean of fires, miles in extent. Flames leapt madly upward and the great sea of conflagration appeared unbroken.'[28]

---

26   www.newhamstory.com, accessed 31 October 2014.
27   ERO C/W 2/3/2, 7, 7–8 September 1940.
28   SE 13 September 1940.

Having fulfilled their mission the raiders had left by 6.30pm and the 'all-clear' sounded. When Paul Rowntree Clifford and his helpers at the West Ham Mission emerged from a basement they faced a terrible sight.

> As we emerged from the shelters after the 'all-clear' the sky was blotted out by a pall of smoke; the air reeked with the fumes of gelignite; the whole district was ringed with a circle of flame. It seemed that we were in the midst of Hell's inferno.[29]

Ivy Hicks and her friend Rene were cycling back from Epping to their homes in East Ham. Reaching Stratford, everywhere seemed ablaze. When they got to Rene's home they were told that her family had been moved out because of a suspected unexploded bomb nearby. They found them in Gainsborough Road School, which no-one was then allowed to leave for two hours. They had been home for only five minutes when the second raid began and they spent the rest of the night in their respective Anderson shelters.[30]

The first wave of raiders had left but a force of bombers, guided to their target by the immense fires below, which were visible from the French coast, arrived just under two hours later. Some 250 aircraft came over in wave after wave until 5.00am the next morning, dropping tons of high explosives, oil bombs and incendiaries into the inferno below. During the night nine major conflagrations, nineteen large fires and about 1,000 smaller ones raged across the area. Molten tar from a Silvertown factory trapped fire engines, ambulances and civil defence vehicles in a sticky mass. Burning barges drifted down the Thames before floating back with the incoming tide.[31] Ships in the docks were hit and set ablaze. East Ham's shopping area was devastated and countless streets were closed by the wreckage of fallen buildings.[32]

F.W. Hurd, a fireman based at Euston, was ordered to East Ham. It was unusual for fire crews to be sent such a distance and he feared the worst. His crew arrived at the blazing Beckton Gas Works:

> And all the time the area was being mercilessly bombed. The road shuddered with the explosions. A.A. shells were bursting overhead. A Royal Navy destroyer berthed in one of the docks was firing her A.A. equipment, as were other ships. The shrapnel literally rained down. It was now about midnight and still this incessant racket kept on. It surprised me how quickly we got used to sensing whether a bomb was coming

29 P.R. Clifford, *Venture in faith: the story of the West Ham Central Mission* (London, 1950), pp. 122–3.
30 I. Alexander, *Maid in West Ham: my formative years 1924–48* (Winchester, 2001), p. 54.
31 C. Demarne, *The London Blitz: a fireman's tale* (London, 1980), pp. 8–9.
32 ERO C/W 2/3/2, 7, 7–8 September 1940.

our way or not. At first we all lay flat every time we heard anything but after an hour or so we only dived for it if one came particularly close.[33]

It was not just the dockside boroughs that were pounded on this apocalyptic night; the Essex Thames remained a key target, with the Anglo-American Oil Works at Purfleet being attacked for an hour. Six hundred firemen fought the huge blazes, during which 200 firemen were overcome by fumes and six people were killed.[34] At 5.40pm the message 'Fire Raging Furiously out of control' was despatched to county HQ and at 11pm ten oil tanks were ablaze along the river front.[35]

The raid ended at 4.52am, after ten hours of concentrated bombing. In the second raid alone the Germans had dropped 625 tons of high explosive bombs and more than 800 incendiary bomb canisters, each containing 795 pounds of explosive.[36] Gladys Strelitz and her brother and sisters left the church where they had sought shelter: 'As we got out of the crypt, we could see the Home Guard actually digging out bodies. And the smouldering flames and the stench was terrible and the sky was all lit up with flames.'[37]

The *Stratford Express* reporter who had watched the raid from his home made his way to the area on the day after:

I came upon street after street of derelict houses, blasted into piles of rubble, or with the inside so disintegrated that they were totally uninhabitable. The occupants for the most part had scraped what few articles remained to them and left, and through shattered windows and torn curtains and blinds, messengers of distress, and here and there could be discerned furniture in grotesque positions.[38]

Fires were still raging in West Ham and along the Thames, and Rest Centres were overflowing. Silvertown was ablaze. Those whose homes were undamaged or who defiantly chose to stay often had no supplies of gas, water or electricity and their streets were blocked by debris. Thousands of people had already left, although often only temporarily; they became known as 'trekkers', and that morning and throughout the day they were found trudging into Essex to safety, clutching or pushing in barrows and prams what few possessions they had left. Some 3,000 were accommodated in Chingford on 8 September, and another

---

33   IWM 4833, F.W. Hurd, 'Blitz Over London: An impression of the first of these large-scale Night raids in the capital, 7 September 1940'.
34   R. Reynolds and J. Catton, *Thurrock goes to war* (Wickford, 1997), pp. 45–7.
35   ERO C/W 1/3/10, Extra-Metropolitan Essex: County Chronological Files, 7 September 1940.
36   Gardiner, *The Blitz*, p. 14.
37   Quoted in Stansky, *Blitz*, p. 93.
38   SE 13 September 1940.

3,000 arrived over the following four days.[39] Those who reached Epping Forest found makeshift facilities put up by Essex County Council. There were three small camps equipped with incinerators, latrines, kitchens, canteens, standpipes and 'ablution benches'.[40] Many refugees moved just far enough away to return to work during the day. East Enders moved out only a small distance and in September half the population of Stepney fixed notices on battered front doors giving addresses in Becontree, Chadwell Heath, Dagenham and East Ham.[41] Some workers from the Tate & Lyle sugar factory at Plaistow were evacuated as far away as Finchley, but the majority continued to report for work.[42]

Metropolitan Essex bore the brunt of that first night of the Blitz, although fatalities were astonishingly light. The Group 7 operational report listed 26 dead, although the situation was so chaotic in West Ham that no figures were listed.[43] This was out of a total of 436 people killed in London. Even by the end of September there were still 1,206 casualties in West Ham that had not been allocated among the three categories of dead, serious or slightly injured, largely because of the inadequacies of the compilation of information in the borough. They may well have included those of the South Hallsville School bombing, which is discussed below.[44] Nevertheless, in spite of the ferocity of the attack and the extent of the devastation, the casualty figures were far below the official predictions, based on which the government had planned mass burials.[45]

After the devastating attack on 'Black Saturday' the Germans launched a remorseless bombing campaign on London, which inevitably affected the Home Counties, including Essex. Daylight raids over Metropolitan Essex declined, although they did not entirely cease.[46] However, it was night raids, which are now indelibly associated with the Blitz, which formed the core of the Luftwaffe's campaign. The sirens usually sounded at about 8.00pm each night and the all-clear did not take place until about 5am the next morning. Along with the rest of London, Metropolitan Essex was attacked for 57 consecutive nights up to 2/3 November and 35 of the subsequent 50 nights up to Christmas Eve. Clear, moonlit nights, the nights of the so-called 'bombers' moon', were believed to be particularly attractive to the enemy, but in reality the Luftwaffe often came even when the weather was less favourable. For instance, an all-night raid occurred on 16/17 October, when there was heavy cloud and rain. However, from about November the Germans' focus on ports and provincial towns and cities,

39   ERO C/W 2/3/2, 7–8 September 1940.
40   ERO C/W 4/8, maps showing uncontrolled evacuation camps at Epping Forest.
41   T. Harrison, *Living through the Blitz* (London, 1976), p. 65.
42   O. Lyle, *The Plaistow story* (London, 1960), p. 207.
43   ERO C/W 2/3/2, 7–8 September 1940.
44   For West Ham, www.newhamstory.com; for other areas ERO C/W 2/3/2, 7 September 1940, and ERO C/W 2/4/1, Group 7 general file, casualty figures 1940–41.
45   A. Calder, *The people's war: Britain 1939–1945* (London, 1969), p. 165.
46   The following analysis is based upon civil defence reports of air raids in ERO C/W 2/3/2.

combined with a sustained deterioration in weather conditions, contributed to a marked reduction of attacks. The area was still bombed, but during January and February 1941 raids fell to an average of about one every four nights, and from March to May it was one night in every nine. Nevertheless, the Germans launched one last ferocious campaign in the spring of 1941 and, on the nights of 19/20 March and 19/20 April, Metropolitan Essex, along with London, suffered two of the heaviest raids of the entire Blitz. The raid of 19/20 April exceeded all others in its violence and, once more, it was disastrous for Metropolitan Essex. During seven-and-a-half hours 232 high explosives, 77 parachute mines and thousands of incendiaries were dropped. In West Ham many factories, schools, cinemas and churches and hundreds of houses were destroyed or damaged. Forty people were killed and more than 200 injured. In East Ham 64 died that night. In total 259 people were killed and 859 were injured in Group 7.[47] On 10/11 May a further 58 people were killed and 219 injured in what proved to be the final raid of the Blitz, following which major Luftwaffe units moved east to prepare for the invasion of the Soviet Union.[48]

The government's provision of shelters was still incomplete when the Blitz began, although a variety of shelters had been provided and any safe place was used as raids developed. A survey of seven of the boroughs in Group 7 carried out on 6 January 1941 revealed shelter provision for almost 700,000 people. Most of this provision comprised Anderson shelters for 570,000 people. The Anderson shelter was designed for suburban areas where residents had gardens. They were made of panels of galvanised corrugated steel set four feet deep in the ground and covered on the top and sides with a minimum of fifteen inches of soil. They were free to anyone earning less than £250 a year, which covered a large proportion of the population. Surface shelters or reinforced basements in homes had been provided for 30,000 people, and public shelters capable of holding almost 100,000 people had also been erected, largely for those with no gardens.[49] Soil conditions in parts of Essex were unsuitable for shelters and in the autumn of 1939 those at Romford were two feet deep in water. On 23 October 50 women carrying banners on which were painted 'Shelters not death traps' and 'Is pneumonia better than bombs?' marched to the Town Hall to protest.[50] This problem was not unique to Essex and the government's solution was to reset shelters in a concrete tank, placed in the soil up to ground level, to act as a waterproof foundation. Essex County Council approved this method for the county's damp areas.[51]

---

47   ERO C/W 2/3/2, 19–20 April 1941.
48   ERO C/W 2/3/2, 10–11 May 1941.
49   ERO C/W 2/13/1, Group 7 shelter surveys, 6 January 1941.
50   BA 28 October 1939.
51   BA 15 November 1939.

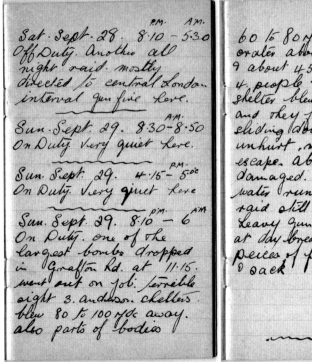

Figure 2.5a. Extracts from the Blitz diary of William Riddiford, ARP warden in Dagenham, revealing some of the horror that he experienced (Part 1). (London Borough of Barking & Dagenham Archives and Local Studies Centre)

Figure 2.5b. Extracts from the Blitz diary of William Riddiford, ARP warden in Dagenham, revealing some of the horror that he experienced (Part 2). (London Borough of Barking & Dagenham Archives and Local Studies Centre)

No type of shelter was invulnerable, however. Anderson shelters were capable of withstanding the effects of bombs which exploded nearby but they were not designed to withstand direct hits. During the Blitz there were direct hits on 33 Anderson shelters in Essex, killing 82 people and injuring 47. Direct hits on six surface shelters killed 23 people and injured 121.[52] These direct hits affected only a tiny fraction of shelters but the victims were no longer around to debate their extreme statistical misfortune.

Anderson shelters had advantages over houses in that the weight of materials in a collapsed house could be lethal to its occupants. Nevertheless, they were deeply unpopular with most people. They were invariably cold, cramped

---

52   Based on an analysis of information in ERO C/W 2/3/2, September 1940–May 1941.

and uncomfortable, and, above all, they were not designed to keep out the tremendous racket of exploding bombs and anti-aircraft fire that went on for hours at a time. They had been intended to accommodate people during short raids, but, as enemy aircraft appeared throughout the night, shelterers were compelled to take up residence for long periods. Mary Hoodless of Hornchurch went to the Anderson shelter at first but then stayed in her house. The shelter gave her terrible back ache and leg pains, and on one occasion a bomb blast made her neighbour's nose bleed for two days. Her diary records the utter misery which the incessant noise of the sirens, guns, bomb-blasts and shrapnel caused her.[53] Helena Britton from Walthamstow told her daughter in America, 'It's about nine weeks now since dad and I undressed to go to bed … We made it [the shelter] as comfortable as possible, but we all get so stiff owing to restricted movement.'[54] By the end of December 1940, even though there had been heavy raids in that month, a Group 7 survey revealed that only about a third of potential shelterers were using Andersons; most people preferred to accept the risks of sleeping in their own homes.[55] This was in line with the results of London's first 'Shelter Census' in November, which had revealed that just 27 per cent of people used them.[56]

German tactics also wrought a profound change in the way that public shelters were used. Originally they were intended for use by those caught outside during an attack. However, as heavy raids developed, people began taking shelter throughout the night, bringing bedding and belongings with them, and treating the shelters like dormitories. This prompted local authorities, some of them slowly and reluctantly, to accept that they had a responsibility to make them more habitable. In November 1940, for instance, Barking Town Council bought several hundred three-tier bunks to sleep almost 3,000 people and within a short time it was issuing shelterers with tickets to 'book' a bunk.[57] The government was resistant to the idea of 'deep' shelters and the use of tube stations as shelters in case a 'shelter mentality' paralysed the war effort, but Professor J.B.S. Haldane, a distinguished scientist and leading Communist, pointed out the inadequacies of air-raid provision in London and the Communist party campaigned for deep shelters and the use of Tube stations. Unable to counter this campaign and faced by people storming the Tubes once the Blitz began, the government granted *de facto* recognition of their use.[58]

53   W.A. Hoodless, *Air raid: a diary and stories from the Essex Blitz* (Stroud, 2008), pp. 27, 31–5, 42–3.
54   Quoted in J. Gardiner, *Wartime: Britain 1939–1945* (London, 2004), p. 349.
55   ERO C/W 2/13/1, Group 7 shelter survey, 6 January 1941. A survey on 3–4 June 1941 actually revealed that the number of shelterers had increased to 278,000.
56   Calder, *People's war*, p. 181.
57   SE 29 November, 6 December 1940.
58   J. Gregg, *The shelter of the tubes: tube sheltering in wartime London* (London, 2001), pp. 6–7; Calder, *Myth of the Blitz*, pp. 83–4.

There were only two 'underground' Tube stations in Metropolitan Essex, at Stratford and Leyton. The Central Line had been extended before the war but in 1939 it ended at Leyton, and the underground part of the station was unfinished when war broke out. As West Ham began to take a terrible pounding large numbers of people entered the Stratford tube each night, even though nothing had been done to make it habitable. The tunnel reached almost as far as Leyton. At first it was fenced off, but at the Leyton end shelterers broke the fences and sought the safety of the deeper parts of the tunnel, towards Stratford. In September 1940 it was claimed that 8,000–10,000 people sheltered there every night. Conditions below were appalling. Leyton's medical officer visited the tunnel and noted that:

> All along the tunnel there are cushions, rugs, blankets, mattresses, and other forms of domestic clothing to provide warmth. Many of these are not only dirty but verminous. Scraps of bread, fruit and other forms of food are strewn among the bedding and on the floor of the tunnel, and I fear this will attract rats unless some steps are taken.... Water is lying in puddles of varying depth all along the concrete floor of this tunnel, and judging from its appearance this water has been contaminated by human excrement.[59]

Further reports suggested that there was widespread dampness, while at the Leyton end air circulation was so poor at first that people fainted.[60] In spite of its sleaziness, however, the shelter was a paradise compared with Stepney's Tilbury shelter, which was notorious not only for the dreadful environment but also for violence, prostitution and criminality.[61]

Conditions in West Ham were dire in consequence of the severity and frequency of raids, the degree of destruction and the high level of homelessness. In the first week of the Blitz, Feeding Centres provided three meals a day to some 10,000 people.[62] Not surprisingly, shelters assumed critical importance to these people and hundreds who used the tunnel signed a petition demanding the provision of decent facilities. At first West Ham Town Council refused to cooperate because the use of tube stations as shelters was not official government policy.[63] This led to the creation of the West Ham Deputation Committee, which campaigned for facilities in the tunnel. The Labour-dominated town council

---

59 TNA HO 271/721, Leyton Borough Public Shelter, West Ham and Leyton Tunnels. Leyton Medical Officer report, 'Cleansing of Shelters', 26 September 1940.
60 TNA WO 189/2141, 'Report on Air conditions in the Leytonstone–West Ham Shelter Tunnel: investigation carried out on the night of 8–9 April 1941'.
61 Gardiner, *Blitz*, pp. 72–4.
62 SE 1 November 1940.
63 SE 5 July, 18 October 1940.

interpreted the committee's demands as overt criticism of its overall handling of the emergency. Councillors were alienated further by the committee's left-wing ideology, typified by a demand that the government should use the Soviet Union as a mediator 'to ask on what terms they would use their services in the interests of a solution of war honourable to the people and not submitting to Fascism'.[64] The demand reinforced the council's view that the committee was influenced by Communists and it steadfastly refused to recognise the committee as the legitimate representative of underground shelterers.[65]

The ruling Labour council at Leyton had also been working to adapt small sections of the Gainsborough Bridge (Leyton) Tube station as air-raid shelters.[66] Thousands of local residents flocked to the tunnel and even in the spring of 1941, when the worst of the Blitz was over, there were still about 2,000 regular users each night.[67] One visitor to the area wrote that, 'Had I been a stranger to this part of High Road, Leyton, I should certainly not have found it necessary to inquire my way to the tunnel. It was merely a case of following the crowd.'[68] One reporter visited it in late September 1940:

> The wholesale nightly migration of people of all types to these tubes is a spectacle comparable to a football Derby day. From all directions, as darkness begins to descend, comes a procession of young and old, bowed down like pack horses with the oddest collection of articles to make the nights more tolerably comfortable. Despite all they can do the standard of comfort is very low, but these nightly wanderers care little for this. The discomfort that comes of herding, the stone-covered floor, and the foetid atmosphere, are nothing compared with the peace of mind which comes from the security these steel girt chambers hold out[69]

To improve conditions the shelterers at Leyton followed West Ham's example and formed the Gainsborough Bridge Tunnel Shelter Committee. Leyton Town Council alleged that the committee had been infiltrated by Communists and refused to recognise it. When a group of councillors, accompanied by a local MP, R. Sorensen, visited the tunnel, they were criticised by other councillors for lending legitimacy to the Shelter Committee. The West Leyton Labour Party hit back at those who denounced Sorensen's visit by stating that he supported those 'who are doing all possible to make their lives more tolerable and happier under existing conditions'. Miss A.P. Flaherty, the secretary of the Shelter

---

64   SE 4 October 1940.
65   SE 4 October 1940, 31 January 1941.
66   SE 5 July 1940.
67   SE 21 March 1941.
68   SE 4 October 1940.
69   SE 27 September 1940.

Committee, rejected the council's allegations, arguing that the formation of the committee had been spontaneous because of the need to pressurise the council into making the tunnels habitable.[70]

Unfortunately this political controversy was not the only example of disharmony in Leyton. An unseemly rift developed between those who used Anderson and public shelters on the one hand, and the Gainsborough Bridge shelterers on the other. Its cause was the fact that the Gainsborough Bridge shelterers seemed to get preferential treatment from the council. A letter from one resident who took to her Anderson shelter each night pointed out:

> They don't get cheap food. They don't get music, except for the row of the guns and bombs, but they are prepared to carry on and at the same time to be on the top with a view to rendering such assistance as they can to their neighbours in an emergency. The people in the smaller shelters haven't got canteens, wireless and cheap cups of tea.[71]

The implication that tunnellers were selfish spongers saving their own skins by abandoning all communal responsibilities while living in security led them to be nicknamed 'divers', with its obvious connotations. A.J. Stanley, the vicar of Leytonstone, complained of the 'shelter mania' displayed by those who took refuge in the tunnels even when there was no raid.[72] Some people accused the tunnellers of contributing nothing to the war effort. A letter from T. Conway of Leytonstone refuted this by asserting that:

> Among these people are bus, tube, tram drivers and conductors, railway guards and signalmen; aircraft, munitions and shipping industries are well represented down in the tunnel, also soldiers, sailors and airmen when on leave.[73]

In mid-March 1941 the Leyton Tube shelterers were suddenly given a week to quit so that war production could take place in the tunnel. The committee argued that

> these tunnels are regarded by the local residents as the only safe and adequate air raid shelter in the locality … and there is a strong feeling in the neighbourhood that the tunnels as they are occupied at the moment should be maintained as hitherto, for it has proved in the

---

70   SE 31 January, 7, 14, 21 February 1941.
71   SE 31 January 1941.
72   SE 21 February 1941.
73   SE 7 March 1941.

event of a severe air raid [that] many people flock to these tunnels in preference to any other place of refuge.[74]

Four members of the Shelter Committee travelled to London to see Ellen Wilkinson MP, supported by a petition signed by 6,798 people. The government reversed its decision and the tunnels were still in use in April.[75]

Essex outside Group 7 ('Extra-Metropolitan Essex') was also bombed, and there was hardly a town or village which did not experience at least one 'incident'.[76] These raids did not have the same impact as those on Metropolitan Essex because enemy bomb-loads were scattered over a largely rural landscape with a dispersed population. Between October 1940 and May 1941 about 50,000 hostile devices were dropped outside of the metropolitan area. Of these, about 7,500 were high explosive bombs, roughly 40,000 were incendiaries, 261 were parachute mines and 334 oil bombs. More than a quarter of all these missiles fell harmlessly on agricultural and waste land, and more than 500 ended up in rivers and the sea.[77]

German attacks on the county followed a similar pattern to those on Metropolitan Essex. Attacks occurred nightly throughout September, October and November. Although consecutive nightly raids on Metropolitan Essex paused briefly from 2/3 November, it was not until 18/19 November that this happened in the rest of the county, ending 73 consecutive nights on which bombs fell somewhere. Between then and Christmas Day bombs were dropped on the county on 25 of the next 35 nights.[78]

The perceived wisdom concerning the dropping of German bombs on rural Essex is that Luftwaffe pilots dropped what was left of their bomb-loads, lightening their load as they sped back to safety. This is what contemporaries believed. One person said, 'I remember nights spent in the passage listening to aircraft going round and around overhead. They funked going into the London defences and so they circled round and round and they dropped their bombs before going home.'[79] Herbert Maxwell Scott agreed, writing on 2 October 1940, 'At Home we have been quiet in the daytime … old Herman keeps droning about at night on his way there or on his way back and he seems to drop a certain amount of stuff at random.'[80] The official history of civil defence also accepted this idea,

---

74   TNA HO 271/721, letter from Gainsborough Bridge Tunnel Shelter Committee to E. Wilkinson MP, 14 April 1941.
75   SE, 21, 28 March, 4 April 1941.
76   The innocuous term 'incident' was used on any occasion when an enemy missile fell. 'Incidents' were recorded even when there were no casualties or no damage inflicted.
77   Based on author's analysis of the Essex police record in ERO T/A 679/1, Daily Situation Reports by Essex County Constabulary HQ to Sub-divisions, 3 October 1940–30 April 1945, which provides a comprehensive account of where, how many and what type of missiles fell on Extra-Metropolitan Essex throughout the war.
78   The information in this paragraph is based on a study of ERO T/A 679/1.
79   ERO SA 24/1319/1.
80   Maxwell Scott, *Pa's wartime letters and this & that*, p. 59.

asserting that after the introduction of the capital's anti-aircraft barrage bombers flew higher and avoided entering the inner artillery zone, releasing their bomb loads elsewhere.[81] Little Horkesley church, near Colchester, destroyed in 1940, was probably the victim of the Luftwaffe's policy. This theory has something to recommend it, but it does not explain everything. Throughout the Blitz four areas of Essex outside the metropolitan area suffered persistently and sometimes heavily: the area around Brentwood and further south, including the urban sprawl around Romford and Hornchurch; the Essex Thames region and its hinterland, encompassing all the great oil refineries; the Tendring coast around Clacton and Harwich; and a central swathe of the county enclosed by a quadrilateral demarcated by Stansted Mountfitchet, Halstead, Maldon and Ingatestone, which included the light urban-industrial areas of Chelmsford, Witham and Braintree. The first two of these areas were bombed repeatedly during 1940–41. The Tendring coast was the object of regular attacks by single and small groups of aircraft, often during daylight hours, and the central area was hit over and over again during the Blitz. In reality, however, nowhere was safe from attack, and bombs fell regularly on places outside these areas.

Nevertheless, it is true that the location of bomb drops on many nights seemed random. For example, on 22/23 December 1940 high explosives and incendiaries fell on several widely scattered places, none of them remotely vital targets: Romford; Mayland, on the Dengie peninsula; Nazeing, near Harlow; Tolleshunt Knights, south of Colchester; and Kelvedon Hatch, between Brentwood and Ongar. The small number of bombs – five high explosives and 200–300 incendiaries – suggests that they were almost certainly off-loaded by returning aircraft.[82] Missiles from a single plane could land close together or be widely separated, so that many places could be hit by bombs from a single aircraft.

The largely rural nature of Essex meant that casualties were much lighter than in the metropolitan area. However, there was still the same relentless roll of death. The worst single incident occurred during the great raid of 19/20 April 1941, when 38 people were killed by a parachute mine which destroyed part of Essex Road in Collier Row. Twelve of the bodies were never identified and they were buried in four mass graves. Six others were killed in another Romford street, and at Hornchurch nine members of the Gill family were killed by a direct hit on their Anderson shelter. They included seven children, whose ages ranged from eleven years to 23 months. During that horrific night, when there was so much destruction and so many fatalities in both parts of Essex, eight parachute mines, three high explosive bombs and a large number of incendiaries fell on Romford. Ninety-three houses were demolished and

81   T. O'Brien, *History of the Second World War: civil defence* (London, 1955), pp. 388–9.
82   ERO T/A 679/1, 22–23 December 1940.

Figure 2.6. The stark shell of part of South Hallsville School, after the disaster of 9–10 September 1940. (Newham Heritage & Archives)

about 2,000 damaged. Such was the severity of the raid that the town sustained 20–25 per cent of its total war casualties and damage in this one night.[83]

The individual human tragedies are illustrated by these air-raid reports from the Harwich Report Centre in 1941:

> 4 May 12.25am Please send mortuary van for body of child.
>   12.31am Please proceed with van to Cliff Road Main Road [Dovercourt] end, body of child expected to be recovered at any time now. Afterwards proceed to Cottage Hospital to remove body of man.
>   1.52am Body of boy recovered at 1.35.[84]

The victim was named Roy Neville, just ten years old.

The Essex press responded belligerently to the Blitz. 'Goering's air murderers' was the *Essex County Telegraph*'s description of the Luftwaffe.[85] The anger was caused by people's perception of German motivation. One Grays resident

---

83 G. Richards, *Ordeal in Romford* (Romford, 1945), pp. 12–13; P. Watt, *Hitler v Havering 1939–45* (Romford, 1994), pp. 60–63.

84 ERO A5903, Box 1, air raid reports, Harwich Report Centre, 22 June 1940–20 February 1941; Message book 10, 4 May 1941.

85 ECT 14 September, 5 October 1940.

bemoaned the destruction in London, particularly of its cathedrals, churches and palaces.[86] The disquiet at the scale of the early raids was heightened by the fact that the fires which resulted created an eerie red glow that could be seen on the skyline throughout much of south and west Essex. On 7 September darkness did not fall over Romford and Hornchurch because the glow from the burning docks was so bright. The wind brought burnt remains of industrial materials, such as sugar packets, fluttering down in the area.[87] Secondhand reports of the devastation were no less terrifying. Margery Allingham sent two men from Tolleshunt D'Arcy to deliver furniture to central London shortly after the first raid. What they witnessed on their journeys affected them profoundly. 'Their horror was far more impressive to us than any mere recital on the wireless, or even the photos in the newspapers,' she said. 'I looked petrified for days.'[88] When the abridged version of the official history of Britain's civil defence was written it readily acknowledged the immense strain that civilians had been under during the Blitz.[89] The *Stratford Express* recognised this when it commented that 'It requires courage of a high order to listen to this night after night without blanching, and it is to the everlasting credit of the people in the districts haunted by it that they have stood up to it so well.'[90]

The severity of the Blitz added a new urgency to the debate about shelter provision. The *Woodford Times* advised people caught in the open during a raid to

> [k]eep calm, make use of the best protection near at hand, and above all lie flat on the ground.... Lie flat, face downwards, supporting the head on folded arms, keeping the chest just off the ground, to avoid the earth shock of an explosion.[91]

However, for most people more substantial provision was required. Billericay Urban District Council (UDC) planned to dig four deep shelters by tunnelling into the hills in the district, but this was abandoned because of the cost.[92] Colchester's Labour party appealed for deep shelters, but the Home Office argued that the area's soft clay was unsuitable.[93] In Chelmsford widespread disquiet concerning shelters led to the creation of a Citizen's Air Raid Shelter Committee, supported by trade unions, religious bodies and political parties. Although more than 5,000 residents urged the immediate provision of deep shelters, the council

86   MOA diary 5414, 10 September 1940.
87   Watt, *Hitler v Havering*, p. 35.
88   M. Allingham, *The oaken heart* (London, 1941), pp. 217–18.
89   HMSO, *Front line 1940–41: the official story of the civil defence of Britain* (London, 1942), pp. 60–8.
90   SE 13 September 1940.
91   ERO T/P 218/6, Newspaper cuttings from the WT 25 October 1940.
92   ERO A12402, Box 1, Billericay UDC minutes, 28 December 1940.
93   CBC minutes, ARP Committee, 10 December 1939.

rejected them as too costly.[94] As in Leyton and West Ham, allegations were made that the Shelter Committee was run by Communists. One supporter of the committee wrote that, 'The fact that most of our workers in this effort are either Socialists or Communists, is only because they appear to be more interested in the provision of adequate shelter for the people than members of other parties.'[95] At least Chelmsford Borough Council recognised the vulnerability of streets in the vicinity of the town's three great factories.[96] All 848 houses within a 250-yard radius of these works were strengthened by the building of blast walls and six-person communal shelters, costing almost £6,000.[97]

Dissatisfaction with air-raid provision in rural Essex centred on the government's refusal to provide either school shelters or sirens in the countryside. Its reasoning was that rural areas were not sufficiently vulnerable to merit either form of protection. A public meeting in Bardfield passed a resolution criticising Braintree Rural District Council (RDC) for its failure to provide a school shelter. Stanley Wilson, a Saffron Walden county councillor who became an unofficial spokesman for villages, addressed the meeting and said, 'Rich people have been wise. They have built shelters for their children, but I want shelters for all children, rich and poor.'[98] Many parents challenged the authorities and at the risk of being prosecuted kept their children off school until shelters were built.[99]

The problems associated with shelter provision were just a part of a wider discontent which was thrown up by the Blitz, particularly in those areas affected most severely, such as West Ham. The initial impact of intensive bombing shocked people in these areas. Doreen Idle, Labour party activist and investigative reporter, spent time in West Ham during the Blitz. She wrote that

> it was more than bricks and mortar that collapsed in West Ham on the 7th and 8th of September 1940; it was a local ordering of society which was found hopelessly wanting, as weak and badly constructed as the single brick walls which fell down at the blast as though a gigantic Goering had literally laid his heavy hand upon them.[100]

This may well have been attributable to deficiencies in local government, but was also due to the fact that no amount of planning could have coped with

---

94 ECC minutes, 15 November 1940; ERO D/B 7 M2/22/2, ChBC Domestic Air Raid Shelters 5 December 1940; ECT 7 December 1940.
95 EC 20 December 1940.
96 In the Home Office circular, 'Your Home as an Air Raid Shelter', mentioned in ChBC minute, 31 July 1940.
97 ERO D/B 7 M2/22/2, 5 December 1940; ChBC minute, 31 July 1940.
98 EC 13, 27 September 1940.
99 ChBC minute, 7 October 1940.
100 E.D. Idle, *War over West Ham: a study in community adjustment* (London, 1943), pp. 6–7.

the catastrophe of that first raid. West Ham was burdened by the legacy of inter-war financial problems and in addition it had to assume all the financial responsibilities of ARP provision. In common with other local authorities, it was beset by fears that seeking a new loan to pay for it would hang an even heavier millstone around its neck.

West Ham Borough Council was dominated by the Labour party before the war. Its pacifist traditions had meant that ARP provision had been unenthusiastic and inadequate, even after war had begun. Of the 64 councillors 57 were Labour, and the borough's political life had stagnated as a result. In Doreen Idle's opinion, the average age of the councillors – 60 – meant that they were too old to meet the challenge of the Blitz. Lacking, as she put it, 'mental elasticity', the council's responses and solutions to the severe problems created by air raids were slowly and reluctantly reached.[101] Some councillors, perhaps between a third and a half, evacuated themselves when the raids began. A meeting in late November 1940 had 25 absentees, and there were references to those who had moved to Devon and Cornwall.[102] Its post-raid provision was flawed. When the Blitz began the neighbouring borough of East Ham had adopted a policy of centralisation for dealing with all enquiries about post-raid provision.[103] In West Ham the council had opted to decentralise such services in order to serve the borough's outlying areas. The result was that bombed-out families seeking solutions to feeding, homelessness, clothing, furniture and identification had to visit council departments scattered around the borough. The borough was also slow to provide first-aid repairs to damaged houses, clear debris from the streets and provide adequate feeding facilities. It was six months after the Blitz had started before many public shelters were made habitable.[104]

A much graver issue concerned the West Ham ARP Controller. The borough's overwhelming problems meant that four controllers were appointed in quick succession. Nevertheless, borough councillors tended to focus on their own prestige rather than effective administration. The regional commissioners believed that town clerks made good controllers, but West Ham's councillors feared that the government would use them to undermine their authority. A long dispute with Sir Will Spens followed. The council was eventually persuaded to appoint the deputy town clerk as controller and the mayor as chairman of the Emergency Committee, and things proceeded comparatively smoothly into the spring of 1941. However, when the borough was severely hit in the raid of 19/20 March the controller was visiting his evacuated daughter. In the administrative chaos that followed, Herbert Morrison threatened to

---

101   Idle, *War over West Ham*, p. 60.
102   SE 29 November, 27 December 1940.
103   SE 28 February 1941; Idle, *War over West Ham*, p. 65.
104   Idle, *War over West Ham*, pp. 59–67.

strip the council of its responsibility for civil defence. He had recently done just that in the borough of Stepney and, with this example in mind, the chastened councillors appointed as controller W.W. Paton, a much respected and charismatic local clergyman nicknamed 'The Guv'nor'.[105]

The Blitz demonstrated the acute danger from incendiaries and in some areas fire-watching parties were formed by residents willing to keep a night-time vigil. The first Fire Watchers Order of September 1940 made fire-watching compulsory in factories and warehouses. In Maldon every firm was required to inform wardens of the location of keys, ladders and stirrup pumps.[106] At Ford in Dagenham the arrangements eventually combined its fire brigade, fire-watchers and spotters all working together, supervised by 35 ARP wardens.[107] Nevertheless, the huge raid on the City of London on the night of 29/30 December 1940, which caused immense damage, suggested that voluntary fire-watching had failed and in 1941 it was made compulsory for all men between 18 and 65, and was later extended to women. Men could now be forced to fire-watch for up to 48 hours a month. By the New Year of 1941 12,000 people had enrolled for residential fire-watching in Leyton and 7,000 in Barking, where the town's firms also created their own scheme.[108]

People soon began to adjust to the Blitz. Morale was helped by the realisation that casualties were far less than pre-war predictions. People accepted as normal the unusual nature of their changed circumstances. The ability of people to adapt was helped by the predictability of German air raids, which allowed people to return from work and prepare for the night ahead. This unchanging routine is typified by a description of those sheltering in Chelmsford's Shire Hall:

> Some come early in the afternoon to stake their claim. Some wheel perambulators containing crying infants; others carry bedclothes. After their night's sleep, the 'shelterers' depart, and the keepers clear up, ready for the night to come. The same faces will be seen again, in the same places, and at almost precisely the same hour.[109]

From Walthamstow Helena Britton wrote to her daughter on 12 November: 'Lots of people are leaving town … but I don't want to leave our little home if it's possible to stay … you mustn't worry about us, dear. We shall pull through.'[110] The Adams family from Epping adapted to a new lifestyle, as one member recalled:

---

105 Idle, *War over West Ham*, pp. 63–4; SE 29 November, 27 December 1940.
106 ERO D/B 3/5/36, Maldon Town Council minute, 10 December 1940.
107 H. Jones, *British civilians in the front line: air raids, productivity and wartime culture 1939–45* (Manchester, 2006), p. 103.
108 SE 31 January, 14 February 1941.
109 EC 15 November 1940.
110 Quoted in Gardiner, *Wartime*, p. 349.

In fact we arranged life very differently. We fitted everyday things like that around to make it convenient … You cooked to be ready, and you slept when you could, and you played when you could. You learnt to be ready for anything that cropped up.[111]

Just how successful was the German bombing campaign? The amount of destruction that the Luftwaffe inflicted on Essex was enormous, yet not catastrophic. By December 1941 almost 16,000 buildings had been completely demolished, 226,000 were damaged but repairable and 346,000 had been slightly damaged.[112] In spite of the widespread devastation the number of people rendered homeless was relatively small and damage to the industrial, retail and communications infrastructure was repaired quite quickly or alternative outlets were obtained. What of the human cost? Between 1 September 1940 and 11 May 1941 a total of 1,906 residents of Metropolitan Essex died, 3,824 were hospitalised with serious injuries and 7,538 were slightly injured. The rest of Essex was more fortunate, with only 303 fatalities and 1,169 injured.[113]

However, these statistics hide the often terrifying reality of the Blitz. Thousands of Essex residents shared Evelyn Jessie Grubb's experience when her house was damaged by the blast of a land mine:

All our ceilings and most of the roof went. All of us safe … The staircase had an avalanche of ceiling down it. I thought 'This is it!' Glass fragments right through curtains and hall picture and all in some butter I left on the kitchen table. All windows gone. A hole over Pat's bed. Good job she wasn't in it.[114]

A parachute mine landed on an Anderson shelter in a garden in Barking, blowing apart the bodies of the six family members inside. The torso of one of them landed on the roof of what had been their home. An arm was found with an engagement ring on it belonging to a girl who was due to have been married only a few days later. The rescue van had only one shroud, so the body parts were placed inside potato sacks which came from a nearby greengrocer. A dustcart was used to transport the remains to the mortuary.[115]

111 ERO SA 24/1319/1, Adams family, Epping.
112 ERO C/W 2/15/1, Group 7 repair of war damage, December 1940–December 1941; Essex County Council, *A report of the ARP committee*, pp. 26–9.
113 ERO C/W 2/4/1, Group 7 general file; ERO C/W 2/3/2, Operational report 1939–45. In addition, there were 1,206 casualties in West Ham in September 1940 that were not included in these three categories because of the vagueness of the information from the authorities there. The figures for Extra-Metropolitan Essex are calculated from ERO T/A 679/1, although the crucial period 7 September to 1 October 1940 is not included.
114 Diary of Evelyn Jessie Grubb, 11 May 1940.
115 Gardiner, *Wartime*, p. 343.

The personal tragedies are too many to relate, as the bombs carried off the great and the humble. On 13 October 1940 the mayor of Chelmsford, John Ockleford Thompson, and his wife, son and grandchildren were killed when their house suffered a direct hit. He had been elected mayor for a record eighth time only a few days earlier.[116] Even small villages were not immune from disaster. Three schoolchildren from Lexden, near Colchester, who had been evacuated to rural Rushden in Northamptonshire were killed when the school there was hit.[117] There was a much heavier toll of children who were not evacuated. At Romford and Hornchurch one in every three fatalities was under the age of twenty.[118] The pathos of this simple entry made by the vicar of St Peter's, Upton Cross, is striking: 'Funeral. One unidentified body killed September 1940, discovered in debris, Mortlock Road, E.16, June 13 1941.'[119]

Essex's worst disaster during the Blitz occurred in West Ham on the night of 9/10 September 1940. Refugees from Silvertown had taken shelter in South Hallsville School in Canning Town. They were traumatised, or, as the condition was referred to at the time, 'bomb-shocked'. On the second night of raiding the school became even more crowded. Ritchie Calder, the crusading journalist who was a member of the Labour party's committee on air-raid precautions, and his friend, the combative West Ham clergyman W.W. Paton, visited the school on 8 September. 'From the first glance it seemed to me ominous of disaster,' Calder later wrote, calling it 'a bulging, dangerous ruin'.[120]

> In the passages and the classrooms were mothers nursing their babies. There were blind, crippled, and aged people, pensioners … Whole families were sitting in queues, perched on their pitiful baggage, waiting desperately for coaches to take them away from the terror of the bombs.[121]

He wrote that 'I knew that Sunday afternoon, that as sure as night would follow day, the bombers would come again with the darkness, and that the school would be bombed.'[122]

Calder went to Whitehall, where he warned the authorities about the school's extreme vulnerability. Arrangements were made to remove the refugees by bus, but they were muddled. On 9 September some of the refugees were removed but only to make room for more people made homeless the previous night. In

---

116   EC 18 October 1940.
117   L. White (ed.), *Lexden in wartime: memories of local people*, vol. 2 (Colchester, 2008), pp. 2–3.
118   Watt, *Hitler v Havering*, p. 91.
119   ERO D/P 593/1/29, St Peter, Upton Cross, register of services, 14 June 1941.
120   R. Calder, *The lesson of London* (London, 1941), p. 16.
121   Calder, *Lesson*, pp. 17–18.
122   Calder, *Lesson*, p. 18.

consequence the school was still crowded when the raid began that night.[123] Calder's worst fears were realised when a bomb fell on it, collapsing it inwards. The message which reached Group 7 HQ at 7.40am stated that:

> Verbal reports from Controller who states that major occurrence at Hallsville School resulted in 200 casualties, mainly children. Imperative that other refugees are evacuated without delay. Arrangements for this [are] going forward. Otherwise situation still obscure.[124]

By 12.30am it was reported that there were 626 casualties, including 200 refugee children, although the 'proportion [of] killed/wounded [was] not known'.[125] For the next twelve days the rescue services dug in the rubble for survivors. Calder was beside himself with rage at what he regarded as the criminal negligence of the borough authorities and the government. He returned to the scene, where he 'saw the gaping bomb crater, where stood a school used as a shelter centre, containing still uncounted bodies – familiar families wiped out they waited for transport which never came. He saw the … tomb of whole families'.[126] Calder claimed that 450 people died in South Hallsville School. The local authority listed 73 dead. Local people believed that there was an official cover-up and the *Stratford Express* alleged that between 400 and 600 had died.[127]

Essex's proximity to London, the presence of the East End docks and oil refineries within its borders and its location on the Luftwaffe's flight path all combined to ensure that its experience of the Blitz was far more intense than most other counties. The battering it received occurred over several months, including over 100 nights in 1940, and included the three worst raids of the entire Blitz. The raid on 'Black Saturday' equalled or exceeded in ferocity and destruction raids such as those on Coventry, Liverpool, Sheffield and Southampton. Indeed, given that most places in Essex experienced one or more 'incidents', its experience was also more wide-ranging than that of most counties.

The Blitz inflicted death and destruction upon the people of Essex and pushed its population to the brink of their endurance. One leading Civil Defence officer in Group 7 noted that 'The atmosphere grew tense with suffering and struggle … an immense weariness at the relentless regularity of the attack.'[128] However, on reflection it is hard not to admire the courage and resilience that people displayed. The disruption to their daily lives was enormous and the threat of death hung over them for nine long months.

---

123 Calder, *Lesson*, p. 19.
124 ERO C/W 1/5/11, Group 7 Situation reports, 10 September 1940.
125 ERO C/W 1/5/11, Group 7 Situation reports, 10 September 1940.
126 Calder, *Lesson*, p. 19.
127 SE 13 September 1940.
128 O'Brien, *Civil defence*, p. 389.

However, civilian morale, that vital element in modern warfare, survived in spite of the Luftwaffe's efforts. Herbert Maxwell Scott recognised this in a letter he wrote to a Canadian army officer on 2 October 1940. He noted that, in his opinion, the Blitz 'so far [seems] to have been a complete failure … even if it has made the old knees wobble a bit at times!' Even in London his business had not been too disrupted:

> In mid-September it was a bit of a problem getting about and I was lucky to find a neighbour who had to go up by car and who had the petrol to do it. Trains were uncertain and usually pretty late … but [raids] seem to make little difference to getting about.[129]

It is difficult to generalise about how contemporaries viewed the Blitz, but perhaps we may suggest that this part of a poem, written at the time by Margaret Fowler of Wickham Bishops, gets near to it:

> What have we seen in Essex?
> The wreck of houses small,
> The wreck of lovely churches,
> Danbury, Coggleshall;
> Dead cattle on the marshes,
> Deep craters by the lanes,
> And parachutists falling,
> And flaming aeroplanes.
> These have we seen, but still we go
> With heads erect and hearts aglow.[130]

---

129 Maxwell Scott, *Pa's wartime letters*, p. 58.
130 CLSL, *Essex Review*, vol. 50, 1941, p. 143.

3

Fortress Essex

Consolidation of defence

Fears of invasion, which, as we have already seen,[1] were widespread in the summer of 1940, had abated somewhat by the autumn, but preparations continued for just such an eventuality. Even Germany's invasion of Russia in June 1941 and the entry into the war of the United States in December 1941 were unable to eliminate official concerns, which had been intensified in May 1941 when the Germans carried out a successful airborne invasion of Crete.[2] The *Essex Chronicle* issued an ominous warning, arguing that 'If 1942 is to see any climax to the war, and not be spent by the enemy in playing for time the probability of an attempted invasion of this country by the Germans in the coming spring is very real.'[3] In January 1942 Sir Will Spens, the Regional Commissioner, issued an official statement: 'Do not persuade yourselves, and do not allow others to persuade you that invasion is improbable.'[4] Consequently, in the summer of 1942 Walthamstow Town Council issued a leaflet to all householders warning of an invasion, 'whether it be as a last desperate gamble by the enemy or as a counter-attack when the Western Front is opened'.[5]

Following the example of the Great War, in 1941 all villages and even large towns were ordered to form Invasion Committees. Work on forming these committees was certainly under way soon after the German attack on Crete, although they were initially described as 'preparatory and consultative'.[6] Local councils were given the responsibility for forming them under the overall direction of the county council. Much of their work went over the old ground of air-raid precautions, food supply and billeting, but they nevertheless tried

---

1   In Chapter 2.
2   EC 6 June 1941. Herbert Maxwell Scott estimated that a successful airborne invasion would require 2,000 German planes, each carrying fifty paratroopers, to convey a force of 100,000 men. For this reason he did not think that such an assault was feasible: S. Maxwell Scott, *Pa's Wartime Letters and this & that* (2010), p. 73. This was written on 26 January 1941.
3   EC 9 January 1942.
4   ECS 24 January 1942.
5   ERO C/W 2/11/9, Invasion Defence papers 1941–3, Walthamstow Invasion Defence Scheme.
6   ERO A12978, Papers of Alderman William Russell, Romford 1936–46, File 8 (Parish invasion schemes), 16 October 1941.

to keep local populations as focused and alert as possible. The composition of Invasion Committees varied from place to place. At Fordham all parish councillors and the heads of local civil defence services were co-opted on to it.[7] At Canvey Island, which had a much more strategic position on the Thames, the committee included air-raid wardens and representatives of the army, the Home Guard, the national fire service and various utilities.[8]

The Danbury Invasion Committee was particularly thorough in carrying out its duties. In the autumn of 1942 it issued an 'invasion sheet' to all householders entitled 'Are You Ready?' Villagers were urged to pack a bag in readiness and arrange to go to a friend's home if their own was destroyed. Fire-fighting equipment had to be made ready and provision made for food, fuel, transport and first-aid materials. Crude slit trenches were recommended as shelters. The committee gathered emergency rations for eight days to be used as a last resort, acquired 73 stirrup pumps and created a road clearance group, a central demolition gang and five area road gangs to repair damaged roads. It cooperated with the Home Guard in the 'Danbury Defence Scheme'. The positive tone of the committee's activities was summed up in its invasion leaflet, which concluded with the words 'Stand Fast, Keep Your Head, and Be Cheerful'.[9] The efforts of these committees were not always recognised and their meetings were often poorly attended. Some found them laughable. The ever sceptical Eric Rudsdale was told about the work done by the Boxted committee and he found the whole thing distinctly ridiculous:

> Almost all the talk was of an invasion, or at least the invasion of Boxted. I never heard such nonsense. They have been holding meetings, arranging billets for refugees, scaring old people half out of their wits, instructing people to burn their houses, bury food in the garden and perform all manner of strange antics. The parson has been asked to prepare grave spaces for the dead, and to be ready to arrange committal services.[10]

Urban invasion schemes were necessarily more complex than rural ones. Romford's Scheme was drawn up to cope with a human catastrophe – namely,

> to meet the situation when outside assistance is no longer available; when gas and electricity have failed; when the normal supplies of food and water have ceased …; when the casualty roll is beyond the capacity

---

7   ERO A12978, 20 September 1941.
8   ERO D/UCi 1/1/18, Canvey Island Invasion Committee minute, 25 February 1942.
9   ERO D/Z 12/1 Danbury Invasion Committee minutes, 12 May, 15 October 1942.
10 ERO D/DU 888/25/1, Rudsdale journal, 10 March 1942.

of the normal medical and mortuary services; when fires have broken out which, if they are not controlled at an early stage, will be altogether beyond the resources of the local fire service; when the number of homeless persons is far too great to be accommodated in the normal rest centres; and when there are possibilities of panic, which if not speedily checked, might spread to an uncontrollable and dangerous extent.[11]

Wanstead's scheme divided the town into six areas, the idea being that each one should be self-supporting 'for a considerable time'. It emphasised that '[l]eadership of the people must be personal and must be directed by one leader at each level'. Posts of Invasion Defence Officer, Invasion Defence Warden and Post Invasion Defence Warden were created, and below them was a network of street leaders to take charge of volunteers from each street. Although there was some criticism that invasion committees were too secretive, this scheme pointed out that 'The fact that an invasion defence organisation is being set up in the London Region cannot be widely known, and the local population should be made aware as soon as possible of the aims and objects of the scheme.' Nevertheless, although the public's cooperation was encouraged, it noted that 'the detailed invasion arrangements should not be made public'.[12] West Ham's Scheme noted that 'The general military plan is that there will be no withdrawal.'[13] Similarly, at Dagenham the scheme's aim was 'to defend the area to the last man and last round or bomb'.[14]

This county-wide structure of Invasion Committees was merely one part, and a fairly minor one at that, of a much wider defensive system which had been created in the summer of 1940 and which was developed over the next two years. In late 1940 and early 1941 official policy was to hold the beach areas lightly and maintain mobile reserves in the rear to counter-attack wherever the danger was greatest. Other mobile reserves were created to deal with possible thrusts towards the county's fighter airfields. To defend the beaches, County Beach Divisions were established. For example, battalions of the Northants, Suffolk and Essex Regiments were formed into 221 Infantry Brigade of the Essex Beach Division. The coast of north-east Essex was divided up into a number of defensible positions with each one allocated to units of the Division. G. Elcoat, who served with the Essex Beach Division, recalled that one unit guarded the line from Walton to Jaywick, with another unit to the west. Another unit held five miles of coast from Holland-on-Sea to Butlin's holiday camp at

---

11   ERO A12978, File 8 (Parish invasion schemes), memorandum, 29 January 1942.
12   ERO C/W 2/11/9, Invasion Preparation papers 1941–3, Wanstead and Woodford, 'Organisation of Civil Population in Invasion Scheme, 1942'.
13   ERO C/W 2/11/9, West Ham County Borough Invasion Defence Scheme, 5 January 1944.
14   ERO C/W 2/11/9, Borough of Dagenham Home Defence Organisation, May 1944.

Clacton-on-Sea. The Holland–Clacton unit was responsible for denying the pier to the enemy. These defences were strengthened by the Home Guard and by the use of some rather unorthodox methods. The crude Fougasse Flame Thrower, a 40-gallon petrol drum which was ignited by an electrical charge, was used by these units; steel tubes filled with high explosives which were designed to be detonated under armoured vehicles were left in the road. The Spigot Mortar and its cousin the Blacker Bombard, light and relatively easily operated weapons, were devised to be used against tanks or as anti-personnel weapons. The latter was issued to both regular and Home Guard units during 1941–42. By 1941 ammunition was more plentiful than in the famine year of 1940, when some units had only five rounds per man which had to be carried everywhere, on and off duty, together with the man's rifle, gas mask and steel helmet.[15]

The other component of the county's defences was the Home Guard. As part of that organisation clandestine 'underground' auxiliary units capable of carrying on military activities against the enemy were created. These units would have fought on even after invading forces had occupied the area.[16] Those men chosen were capable of living off the land, making the most of hiding places and using all forms of weaponry. For instance, Capt W.K. Seabrook was Group Commander of 202 Battalion, which covered Great Leighs, Silver End, Tiptree, Boreham, Terling, Hatfield Peverel and Wickham Bishops. The 43 men in the battalion were drawn from a wide range of occupations, including farmer, farm labourer, bus driver, welder, gardener, clerk, butcher, carpenter and bricklayer. Their ages ranged from twenty to 44, with about 60 per cent being 30 and over. The men were to operate with a ration box with twelve days' supplies containing sugar, tea, milk, cheese, jam, pilchards, bacon, meat and vegetables, toilet paper and biscuits.[17]

After 1940 the Home Guard was changed from a rather ramshackle group lacking uniforms and weapons into a military unit which was trained and organised, and had at least the semblance of being capable of putting up a fight should the enemy arrive. Fixed defences for the Home Guard to defend were essential, but progress was slow at first. In July 1940 the Lord Lieutenant, Sir Francis Whitmore, complained bitterly about the lack of cooperation from civilian contractors in building road blocks and strong points. In the Danbury area only seventeen out of the planned 88 pill-boxes were built and manned in the summer of 1940. At Clacton one contractor misread the plans and built the pillbox upside down.[18] The Home Guard's responsibilities accumulated rapidly.

15   ERO Box Z11B, G. Elcoat, 'Invasion preparations on the Essex Coast 1940–41' (1960).
16   P. Summerfield and C. Peniston-Bird, *Contesting home defence: men, women and the Home Guard in the Second World War* (Manchester, 2007), pp. 44–5.
17   ERO T/B 536/1–2, Secret wartime notebooks of Capt W.K. Seabrook, Group Commander, 202 Battalion, underground auxiliary Home Guard unit 1940–44.
18   P. Finch, *Warmen courageous: the story of the Essex Home Guard* (Southend, 1951), pp. 30–31.

Figure 3.1. The Home Guard erect road barriers at Woodford Wells in Metropolitan Essex. (Imperial War Museum)

In the words of the army these were:

> Observers and local parachute hunters: defenders of road approaches to towns and villages: nucleus of defended localities: traffic control: anti-sabotage guard of telephone exchanges, electric light and waterworks, factories and the like: guides to mobile columns.[19]

Throughout the war the Home Guard's various units evolved into larger groups and were often merged or subdivided as the need arose. It was also expected to conform to a number of different defence plans, each one replacing a predecessor. Something of the mild irritation that this engendered can be sensed in part of a poem entitled 'Home Guard Training', written by one of its volunteers:

> The Brigadier we had last Spring
> Said 'Static roles are not the thing;
> As mobile as the midnight flea

---

19 Finch, *Warmen*, p. 17.

Is what the Home Guard ought to be.'
He went; another came instead
Who deemed mobility quite dead,
And thought the Home Guard, on the whole,
Far safer in a static role.
No doubt some high strategic plan
Beyond the ken of common man
Dictates these changes in our job
From 'mob' to 'stat' and 'stat' to 'mob'.
Still, it would help us all to know
More positively where to go,
In case, when Boches do appear
We cannot find a Brigadier.[20]

Nothing was overlooked in terms of the Home Guard's instruction. An early order emphasised that 'an enemy in your vicinity is a stranger surrounded by his enemies. He will therefore be more alert than you who are surrounded by your friends.' It added, 'Talk as little as possible and don't smoke. A lighted cigarette is visible for 300 yards at night.'[21]

In many ways the Home Guard was never able to escape from its amateurish origins. Its uniform was a case in point. When steel helmets were slow to arrive an order was issued suggesting that they could be bought from a reputable company. But, as one officer reported, 'this order, I fear, was interpreted very broadly and many equipped themselves, at considerable expense, with fanciful variations which – despite an impressive appearance – would not have stopped the missile from a peashooter'.[22] When one unit in the so-called Estuary Sector – which was responsible for defending areas such as the Thames – was inspected by a General 'The platoon commander was in the guise of a cross between a Balkan bandit and a Texas cowhand, having a large Service Webley suspended from a belt studded completely around with .45 cartridges.'[23] Officers made constant complaints about the mishandling of rifles and the failure to keep them clean. Saluting of superior officers was frequently decried as 'slack' or 'slovenly.'[24] Even after the threat of invasion had passed the Home Guard continued in existence and in 1942 compulsory enrolment was authorised where units were below strength. Attendance at parades and all duties remained compulsory and men who failed to appear were often taken to court.

---

20 Finch, *Warmen*, pp. 32–3.
21 Finch, *Warmen*, pp. 80–1.
22 Finch, *Warmen*, p. 82.
23 Finch, *Warmen*, p. 99.
24 ERO C 1412, Essex Home Guard, Battalion Orders no. 1 (21 June 1942), no. 5 (25 February 1942), no. 11 (10 April 1942).

Figure 3.2. King George VI enjoys a close view of Essex Home Guard men being trained in unarmed combat. (Essex Record Office)

However, there was no absence of a Captain Mainwaring-style sense of mission designed to sustain public morale. A march past of the Colchester Home Guard led Alderman Percy Sanders to proclaim that 'Colchester's citizens can, I am sure, feel more secure now by reason of having this splendid Company of men ready to do whatever may be required of them should necessity arise.'[25] In June 1942, when the Halstead and Great Yeldham companies were subdivided from the Colchester Battalion, one senior Home Guard officer asserted that 'In splitting this battalion in two therefore, I feel that one more nail has been hammered into Hitler's coffin.'[26]

The wartime economy

Essex was a farming rather than an industrial county but it contained sufficient resources to make a significant contribution to the war effort. In south Essex lay the London docks and the Ford factory at Dagenham, as well as oil refineries and multifarious industrial concerns, and along the

25   ECS 12 July 1941.
26   ECS 19 September 1942.

Figure 3.3. Wings for Victory week in Colchester in May 1943. The final total of almost half a million pounds is shown as having exceeded the town's original target of £300,000. (Essex Society for Archaeology and History)

coast its small ports, idle and depressed before the war, were rejuvenated by war contracts. The towns of Colchester, Braintree and Chelmsford also contained large numbers of factories; in particular, at Chelmsford were the crucial Hoffmann ball-bearing plant and Marconi, where vital war work was done. For all the Luftwaffe's attentions, none of these concerns were put out of action permanently during the war.

In 1939 the government launched the War Savings Campaign, encouraging people to buy National Savings Certificates, War Bonds and Defence Bonds. The watchword was 'Lend to defend the right to be free'. The failure to invest was almost seen as unpatriotic. For instance, a Miss Fairhead, who ran the grocer's shop at Writtle, would return people's change only if they insisted and always suggested that her customers allow it to be invested in savings stamps.[27] Savings became a national obsession. At Colchester more than £964,000 was raised in savings between 1 January and 7 December 1940 and by the end of 1941 this had increased to £2.4 million.[28] Prior to the war there were 54 Savings Groups in the town with a membership of 2,616; by October 1944 there were 350 groups with 16,453 members.[29] In reality the government approved of national savings because it was a useful anti-inflationary device, while at the same time

27 EC 19 February 1943.
28 ECT 14 December 1940; ECS 31 January 1942.
29 H. Benham, *Essex at war* (Colchester, 1946), p. 138.

investors had much less to spend their money on, as shortages became more acute, and therefore saving made a virtue out of necessity.

Even more colossal efforts were made in the national drives which regularly punctuated the war. The impetus for these came from local communities during the Battle of Britain, when funds such as Colchester's 'Spitfire Fund' were launched. This fund reached its initial target of £5,000 in just seven weeks, prompting the *Essex County Standard* to say 'this had been raised not by the few but by the many'.[30] The government, eager to encourage such unstinting patriotism and to add another arrow to its anti-inflationary bow, formalised such activity with regular national fundraising drives. The first of these, 'War Weapons Week', was introduced in 1941, and was followed by 'Tanks for Attack'. 'Warships Week' and a second 'Tanks for Attack' were launched in 1942, 'Wings for Victory' in 1943 and the last drive, 'Salute the Soldier', in 1944.

Every town and village participated in these drives, each setting huge targets and usually exceeding them. At Frinton and Walton 'War Weapons Week' raised almost £320,000 – at £79 per head of the population, it was the most generous of any community in Britain. This had been made possible by a donation of £150,000 from Sir Edward Wilshaw, a wealthy Frinton resident. The small villages of Kelvedon and Feering exceeded their target of £15,000 by almost two-thirds in just two days. By the end of the week they had raised £46,000.[31] The week raised £10 million in Essex, with the metropolitan area contributing 30 per cent of this.[32]

The annual drives brought the best out of a war-weary population. The 'Tanks for Attack' drive in 1942 saw places such as Dagenham raise 40 per cent more than for 'War Weapons Week', with Brightlingsea increasing its amount by a staggering 75 per cent.[33] However, some people felt that there were limits to these fundraising bonanzas. In late 1943 both the chairman and publicity officer of Chelmsford RDC Savings Committee resigned when the 'Raise the Standard' campaign required the authority to enrol another 6,666 members. The two men described such an expectation as impossible.[34] Nevertheless, the last of the national drives, 'Salute the Soldier', still raised vast sums, even though by then people had grown used to the idea that the war was as good as won. At Colchester £574,000 was raised, a sum which exceeded the previous highest amount in 'War Weapons Week' by almost £60,000.[35]

The annual average of wholesale prices of all goods rose by about half between 1939 and 1941 and the cost-of-living index by a third by the end of

---

30   ECS 19 October 1940.
31   ECS 9 August, 17 May 1941.
32   ECS 11 October 1941.
33   ECS 17 October 1942.
34   EC 29 October 1943.
35   ECS 28 July 1944.

the war. This was due partly to scarcities but also to increasing full employment and wage rises in some areas of the workforce.[36] Ernest Bevin used his influence to prevent the government from introducing a wage freeze and during the war wages effectively doubled while salaries rose by 30 per cent, partly as a result of the demand for labour and the government's use of price controls and subsidies.[37] Employees were eager that their wages and salaries should not fall behind the cost of living and, as in the Great War, local authorities compensated for this by paying war bonuses. For example, in early 1940 Essex County Council agreed that the standard of living of its lowest paid employees must not be 'unduly impaired'. In its estimation all employees who received up to a maximum of £208 a year would find it difficult to withstand the rise in the cost of living. Based on the existing cost-of-living index, the war bonus was set at 4s 6d a week. When the index varied by nine points either way the war bonus would be increased or decreased proportionately; however, two years later the county council decided that its original decision had led to hardship and this was reduced to four and a half points. On this occasion the scheme was extended to employees earning more than £208 a year.[38]

All local authorities operated war bonuses. Colchester Borough Council granted them on twelve occasions between March 1940 and February 1945.[39] War bonuses were not uniform, nor were all employees covered by them. Essex County Council's scheme excluded all its workers who were governed by national awards and those in the armed forces. Colchester Borough Council sometimes granted war bonuses to separate groups of employees, such as, in March 1940, its caretakers and cleaners.[40] East Ham Town Council adopted a similar approach, awarding its manual workers a second war bonus in early 1941.[41] The system did not always run smoothly. When Barking Town Council granted an additional war bonus of 5s in May 1940 there were allegations that the trade union which requested it had two councillors on the town council, and that it was exploiting the situation.[42]

Much more controversial were the wartime pay rises awarded to the chief officers of local authorities. In late 1940 the granting of a pension of £1,000 a year to the clerk to the county council after he had completed only six years' service was greeted with fury. Labour Councillor Stanley Wilson, from Saffron Walden, complained at the award:

---

36 A. Calder, *The people's war: Britain 1939–1945* (London, 1969), p. 239; J. Gardiner, *Wartime: Britain 1939–1945* (London, 2004), p. 174.
37 Calder, *People's war*, p. 351; R. Mackay, *The test of war: inside Britain 1939–1945* (London, 1999), p. 155.
38 ChBC minutes, General Purpose Committee, 22 January 1940, 7 April 1942.
39 ECS 30 March 1940, 22 March 1941, 10 January, 4 July 1942, 14 April 1944; CBC minutes, 18 January, 31 May, 24 September 1943, 11, 25 January, 31 March 1944, 28 February 1945.
40 ECS 30 March 1940.
41 SE 28 February 1941.
42 SE 30 May 1941.

I have been a good deal about Essex and I know something about it. I have seen some of the people who will have to pay this very generous pension – peoples with bundles in their arms – reminding me of France. People have no homes. I don't suppose they will have heavy pensions, nor will the shopkeepers who have no trade.... I am opposed to the granting of these generous pensions whilst the great mass of people go hungry and many are homeless.[43]

Three years later there was another outcry when some county councillors proposed that the press be excluded from the discussions of the salaries of its leading officials. Stanley Wilson, again in the front ranks of opposition to this move, cried that 'It is striking at democracy. It is just the sort of thing Hitler and Mussolini would have done.' One councillor argued that, with the county's population increasing, the 'best brains' had to be employed to govern it. Wilson rejected this argument: 'It is class society that is rotten to the bottom,' he railed. 'It causes wars and poverty. The parson is on his last legs and the squire is on the dole. We are building up a new aristocracy.'[44]

Ordinary people, however much they resented such pay rises, were more concerned at a time when prices were rising at an unprecedented rate with having access to the necessities of life. Only when this occurred would the country's war effort function efficiently. Rationing, which was based on the successful scheme that had operated in the Great War, was imposed on many foodstuffs.[45] Aided by government subsidies that were used to keep down the price of bread, potatoes and meat, between 1939 and 1941 it guaranteed that people had access to the basics. Milk, tobacco, beer, fruit and vegetables, poultry, fish, sausages and offal were never rationed. It was these unrationed foodstuffs that resulted in the endless queueing endured by housewives which became a major wartime grievance of women.[46] In a survey in Dagenham in late 1941 that touched on shopping one woman noted that the queueing was awful, but that it was improving. She had been in the habit of taking a magazine with her to the shops, and on one occasion she read fourteen pages while waiting to be served. Nevertheless, she still found queueing very depressing.[47] Relations between shopkeepers and their patrons were not always amicable; the same woman commented that in her experience shopkeepers had to deal fairly with their customers because local women watched for any signs of unfairness and

43   EC 22 November 1940.
44   ECS 8 October 1943.
45   Butter, sugar, bacon and ham in 1939, meat in 1940, cheese and preserves in 1941, tea, margarine, cooking fats in 1943.
46   I. Zweiniger-Bargielowski, *Austerity in Britain: rationing, controls and consumption 1939–1955* (Oxford, 2000).
47   TC1 1/3/H Housing 1938–48, Becontree and Dagenham 1941–2.

were quick to voice their opinions.[48] The problem facing consumers from 1940 was summed up by this humorous ditty:

> Britain's gastronomic passions
> Had to undergo a change
> When the handicap of rations
> Puts so much outside our range.
> Diners can't go cock a hoop on
> Dishes measured by the ounce;
> Nor may they exceed their coupon
> While inspectors wait to pounce.[49]

Failing to economise was seen as unpatriotic, as this comment from 1943 reveals:

> What does this mean to you – to you who cut off a slice of bread at random, when you are no longer hungry? To you who throw away bread 'not quite as fresh as it was?' To you who nibble on a roll when there are potatoes on your plate? And to you who still turns up your nose at the crusts which are not cut off your bread?[50]

Most people dabbled in the black market but it was shopkeepers and small businesses that people relied on for rationed goods. As in the 1914–18 war, retailers experienced a difficult time. They were suffocated with complex official regulations, simple oversights of which could lead to prosecution.[51] Their male workforce had also been drained away. By the spring of 1940 the Colchester Co-op had lost 100 men to the Forces and by 1943 more than 300 employees had gone, most of them men.[52] Colchester's butchers took out a front-page advertisement in the *Essex County Standard* requesting that their customers take their own meat home because of the shortage of delivery men due to conscription and in 1943 household deliveries of foodstuffs were totally prohibited.[53] In mid-August 1942 shops in Colchester town centre, especially drapers, milliners and ladies' and gentleman's outfitters, closed for a week because of a combination of staff shortages, shortage of supplies and their depleted workforces' need for a holiday. When in 1942 registration for national service reached women born in 1899 some were drafted into these shops to

---

48   TC1 1/3/H Housing 1938–48, 21 October 1941.
49   BA 21 December 1940.
50   ST 3 February 1943.
51   S. Hylton, *Their darkest hour: the hidden history of the home front 1939–1945* (Stroud, 2001), pp. 192–3.
52   ST 27 April 1940, 30 April 1943.
53   ST 4 May 1940; again with the exception of bread and milk.

replace women who were now in the Forces.[54] Nevertheless, in spite of what were severe problems, traders often co-operated with one another. At Barking, butchers, grocers and provision merchants formed Mutual Assistance Pacts to provide both a service to customers of destroyed shops and temporary work for employees of these shops, and arranged to hand back customers when shops were re-established.[55]

The problems facing individual shops were typified by what happened to the Maldon and Heybridge Co-operative Society. Like local authorities, it paid war bonuses to its employees at various times during the war.[56] When its customers had to undertake new registrations for bacon, butter, sugar and meat rationing in the summer of 1940 numbers had fallen by ten per cent because of evacuations.[57] Because of conscription there was considerable change in staffing at the Society's shops. Before the war it employed 96 males and 32 females. Two years later there were 83 men and 53 women. By then 145 employees had either been employed or had left – an average of three a week.[58] The Society sometimes had difficulty in obtaining supplies. In November 1940 it temporarily solved its milk problem by reaching an agreement with a local farmer to buy 36 gallons a day from him, although it was another six months before it received additional official supplies in order to meet the permitted quota of one pint per customer.[59] Nevertheless, within another six months its milk supply was cut by fifteen per cent and a new agreement had to be reached with the supplier.[60] Coal was often particularly difficult to obtain. On one occasion the Society agreed to accept a third of its allocation in Welsh coal, which was considered inferior for heating purposes; the Society's minute noted that it 'was not likely to be greeted favourably in this area'.[61]

The Maldon and Heybridge branch, like all other businesses employing more than 50 employees, was obliged to make extensive preparations for air raids. A small committee was set up to participate in a proposed scheme of mutual assistance to ensure that local bread deliveries were maintained after an air raid.[62] It was arranged that shops would stay open after normal closing hours following a severe raid and, in fact, the Society's shops at Maldon, Burnham and Southminster were hit on the night of 26/27 September 1940, causing £600 worth of damage.[63] Air-raid warnings proved to be far more disruptive

54   ECS 1, 15 August 1942.
55   SE 20 September 1940.
56   ERO D/Z 187/2/19, Maldon and Heybridge Cooperative Management Committee minutes 1939-44, 2 February,
       22 March 1940.
57   ERO D/Z 187/2/19, 26 July 1940.
58   ERO D/Z 187/2/19, 8 August 1941.
59   ERO D/Z 187/2/19, 29 November 1940, 9 May 1941.
60   ERO D/Z 187/2/19, 14 November 1941.
61   ERO D/Z 187/2/19, 1 November 1940, 20 June 1941.
62   The scheme was abandoned without ever having been operational: ERO D/Z 187/2/19, 6 September 1940.
63   ERO D/Z 187/2/19, 27 September 1940.

to business than actual raids, however. At the start of one week in mid–October 1940 more than nine hours were lost as staff and customers took shelter. The management committee did urge staff to keep shops open for as long as possible and employees who voluntarily worked through a raid were paid time and a half. During October all its staff, including female employees, agreed to participate in a spotting system to give early warning of enemy aircraft and in early 1941 some offered to take part in the new fire-watching system.[64] At least air raids provided some benefit for the Co-op's customers. In 1941 it held several grocery salvage sales of jellies, custard powders, soups, macaroni, starch, canned goods and dried fruit, using produce purchased from damaged warehouses. The first two raised £144 and £160 respectively.[65]

Other economic enterprises found their activities affected by the war. The Colchester Equitable Building Society operated on a restricted scale, husbanding its resources by granting fewer mortgages. In 1941 it granted only fourteen. Its conservative approach was influenced by the large amounts of income tax, national defence and war damage contributions it had to pay, which totalled £9,190 in 1941. As part of this policy it cut the interest on both its share capital and deposits.[66] Daniell's, the Colchester brewing company, which had large and valuable east coast interests, found its operations there greatly reduced by adult evacuation, although this did at least enable it to delay rationing to its other pubs. Beer duty was twice increased in 1940, which meant that the company paid £43,000 more in tax than in 1939. Its sales of bulk beer declined by ten per cent in the first year of the war and a shortage of labour meant that, like many businesses, it carried out only those repairs that were absolutely necessary. In 1941 its beer stocks almost ran out on several occasions and the government's prohibition on imported wine and spirits forced the company to use its stocks, thus depleting a valuable source of investment. Although its gross profits from beer, wine and spirits was a record, much of this resulted from wartime inflation rather than rising sales.[67]

Newspapers, too, faced difficulties. In 1939 the *Burnham Advertiser* complained that every week the government was urging it to fill its advertising space with official advertisements and notifications. As a small newspaper almost entirely devoted to local affairs it was unable to print the huge amount of material requested. In that one week in December in which its complaint appeared it had received long articles from the Ministries of Food, Agriculture and Information about avoiding waste, growing food, evacuations and avoiding

64   ERO D/Z 187/2/19, 12, 19 October 1940.
65   ERO D/Z 187/2/19, 6, 27 June 1941.
66   ECT 3 March 1942.
67   ECS 29 March 1941, 28 March 1942.

eyestrain brought on by the blackout.[68] In 1940 newspapers were allocated less paper following the fall of Norway and the cutting off of Scandinavian timber supplies. Then, in March 1942, paper supplies were cut by a further ten per cent and advertising space was rationed by government order. The *Essex County Standard* imposed advertising rate increases and less space on its customers. To minimise the effects of the change, one issue a month was reduced from eight to six pages.[69] To save paper the *Stratford Express* stopped its mid-week issue.[70]

As in the First World War, Essex's coastal region was severely affected by depopulation. Businesses in seaside resorts were devastated by the evacuations of 1939–40, when Clacton's population fell by between 80 and 90 per cent, Walton's by 70 per cent and Frinton's by half. It was not until the end of 1944 that about half of Clacton's residents returned. There were more than 150 businesses in early 1940 but five years later the town's Chamber of Commerce had only 34 members, although this had grown to more than 200 by the end of the war.[71] The Chief Constable of Southend estimated that about 80,000 of the resort's population of 135,000 had left in 1940.[72] As in Essex's other resorts, this caused profound problems for the town's economy and local authorities.

The coastal maritime industries were particularly subjected to severe restrictions. In the fishing industry the first sprat catch of the season suffered from markets badly depressed by the war and much of it was used as manure, although by early 1940 sprats were being shipped to Sweden from ports such as Brightlingsea.[73] Colchester's oyster industry was buoyant in the first few months of the war, selling over 67,000 more than the previous year, but the unusually savage winter of 1939/40 caused widespread damage and recovery took a year. Nevertheless, by early 1942 the Colne Fishery had experienced record prices and great demand. Even though the industry was hit by a shortage of labour and boats and severe frosts, the oysters had survived and the company's prices were the highest on record, with Colchester oysters fetching £3 11s 8d per hundred. This resulted not from profiteering but from increased demand, price rises, extensive shortages and several years of costly cultivation.[74]

By late 1941 only one fishing boat, the *Sunbeam*, was left working at Brightlingsea. Many of the town's seamen had been called up and others were transferred into shipbuilding, resulting in most boats being laid up.[75] However, the port's fortunes were revived by the renewal of naval shipbuilding, which

68 BA 16 December 1939.
69 ECS 14 March 1942.
70 SE 20 March 1942.
71 C. Thornton, 'The Resorts in the Second World War', in C. Thornton (ed.), *The Victoria History of the County of Essex, vol. xi, Clacton, Walton and Frinton: north-east seaside resorts* (London, 2012), pp. 178, 188, 192.
72 ST 20 June 1945.
73 ECS 13 January 1940.
74 ECS 23 September 1939, 2 March 1940, 1 March 1941, 28 February, 12 September 1942.
75 ECS 4 October 1941.

Figure 3.4. The launch of minesweeper J537 at Wivenhoe shipyard, possibly in 1942. The town's local dignitaries were out in force. (Mersea Museum/Leo Michael Smith)

saw the construction there of 5,500 pontoons for the army.[76] The Royal Navy returned in February 1940, with a small flotilla that tackled German magnetic mines. The town's naval base, named HMS *Nemo*, was home to between 400 and 650 personnel at any one time between 1940 and 1942. Many were Wrens who worked as typists, clerks, telephonists, radio operators and drivers, and this naval establishment helped to support local businesses generally.[77] The war also rescued nearby Wivenhoe from its pre-war doldrums when the Admiralty commandeered the upstream shipyard; in January 1940 Wivenhoe Shipyard Limited, an offshoot of Rowhedge Ironworks, was established. It produced over 24 wooden minesweepers to fight the menace of magnetic mines, as well as motor torpedo boats and four decoy submarines. Vosper Limited, which was bombed out of Portsmouth, also opened up there in 1941, constructing fifteen motor torpedo boats and carrying out repair works.[78] Similarly, at Rowhedge

---

76 P. Brown, *The fighting branch: the Wivenhoe to Brightlingsea railway line 1866–1964* (Romford, 1975), p. 46.
77 J.P. Foynes, *Under the white ensign: Brightlingsea and the sea war 1939–45* (author, 1993), pp. 9, 51, 56. HMS *Nemo* was closed on 16 May 1945, although Royal Navy personnel were still present in the autumn of that year (p. 103).
78 N. Butler, *The story of Wivenhoe* (Wivenhoe, 1989), pp. 254–5.

more than 300 workers were employed in two yards building minesweepers and cargo coasters, and the Rowhedge Iron Works resumed building steam engines for the first time since 1918.[79]

The port of Harwich experienced a civilian evacuation similar to that that took place in the resorts, but, as in the Great War, it became a military and naval stronghold. Parkeston, from where the London and North Eastern Railway's (LNER's) ferry passenger services to the Continent left, was requisitioned by the Admiralty, and all ferries were turned over to the Royal Navy for wartime use. Osea Island in the Thames also became a naval base again, repairing and maintaining small coastal motor boats. Local firms were put on a war footing to produce spares and equipment. Only a handful of small boats and Maldon fishing boats, licensed by the Admiralty and marked with a large 'M' and an official number painted on both prows, were permitted to ply the river Blackwater.[80]

Essex's industrial firms, large and small, were incorporated into the country's war effort. Marconi's first military orders came in 1938, as the government made use of the company's pre-eminence in the field of communications to produce transmitters and receivers for ships. Demand for the company's skills was more extensive than in the Great War but, like all other firms, Marconi was handicapped by the loss to the Services of many of its physicists, engineers and technicians. By 1943 the company had lost 500 skilled workers, although by the end of 1944 the company's workforce had expanded by 400 per cent to 6,000.[81] One of the company's first war jobs was the conversion of ten luxury coaches into two heavy mobile field stations for the army, with transmitter, power plant, central telegraph office, receiver and accommodation coaches. A job that would normally have taken five months was completed in just one. In total, the company converted 380 commercial vehicles, each with short wave transmitters. It produced material that was invaluable in the prosecution of the war, such as the TR 1154/1155 transmitting–receiving set which was fitted in every British bomber and Coastal Command aircraft. Marconi also helped to produce a new generation of ASV (Aid to Surface Vessels apparatus) in 1942 which allowed aircraft to detect U-boats that had surfaced at night. However, its greatest contribution to the destruction of the German U-boat menace was the building of a naval radar set which was fitted to all corvettes and destroyers. The first model was delivered to the Admiralty in April 1941 and within a few months 250 were in use.[82]

---

79   R. Douglas Brown, *East Anglia 1943* (Lavenham, 1990), p. 89.
80   J. Wise, *The story of the Blackwater Sailing Club* (Maldon, 1999), pp. 71–2.
81   W.J. Baker, *A history of the Marconi Company* (London, 1970), p. 306; G. Godwin, *Marconi 1939–1945: a war record* (London, 1946), p. 23.
82   Godwin, *Marconi*, pp. 11–13, 17, 48–9, 52.

Figure 3.5. An anti-aircraft gun on the roof of Crittall's factory. In the background are the roof tops of Braintree. (BRNTM 2012.1089.6, Braintree District Museum Trust)

There were more than 70 factories engaged in war production in Chelmsford alone during the war. Hoffmann made munitions as well as bearings. It employed more than 9,000 people and during the conflict made two and a half million balls and rollers. These were used throughout the British armed forces – by Fighter Command in the engines of its aircraft, in submarines, tanks, landing craft, radar equipment, searchlights and heavy guns.[83] In the Courtaulds textile mills at Halstead and Braintree 60 per cent of looms and 52 per cent of employees were directly engaged on war production. Thirty per cent of the remaining looms turned out Board of Trade 'utility' fabrics for civilians.[84] Crittall at Silver End changed from manufacturing window frames to producing steel ammunition boxes, parts for Halifax bombers, Bailey bridges, shells of various calibres and steel landing mats for the beaches.[85] At Colchester the firm of Davey and Paxman took on a variety of manufacturing contracts, including building engines for tank landing craft.[86]

83   M.R. Innes, 'Chelmsford: a geographical and historical survey to 1951', unpublished typescript (1951), p. 438; EC 18 May 1945.
84   D.C. Coleman, *Courtaulds: an economic and social history, vol. III, crisis and challenge 1940–66* (London, 1980), p. 5.
85   B. Stait, *Silver end: the war years* (author, 1995), pp. 28–9; D.J. Blake, *Window vision* (Braintree, n.d.), pp. 80–1.
86   K. Waddy, 'What were women's experiences at Davey and Paxman and Company during World War Two, and what impact did the presence of women workers have on the firm?', BA dissertation (Essex University, 2008), p. 2.

The Ford factory at Dagenham had been operational for eight years when war broke out. Its sixteen-acre plate glass roof was first darkened and then substituted by metal sheets. To confuse the Luftwaffe an elaborate picture was painted on the roof to make it seem as though it was marshland with metal tracks running through it. Its location near the docks made it apparently vulnerable to enemy air raids, but in June 1940 it received large contracts for wheeled vehicles. When raids did begin the factory continued functioning just as effectively as those of other firms. Almost 350,000 vehicles, tractors and carriers were built by 1945. The company produced a huge range of wartime equipment – RAF machinery used to attack magnetic mines, chassis to move barrage balloons, tractors which pulled bombers and bomb-trains and the Ford Emergency Food Vans. Landing craft powered by Ford engines were first used on a commando raid in Norway in 1941 and subsequently in great numbers in all further landings. The company also solved a serious problem facing the army – how to waterproof the electrical equipment in its vehicles. It discovered a new compound – Trinadite – which did the job and had it coated over all the equipment. During the war the slag which was the by-product of its blast furnace was converted into Tarmacadam and used to build 56 airfield runways. In answer to the critical matter of food production, the company also built twice as many tractors – 130,000 Fordsons – during the war as it had in the five years preceding it. The farm at Boreham near Chelmsford, which the company had purchased in 1931, trained young men and members of the Women's Land Army.[87]

Working conditions in Essex factories were far from ideal, although efforts were made to cater for their growing workforces, especially as most of the increase was female. At Davey and Paxman at Colchester a new canteen was built and a tea trolley brought refreshments. Employees were not paid extra for overtime, but did receive an additional meal instead.[88] At Crittall's at Witham the hours were long and employees had to work all day Saturday and alternate night and day shifts.[89] In the winter of 1940 German air raids led to a serious loss of working hours at Ford. The company had built indoor and external shelters, but the employees refused to work unless they were warned when the enemy was actually overhead. A system to achieve this was thus quickly instituted by the management. It also altered working shifts from three eight-hour shifts to two twelve-hour ones to minimise employees' travel during raids.[90] Marconi tackled the problem of worker fatigue by instituting rest intervals and rest rooms staffed round the clock by trained

---

87 St G.H. Saunders, *Ford at war* (London, n.d.), pp. 6, 10–11, 18–20, 35, 47–9, 54.
88 Waddy, Davey and Paxman, pp. 25–6.
89 Stait, *Silver End*, p. 29.
90 Saunders, *Ford at war*, p. 30.

nurses. Artificial daylight was used to minimise the ill-effects of unfriendly bright lights.[91]

Although industrial relations were fraught with tensions, government legislation, wartime patriotism and wage increases took the edge off them. Industrial unrest in Essex workplaces never reached the pitch that it did in the coal mining industry, or even in newer, technologically advanced enterprises.[92] A handful of strikes involving small numbers of workers occurred, although they were quickly resolved. For instance, in May 1940 bus drivers at the Grays Green Line depot went on strike in protest at revised bus timetables which they claimed would result in them working longer hours for the same pay. The strike inconvenienced thousands of workers at Thameside factories, but its duration was very short.[93] In 1943 workers at Crittall's walked out amid complaints of excessive supervision by management, including timing women in the toilets, where it was asserted that they were wasting time by making themselves up prior to stepping onto the shop floor. One of the problems was that not all the workforce was unionised, and although the company had prevented a closed shop before the war the conscripting of new men and women was undermining this.[94] All Crompton-Parkinson's 3,000-strong workforce walked out in 1943, claiming that a pay award conceded in March had still not been paid. Arbitration produced a quick and satisfactory solution.[95]

A strike occurred at Ford's in May 1944, just two weeks after the company reached an agreement with the trade unions. The dispute, which affected only 300 employees, happened after one worker was disciplined, although, once again, it was all over in a couple of days.[96] The long working hours and Marconi's autocratic management style, with its imposition of compulsory overtime and rules concerning manual and technical workers, produced a tense situation. Reginald Olive, a shop steward, proposed joint industrial action by all unions, but the union's district secretaries prevented this. Union activists Fred Roberts and his wife Olive suggested the creation of a joint shop steward's committee of all employees, not just manual workers, and Fred was elected as its convenor. When Roberts was threatened with the sack the Trades Union Congress (TUC) general secretary, Walter Citrine, became involved in the problem, and Marconi compromised, agreeing to accept the Engineering Employers' agreements for manual workers, although it continued to refuse to recognise white-collar staff

---

91   Godwin, *Marconi*, p. 124.
92   Mackay, *The test of war*, pp. 88–9.
93   BA 4 May 1940.
94   EC 12 March 1943.
95   EC 8 October 1943.
96   EC 5 May 1944.

unions.[97] Workers were alert to the possibility of war priorities being used to undermine their rights. In 1943 the Colchester Trades Council rejected an official request to organise a 'Production Week'. The Trades Council, which represented some 8,000–9,000 workers, asserted that 'We will not … tolerate any incursions upon our hard–won rights and privileges if made under the auspices of a supposed war effort.' It argued that a 'concentrated, sustained effort' was more valuable than 'a spasmodic week in which the workers are keyed to such a pitch that the natural reaction is a general slackening'.[98]

The war caused severe transport problems for individuals and businesses. The U-boat campaign threatened Britain's oil imports and, in addition, the military's needs were prioritised over those of civilians. Petrol was rationed from the outset and the use of petrol in private cars was completely banned in 1942.[99] To counter this, the government encouraged firms and enterprising individuals to convert their vehicles to 'producer gas' made from anthracite. W.J. Morrison, an employee of the National Omnibus Company at Chelmsford, invented a contraption allowing buses, lorries and cars to run on this fuel. By 1942 the company's buses operated on producer gas from its Maldon depot. By then 21 modified buses were in operation, saving 78,000 gallons of petrol a year. Unfortunately, in due course coal shortages brought an end to this novel experiment.[100]

Bus companies experienced various problems. The wages paid by Westcliff-on-Sea Motor Services increased from £8,668 to £12,675 in the first year of the war, but even before the end of 1939 fifteen of its 21 routes showed a decrease in fares as a result of evacuation.[101] In early 1940, in order to attract more passengers, the company applied for permission to revise its fares, replacing them with a 2d workmen's fare on all routes.[102] From 1942 a bus curfew was introduced to save fuel and from then on buses could not leave Chelmsford, Colchester, Maldon or Southend after 9pm. Christmas Day bus services had been scrapped in 1939 but from 1942 no Sunday bus services could depart before 1pm and they, too, stopped at 9pm. This was much resented by people who travelled to church services, but in the countryside at night the absence of both cars and buses seemed to restore a lost pastoral air.[103] The harsh economic conditions led the government to urge bus companies in the same area to cooperate to avoid the duplication of routes and subsequent waste of petrol. Until the summer of 1942 Southend Corporation, Eastern National

97   M. Wallace, *Nothing to lose, a world to win: a history of the Chelmsford and District Trade Union Council* (Chelmsford, 1979), p. 96.
98   ECS 20 February 1943.
99   E.R. Chamberlain, *Life in wartime Britain* (London, 1972), pp. 106–8.
100   EC 8 May 1942.
101   ERO D/F 271/1/WMS/5, Papers of Westcliff-on-Sea Motor Services.
102   ERO D/F 271/2/7, Westcliff-on-Sea Motor Services, correspondence, 1939–45.
103   EC 6 November, 4 December 1942.

and Westcliff-on-Sea Motor Services operated as three separate undertakings but subsequently a Joint Committee was set up to establish a cooperative fare-sharing venture; however, a draft agreement had still not been signed by February 1945.[104]

Nevertheless, people were not deterred from using buses, and shoppers often hogged seats to the disadvantage of war workers returning home. Southend Town Council supported the idea of 'priority travel' for weekly and season ticket holders whose war work was being compromised by casual travellers and Canvey UDC requested that the island's essential workers be given coloured permits giving them priority in bus queues, but neither request was granted.[105] So many passengers travelled between Chelmsford and Brentwood that Brentwood UDC requested shelters in the High Street; a census in Brentwood in January 1944 revealed that during one hour 788 people queued for a bus, with the largest number in the queue at any one time being 125.[106] In the longer term many bus companies prospered because of the huge increase in war workers and the ban on cars. Moore's of Kelvedon transported war workers to factories in Braintree, Chelmsford and Colchester. New buses were no longer being manufactured, so the company had to buy second-hand double-deckers.[107] Nonetheless, the war did sound the death knell for Southend's tramways, which had been losing money well before war began. The council began replacing them with more economical trolleybuses and buses in 1938–39 and by mid-1941 it decided to close the tramway, which was shut down in April 1942.[108]

The government urged more people to use trains but it was not a popular suggestion. Train services were cut by a third during the war and were often overcrowded with war workers and servicemen and women. Services were frequently late, owing to air-raids, and fares were three times higher than pre-war prices. Nevertheless, the county had far more branch lines at this time than before the Beeching 'axe' descended in the 1960s and they were vitally important to the war effort. The Saffron Walden railway handled primarily agricultural freight. Tinned food and dried milk were brought to the town and distributed by lorry to Ministry of Food storage depots. It also handled war supplies, which arrived and were unloaded at night for nearby airfields at Debden, Duxford and Wethersfield. Petrol sidings were installed half a mile east of the town, where fuel bays were capable of accommodating six tank wagons each. Many of the trains operated via Shelford and Bartlow so that

104 ERO D/F 271/2/38, Southend Transport Proposed Coordination of Services.
105 ST 3 February 1943.
106 EC 4 February, 30 June 1944.
107 B. Everitt, *Moore's: the story of Moore brothers, Kelvedon, Essex: passenger carrying through five generations* (author, 1998), pp. 84–5, 91–2.
108 ST 3 September 1941; V.E. Burrows, *The tramways of Southend* (Southend, 1965), pp. 162, 164–5, 169.

the dangerous high octane fuel did not pass through the town.[109] The Maldon East–Witham branch carried troops around the area – to and from Osea Island, for example. It also ferried agricultural produce and supplies to Maldon firms building motor torpedo boats.[110] The Braintree branch line transported thousands of tons of rubble to build the runways of Saling airfield, and every night trains carried bomb loads for the same destination.[111]

After D-Day the Bishop's Stortford–Dunmow–Braintree line was used by ambulance trains working to and from Harwich and Parkeston Quay, bringing casualties from northern Europe to military hospitals at Bishop's Stortford.[112] The Colne Valley and Halstead Railway experienced a huge increase in war traffic, most of it consisting of ammunition and petrol. By May 1943 Earls Colne station had become an ammunition dump for about 30 airfields in Essex and Suffolk. There was such a surplus of bombs that the Unites States Army Air Force (USAAF) was forced to disperse them in heaps on quickly built concrete stands on country roads, especially around the villages of Pebmarsh, Bures and White Colne.[113] In the two months before D-Day some 10,000 bombs were stored at Earls Colne and White Colne.[114]

In spite of petrol restrictions and, later, a shortage of rubber for tyres, motor transport companies remained essential for the economic life of the nation, as much rail freight had to be unloaded and then taken by road to its final destination. Firms such as Bloomfield Transport of Brentwood were kept constantly occupied. The company delivered army huts over a very wide area and, in common with many other firms, it was involved in airfield construction, particularly after the arrival of the Americans. One of the firm's contracts was to keep a certain number of lorries loaded with hardcore overnight to fill bomb craters at airfields; another stipulated keeping empty lorries at the disposal of the authorities and having cars available to ferry army officers to and fro. In 1944 the company built highly secretive sites around Bradwell airfield as emplacements for A.A. guns to shoot at doodlebugs.[115]

Many of the local authorities' responsibilities were increased as a result of the war. One of the most onerous was salvage. The government was eager to avoid waste in everything – food, clothing, paper, metal – and local councils thus organised the salvage of these materials. East Ham, for example, began a collection of food scraps and in the first week twelve tons was collected from the

109   P. Paye, *The Saffron Walden branch* (Oxford, 1981), pp. 50–3.
110   D.L. Swindale, *Branch lines to Maldon* (Colchester, 1977), p. 35.
111   C. Lombardelli, *Branch lines to Braintree* (Colchester, 1980) p. 26.
112   P. Paye, *Bishops Stortford, Dunmow & Braintree branch* (Usk, 1981), pp. 51, 53–4.
113   My friend Derek Wolstencroft showed me the remains of some of these concrete stands by the side of roads around Bures.
114   E. Willingham, *From construction to destruction: an authentic history of the Colne Valley and Halstead railway* (Halstead, 1989), pp. 88–91.
115   D. Bloomfield, 'Bloomfield transport 1927–49' (unpublished manuscript, 2012).

borough's 15,000 houses.[116] The collection of scrap metal, which necessitated the removal of gates and railings, was controversial. The public was told that their removal was essential so that the metal could be used in war production; and, indeed, one of the *Essex County Standard*'s columnists argued that it was better to defend the Empire than retain the railings, which he described as 'ugly superfluities'.[117] Removal was preceded by an official survey resulting in a list of scheduled and unscheduled railings, the former being the ones to go. At Brentwood the survey scheduled 307 tons of iron for removal, comprising more than 99 per cent of the town's railings.[118] Opposition, which was widespread and involved individuals, religious groups and local authorities, was based on both artistic and safety grounds. Barking Town Council protested at the removal of unscheduled railings. At East Ham the council opposed removal on safety grounds, whereas the West Ham Property Owners' Association objected on principle.[119] Charles Kay, a Wivenhoe resident, also opposed removal, especially from around graves. He pointed out that there were already large unused piles of scrap iron from bombed-out houses. People were particularly unconvinced by official claims that the scheme was essential when they saw the scrap iron seemingly abandoned in mounds around the county.[120] Peter Tweed of Lexden, near Colchester, was a teenager during the war. He recalls that

> Aluminium saucepans disappeared to make Spitfires and people also gave up their railings for the war effort, but there was little point in it. They brought them to a plot of land where the pill box had been built, dumped it in great piles, and in time weeds and brambles grew up. The railings disappeared from view and were still there at the end of the war.[121]

Nevertheless, in spite of widespread cynicism Essex topped the national scrap metal drive in 1942, raising 181 cwts per 1,000 of the population, a significant increase on the national average of 148 cwts.[122] In October 1942 the Ministry of Supply inaugurated a book recovery drive to replace the stocks of blitzed libraries and to provide books for children's homes, schools and servicemen and women. Essex was asked to donate three and a half million books but within six months it had doubled its target.[123]

---

116   ECS J July 1940.
117   ECS 22 August 1942.
118   EC 8 May 1942.
119   SE 6, 20 February, 17 April 1942.
120   ECS 25 October 1941.
121   Tweed quoted in L. White (ed.), *Lexden in wartime: memories of local people, Vol 2* (Colchester, 2008), p. 5.
122   ST 31 March 1943.
123   ST 24 March 1943.

Some local authorities struggled financially as their rates revenue was badly affected by the war. Thanks to government grants, Southend Borough Council managed to peg the rates at 6s 11d in the pound from 1940 until the end of the war.[124] Harwich Borough Council kept its rates at 8s from 1940 onwards.[125] Economising measures were undertaken by all councils as a means of restraining rate demands. They were assisted by the blackout, which reduced lighting costs, by evacuation, which cut expenditure on education, and by the government's decision to fund most of the cost of civil defence spending. Colchester Borough Council saved almost £7,000 on its fire brigade once it was taken over by the government.[126]

Outside Metropolitan Essex and the resorts the single most important factor affecting the level of rates was the Essex County Council precept, which formed the largest proportion. For instance, in 1942/3 Burnham UDC's 1d rate produced £13,361, of which £10,445 was due to the county council, leaving Burnham with just under £3,000 for all its needs.[127] Councils were usually only able to keep rates at the same level as the previous year or decrease them when the county council precept was lowered, as it was in the three years 1940/41, 1941/2 and 1942/3. Local authorities in two areas of Essex, the county's resorts and Metropolitan Essex, were so badly affected by disastrous falls in rates during the war that fluctuations in the county council precept were not major considerations. Resorts such as Southend, Clacton, Frinton and Walton were affected by the large-scale evacuation of their population in 1939–40. In July 1940 the government released people evacuated from these areas from having to pay rent, rates or utility charges until they returned and during the next six months 600 reductions to Clacton's rating list reduced the UDC's income by £6,000. The government eventually provided assistance for coastal resorts and in November 1940 Clacton was granted £5,500 for that month's difference between income and expenditure. Further sums arrived periodically and by the end of the war government aid totalled £100,000. Walton, too, was badly affected and by the summer of 1942 it had received more than £18,000 in government grants.[128]

Southend's situation was even worse. As at Clacton, mass evacuation led to a catastrophic fall in traders' income. Problems began with the evacuation of 1939, which left between 4,100 and 5,100 empty properties in the town. By the following summer the number of rate cases written off by the council as irrecoverable was 10,541, accounting for one in ten of the rate-paying population

124 SSt 11 April 1940, ST 25 April 1945.
125 ERO D/B 4M1/1, Harwich Borough Council minutes 1936–45, various.
126 ECS 4 April 1942.
127 BA 1 August 1942.
128 C. Thornton (ed.), *The Victoria History of the County of Essex, vol. xi, Clacton, Walton and Frinton: north-east seaside resorts* (London, 2012), p. 195.

and totalling over £58,000. By early November about 1,000 tradesmen, including some of between twenty and 40 years' standing, were summonsed for non-payment of rates.[129] The council had overspent by £200,000 and it had an overdraft of £36,000 and a £200,000 bank loan.[130] By the spring of 1941 more than £131,000 of rates had been written off as irrecoverable, of which £121,000 was from empty property.[131] Gradually government aid started to rise: during the financial year 1940/41 the council received £144,000 in aid and in 1941/42 £280,000. In April 1942 it was given another £206,000, and £92,000 a year later.[132] Fortunately, from 1942 the town's economic position began to improve. As invasion fears waned residents began returning and the rates collected for 1941/42 increased by almost £70,000. By December 1942 the £90,000 in rates collected that month represented a rise of £35,000 on the same month the previous year. The fact that those ratepayers who returned still had to pay their outstanding rates since their departure was not popular. Many felt that when the authorities pressurised them to leave in 1940 they were not incurring such a liability, especially as they had to pay rates or rents in their places of evacuation.[133] However, by 1943 a concession was made to some people that allowed residents who had left after 16 July 1940 to pay only half their outstanding rates.[134]

The two boroughs most affected by the war were East and West Ham. The Blitz caused widespread devastation in both boroughs, destroying or damaging thousands of houses and leading to an exodus of population. Until 1941 East Ham was the only local authority in Metropolitan Essex to receive government aid, which caused great bitterness in West Ham.[135] The latter borough had suffered more damage than its neighbour, its rate collection in 1940/41 had fallen by £220,000 compared with 1939/40 and it already had an overdraft of £200,000. In addition, it was struggling to repay the inter-war Goschen Loan, which had been used to relieve distress resulting from unemployment. As an indication of the borough's difficulties, a rate of 21s 6d in March 1939 raised £1.54 million; in the financial year 1940/41 it brought in a third of that figure.[136] In March 1941 the government provided £350,000 on the grounds that it was a distressed area – the first of many advances to keep the Borough Council afloat financially. These were designed to meet deficiencies in the borough's rate fund; 75 per cent of each was a grant, and the rest was an interest-free loan. By the end of 1941 the borough had received nine advances

129   BA 9 November 1940; SD 23 May 1940.
130   Douglas Brown, *East Anglia 1940*, p. 130.
131   SSt 26 March 1941.
132   ST 18 March, 22 April 1942, 28 April 1943.
133   ST 30 September 1942.
134   ST 28 April 1943.
135   SE 28 March 1941.
136   ST 26 September 1941.

Figure 3.6. An incident inquiry post next to the Green Man public house in Waltham Holy Cross, manned by female wardens. These posts were created to assist the public after a serious 'incident'. (Waltham Abbey Historical Society)

totalling £974,000, a colossal sum of money. By 1946 its accumulated deficit was £1.36 million, of which £1.23 million was met by the government.[137]

Home, field and factory

The experience of Essex women during the war was little different from that of women elsewhere in the United Kingdom. As a farming county, locals were included among the several thousand women who comprised the Women's Land Army in Essex. They formed an even larger labour force in the county's factories, especially in Chelmsford, and in the many industrial concerns which were turned over to war production after 1939. Some of those not in essential war work were found in the Women's Voluntary Service (WVS) or Women's Institutes, organising all manner of patriotic and practical activities. Female teachers were evacuated, along with their charges, and many spent the entire war out of the county. Like every other resident of Essex, women faced the terrors of the Blitz and, from 1944, the menace of the V–1s and V–2s.

---

137 TNA HLG 52/1511 West Ham County Borough, possible breakdown of essential services due to financial difficulties.

During 1939 and 1940 many women held back from entering employment or joining the services, although the government continued to encourage them to come forward voluntarily. Some did, but not enough. The Registration of Employment Order in March 1941 saw the beginnings of registration of women aged twenty and 21 for essential work, but it was not a success. By mid-1941 the government estimated that, nationally, 1.5 million women were required to replace conscripted men in most areas of employment. Women had to provide half the number needed in munitions and 750,000 in other industries.[138] Consequently, in December 1941 Britain became the first nation in the conflict to conscript women. Single women and childless widows between the ages of twenty and 30 were made eligible for military service or direction into industry or Civil Defence, and by 1942 ten million women aged between nineteen and 50 were registered for war work.[139] Industrial concerns in Essex eventually hired women in large numbers. At the Tate & Lyle sugar factory in Plaistow the 873 female employees were outnumbered three to two by males in 1939 but during 1941 and 1942 government legislation meant that females formed about 53 per cent of all workers.[140] At Ford's Dagenham car factory the company had refused to employ women before the war because Henry Ford believed they should be at home raising a family. The war forced it to abandon this policy; in September 1941 a total of 1,100 women had been hired and by the end of the war there were 3,500 female employees.[141]

The demand for women factory workers became so great that more than 100 were applying for each course vacancy at the North East Essex Training College at Colchester. They received an allowance during training, allowances for any dependants and travelling expenses.[142] When government officials visited another training centre near Leyton they were impressed when they saw that '[g]irls and young women [were] efficiently tackling oxy–acetylene welding, instrument making and other intricate jobs on modern machinery, and liking it'.[143] Many women in Essex factories were local. In recordings made some time after the war, some of them remembered their wartime efforts. For example, in 1941 Ethel Dyer registered for national service in Colchester. At the time she was working in the town at Crowther's factory, making uniforms, but she was directed to work at Hoffmann's in Chelmsford, where she remained until April 1945.[144] Secrecy was emphasised and most of the time the women were kept ignorant of what it was that they were producing. Ivy Kelly worked at

138   Gardiner, *Wartime*, p. 499.
139   Gardiner, *Wartime*, p. 519.
140   O. Lyle, *The Plaistow story* (London, 1960), p. 223.
141   Saunders, *Ford at war*, p. 21.
142   ECS 5 September 1942.
143   SE 24 October 1941.
144   ERO SA 8/965/1.

Crompton's, spending most of her time in the switch gear shop making items in steel and brass; she had no idea of their purpose.[145] Jeanette Roberts moved to Chelmsford when her husband got a job at Marconi and also worked for the company in its Crystallography Department at Baddow. She recalled that, although she and her female colleagues were not certain, they believed that they were working on the production of crystals used in radio transmitter sets dropped behind enemy lines. They never did find out because they were told not to ask questions. Chatting was discouraged in case they overworked and ruined the crystals.[146]

An unnamed Chelmsford woman aged 45 worked in a factory from 9am to 6pm Monday to Friday and from 9am until 1pm on Saturdays. She worked full-time, but because her husband worked full-time she always went home and prepared a hot meal for him. Her peacetime domestic habits were largely unaffected by the war:

> I dust the house each morning, and one morning a week do the washing, another evening the ironing. My shopping I do in the lunch hour on the way home, and Sunday is my day for doing the house thoroughly. I enjoy my work, both at home and at work, and find no strain whatever, and my friends tell me they see no difference, although I will admit I was very particular before the war.[147]

On the other hand, 40-year-old Mollie Pinnick, from Heybridge, who had been recruited by the Ministry of Aircraft, admitted that 'a spick-and-span house [was] a pre-war luxury'.[148]

As in all areas of employment where women replaced men they faced varying degrees of male hostility. This was partly based on the belief that women were less practical than men and could not be trusted with skilled work. Sybil Olive got a job on a lathe in the machine shop, but it was a male 'setter-up' who got the lathe ready for her. She found the men in general unwelcoming and female workers were not kept informed of what they were doing.[149] The Maldon and Heybridge branch of the Amalgamated Engineering Union (AEU) was critical of attempts to recruit women into engineering because it claimed that such work could not be done after only a few weeks' training.[150] At Crittalls' Silver End factory near Braintree women worked alongside men in spite of the latter's disapproval. They made parts for radar sets that were used by the

---

145 ERO SA 24/1455/1.
146 ERO SA 24/1459/1 Jeanette Roberts interview.
147 EC 28 August 1942.
148 EC 11 September 1942.
149 ERO SA 24/1457/1.
150 EC 4 December 1942.

RAF to transmit signals picked up on the ground; in particular, to overcome interference in aircraft a small copper sleeve was made using female skill in 'stitch welding'.[151] By the end of 1942 the *Essex Chronicle* felt able to declare more positively that male prejudice against female workers had almost vanished in Chelmsford because they had proved their worth.[152]

How Essex women felt about factory life is impossible to assess accurately, although anecdotal evidence suggests that they were positive about in it general. In an interview for the *Essex County Telegraph* 21-year-old Jean Thorpe from Colchester said, 'You get used to the noise. One advantage is that you get used to it gradually.'[153] Joyce Read, a 23-year-old Colchester woman, remarked, 'I think engineering appeals to me most because it is closer to the war. You soon get accustomed to the work.'[154] Joyce Ward had been a cinema usherette before the war. She commented that she was 'enjoying the work immensely and it helps to pass the time'[155]. Since her husband was a sailor and spent a great deal of time at sea, the work partially filled a void in her life.[156] Jeanette Roberts was able to meet a wide range of women she would not otherwise have met, particularly from middle- and working-class backgrounds. Eventually, however, she found that the people she worked alongside grew tiresome; there was a great deal of what she termed 'low sexual talk'. Nevertheless, years later, when she was asked if she had enjoyed her war work, she replied:

> Yes, I did, because it was a change for me. I'd enjoyed teaching and I would have like to have gone back … but of course [as] a married woman with children you didn't. I didn't particularly like being at home with young children, I found that boring, and so I preferred the company of other people and different experiences, and so the war work gave me an opportunity to experience contact with other people and other ways of life.[157]

Apart from providing huge numbers for the factory labour force, women were also a reservoir of labour for the farmer. The Women's Land Army (WLA), which had existed during the First World War, was re-established on 1 June 1939. Official efforts to make the work look glamorous by emphasising the healthy outdoor life did not square with the reality of work on the farm, which was dirty, back-breaking and, in winter, cold. Until WLA hostels were built

---

151   Stait, *Silver End*, p. 29.
152   EC 18 December 1942.
153   ECT 5 July 1941.
154   ECT 5 July 1941.
155   ECT 5 July 1941.
156   ECT 26 July 1941.
157   ERO SA 24/1459/1.

Land Girls were billeted in farms and cottages which middle-class women found primitive. The WLA were paid less than their male counterparts. At the start of the war agricultural labourers got 38s a week, which was less than half the national average, and Land Girls aged eighteen and over received only two-thirds of that figure. The basic working week was 48 hours in winter and 50 in summer, with anything over that paid as overtime, and to begin with there were no guaranteed holidays.[158] Given the low wages, recruitment was slow at first and by December 1939 there were fewer than 100 Land Girls working on Essex farms.[159] Nevertheless, progress was made and by 1943 more than 4,000 women had been registered in the WLA, part of a national force of 80,000.[160]

The need to attract and retain Land Girls led to a gradual improvement in conditions. Cottage billets were superseded by the building of WLA hostels; there were fourteen by 1942.[161] The hostels ensured, among other things, that the women were properly fed; at first there were complaints that they were expected to work all day on two cheese sandwiches and a tomato.[162] Although many Land Girls came from rural backgrounds, this was certainly not the case with all of them. In 1943, twenty of them received special armbands recording four years' service on Essex farms as part of a rolling programme of awards carried out throughout the county. Only six came from villages in the county; four came from London and one from Wiltshire, while the other nine had lived in either Metropolitan Essex or small Essex towns before they took up farming.[163] Their work was immensely varied. Marjorie Geere had been secretary to the mayor of Chingford before she was sent to Witham in 1941 to do farm and dairy work. She cleared derelict land, milked cows, bottled milk, mended hedges and fences, harvested and even transplanted 10,000 cabbage plants by hand.[164]

Nevertheless, the war opened up new opportunities for women. When Nazeing Common was ploughed up 21-year-old Gladys Kempton, from Westcliff, worked there as the first female driver of an earth excavator in the county. Gladys, who before the war had been a knitting machinist, lived nearby with another Land Girl in a caravan.[165] Caroline Evans applied to drive tractors. Faced with a six-month waiting list, she instead went into market gardening on a farm near Southminster. Then, when a vacancy appeared at a tractor

158 EFJ December 1939.
159 EFJ December 1939.
160 ECS 19 November 1943; in August 1943 the government, believing that too many young women were evading the Forces or factory work by working on the land, banned further recruitment into the WLA: G. Clarke, 'The Women's Land Army and its recruits 1938–50', in B. Short, C. Watkins and J. Martin, *The front line of freedom: British farming in the Second World War* (London, 2006), p. 105.
161 G. Owen, *Writtle: a village of distinction* (1993), p. 88; ECS 14 March 1942.
162 ECS 15 October 1943.
163 EC 29 October 1943; this partly accords with Clarke's assertion that one-third of all WLA recruits came from London and the industrial north: 'Women's Land Army', p. 107.
164 M. Geere, *Reminiscences of a Land Girl in Witham* (Witham, 1987), p. 9.
165 EC 7 August 1942.

depot, she trained and then worked for the Essex War Agricultural Committee (EWAC). She drove tractors around the countryside, often towing three trailers delivering farm tools. She learnt how to use caterpillar tractors and Fordson tractors and eventually became a Grade A driver.[166]

Some farmers came to appreciate their Land Girls. One man abandoned his stereotyped views of them:

> I have seen them at work in the root fields in the early summer and I have seen them clearing derelict land of its cursed bushes and digging ditches and watercourses that had been blocked for years. I have seen them doing work which I never believed women could have done. They have helped to alter the appearance of the Essex countryside and made it a joy to everyone who understands and appreciates cultivations.[167]

This male writer felt that, despite their very practical achievements, women retained their feminine sensitivity even when engaged in vital war work:

> I watched her hoeing in the wheat,
> An English girl so fair:
> The sea of grass enwrapped her feet,
> And golden gleamed her hair.
> The larks were singing in the sky,
> She did not seem to heed:
> But bending down unceasingly
> She hoed and hoed the weed.
> But when I heard the distant drone,
> As winged men rode the air,
> I saw that as she stood alone,
> Her lips moved, as in prayer.
> And down her cheek a teardrop wound,
> I turned my face away,
> That field of wheat seemed holy ground,
> I could no longer stay.[168]

On the other hand Pamela Russell, who farmed at Stubbers, near South Ockenden, found Land Girls rather a trial. They certainly seemed to come and go with regularity, although one can only speculate about whether it was because they were unsuited to the work or whether Russell was a hard

---

166   ERO SA 24/763/1.
167   ECS 9 January 1943.
168   ECS 18 June 1943.

Figure 3.7. Mary Page, of the Women's Land Army, milks one of the Guernsey cows on a farm at Pebmarsh, near Colchester. She came to the area from Northamptonshire Agricultural College. (BRNTM 2014.869.2, Braintree District Museum Trust)

Figure 3.8. These Women's Land Army volunteers get to grips with the mechanical side of farming at Bower Hall Farm on Mersea Island. (Mersea Museum/David Green)

taskmistress. 'My latest cow-lady rather a pain and grief as she arrived quite unable to milk, and hardly knowing one end of a cow from the other,' she wrote, 'but had a great reputation at her agricultural college where she has absorbed the theory of farming very industriously.' She continued her complaint: 'She has been here nearly a fortnight and I still have to strip the cows daily for her. She is really an office-wallah and knows several foreign languages. Of Irish extraction, but with a dreadful accent, and very dull, but talks incessantly.' About six weeks later she wrote that her 'mincing-fur lined glove wearing Land Girl' had left and she now had the full-time job of dealing with the cows in addition to her other work. She resorted to using a boy scout to do odd jobs and he even had a go at milking. There was no further mention of Land Girls in her letters after that.[169] Mrs J.L. Stevens, who, as a Land Girl, was on the other side of the fence, also found her experience rather trying:

> The farmer's wife who seemed to have nothing better to do than spy on us through binoculars for most of the day and who would tell us before we went home how long we had spent in the ditch going to the toilet, and how many times we had been and how long we had taken to eat our lunch sandwiches, no cosy barn here just the shelter of hedge or ditch.[170]

Land Girls took their own form of revenge on unsuspecting civilians. When working at Waltham Abbey, Stevens wrote: 'The amusement we felt each evening for six weeks after mucking out cow sheds when we six girls walked into the last carriage of the District Line train at Upminster and all the other passengers got out.'[171]

The journals of Eric Rudsdale reveal something of the difficulties that farmers and the authorities experienced with Land Girls. In 1942 he was appointed to the Lexden and Winstree District Committee of the EWAC, thus gaining first-hand experience of farming problems. His views on Land Girls have to be weighed carefully. His comments were invariably critical and, like other EWAC officials and some local farmers, he regarded Land Girls as lazy and untrustworthy. Problems arose because some Land Girls were resentful of the fact that they could earn more in factories, and in less primitive conditions. There was no effective discipline that could be imposed by the EWAC or farmers, and those who were minded to be uncooperative generally got away with it. In the summer of 1944 Rudsdale complained about the 'long stream of phone calls for me to answer, mostly about WLA. What little bitches they are.'[172] In January

169 ERO D/DRu C5, Letters of Pamela Russell of Stubbers, 21 May, 1 July 1941.
170 IWM 1237, J.L. Stevens.
171 IWM 1237.
172 ERO D/DU 888/27/4, journal, 17 August 1944.

1943 one farmer rang Rudsdale's office to say that two Land Girls had failed to turn up for work and two had left early because it was too cold, leaving him with only sixteen women.[173] One woman complained that two of her Land Girls had left the farm with their luggage with two Americans in a jeep and had not been seen again.[174] A farmer named Crawford phoned to complain that after he had been compelled to hire Land Girls his pension was cut. 'We might just as well have Hitler here,' said Crawford. 'In fact far better, because the girls would then have to keep some sort of discipline, which they don't now.'[175]

The conscription of men led to some modest improvements in the position of women in the professions and the white-collar sector. For instance, Colchester Borough Council withdrew its pre-war ban on married women teachers: in 1941 Miss E.P. Milsom was allowed to continue as an assistant teacher after her marriage, but only for the duration.[176] It was not until the spring of 1942 that any married woman was able to continue teaching without the council investigating the merits of her case.[177]

One of the most contentious issues concerning women was whether or not they should be employed as police officers. Women police officers had existed during the First World War but by 1924 only 110 were still employed throughout the country. Nationally, both local and police authorities had publicly stated their opposition to employing women officers. In Essex the Essex Joint Standing Committee (EJSC), comprising the Chief Constable and county councillors, had oversight of the county police force, and it opposed supplementing the force with women officers from the start of the war. There was never any question of women replacing men. Lady Rayleigh, one of the most influential women in the county, urged that female police officers be appointed and issued with motorcycles so they could disperse women who loitered near army camps. The Chief Constable, Major A.P.W. Wedd, was an implacable opponent of women police officers. He said,

> I told them that if I had a hundred women police officers I would not know what orders to give them. My own view is that although there are certain aspects of police work in which they might be useful, patrolling the streets in uniform is not one of them.[178]

Like others on the EJSC, he believed that, if they had to concede the issue, women should be employed only in secretarial, transport and domestic duties.

173 ERO 888/26/1, journal, 13 January 1943.
174 ERO D/DU 888/26/4, journal, 24 June 1943.
175 ERO D/DU 888/26/3, journal, 2 April 1943.
176 EC 1 March 1941.
177 EC 28 February 1942.
178 EC 6 December 1940.

The EJSC deferred a decision on the subject until the spring of 1941, when it rejected the idea outright.[179] More than two years passed before it reconsidered its decision, by which time it was coming under pressure from the press, local justices and women in general. The Braintree and Tendring magistrates criticised its refusal to appoint women; the Essex Federation of Women's Institutes protested to all Essex magistrates; and various women's organisations wrote to their MPs asking them to put pressure on the Chief Constable.[180] In September 1943 the EJSC decided to further examine the issue 'in view of the exceptional war conditions and of recent expressions of public opinion',[181] but the views of some of its members remained implacably hostile to the employment of women police. H.C. Carruthers, a male member of the EJSC, said that, rather than women, 'We want strong, well developed men of intelligence in our police force.'[182] Not surprisingly, this re-examination achieved nothing and it effectively shelved the issue once more. The ludicrous position of the EJSC was highlighted when a court official from Colchester, which did employ auxiliary female police officers, wrote to the *Chronicle* to say that 'Our policewomen are not merely uniformed ornaments. They are human beings – they sympathise, they plead, and above all, they understand. They are, however, not lacking in firmness when a firm hand is absolutely necessary.'[183] The writer noted that in the previous six months more than 400 women had sought the help and advice of the borough's policewomen.[184] The EJSC dismissed such evidence and alleged that these policewomen did not do 'real' police work but rather things such as 'vetting' girls who were trying to get into dances, chaperoning those who did and escorting them home afterwards.[185]

Nevertheless, in May 1944 the EJSC was under pressure once again. Following a communication from Tom Driberg, the Independent MP for Maldon, the home secretary Herbert Morrison intervened. At a special meeting of the EJSC a letter from Morrison was read, which was said to have stated his policy 'in no uncertain terms'. As a result it was decided to create a Women's Auxiliary Police Force in Essex comprising a regular female inspector, a sergeant and 23 constables. To meet the EJSC's objections the women were added to the establishment and did not replace male officers.[186] There was little local enthusiasm and when a police sergeant and two constables were appointed, they came from the Metropolitan area and Lancashire.[187]

179 EC 8 March 1941.
180 EC 30 May 1941.
181 ECS 10 September 1943.
182 ECS 10 September 1943.
183 EC 29 October 1943.
184 EC 29 October 1943.
185 ECS 3 December 1943.
186 EC 5 May 1944.
187 EC 4 August 1944.

During the war women were employed across the whole range of occupations. At Colchester Post Office by Christmas 1942 many of the jobs were undertaken by women.[188] In the summer of 1940 more than a thousand women, referred to by the *Chronicle* as 'conductorettes', formed a queue in Romford hoping for jobs on Green Line Coaches.[189] Colchester Borough Council was employing female conductors by 1942 to replace men who had been called up.[190] One Eastern National conductress, Mrs E. Clark, nicknamed 'The Little Commander', became famous for her exploits. She worked at Tilbury during the Blitz and her bus always ran. It was claimed that she and her passengers, usually sailors heading back to the docks, rocked the bus from side to side to help the driver get through debris on the road while bombs fell all around them. By 1942 she was working at Chelmsford, supervising the company's 120 conductresses. She lived several miles away from Chelmsford, at Hatfield Peverel, and to arrive for the first bus to leave at 5am she left home at 2.45am to walk there.[191] Women even penetrated the male bastion of the railways. Thirty-five-year-old 'Dolly' Palmer was the first signalwoman appointed in the Eastern Region as well as being a porter at Althorne station. Prior to that she had been the temporary stationmistress at Fambridge. Before the war she had worked in the clothing alterations department of a London store.[192]

Women still populated the traditional female spheres of employment, however. They ran the British Restaurants which were set up in towns during the war; they worked in the many new school canteens which sprang up; and they were found in the nurseries which were opened in the second half of the war. Doris Martin joined the Red Cross full-time after the outbreak of war and worked throughout the war at the emergency maternity hospital which had been set up at Danbury Park. The staff dealt with about 40 expectant mothers each month and the Queen visited when the 2000th mother gave birth.[193]

By 1941 the need for women workers meant that married women were included in the government's national service scheme. Like many young women with small children, Jeanette Roberts did part-time work at Marconi in the mornings, while her friend looked after her children. She then left work at lunchtime and looked after her friend's children.[194] Marconi had no objection to this sort of arrangement. Not every employer was able to do this and nursery provision was essential if this untapped reservoir of female labour was to be used. Nurseries did not really exist before the war, as it was assumed that married

---

188   ECS 3 January 1942.
189   ECS 12 July 1940.
190   CBC Transport Committee minute, 21 July 1940.
191   EC 20 March 1942.
192   EC 5 March 1943.
193   ERO SA 24/1454/1 Doris Martin.
194   ERO SA 24/1459/1.

women with children would stay at home to look after them, continuing to do so even when the children went to school. At the start of the war the nurseries which were opened were very much *ad hoc* affairs; they tended to be short-lived and were operated by voluntary means or by local authorities outside Essex. A short-lived nursery class at Great Baddow that catered for infant evacuees from Tottenham was funded by Tottenham Education Committee. However, when numbers declined it was closed down.[195] Colchester, with its numerous factories and engineering works, had struggled to open and sustain wartime nurseries. Ruth Bensusan Butt, a prominent Colchester doctor, was using her home; 22 children attended, and she had to turn mothers away daily. She blamed government rules, which insisted on a trained nurse being present, for hindering the growth of voluntary nurseries. In her opinion they could be run with the application of common sense.[196] Children were also being looked after at three schools in the borough by teachers and helpers who stayed on after school for the purpose. Their mothers worked in the town's engineering works.[197] At the end of 1941 the council had attempted to ascertain the need for nurseries in the town but, as few firms responded to its enquiries, no steps were taken.[198] The Ministry of Health disagreed with the council's decision and instructed it to set up three, each catering for 40 children.[199] The first of them – the Brook Street nursery – opened in September 1942.[200]

Both Essex County Council and Colchester Borough Council took a relatively positive and active approach to nurseries, unlike Chelmsford Borough Council, which courted intense unpopularity by resisting them.[201] In September 1940 a resolution requesting the borough's Education Committee to prepare a scheme for nursery schools was defeated and another year elapsed before the council decided that a full-time nursery was needed.[202] This was almost certainly influenced by a circular from the Ministry of Labour that was sent to all local authorities whose areas contained essential industry instructing them to establish nurseries. Within weeks Chelmsford Borough Council approved plans to erect two wartime nurseries for 80 children, although shortages of materials meant that the first one was delayed by a year.[203] The council's slow progress infuriated and exasperated women in Chelmsford and some of the more vocal ones set up a local pressure group,

195 EC 1 March 1940.
196 ECS 4, 15 July 1942.
197 CBC minutes, 18 June 1941, 27 May 1942.
198 CBC minutes, 17 December 1941.
199 CBC minutes, 20 May 1942.
200 CBC minutes, 14 September 1942.
201 J. Wilkinson, 'Women at war: the provision of childcare in Second World War Chelmsford', *Essex Journal*, autumn 2007, pp. 38–44, provides a very good account of this issue.
202 ChBC 12 November 1941; EC 27 September 1940.
203 EC 11 February 1942.

the 'Women-at-War Committee'. In February 1942 three mothers wrote to the *Chronicle* bemoaning the inability of married women in Chelmsford to respond to the national appeal for labour. They demanded day nurseries for under-fives, school meals and better shopping facilities for women workers.[204] The committee wrote to the town's MP and in March formed a deputation that lobbied Chelmsford Borough Council.[205] Yet the hostility of some men to nursery provision was intense. One local man, Frederick Hammond, wrote to the press, saying:

> The money spent on war-time nurseries in Chelmsford is a waste of public money. To my mind such schemes are an endeavour to drive the wedge of Socialism well into our public life, and will, if pursued, after the war, be detrimental to the sanctity of home life. You will have your children, turn them over to the authorities, and go your way.[206]

In spite of such opinions, the first nursery was opened in Corporation Road in August 1942. In total three nurseries were established, providing 160 places. Women such as Jeanette Roberts, who chaired the Women-at-War Committee, felt that it was a real achievement. The children were safe and cared for while their mothers were able to perform a patriotic duty, earn a reasonable wage and enjoy the company of other women.[207] By 1943 the Chelmsford and Colchester nurseries were part of over 1,300 established nationwide.[208]

Nevertheless, when the Women-at-War Committee tried to persuade the borough council to open play centres at schools it came up against the same brick wall. Its appeal was rejected on the grounds that

> the general policy to relieve mothers of the responsibility for the care and welfare of their children is to be strongly deprecated, despite wartime labour requirements, as it will inevitably result in the destruction of the family home life.

Thus, according to the council, a woman's place, despite the war, remained firmly in the home. It maintained a reactionary policy towards women throughout the war, in late 1943, for example, voting eighteen to ten against a proposal to co-opt three women representing the WVS and Cooperative Guild on to the Housing Committee. The decision prompted cries of 'Women

---

204   EC 13 February 1942.
205   ERO SA 24/1459/1; EC 27 March 1942.
206   EC 11 September 1942.
207   EC 16 October 1942, 1 September 1944.
208   Gardiner, *Wartime*, p. 519.

Haters!' from the public galleries.[209] Nevertheless, in 1944 Mrs Beryl Sturley was chosen to replace a councillor who had died in office.[210]

Two issues that plagued women war workers in towns were the inter-related problems of shopping and bus travel. In pre-supermarket days women had to visit a variety of shops to obtain everything they needed and, without fridges and freezers to store their perishables in, they had to shop every day. They had no choice but to shop in their lunch hour or after work. Many war workers travelled home by bus at the end of their shift but the situation was complicated because shoppers who did not work often used the same buses.[211] Sylvia Lambert, representing the women workers of Paxman, in Colchester, wrote complaining of 'shoppers and picture-goers' using buses during the rush hour. Combined with the severe restrictions on bus services, this meant that many workers missed their bus and faced a long walk home.[212] In 1942 Maldon bus conductresses threatened to strike because unnecessary civilian travel meant that they arrived home extremely late.[213]

In whatever capacity they worked, women doing the same as men received only a proportion of what their male counterparts earned. While Land Girls benefited from the wage increases of the male agricultural workers (by July 1940 their weekly wage was increased to 36s and it went up to 48s from December 1943) it did not keep pace with that of the men. Just as in agriculture, women who worked in factories or as office workers received only a proportion of the pay that men received.[214] In 1941 female employees of Colchester Borough Council, who were already on a lower wage than men, were given a war bonus that was only a third of that awarded to the men. The war bonus did gradually increase but from 1943 to 1945 it was still only 70–81 per cent of a man's bonus.[215] The differentials in these latter percentages seem to have been fairly standard for war bonuses. East Ham Town Council gave women employees 81 per cent of a man's war bonus.[216] In teaching the differentials remained the same, with male teachers earning at least a fifth more than their female counterparts.[217] Married women employees of Essex County Council whose husbands were in the Forces were also disadvantaged. Although they were granted two weeks off work when their husbands came home on leave, this was taken off their holiday allowance.[218]

---

209 EC 27 November 1943.
210 EC 2 June 1944.
211 EC 11 December 1942.
212 EC 6 October 1944.
213 EC 30 October 1942.
214 EC July 1940; ECS 9 January 1943.
215 CBC minutes, 30 January 1941, 24 September 1943, 28 February 1945.
216 SE 24 October 1941.
217 ECC minute, 4 January 1944.
218 ECC minute, 23 April 1942.

As well as meeting the challenges of working at new jobs in a testing environment, married women retained the responsibility for looking after their children, for cooking and for housework. As soon as war began local newspapers began a weekly column designed to aid women in the emergency. Margaret Vernon was the 'editress' of the 'Page for Women' in the *Billericay Times*. In her first column she exhorted women not to hoard or waste, but to use culinary ingenuity.[219] Common-sense articles appeared on subjects such as 'Does Your Child Cough?', 'Your Lungs In Winter' and 'How to deal with Cuts'.[220] The phrase 'kitchen front' was used to describe the vital domestic role played by women in the war, and in 1943 there were nearly nine million women who were full-time housewives, most of whom had children under fourteen.[221] Feeding the family was vital and it was women who shopped, who made the best of coupons and who queued to get whatever was available. Sybil Olive found that rationing was boring, but her family never went hungry. Bread and potatoes were always available and they kept chickens. As chicken feed was rationed she fed them on scraps. Unable to kill them herself, she got a neighbour to do it.[222] Jeanette Roberts found that meals had to be planned to cope with shortages but she, too, found the food monotonous. She detested shopping. On one occasion she joined a queue without knowing what it was for. Hoping for food, she ended up with a new saucepan.[223] On 28 January 1943 one of the longest queues ever seen in Chelmsford gathered for whiting and rock eel. Many customers began arriving before nine, although the shop did not open until ten. Fish had been in short supply and this was quite an occasion.[224]

To assist with the 'kitchen front' food economy committees were set up. The North-East Essex Committee organised food demonstrations. Even schoolchildren participated. The girls of Colchester County High School, inspired by the 'Home Science' department, gave exhibitions on 'helpful hints in Wartime', which involved potato pastries, scalloped cabbage, a haybox that 'cooks while you sleep' and home-made cleaning substances and polishes.[225] Not all women were enamoured of these campaigns. Councillor Mrs Duncan of Barking found them condescending:

> They knew all they needed to know about economical cooking. They had to know. There was nothing they could afford to waste. No

219 BT 16 September 1939.
220 BT 8, 15 January, 12 February 1944.
221 Gardiner, *Wartime*, p. 182.
222 ERO SA 14/1458/1 Sybil Olive.
223 ERO 24/1459/1.
224 EC 29 January 1943.
225 ECS 27 April, 25 May, 8 June 1940.

working class housewife could be taught anything in that direction. They knew how to scrape and make the best of anything they got.[226]

Even better-off women had to adapt their cooking habits. In an article in the *Woodford Times* entitled 'No Food Snobs', the writer asserted that women could no longer be choosy:

> Well-dressed women sally forth with their shopping baskets and unashamedly ask for shin, flank or brisket of beef. Scrag-end, best value of all the cheap cuts of mutton, has been promoted to an important place in middle-class menus for it makes grand Scotch broth and stews.[227]

The grimy work and unflattering clothes that accompanied work in factories and fields did not deter women from cultivating as feminine an appearance as possible. This was achieved even though cosmetics were severely restricted and clothes were rationed. In 1940 a young woman was heard to comment that stockings were dreadfully expensive, particularly as she had just laddered the ones she was wearing. She resolved to use the new paint that was available to draw the stocking line down the back of her legs. One of her companions replied that her sister had gone to work wearing it and nobody had noticed.[228] Some men did notice such niceties, however, and in 1943 it took a full council meeting at Saffron Walden to permit women to wear slacks in its offices because a shortage of coupons meant that women were unable to buy stockings and their legs were cold.[229] When the *Essex Chronicle*'s young female journalist Junella Chapelle provided a description of the 'typical' female factory worker, she was full of admiration for her ingenuity:

> Miss Chelmsford is a munitions worker, one of Mr Bevin's volunteers. In the factory her curls are hidden beneath a large and unbecoming cap, but that does not keep her from visiting the hairdresser once or twice a month. Owing to the Government's 75 per cent cosmetics cut, there is a shortage of shampoo so while the West End beauty salons ingeniously make do with a concoction of four eggs, mixed with rum, Miss Chelmsford gets plain soap and water. She finds metal hair clips also hard to obtain, so she had adopted the new 'pompadour' style, and uses the curved tortoiseshell combs of [her] grandmother's day.[230]

---

226 SE 14 June 1940.
227 WT 1 November 1940.
228 MOA Diarist 5414, 12 July 1940.
229 Douglas Brown, *East Anglia 1943*, p. 118.
230 EC 14 January 1941.

The Colchester Cooperative Society sold the 'Jamal' machine-less permanent wave contraption, which did not require mains electricity and could therefore be kept on the head and used even if one had to dash for the shelter.[231] Pam Hobbs' sister used soot for mascara, melted and reused stale lipsticks and restored dried-up rouge by mixing it with water.[232]

Under the pressure of clothing restrictions and official exhortations to 'make do and mend', women had to be adaptable to look fashionable or at least presentable. Pamela Hobbs's slippers were made from scrap material or padded cloth, with felt or string for soles.[233] Women's Institutes often invited speakers who were able to provide handy tips on how to make the most with the least. In 1944 the Galleywood branch was entertained with a talk on wartime handbag and shopping bag making.[234] By early 1943 Pamela Russell bemoaned the fact that anything leather

> is absolutely prohibitive, so buying a new bag simply doesn't enter our mind, especially as all the papers from Vogue downwards urge one to make exquisite shoulder bags out of a re-knitted jersey, or a piece of sacking adorned with raffia work or sequins (neither of them quite my pigeon).[235]

When her friend Marjorie gave her a bag as a birthday present she was ecstatic:

> Now I shall be able to cut a great dash in London on my too infrequent visits, with my new black bag and my last word in 'creations'. A most eminently fashionable ensemble made out of a black coat and frock of Aunt Lily's with a striking front-piece of gorgeous silk from the lining of an old velvet cloak of mothers.[236]

There were moments in which she felt quite despondent about her appearance, although she always managed to retain her sense of humour.

> We all go around looking shabbier and shabbier ... and our clothes hang about us in such characteristic bags and folds, that soon we shall send our old suits to represent us at meetings – they will make such

231 ECS 19 October 1940.
232 P. Hobbs, *Don't forget to write: the true story of an evacuee and her family* (London, 2009), p. 254.
233 Hobbs, *Don't forget to write*, p. 296.
234 BT 18 March 1944.
235 ERO D/DRu C5, Russell letter, 24 May 1943.
236 ERO D/DRu C5, Russell letter, 24 May 1943.

quiet and sympathetic gatherings and the chairman will be able to get through his work far more quickly.[237]

Her friend Violet used her ingenuity to make a 'complete trousseau' of white underwear from the surplice her son had worn in the village choir.[238] Pam Hobbs's sister Violet worked in a rubber factory making inflatable dinghies and parachutes, and occasionally she smuggled parachute silk out of the factory under her trousers in order to make underwear.[239] Making do and mending extended to everything. When Violet Hobbs was married in 1943 she borrowed her headdress and veil and a fellow worker provided her wedding dress. Her bridesmaids wore borrowed outfits and the wedding cake consisted of plastered cardboard mounted over a tiny sponge cake.[240]

A significant outlet for the energies and patriotism of women was the Women's Institute. The organisation had grown enormously during the inter-war years, reaching 290,000 members. Its function had been to provide leisure activities, but after war broke out its activities spread much wider. At the outset Mrs Marriage, the chairman of the Essex Federation, stated that 'If we are to maintain our individual balance and sense of proportion, we must hold on to whatever is normal and of permanent value, while keeping our eyes open for the many ways in which we can be of national service.'[241] There was no shortage of the latter. In 1940 there were 15,000 members in Essex and throughout the war there were about 201 branches in the county. Its 'Jam and Jerusalem' image was taken to new heights as branches became reception points for wartime fruit harvests. These gluts were passed to more than 160 preservation centres where they were turned into a variety of products. In 1940 the unused kitchens at Birch Hall, near Colchester, were used by the Birch and Layer Breton branch, which from two and a half tons of surplus fruit made 4,000 pounds of jam and jelly and 1,000 cans and 200 bottles of fruit. The branch's work was led by four ladies who had attended a three-day course on preserving at the Ministry of Agriculture.[242]

However, the Women's Institute was not merely a quiescent, conservative group of kitchen enthusiasts. During the war it also participated in the social and political debates that preoccupied the country, being in the forefront of the campaign for women police in Essex. In 1941 the Lambourne Women's Institute called for a more adequate representation of women on urban and rural district councils.[243] At Bures there was a demand that '[a]fter the war

---

237 ERO D/DRu C5, letter to Ellery Sedgewick, 24 April 1944.
238 ERO D/DRu C5, Russell letter, 24 April 1944.
239 Hobbs, *Don't forget to write*, p. 256.
240 Hobbs, *Don't forget to write*, pp. 262–4.
241 BA 23 September 1940.
242 ECS 2 November 1940.
243 EC 30 May 1941.

equal payment should be made to all workers on any one job, irrespective of the workers' sex'.[244] Women's Institutes also called for the creation of a fairer post-war society. In 1942 the Wivenhoe branch urged:

> That to discourage future wars British women should unite to insist that the Crown take complete control of wholesale industrial enterprises (with recompense to the owners) at the close of this war, thus preventing the sale by individuals to potentially hostile nations of the future means of waging war against ourselves.[245]

The Women's Voluntary Service (WVS) plugged another critical gap. It was created in 1938 when the Home Office asked Stella, Marchioness of Reading to start an organisation to draw women into ARP services. The Essex WVS was headed by Lady Rayleigh, wife of the landowning and farming magnate, Robert Strutt, Baron Rayleigh. Local councils provided free premises and furniture. Many well-off women gave their services freely and anyone of note was keen to be associated with it. In Colchester 949 women were involved by 1942.[246] All appointments were made from above and the organisation's structure went right down to village and street leaders. The WVS surveyed accommodation in reception areas and participated in the evacuations of 1939 and 1940. It established street salvage groups and helped to make wattle hurdles during the invasion scare of 1940. It sponsored the 'Housewives' Scheme', which provided help in an emergency and administered the type of first-aid to women that it was thought inappropriate for male wardens to give. Later it organised national savings street groups and in Colchester it was in charge of a voluntary car pool that was used following the abolition of the basic petrol allowance. At the town's North Station the WVS ran a canteen seven days a week, 24 hours a day. Five women were always on duty in five shifts. These activities were but a fraction of what the WVS contributed during the war.[247]

At Leyton the borough council asked Jenny Hammond to form the local branch of the WVS and eventually about 500 women from all age groups joined. She had to start the whole organisation from scratch, although the borough council provided premises and paid the rent. During air raids the WVS manned the telephones, receiving information from wardens which was then directed to WVS members throughout the town. A clothing store was available to assist families who had been bombed out and it found places for

---

244   ECS 21 February 1942.
245   ECS 7 March 1942.
246   ECS 12 September 1942.
247   Benham, *Essex at war*, pp. 118-20.

them in Rest Centres and temporary billets. The town's WVS headquarters had links with Spilsby and adjoining villages in Lincolnshire, which 'adopted' Leyton and provided second-hand furniture for bomb victims. On one occasion fourteen lorries carrying four tons of furniture each arrived in the borough. The WVS also ran Emergency Feeding Centres and sometimes kept them in operation for several days following a heavy raid.[248]

The war thus provided women with opportunities not seen since the Great War. They replaced or worked alongside men in factories, in engineering, workshops, buses, trains and on the land, and they participated in Civil Defence. They were lauded as heroines who combined the duties of housewife and mother with their contribution to war work. They were well aware, however, that they were not full partners in total war. Their pay was kept below that of men, much of their work was considered to be of an inferior quality to that of men and many of them feared that, as in 1918, their services would be disposed of with indecent haste once the war was over.

Farming: patriotism and protest

Prior to the Second World War farming in Essex had been at a low ebb for almost twenty years. Previously the Great War had rescued it from a 40-year depression caused by the import of cheap corn from the New World. Aided by guaranteed prices for cereals, which were briefly enshrined in the Agriculture Act of 1920, farmers boosted the country's self-sufficiency and enabled it to combat Germany's U-boat campaign. But, unfortunately, the Agriculture Act was repealed the next year, foreign imports resumed and wheat prices collapsed. The Depression only worsened matters and by 1934 wheat prices were at their lowest since the nineteenth century.[249] The state of Essex farming was worse than it had been in 1914 and it was saved only by farmers changing from arable to dairy farming. Consequently, when war broke out pasture covered almost half of all farmland in the county and only a quarter of farmland was used to grow cereals. The remainder was derelict.[250]

The government's revitalisation of farming during the war rested on a policy of decentralisation based on the formation of county agricultural committees similar to those of the Great War. Their fundamental role was to free all the shipping space that was being used to import food so that war materials could be brought in instead. To this end scientific and high-

248   ERO SA 9/449/1.
249   Calder, People's war, p. 4181–9.
250   P. Wormell, Essex farming 1900–2000 (Colchester, 1999), p. 48.

production methods, rather than any large-scale land reform, were adopted.[251] The Essex War Agricultural Committee (EWAC) was activated as soon as war broke out. To supervise the agricultural development of the whole county the EWAC delegated responsibility to thirteen district committees made up of experienced and knowledgeable farmers. It was these men who oversaw the government-inspired revolution in farming.[252] To increase the amount of time that farmers could work the government introduced Summer Time in 1940, setting the clocks one hour ahead of GMT on a permanent basis instead of just from April to October. In 1941 another hour of daylight was added (Double Summer Time), so that work on the land could go on far into the night.[253]

The EWAC's first duty was to identify the 40,000 acres that it was ordered to plough up to create more arable land. This amounted to about 10 per cent of the existing grassland in the county. District committees decided on a local allocation, although the unusually wet autumn of 1939 and severe cold snap of early 1940 delayed the ploughing-up process, as did the nature of the Essex soil – mainly heavy and intractable clay.[254] Consequently, Essex was one of only five counties that failed to meet its initial target.[255] Even so, the EWAC was informed in August 1940 that a further 28,000 acres had to be ploughed. The government's demands continued to increase. At the end of 1940 a further 61,000 acres was allocated, effectively doubling the amount already set down.[256] By the end of the war the total area under crops had increased by 140,000 acres. Unsurprisingly the amount of pasture fell by 27 per cent, a drop of 143,000 acres.[257]

The difficulties involved in ploughing up this ever-growing acreage of land varied throughout the county. For example, the poorly drained, heavy London clay areas were either grassland or had been colonised by thorn and brambles. Ralph Sadler, the EWAC's District Officer for Lexden and Winstree, recalled his efforts to reclaim land for arable farming in his area. Using a Fordson tractor alongside gang labour comprising RDC roadmen, Land Girls, conscientious objectors and Italian prisoners of war, the thorn bushes and brambles were dug up, piled in great heaps and burned – in daytime, of course. None of the land was fit to crop in 1940, but in the following year a good harvest was obtained.[258] The same was true of other areas. When the minister of agriculture, Robert

251 B. Short, C. Watkins and J. Martin, 'The front line of freedom: State-led agricultural revolution in Britain 1939–45', in B. Short, C. Watkins and J. Martin, *The front line of freedom: British farming in the Second World War* (London, 2006), p. 1.
252 Sir W. Gavin, *Ninety years of family farming: the story of Lord Rayleighs and Strutt and Parker Farms* (London, 1967), pp. 200–1.
253 EFJ April 1940, April 1941.
254 J. Martin, 'The structural transformation of British agriculture: the resurgence of progressive, high-input arable farming', in B. Short, C. Watkins and J. Martin, *The front line of freedom: British farming in the Second World War* (London, 2006), p. 25.
255 B. Short, C. Watkins and J. Martin, *The front line of freedom: British farming in the Second World War* (London, 2006), p. 25.
256 EFJ November 1940.
257 Wormell, *Essex farming*, pp. 74–5.
258 R. Sadler, *Sunshine and showers: one hundred years in the life of an Essex farming family* (Chelmsford, 1998), p. 61.

Hudson, visited the county in 1942, the EWAC took him to One Tree Hill in Laindon, near Basildon. Looking east, south and west he was shown 1,000 acres of derelict land which had been worked in the Great War and then abandoned, and had since become overgrown with impenetrable thorn. Hudson told them: 'Get it cleared and cropped now; you may never get another chance.' Every available steam engine was brought in to uproot the thorns, huge American army bulldozers shoved the bushes into heaps and they were set alight. The land had deteriorated to such a degree that when it was being cleared a bungalow and a garage with a car in it was discovered buried by the thorns. The bungalow was demolished, but the garage and car were spared, and in 1943 they were surrounded not by dereliction but by an ocean of wheat.[259]

The neglected state and heavy nature of the land meant that tractors were required in greater numbers to clear and plough it. Between 1939 and 1945 almost 130,000 Fordson tractors were produced at Dagenham.[260] And by 1942 there were 5,668 tractors at work in Essex, although farmers were still using 11,000 horses at the end of the war.[261] Finally the number of tractors in use outstripped the capacity to maintain and repair them, a problem solved by the creation of a repair and servicing department at the EWAC's headquarters. Although farm machinery lay idle and broken all over the county, and although local machine dealers lacked the means to repair them, they were hostile to the creation of a centralised EWAC repair depot. Their protests were ignored.[262] Much of the derelict land that was brought into cultivation was poorly drained, and special machines mole-drained 70,000 acres, while 6,000 miles of ditches were tile drained.[263] Combine harvesters arrived in Britain in small numbers – by 1945 the EWAC had two – and lease-lend binders from the United States were also used to cut the crops.[264] However, carting and stacking were a problem because the EWAC owned few horse-drawn vehicles. After scouring the county they found old farm wagons, coal carts and furniture vans and harnessed horses to them. Other farmers were able to obtain lorries and by hook or by crook the sheaves were taken to designated stack sites. All threshing was done by steam and by existing threshing contractors, helped by Land Girls.[265]

Thanks to the ploughing up campaign, and in particular the use of tractors, the employment of alternative forms of labour and the insistence of improved standards of husbandry, cereal acreage increased enormously. In 1943 the

---

259 Sadler, *Sunshine and showers*, pp. 70–1.
260 P. Dewey, 'The supply of tractors', in B. Short, C. Watkins and J. Martin, *The front line of freedom: British farming in the Second World War* (London, 2006), p. 95.
261 Wormell, *Essex farming*, p. 66.
262 Sadler, *Sunshine and showers*, p. 66.
263 Sadler, *Sunshine and showers*, p. 67.
264 Sadler, *Sunshine and showers*, p. 71.
265 Sadler, *Sunshine and showers*, pp. 60, 62, 64–7, 70–72.

Figure 3.9. The sixth column? An advert from July 1941 emphasising the damage done to domestic food production by this unpatriotic rodent. (Essex Farmers' Journal)

national wheat acreage was at its most extensive, to which Essex contributed 144,000 acres. There was also an additional 53,000 acres of barley and 22,000 acres of oats. Consequently, firms such as Strutt and Parker enjoyed a boom period in the war. The company's gross receipts for cereals crops during 1940–44 increased by 150 per cent compared with those for 1935–39, and its total gross receipts for crops and livestock doubled to £356,000. The firm's gross profits per acre were up too, averaging £5 2s an acre.[266]

The substantial increases in crop harvests and subsequent storage demanded an intensification of the never-ending war between farmers and various types of vermin, who, given half a chance, would consume their farm produce. The EWAC set up a sub-committee to supervise this domestic war, which was waged on insects and plant diseases, too. However, the destruction of some types of pest was the responsibility of the individual farmer or landowner, who was liable to prosecution for failing to do so. In November 1939, for instance, rabbits on the Chesterford Park estate of a Mrs Ethel Gotbe caused considerable

266 Wormell, *Essex farming*, pp. 74, 88, 213.

damage to crops on neighbouring farms. The cost of her failure to control and destroy them was a £10 fine.[267] A National Rat Week, an annual event which dated back to the First World War, was held in early November 1939 and in subsequent years. Farmers were given the choice of leaving the destruction to the Land Army Officer or performing the task themselves; if they chose the latter they could obtain chemical poisons containing Red Squill, a highly toxic rodenticide, or Barium Carbonate, which had a lead base. Mixed with meal, dripping, salt, biscuit or oatmeal and shaped into pieces the size of a hazelnut, they were a potent weapon of the war against the rat.[268]

Rats were only one of many species identified for destruction. 'Rat and sparrow' clubs existed before the war in many parts of the country. In the winter of 1940/41 shoots were organised against rooks and pigeons 'on a more intensive scale than hitherto'.[269] The EWAC could specify a time limit within which a landowner had to kill vermin; failure to do so gave the EWAC the right to enter the land to do the job itself. The EWAC's powers were expanded by the Rooks Order of 1940. Rooks were seen as a nuisance because, where their populations expanded, their natural food resources were exhausted and they resorted to devouring agricultural produce. To counter this the EWAC recommended that landowners shoot about 60–75 per cent of all young rooks in the spring.[270] The EWAC appointed a pest officer whose job was to focus on the destruction of rats and rabbits, whose crop depredations were considered to be the most serious. From the autumn of 1939 it became compulsory for farmers to surround all their corn stacks with wire netting at threshing time to keep out hungry vermin and 3d per rat's tail was paid as an extra incentive to step up the campaign. Such campaigns were supplemented by showings of films organised by the EWAC, such as 'Kill that Rat' and 'The Rabbit Pest', which were shown at the Corn Exchange in Chelmsford.[271] In 1943 grey squirrels were added to the list of creatures that landowners were under a legal obligation to destroy.[272]

In addition to cereal and vegetable production, dairy farming was also crucially important. If the nation was going to be provided with dairy products, particularly milk, farmers had to become increasingly self-sufficient in animal feeding stuffs. By the summer of 1940 farmers were authorised to harvest the grass on railway embankments and roadside verges as hay.[273] Feeding stuffs were rationed in early 1941 and by the following year farmers were being urged to

---

267 ECS 30 November 1939.
268 EFJ October 1939.
269 EFJ December 1939, February 1941.
270 EFJ February 1941.
271 EFJ August 1941.
272 EFJ October 1943.
273 EFJ July 1940.

grow more winter feeding stuffs such as peas, kale and beans, and to produce more silage out of roughage. By the autumn of 1942 there were 80 straw pulp plants operating on Essex farms, and every farmer was being advised to install one because of the shortage of animal feeding stuffs. During the 1943 sugar beet 'campaign' the Anglo-Scottish sugar beet factory at Felsted, which contributed 30,000 tons of sugar, produced 14,000 tons of dried pulp and beet tops as animal food.[274] The situation regarding feeding stuffs deteriorated steadily from 1940. Poultry consumed food but were considered to give little back to the soil, and they were targeted for drastic reductions. By October 1940 feeding stuffs for poultry had been slashed by two-thirds.[275] By the end of the year some poultry farmers and smallholders had gone out of business, and others, especially in the south of the county, were struggling to survive. In mid-1941, in view of further curtailments in imported feeding stuffs, farmers were being urged to cull their inferior cattle. The EWAC was now empowered to supervise the stocking of farms in the interests of good husbandry, and two panels, one for dairy cattle and one for livestock, were established through the cooperation of the EWAC and the National Farmers' Union (NFU) to deal with cases where farmers refused to cooperate.[276] The result of the government's feeding priorities for the nation are revealed in the number of animals which were found in the county towards the end of the war. While there were 10,000 more cattle, there were 106,000 fewer sheep and 76,000 fewer pigs, the latter amounting to a fall of 50 per cent. Chickens had also fallen by half, some 750,000 fewer than in 1939.[277]

The greatest problem confronting farmers faced by the government's production demands was the retention of farm workers. This was particularly urgent in view of the fact that some 8,000 agricultural labourers, a quarter of the workforce, had left the county's farms between the wars in the so-called 'drift from the land'.[278] Before the outbreak of war, farmers were already anxious in case their experienced workers were called up,[279] but at first a wide range of farm labourers over the age of 21 was exempted from military service. In the summer of 1940, as a recognition of the importance of domestic food production, the government lowered the age at which men could be registered in reserved occupations from 21 to eighteen in what the NFU considered to be the more important occupational groups in farming such as ploughman, tractor driver and threshing machine attendant. Other farm workers' ages of reservation

274   EFJ September 1942, January 1944.
275   EFJ July 1940.
276   EFJ June 1941.
277   Wormell, *Essex farming*, p. 75.
278   Wormell, *Essex farming*, p. 69.
279   See P. Rusiecki, *The impact of catastrophe: the people of Essex and the First World War (1914–1920)* (Chelmsford, 2008), pp. 104–5.

were either 25 or 30. However, by 1941 the age of reservation for almost all these occupational groups, including farmers, was raised to 25. It was not intended that this should necessarily result in call-up, as each case was examined on its own merits. Nevertheless, during the war the worst fears of many Essex farmers were realised, as 5,000 agricultural labourers were conscripted.[280] Despite this, however, farm workers actually increased by 6,218 during the war because of the use mainly of the WLA but also of part-time local women and schoolboys, conscientious objectors and Italian prisoners of war.[281]

Throughout the war the EWAC supplemented its labour force with additional workers, particularly at harvest time.[282] While the army was reluctant to lend troops to perform farm duties except during the harvest the EWAC was able to establish a good working relationship with Essex County Council, which during the war agreed to amend school summer holidays to allow secondary and elementary school children to work on farms, especially in rural areas.[283] In 1940 it allowed all schools in the county's pea-growing areas to close so that children over twelve and their mothers could assist in pea-picking.[284] Several appeals were made urging boys who had just left school to work on farms prior to their call-up. In 1940 the EWAC created a more systematic organisation by recruiting boys aged fourteen and fifteen from country towns; this scheme was later extended, with an age limit of nineteen and with boys from all parts of Essex made eligible.[285] The use of conscientious objectors was often unpopular with farmers and farm labourers and not always on philosophical grounds. In early 1942 one Essex farmer produced figures relating to beet harvesting with conscientious objectors. He claimed that beet harvesting with these men was three times more expensive than with experienced farm labourers, because the work of the former was generally slack. The farmer concluded that 'means must be found to secure to the farmer a reasonable amount of work from Conscientious Objectors and others who have come into the land to fill the deficiencies of farm labour'.[286]

Above all else, the recruitment and retention of agricultural labourers required an improvement in their wages. Their minimum pay was increased at Christmas 1939, and again on 31 March 1940, with men over 21 now earning 38s a week. This had been increased to 54s by the end of October 1941, to 60s at the end of December and 70s by the end of the war.[287] However, wages in

---

280 Wormell, *Essex farming*, p. 70.
281 Wormell, *Essex farming*, pp. 69–70.
282 EFJ September 1941, September 1942.
283 EFJ April 1940.
284 EFJ June 1940.
285 EFJ August 1941.
286 EFJ January 1942.
287 EFJ January 1940, April 1940, December 1941, February 1945.

war industries remained higher and made farm workers restive. Although the work was of national importance some labourers adopted an idle or truculent attitude in the hope of getting themselves sacked so that they could migrate to work in factories. In consequence, in 1941 farmers in the Saffron Walden area contacted the national headquarters of the NFU, stating that:

> We desire to register a strong protest respecting the excessive wages paid for labour by Government in this neighbourhood. We most strongly emphasise the disquieting effect this disparity in wages is having on our labour, which is seriously impeding the effort being made by agriculturists in food production.[288]

Nevertheless, farmers were nothing if not inconsistent when wage increases were awarded to their employees. In June 1940 the new minister of agriculture, Robert Hudson, announced that the national minimum wage would be raised to 48s a week. He also increased prices to allow farmers to pay the new rate.[289] However, when farm labourers sought a pay increase they were obliged to resort to the Essex Agricultural Wages Committee, which was made up of the men's representatives, farmer's representatives and independent members. Once a decision had been reached it was then submitted to the National Agricultural Wages Board for its approval. Throughout the war farm workers pressed for pay increases, while the farmers were resistant. The independent members on the wages committee tended to side with the men. In December 1941 farmers expressed their disapproval of labourers' wages being increased twice in two months, 'believing that no case can be made out for the deviation of wages in Essex from those laid down by the Wages Board, and that no increase is justified unless a revision of farm prices is brought into effect by the government'.[290] The assertion that wage increases must be accompanied by price increases was a mantra which farmers had chanted before and throughout the war. When 'RAB' Butler, the president of the Board of Education and MP for Saffron Walden, a farming constituency, visited the Dunmow Farmers' Club, speaker after speaker made it clear to him that they had lost all confidence in the government, and in particular the minister of agriculture, Robert Hudson. Hollis Clayton, chairman of the Essex NFU, called the crisis over prices 'the most serious since the outbreak of war'. On this occasion Hudson assuaged the hostility by providing an additional £2.5 million to the milk industry for the benefit of the small producer.[291]

---

288 EFJ September 1941.
289 EFJ June 1940.
290 EFJ December 1941.
291 EC 7 January 1944.

Nevertheless, by the end of the war farmers' grievances concerning wages were still raw, as this NFU resolution demonstrates:

> The Essex branch strongly urges the need for complete overhaul of the machinery for fixing the wages of farm workers. At the present time wages are being fixed by independent people, often with very little knowledge of the industry, and their decisions are often purely matters of prejudice.[292]

At the root of these grievances was the farmers' deep-seated fear that they would be abandoned by the government once the war was over, just as they had been in 1920. Farmers simply did not trust the government. An old-timer made this point to the agricultural commentator James Wentworth Day as they drank together in the Peldon Rose pub near Colchester:

> Har! Government's a rum 'un. You never know what capers they'll get up to. They lets us chaps on the land down in peace, makes an almighty fuss of us in war, and then I don't doubt they'll kick us up the backside when peace comes again.[293]

There was also an assumption that there were too few ministers and even MPs in Essex who had any understanding of farming. Hollis Clayton felt that Westminster demanded change that was too rapid. 'Hustle has no place in nature's dictionary,' he wrote, 'that is a point I am afraid the rulers in power at the present time do not understand.'[294] Essex MPs who represented farming constituencies also felt the lash of Clayton's tongue. In 1942 he wrote 'I should like to know where they are.' He added,

> I have not seen them during the war years at any meeting I have attended, and I have been to a good many. It may be they do understand the agricultural industry, but if they wish to represent their constituents, they should take some interest in them.[295]

However, the *Essex Farmers' Journal* noted realistically that

> Farming methods today are determined by the nation's needs. At times these methods are contrary to good husbandry. Nevertheless

---

292 EFJ February 1945.
293 J. Wentworth Day, *Farming adventure: a thousand miles through England on a horse* (London, 1943), p. 30.
294 EFJ December 1940.
295 EFJ December 1942.

the guiding principle must be: 'Better to have an island depleted of its fertiliser with a Union Jack flying, though tattered, than a land flowing with milk and honey under the heel of the Swastika.'[296]

Farmers were never able to overcome their distrust of government, and this influenced their actions during the war as much as the need to win it. Throughout the war the Essex branch of the NFU scrutinised like hawks every government pronouncement, every variation of policy, every price change and particularly any reference to post-war farming policy. This mistrust was highlighted in 1940, when the government revealed its plans for farming in the next year. The *Essex Farmers' Journal* wondered how best to interpret this statement – whether 'peace-time policy to war-time stimulation' or 'pre-war neglect to war-time coercion'.[297] There is little doubt that many farmers felt that the government, having neglected the industry, was now both exploiting and underestimating them during the war. In August 1940, only two months after promising that production costs and prices would be linked, Hudson's plans for agriculture in 1941 no longer included such a commitment. The Essex branch of the NFU was dismayed by this 'ill-advised policy', which was stated to be

> an attempt to take advantage of the farmers' sense of patriotism in a way which is expected of no other industry; and in view of the promises which have been made to the effect that prices would be related to increased costs of production, the present proposals can have no other effect than to destroy the farmers' confidence in the Government's good faith and to discourage the efforts which are being made to secure the maximum of food.[298]

The government's milk pricing structure caused aggravation throughout the war. When changes were introduced in 1942 the NFU complained that 'this fantastic structure is only to be explained by the ill-advised influence of distributive interests upon the Ministry of Food'.[299] In the following year farmers complained that the government was doing nothing to prevent rising production costs in the dairy industry and a resolution was despatched to national headquarters which reiterated earlier grievances:

---

296 EFJ January 1943. The *Essex Farmers' Journal* was the official mouthpiece of the NFU, but its opinions did not always coincide with those of the union.
297 EFJ September 1940.
298 EFJ September 1940.
299 EFJ November 1942.

Milk producers are already carrying out one of the most difficult tasks of wartime production, and it appears that the Government are content to trade upon the patriotic motives which have inspired producers to maintain a high level of production in spite of many obstacles.[300]

A few months later the Epping branch of the NFU condemned the government's 'foolhardy attitude' towards milk prices and requested that Hudson 'cease pressing "production targets" upon producers'.[301]

Petrol rationing was another source of discord. When it was introduced special arrangements were made for agriculture. In addition to ordinary supplies, farmers were granted special licences to obtain motor spirit and heavy oil during the harvest. Nevertheless, in 1940, in order to impose further economies, all bulk petrol depots were closed except in large towns, and farmers experienced difficulty in obtaining supplies. Those involved in growing fruit and vegetables for the London market had ordinarily transported their produce by road, but difficulty securing petrol meant that they were pressed to make greater use of the railways. However, horticulturalists complained that in Essex railways were not always conveniently located to provide rapid facilities for loading, transporting or unloading their perishable wares, especially when speed was of the essence.[302] In 1942 the government, needing to save more fuel, ruled that vegetable producers outside a 35-mile radius from London (thus including a large part of Essex) could not transport their goods by road to the capital. The Essex branch of the NFU again argued that the county's railway facilities were inadequate for the handling of large quantities of perishable stuff, but their protests were brushed aside. In January 1943 the NFU's frustrations boiled over and it passed an angry resolution, not devoid of menace, stating that:

If, therefore, the Ministry of War Transport persist in a regulated restriction which is not based on sound economic principles of economy, and which is opposed to the interests of the public and growers, this Committee cannot recommend its members farming outside a radius of thirty-five miles from London to continue the growing of vegetables for the London market in the future; and anticipates that members will request the Essex War Agricultural Executive Committee to release them from the acreages already agreed upon.[303]

---

300 EFJ September 1943.
301 EFJ January 1944.
302 EFJ May 1940.
303 EFJ February 1943.

However, in October the government, responding to protests across the Home Counties, relaxed the restriction so that growers covering most of Essex were allowed a limited amount of road haulage by nominated hauliers.[304]

The EWAC was directly responsible to the Ministry of Agriculture for ensuring that the latter's numerous orders were carried out by farmers. By the end of the war there had been almost 2,000 of these orders.[305] The EWAC's most important responsibilities were to make sure that farmers ploughed up the amount of grassland allocated to them and farmed their land in a manner that would produce the best possible yield. A WAC had the authority to take over or repossess part or all of the land of a farmer who was unable or unwilling to conform to the Ministry's requirements. It would then be handed to another farmer to work or farmed by the WAC itself. There was no complicated legal procedure – all that was needed was the posting of notices on the land to announce the fact that it was in new hands. During the war 5,350 farms totalling 344,000 acres were repossessed in England and Wales, and 2,695 tenancies totalling 226,000 acres were terminated.[306] In Essex the EWAC was farming about eight per cent of the county's agricultural holdings – the amount of land repossessed from owners or where tenants were evicted – by the end of the war.[307] For instance, in the Saffron Walden area, which had 480 working farms, the EWAC took possession of a mere 981 acres, a fraction of what was being farmed.[308] This seems to confirm the judgement of Ralph Sadler, the EWAC's Executive Officer, that Essex farms were generally well run in wartime.[309] The farmer could appeal, but only to the Committee that had dispossessed him in the first place. The NFU supported repossessions as a bargaining tool to secure guaranteed prices and post-war stability, so union support for a dispossessed farmer was unlikely.[310]

The EWAC considered that it had strong scientific and professional grounds on which to base its policy towards individual farmers. Early in the war it surveyed all farms in the county to establish exactly what the situation was. The survey so impressed the Food Production Department of the Ministry of Agriculture that it used it as the basis for its National Farm Survey of 1941–43.[311] The Essex survey graded all farms into three categories: firstly, those that were well farmed (category A); then those regarded as moderately well farmed but

---

304 EFJ October 1943.
305 Gavin, *Ninety years of family farming*, p. 204.
306 B. Short, 'The dispossession of farmers in England and Wales during and after the Second World War', in B. Short, C. Watkins and J. Martin, *The front line of freedom: British farming in the Second World War* (London, 2006), p. 165.
307 Short, 'Dispossession', p. 168.
308 J. Cooper, *Clavering at war: an Essex village 1939–1945* (Saffron Walden, 2012), p. 71.
309 See p. 321-4.
310 Cooper, *Clavering at war*, p. 160.
311 B. Short, C. Watkins, W. Foot and P. Kinsman, *The National Farm Survey: state surveillance and the countryside in England and Wales in the Second World War* (London, 2000), p. 26.

capable of improvement (category B); and finally those that were badly farmed or where the land was derelict (category C). Those with well-run farms were generally trusted to work without interference; machinery, labour, manures and feeding stuffs were made readily available to them. The owners of category B farms worked under periodic supervision, but assistance was also available. Those with farms classified as category C were under the greatest risk of having their land repossessed. In this respect the EWAC's powers were considerable. For example, W. Burrell, who farmed Thorrington Hall, was ordered to 'Plough 39 acres of arable land in a husband-like manner to the satisfaction of the Committee by 31 December, 1941, and crop with an approved crop for the 1942 harvest'. It must have been even more galling when he was placed under the watchful gaze of another farmer: 'Destroy all weeds on 50 acres of land by 20 January 1942,' he was told, 'to the satisfaction of Mr A. Mitchell of St Mary's, Great Bentley, on behalf of the EWAC'.[312]

On the whole Essex farms were well run, although whether or not this was the result of the EWAC looking over farmers' shoulders is hard to say. At the end of 1940 Eric Rudsdale was appointed clerk to the Lexden and Winstree District Committee of the EWAC.[313] He was neither a farmer nor an authority on farming. In general he had little but contempt for the men who were in charge of the EWAC. 'The damn canting snobs,' he wrote. 'To think that a war is being waged to keep their filthy hides safe.'[314] His sympathies lay with the small farmer and he was not, therefore, an impartial observer. Nevertheless, there was a shrewdness about him and as part of his job he visited a large number of farms with EWAC officials and saw the state of them at first hand. Even his amateur eye was able to recognise a farm that was badly run. Therefore, his musings provide us with scattered insights, perhaps no more than that, into the level of efficiency or otherwise of farmers in his district. There is no doubt that some farms were not well run and in that respect they were not seen to be serving the best interests of the nation. At a farm belonging to a man named Filer, who had 200 acres, there was only him and a pensioner to do the work. The stock consisted of five cows and a pet lamb. 'Incredible state of affairs,' Rudsdale commented.[315] A visit to Holmwood Farm, at Chitts Hill near Colchester, revealed that its cows were half starved and the farmer had only mouldy hay to feed them through the winter. Four cows produced only three gallons of milk a day.[316] On a tour of farms on Mersea Island he and another EWAC committee member arrived at Bower Hall Farm. In his journal he wrote:

312   ERO D/DU 746/22/1, 21 October 1941, D/DU 746/22/4, 9 June 1942, EWAC Compulsory Cultivation Orders.
313   ERO D/DU 888/24, journal, 1 January 1941.
314   ERO D/DU 888/24, journal, 31 March 1941.
315   ERO D/DU 888/24, journal, 16 March 1941.
316   ERO D/DU 888/24, journal, 13 November 1941.

In the first field we went into it was just a sea of thistles. Webb said, 'What have you got here, Mr Vique?' 'Oats' was the reply, and there was in fact an oat or two sticking up. 'Well,' said Webb, 'I'll tell you what you've got here Mr Vique, you've got a bloody mess!'[317]

Not surprisingly, the Committee decided to take possession of the land at Michaelmas. By the time that Rudsdale started work the EWAC had certainly begun repossessing land in his district. He wrote, 'I feel nothing but anger at the sight of Government officials working hard and systematically to undermine the agrarian organisation, upon which rests, literally, the whole future of the British people.'[318]

At the start of the war Ralph Sadler was a district officer for the EWAC, and in 1943 he was appointed executive officer. Years later he wrote that, in his opinion, 'With relatively few exceptions the scheme worked well, but for a number of reasons some occupiers failed to cooperate and they were eventually dispossessed.'[319] Nevertheless, he clearly felt that there was a reluctance on the part of the Executive Committee to carry out repossessions in cases of gross inefficiency. Matters apparently came to head when the District Committee of Dunmow recommended that H.B. Turner of Barnston Hall, an elderly, respected and long-established farmer who had been an advisor to the Ministry of Agriculture in the Great War, should be dispossessed. Members of the Executive Committee met Turner but no action was taken. However, after an inspection revealed that conditions on the farm were not ideal it was repossessed. Sadler clearly had no regrets about such actions and said that cases like this were few and far between. 'Most C farmers responded to help and encouragement and I am sure benefited from the committee's actions,' he wrote. He went on to say that 'The unfortunate few were proud, elderly men who had not the physical ability nor the financial responsibility to respond to the committee's directions.'[320]

Repossessions were immensely unpopular with farmers throughout the country and national organisations such as the Farmers' Rights Association and the Farmers and Smallholders Association were created to protest against them.[321] One series of repossessions in Essex proved to be very controversial; indeed, they achieved national headlines. In the early summer of 1943 a number of farmers – how many is unclear – in the Peldon area, near Colchester, were dispossessed. The villagers, led by the vicar J.R. Wilson, took action and sought

---

317 ERO D/DU 888/25, journal, 16 June 1942.
318 ERO D/DU 888/25/2, 12 August 1942.
319 Sadler, *Sunshine and showers*, p. 68.
320 Sadler, *Sunshine and showers*, pp. 68–70.
321 Martin, 'Structural transformation', p. 32.

the advice of James Wentworth Day, who lived nearby. Wentworth Day, who has already been mentioned, was a gentleman farmer, journalist, Conservative party supporter and farming commentator whose right-wing views on agriculture were well known. During the war he rode on horseback all around East Anglia commenting on its history, architecture, agrarian culture and, most significantly for the people of Peldon, the evils of War Agricultural Committees. A year earlier he had written an article in the *Daily Mail* about WACs with the unsubtle title of 'Little Hitlers on the Farm'.[322] He later claimed that he had received more letters complaining about the EWAC than about any other committee in the country.

Wentworth Day detested any form of state interference with the land, believing that farmers were quite capable of doing the job if left alone. To him WACs were the worst manifestation of state tyranny. He described them as a system of 'petty *gauleiters* and self-important officials',[323] whose existence was alien to rural England. Perhaps even worse for him was his conviction that the committee's officials had no idea how to run farming. He described them as 'that cocksure body of self-satisfied wiseacres and their presumptuous minions'.[324] Ministry officials were dismissed as 'diploma-ed deadheads'.[325] However, what enraged him most of all was his belief that the committees were inherently undemocratic, which of course they were. Their activities 'smell of the Star Chamber,' he raged. 'They had almost absolute power,' he wrote, 'and they use it, in some instances, in a manner dangerously near corruption, in others arbitrarily with little regard for the elements of justice.'[326]

Wentworth Day was invited to Peldon by the vicar, who claimed that the parish was 'in great distress'. He met with people who told him that 'farmer after farmer' had been given notice to quit by the EWAC without good reason. Wentworth Day suggested that they form an association, devise rules and set up a committee. Some £75 was subscribed to the cause on the spot. Mr Prior, the village postmaster, was appointed honorary secretary and he travelled all over Essex investigating similar perceived abuses.[327] At Colchester on 10 July the Essex Farmers' and Country People's Association (EFCPA) was formed with the aim of bombarding the EWAC into submission. The EFCPA undoubtedly had local support. A week later a further meeting was held at the Red Lion Hotel at Colchester. A loudspeaker van was acquired and Wentworth Day addressed several hundred farmers in the market. They unanimously passed a resolution urging a government inquiry into the 'high-handed and dictatorial

322 Wentworth Day, *Harvest adventure*, pp. 264–85.
323 Wentworth Day, *Harvest adventure*, p. 5.
324 Wentworth Day, *Harvest adventure*, p. 129.
325 Wentworth Day, *Harvest adventure*, p. 183.
326 Wentworth Day, *Harvest adventure*, pp. 5, 264.
327 Wentworth Day, *Harvest adventure*, pp. 270–2.

methods, injustices, and waste of public money' by the EWAC.[328] The London and provincial press provided good coverage at first. The government ignored it, as did the EWAC to begin with, trusting that the agitation would soon die down. It did not. Meetings were held at Maldon, Braintree and Mersea. Robert Hudson paid a surprise visit to Peldon and, according to Wentworth Day, matters improved after that.[329]

However, Wentworth Day's claim that the protestors had triumphed was almost certainly exaggerated; nor was his support for the agitators as clear-cut as it seemed. Eric Rudsdale, in his capacity as an EWAC official, actually met him in the committee's Colchester offices. According to Rudsdale, Wentworth Day 'went off about "British justice", "Gestapo", "German methods", and all that sort of thing, and blackguarded most of the members of the Committee individually and quite wrongly'. However, after Rudsdale had outlined one or two of the cases to him, presumably noting that the repossessions were justified, Wentworth Day 'had to admit that most of the complainants were utter scoundrels anyway'. The two of them ended up in the Red Lion and Rudsdale claimed that they parted on amicable terms.[330] Considering that Rudsdale's sympathies lay with the small farmer, whom he regarded as being oppressed by officialdom, his comments to Wentworth Day may confirm the necessity for the EWAC's actions. In August Colchester's MP Oswald Lewis commented on the issue, although he does not seem to have visited Peldon: 'I see that the misfortunes of these dispossessed farmers are being used for a kind of journalistic stunt,' he noted sourly, 'supported by meetings at which all sorts of wild and irresponsible statements are being made … and there is something peculiarly distasteful in the deliberate magnification of personal grievances or inconveniences'.[331]

Protest meetings and their kindred disaffection lingered on, occasionally brought to life by news of a new dispossession, until they died a natural death towards the end of the year. There was no 'improvement' as alleged by Wentworth Day. The Peldon dispossessions were not revoked and, as Lewis had forecast, the EFCPA proved to be 'an ephemeral body'.[332] It seems likely that the EWAC considered that its dispossessions were necessary, while, as we have seen, the NFU opted not to support its dispossessed members. The latter's mouthpiece, the *Essex Farmers' Journal*, provided no coverage of it, and, in that part of the journal devoted to EWAC matters, neither did the Committee. Ralph Sadler, who began the war as the district officer for the area which included Peldon, had become the EWAC's executive officer at the time of the

---

328   Wentworth Day, *Harvest adventure*, pp. 272; ECS 16, 23 July 1943.
329   Wentworth Day, *Harvest adventure*, pp. 272–3.
330   ERO D/DU 888/26/4, journal, 12 July 1943.
331   ECS 13 August 1943.
332   ECS 13 August 1943.

controversy. When he wrote his memoirs half a century later he, too, considered the matter unworthy of mention.[333]

The war rescued farming in Essex, and throughout much of the country, from two decades of official neglect and local despair. One historian wrote that:

> Without the Second World War, the Essex countryside would have been an unkempt scrub akin to an African landscape. It would have been dotted with derelict and tumbledown buildings, devoid of crops, covered with rough weed infested fields filled with red poppies, yellow charlock, buttercups, speedwell and cleavers, wild oats and prolific black grass. Thistle would have been carried on the prevailing winds and would have blown from Tilbury to Harlow. Farmers would have settled into a subservient peasant-status.[334]

At the end of the war the *Essex Farmers' Journal* wrote a poignant but proud epitaph for those who had worked the land:

> It will be some years before all the scars of war are healed upon the farmland of Essex, the bomb-craters all bull-dozed back again, the crumbling anti-tank ditches filled in, the aircraft landing obstructions taken away, the concrete blocks removed, and all the farmhouses and buildings restored to their former condition where they are capable of restoration at all. Memories are short, and perhaps these scars will be the only medals that Essex farmers will ever get to show the part they took in the war effort. But they can be proud of that effort, sustained 'under fire' and showing what could be done to feed the people of this country from our own lands.[335]

Between the summer of 1940 and June 1941, when Britain had stood alone against the Nazis, Essex, along with the rest of the country, had been transformed into a fortress, anticipating the possibility of invasion, while undergoing a severe bombing campaign by the enemy. Even after America's entry into the war raised hopes of ultimate victory, Essex continued to undergo agricultural, industrial and social changes that were essential for this to be achieved. As we have seen, these changes were not accomplished without some contention. Industrial workers and farm labourers demanded financial remuneration commensurate with the sacrifices they felt they were making; farmers felt exploited by the government and feared that the latter would abandon them after the war by

333 Sadler, *Sunshine and showers*, pp. 68–70.
334 Wormell, *Essex farming*, p. 65.
335 EFJ May 1945.

resuming the importation of cheap foreign food; women faced male hostility in some traditional areas of male employment and, when they campaigned for nurseries that would have allowed married women to contribute to the war effort, they met opposition there, too. In addition to these disputes, the years from 1940 to 1942 were marked by a sequence of military defeats, evacuations and surrenders which fuelled growing popular discontent with the government's prosecution of the war.

4

Popular protest

Politics and the Maldon by-election of 1942

In 1939 an unofficial wartime truce was agreed between the political parties whereby, following the death or resignation of an MP, the sitting party would put forward a new candidate who would be elected unopposed. The truce broke down almost immediately when the Labour MP for Silvertown, John Jones, stepped down in February 1940 owing to ill health. James Hollins, a West Ham Labour councillor and trade unionist, and a resident for over 30 years, was nominated to replace him. However, both the British Union of Fascists (BUF) and the Communist party put up candidates, the latter being Harry Pollitt, the party leader. The constituency was overwhelmingly working class and solidly Labour, and there was little doubt that the Labour party would retain the seat. Hollins polled more than 14,000 votes, Pollitt just 966 and Tom Moran of the BUF a mere 151. Over and above the predictable result, the election revealed considerable apathy, even cynicism, about the war.[1]

In spite of the entry into the war of the Soviet Union and America during 1941 things continued to go badly. The loss of Singapore to the Japanese in February 1942, with the capture of 100,000 men, followed by setbacks in North Africa, meant that people became increasingly critical of the conduct of the war and restive about the prospects of victory. At the same time the reluctance of the government to open a Second Front to aid Russia conflicted with popular admiration of the Soviet Union. This popular dissent manifested itself in three by-elections in March and April 1942, when Independent candidates defeated Conservatives at Grantham, Rugby and Wallasey. These were but straws in the wind compared with the large number of uncontested wartime parliamentary elections, but they were symptomatic of general disquiet.

It was against this background of growing disaffection that another by-election brought the Essex town of Maldon to the fore in national politics. In May 1942 the sitting Conservative MP, Sir Edward Ruggles-Brise, died. Maldon had been a Conservative stronghold for the better part of half a century and the party's

---

1   TC46 By-Elections 1937–47, Box 4, 46/4/A-E, West Ham, Silvertown by-election.

majority, although it had fallen by over a third in 1935, was still a comfortable 7,808. Ruggles-Brise had farmed a large acreage around Finchingfield and had acquired a reputation for championing the interests of agriculture between the wars. Wartime by-elections were not fully representative because of the large-scale demographic changes that had occurred since 1939. The Maldon constituency was the second smallest in terms of population in Essex; the pre-war electoral register had 45,406 names on it, but many locals were now serving in the forces or were in other parts of the country doing vital war work and the register was much reduced. In 1942 the *Burnham Advertiser* estimated that there were only about 36,000 voters in the constituency; the *Essex County Standard* put it even lower, at about 33,000.[2] Hundreds of young people who would have been able to vote were effectively disenfranchised because a new electoral register was not produced until late in the war. The constituency was predominantly agricultural, although there were significant urban communities within its boundaries. The largest towns (ranked according to size), according to the 1931 census, were Braintree, Maldon, Witham and Burnham. Braintree was the location of the Courtauld silk mill, the largest industrial concern within the constituency, and the large Crittall factory was at Silver End, near Witham.

The Conservatives assumed that their nominee would be elected unopposed in accordance with the electoral truce. The party settled on Reuben Hunt as their candidate. He possessed impeccable credentials. At 54 years old, he was the owner of the Atlas Ironworks at Earls Colne near Colchester, which before the war had manufactured agricultural machinery. As well as being a man of great wealth he also wielded considerable influence in the county. He had been a magistrate for over a decade and was both an alderman on Essex County Council and Chairman of the county council's Finance Committee. He was not a resident of the constituency, instead living in Saffron Walden, where he was chairman of the local Conservative Association.

However, within days two Independent candidates emerged. R. Borlase-Matthews, a firm critic of the government, had a background that suggested that he might also be well received in the constituency. Born in Swansea to a wealthy ship-owning family, he had worked on farms as a boy before going to public school and university. In 1942 he described himself as a 'consulting electro-farming engineer'. He owned an estate of 640 acres that included an all-electric farm involving 67 different uses of electricity. As befitted an engineer responding to a time of fuel shortages he drove around the constituency in a car driven by a gas-producing plant described as a 'chestnut roaster' because of its eccentric appearance.[3]

---

2   BA 6 June 1942; ECS 13 June 1942.
3   BA 30 May, 13 June 1942.

Figure 4.1. The charismatic Tom Driberg, who was able to take advantage of popular discontent with the way the war was being conducted to achieve a sensational by-election victory at Maldon in 1942. (Maldon Constituency Labour Party)

Tom Driberg was the youngest and best known of the candidates. Nevertheless, he was shrewd enough to stress his experience and maturity as well as his comparative youth. 'He is 37 years old,' noted his election flyer, 'old enough to take a sensible, balanced view of world affairs, young enough to tackle with vigour the difficult years that will come after the war as well as the immediate task of winning the war as quickly as possible.'[4] At the time of the election Driberg was working at the *Daily Express*, writing a diary and gossip column under the pseudonym William Hickey. He had at one time been a member of the Communist party and had spent time in Spain reporting on the civil war. Although Driberg spent much of his time in London he had a house in the constituency at Bradwell-on-Sea, which met with local approval. Lord Beaverbrook, the owner of the *Daily Express*, gave Driberg time off from work to fight the election.[5] According to Driberg the only piece of advice Beaverbrook gave him was to wear a hat: 'The British people will never vote for anyone who doesn't wear a hat,' he told him.[6] Driberg quickly

4   ERO A8071 Maldon Constituency Labour Party materials, Driberg election flyer, 1942.
5   T. Driberg, *Ruling passions* (London, 1977), p. 180.
6   Reported by Driberg himself on the BBC World At War series, episode 15, *Home Fires: Britain 1940–1944* (1974).

learned the art of electioneering from Richard Acland, a Liberal MP who had become disillusioned with government policy, whose political views had moved to the Left, and who later formed the Socialist Common Wealth Party in 1942 with J.B. Priestley. Driberg had already joined Acland and Priestley as a member of the '1941 Committee', which had been formed by a group of liberal intellectuals in early May and produced a 'Nine-Point Plan' calling for the publication by the government of post-war plans for the provision of full and free education, employment and a civilised standard of living for all.[7]

The Labour and Liberal parties in the constituency were theoretically bound to honour the electoral truce and recommend Hunt to their members. This the Liberal party did, but the Labour party was completely divided. Some local leaders felt that Hunt's election was by no means a certainty. H.A. Woodcraft, the secretary of the Maldon branch, wrote that 'It is reported in the press that one of the *Daily Express* bright young men may stand as an Independent, knowing the precarious Conservative hold, any freak candidature would stand an even break.'[8] Another Labour member, R.G. Mabbs, noted that there was a large body of opinion locally in favour of voting for an Independent: 'anything to oppose the Government in fact!' He added gloomily that 'I am very much afraid of the present movement as leading to political chaos and opening the way to some form of fascism.'[9] Nevertheless, on 3 June the constituency officers opted to continue the electoral truce, although they tried to pin Hunt down to a commitment to a more progressive policy by formulating a number of questions to be put to him concerning the improvement of workers' rights and living standards during and after the war.[10] The decision that the officials had actually made is revealed in a letter that Mabbs sent three days later. Although the party leaders regarded themselves as honouring the electoral truce, supporting Hunt was a ballot paper too far. Mabbs made this clear when he stated that 'We do not say that we will support Hunt, only that we will not support anyone else.'[11]

The short election campaign, which lasted about five weeks, was fought between Hunt, who campaigned on a 'don't-rock-the-boat' programme, and Driberg and Borlase-Matthews, who both urged the government to change its personnel in order to prosecute the war more effectively. Hunt's slogan, 'Take No Risks! Back Churchill's Choice by Voting for Hunt. Essex Born – Essex Bred', expressed the man's conservatism while at the same time trying to counter Driberg's residential advantage.[12] He attempted to soothe farmers, still fearful

7   A. Calder, *The people's war: Britain 1939–1945* (London, 1969), p. 253; BA 30 May 1942.
8   ERO A8071, letter, 21 May 1942.
9   ERO A8071, letter, 24 May 1942.
10   ERO A8071, minutes of meeting of Labour Party officers, 3 June 1942.
11   ERO A8071, letter, 6 June 1942.
12   BA 20 June 1942.

that they would be abandoned after the war, by promising that there would be no repeat of the hardships of the interwar years. The government opposed all wartime by-elections: Churchill regarded them as distractions from the war effort. Nevertheless, he offered his personal support to the Conservative party candidate. In a letter to Hunt he wrote that 'It is still my convinced opinion that in these days when the future of our country and, indeed, of all civilisation is in the melting pot by-elections are completely out of keeping with the gravity of the times.' He expressed the hope that no-one would 'provoke' an 'unnecessary and meaningless contest'. 'You are known as one of themselves,' Churchill wrote, attempting to present Hunt as a man of the people. In the same letter he praised his work on the county council as well as his wide business and financial experience. Knowing that his letter would be published in the local press, Churchill urged voters to return Hunt 'in proof of their unshakeable resolve to carry the war to a victorious end' and to demonstrate their faith in the government.[13]

Driberg and Borlase-Matthews both believed that this rallying cry to maintain the political status quo by Churchill and Hunt was unacceptable because it covered a multitude of sins at the highest level of government, which was why the war was not going well. Borlase-Matthews fought the campaign on the slogan 'Action and Agriculture' by an 'Agricultural National Candidate'. He claimed to have 'initiative, enterprise and energy', and that he was someone who would criticise 'constructively and fearlessly all waste, inefficiency and incompetence wherever it may be, in high or low places, quite free from the deadening control of Party Whips – responsible only to the Electors of this Division'. He believed that the war was an engineer's war and that, as a farmer and engineer, he was well qualified to fight it. 'Why let a lot of laymen, who mean well but are incompetent,' he queried, 'attempt to deal with these highly technical matters, without assistance from those who know?' In his election advert in the *Burnham Advertiser* he concluded by saying that 'he strongly advocates that the right men should be put in the right jobs, regardless of relationships, friendships and party interests. The situation is of only too tragic urgency, so drastic steps must be taken.'[14]

Driberg shared Borlase-Matthews' belief that positions in government were held by men unfitted for them and who had been chosen by what might be called the 'old school tie' method or simply by the party, rather than by a genuine test of ability and competence. Driberg attacked Churchill's criticisms of the two Independent candidates in a letter to the press:

---

13   BA 20 June 1942.
14   BA 23 May 1942.

It is precisely because times are so grave that Parliament must be reinforced as occasion arises with men who subordinate all prejudices and all profits to total victory, and are in touch with the developing ideas of the younger people who will have to build this peace. Where is the levity in this? It seems to me, on the contrary, frivolous and unpatriotic to suggest that Parliamentary seats must be filled exclusively by party nominees. The interests of nation and constituents should be the sole consideration, merit the only criterion. The people support the Churchill government; but they want to see it still further invigorated and streamlined.[15]

Driberg was singling out for criticism the party faithful who were being elected unopposed at by-elections and whose primary consideration was perhaps a business rather than the war effort. He referred to them as 'dummies' and 'yes-men'. 'Service of the community must replace profit for sale as the motive for all our public work,' he asserted. The war effort was being hindered by men who 'cling to the old, dead idea of self-interest, by firms who put their dividends before the nation's good'.[16]

Driberg's election flyer emphasised that '[h]e is not a busy industrial boss. He is not a busy farmer.' He promised to cut his press work to a minimum and devote all his energies to parliamentary work, and concluded by saying that 'he will be in the constituency, and available to all constituents, whenever he is not at Westminster'.[17] The other weapon in Driberg's election armoury was what he believed to be Churchill's impotence as Prime Minister; he was, as Driberg put it, a 'titular leader'. In his weekly election column in the *Burnham Advertiser* he wrote that:

The truth is that there are two Churchills; one is the great national figure whom no party can claim as its exclusive property; the other is the chief who was forced on the Conservative party by the British people and who naturally finds it convenient to have behind him several hundred dummies who will say 'Yes' to everything.[18]

'I have a profound admiration for Mr Churchill himself,' Driberg wrote, 'but I want to save him from his more undesirable friends.' Later, his supporters wrote that '[h]e is for Churchill, against rackets, red-tape, and "yes-men"'. He described Hunt as 'courteous and amiable', but saw him as conforming to the pattern of

---

15 BA 13 June 1942.
16 BA 13 June 1942.
17 ERO A8071 Driberg election flyer, 1942.
18 BA 20 June 1942.

the old type of narrow, reactionary, commercially-minded Conservative. These men kept Churchill out of office for years. These men obsequiously upheld Baldwin in doing nothing and Chamberlain in doing wrong. These men did all they could to obstruct the alliance with Russia which might have checked Hitler years ago and made this war unnecessary.... How can a Socialist or a Liberal or a progressive Tory vote for such a man?[19]

Both Hunt and Borlase-Matthews ran low-key and lacklustre campaigns and there is little doubt that, of the three candidates, Driberg, who was campaigning on a Socialist platform in a Tory stronghold, and who therefore had the most ground to make up, conducted the most dynamic campaign. He had the support of some national figures and their letters supporting him were published in the local press. J.B. Priestley, a familiar, comforting voice on the BBC in the dark days of 1940 and 1941, supported Driberg and expressed undisguised Socialist sentiments:

It is in reality a people's war, and there must be a people's peace – a social organisation for the benefit of ordinary people everywhere; that means sweeping away many sectional interests and clearing out some of the old gangs who are still trying to preserve them.

George Bernard Shaw urged that people vote to eliminate the two-party electoral system which had dominated for so long, saying that 'It means dropping the party lines and voting for the ablest candidates.'[20]

Driberg organised far more public meetings than the other two men and he turned out to be an effective and eloquent speaker, well able to express his ideas so that ordinary people could follow them. He circulated an election flyer, 'What Are We To Do?', which expressed both the contempt that Driberg and his supporters had for those in high office and their hopes for the future: 'This is our chance to prune out some of the dead wood and graft new shoots of young, vigorous, progressive stock to the tree of our National Life.'[21]

He bought space in the *Burnham Advertiser* and produced a weekly column using the same sort of catchy, pithy language that characterised his William Hickey column. Each had the headline 'Driberg – the only Candidate who lives in the Division'. The column was also used to advertise his meetings and visits by well-known individuals who spoke in support of him. On one evening in June he paid a first visit to Braintree, the largest town in the

19   F. Wheen, *Tom Driberg: his life and indiscretions* (London, 1990), p. 177.
20   BA 20 June 1942.
21   ERO A8071, election flyer, 1942.

constituency, which contained the biggest concentration of Labour voters. A few days later an Anglo-Soviet bookshop was opened in the town. All three candidates were invited to attend but Driberg was the only one to turn up and speak. It was an opportune visit, for there he met his most active local supporter, Father Jack Boggis, the sub-dean of Bocking. Boggis was the secretary of both the local Anglo-Russian friendship society and the town's Labour party.[22] In spite of the decision by his party not to support Independent candidates, Boggis urged it to rethink its decision. On 11 June he wrote to a local Labour party committee member saying, 'I do hope that the Party is going to reconsider the position. Hunt is the worst type of Tory from our point of view; squire *and* industrialist.'[23]

Subsequently Boggis resigned his post in the Labour party and became the organising secretary of Driberg's campaign in Braintree. Boggis's support for Driberg was no petulant whim, but was based on an appraisal of the man's capabilities and political beliefs. In attempting to persuade the local Labour party to back Driberg he had written:

> I have gone very carefully into Driberg's record and find he is and always has been a Socialist and at the time of the Spanish war he went there twice and wrote (even in the *Express*) in favour of the [Spanish] Government – which is surely a real test of Fascist leanings or otherwise. He is a real progressive candidate and to support the Tory against him is political suicide…. To me the choice is between an Independent Socialist and the Traditional enemy of our movement: I shall work and vote for Driberg.[24]

Campaign committees were set up in towns and villages throughout the constituency. To lessen the focus on Driberg's personality, which was always a danger with Independent candidates, and in order to provide some form of democratic machinery, his supporters announced that if he were elected these campaign committees would form the basis of a new, non-party Maldon Constituency Association. They would aim to provide political education and especially to organise meetings at which Driberg would report back on parliamentary matters. Dorothy L. Sayers, the famous Essex crime writer, who lived in Witham, provided the furniture for the committee room there. Reginald Clarke, a future editor of the *Essex County Standard*, but then in the RAF, gave assistance. Tom Wintringham, who had fought in the International Brigade in the Spanish Civil War, and who had been given the responsibility

---

22   Driberg, *Ruling passions*, pp. 181–2.
23   ERO A8071, letter, 11 June 1942.
24   ERO A8071, letter, 11 June 1942.

Maldon Parliamentary By-Election, 1942

TRAGEDY AT TOBRUK

¶ " Something has gone wrong in Libya "—again . . .

¶ " The shipping situation is grave "—but the Government won't tell the British people just how grave, tho' our Allies (and the enemy) know the grim truth.

¶ We " can't afford " to increase the old-age pension—but we *can* afford to pay £66 millions promptly, in hard cash, to the millionaires who owned coal-mining royalties.

¶ Our sons and brothers fighting in far lands hang on desperately for munitions that don't turn up, while profiteers haggle with the Government at home.

¶ Something is wrong indeed, *near the top.* . . . The British people are deeply troubled by the continuing tale of disasters; after nearly 3 years of " total war," they resent such things as the legal loopholes by which the rich can still eat sumptuously in London restaurants; they demand a fairer deal for Service men and their dependents.

THE *above is true, every word of it. We all know it. The thing is, what's to be done about it ?* One immediate step that electors in the Maldon Division can take is to vote for Tom Driberg on Thursday.

Hunt . . ? He belongs to the lot who say we " can't afford " higher old-age pensions—who kept Churchill out of power for years and always stood against co-operation with Russia. He " promises nothing "; he has " no policy "; he would simply vote as the Tory Party Whip told him to.

Matthews . . ? He promises pretty well everything. He lives far from the Maldon Division, and has tried to get into Parliament at various other times and places. You must " vet " an Independent carefully : you can judge him by his friends.

Driberg is backed by respected and thoughtful people of all parties in the Division, and by nationally famous men like J. B. Priestley, Bernard Shaw, Hannen Swaffer, and Vernon Bartlett. Such names are a guarantee of his worth : so is the job he has done for years as " William Hickey " of the Daily Express.

Driberg has a policy which puts service before profit. He does not descend to personal vilifying of his opponents. He lives in the Division,

Figure 4.2. The leaflet that Driberg and his supporters rushed to distribute after the fall of Tobruk to Rommel, a reverse that shocked the nation. (Maldon Constituency Labour Party)

for setting up the national Home Guard training school at Osterley Park, accompanied Driberg on a lightning tour of the constituency.[25]

Only five days before polling day an appalling military disaster befell the Allied cause: the Libyan port of Tobruk, after a lengthy siege, surrendered to Rommel on 21 June. Some 30,000 Allied soldiers were captured. The news, reported on the BBC the next day, hit the British people like a bombshell, arousing great anger and soul-searching.[26] For Driberg and his supporters the fall of Tobruk symbolised everything that was wrong with the government and its prosecution of the war. They immediately circulated throughout the constituency a second election flyer bearing the headline 'Tragedy at Tobruk'. The military problems facing the British in North Africa were highlighted, profiteers were attacked and it was alleged that the truth about shipping losses was being kept from the public.[27] On the eve of the poll Driberg managed to attend five meetings – at Burnham, Maldon, Witham, Silver End and Braintree. He did not arrive at Braintree until 10pm, where he found 6,000 people waiting for him in the market place. As part of his speech he reported an alleged conversation he had had with a leading Conservative, who had said that things were going badly in North Africa because Britain was sending too much aid to the Soviet Union. The crowd was suitably outraged and Harold Quinton, the secretary of the local branch of the Communist party, said that he would have to abandon the electoral truce and vote for Driberg.[28] The election result was a sensation:

Driberg Independent 12,219
Hunt Government Conservative 6,226
Borlase-Matthews Independent 1,476

In the course of just a few weeks he had overturned the Conservative majority of almost 8,000 and acquired a majority of 6,000. The Conservative vote had fallen significantly and at the same time Driberg had attracted support from a huge number of voters. Borlase-Matthews lost his deposit.

How was Driberg able to achieve such a landslide victory? His ability as a public speaker was a major factor, as was, as the *Essex County Standard* put it, his 'commanding and engaging personality'.[29] Being the youngest of the candidates may have influenced voters, particularly as he constantly stressed the need for fresh blood in parliament, and he had campaigned tirelessly. By

---

25   Driberg, *Ruling passions*, pp. 182–3.
26   Calder, *People's war*, p. 299.
27   ERO A8071, election flyer, 1942.
28   Driberg, *Ruling passions*, p. 184.
29   ECS 4 July 1942.

comparison, Hunt's campaign was lacklustre, perhaps as a result of complacency. His supporters organised only twelve meetings during the entire campaign and Conservative canvassing was said to have been less vigorous than in the past. Perhaps of even greater significance was the disaster at Tobruk, which increased many people's disillusionment with the conduct of the war and probably swayed the attitude of many who were undecided. Driberg himself was in no doubt about why he won. In his victory speech at the Maldon Parish Hall he said,

> I believe that this decision reflects the mood of the British people. They are aware of the urgent gravity of the situation. They know that free and constructive criticism can help the Government to make total war more effectively. They are determined that no consideration of private interest or profit shall block any longer the path to speedy victory or a decent peace.[30]

He countered the accusations that he had exploited the fall of Tobruk by saying that 'It was impossible not to mention Tobruk. It was the latest, ghastliest illustration of the kind of thing that my whole campaign was directed against. It was strictly and seriously relevant.'[31]

The Conservative *Essex County Standard* felt that the result demonstrated 'shakiness', but dismissed it as a serious threat to the government's credibility. It was certainly contemptuous of those who had voted for Driberg:

> He was clever enough to convince a number of simple-minded country folk that if they voted for Driberg they would, as he himself put it, 'go straight ahead for victory.' This is an interesting expression of delusion, due to nerves and disappointment. It does not show a high degree of intelligence and of fortitude on the part of those who voted for Mr Driberg.[32]

National newspapers were divided over the significance of the result. *The Times* saw no reason for alarm:

> The return of a critic of the National Government is no sign of disunity in the nation, but rather one more plea, urged at a moment of perplexity and disquiet, for achievements and a progressive capable of commanding, preserving and promoting national unity.

30   ECS 4 July 1942.
31   BA 4 July 1942.
32   ECS 4 July 1942.

On the other hand, the *Daily Mirror* was elated that Driberg had defeated 'the official Conservative, the Party machine, and the dispensers of dope about union in pursuit of failure. We congratulate Tom Driberg; we salute William Hickey. The public is sick of yes-men armed with rubber-stamps.'[33]

There is no doubt that Driberg's words took root in fertile soil, and not just in the Maldon constituency. A Chelmsford resident asserted that a Socialist government was needed, and echoed Driberg by saying that it must be composed not of political hacks but of men of wisdom and far-sightedness.[34] A Colchester woman also supported Driberg's views when she described the need to sweep away the current unrepresentative government, replacing it with a government untrammelled by political ideologies.[35]

Two and a half years later, with the war moving to a victorious close, events conspired to force a further by-election at Chelmsford. It was caused by the death of Col. Jack Macnamara, the town's MP since 1935, who was killed on active service in Italy in December 1944. Once again the political truce broke down. The Commonwealth party, formed in 1942 by Richard Acland and which had already won a couple of by-elections since then, entered negotiations with the local Labour party to put forward a candidate acceptable to both. Negotiations floundered and the Commonwealth party chose instead Norman Hidden, a man of pronounced left-wing views.[36] When Hidden resigned from the Commonwealth party to stand as a Labour candidate in the Harwich constituency, the Commonwealth party selected an RAF officer, Wing Commander Ernest Millington.[37] The Conservatives also chose a serving RAF officer, 34-year-old Flight Lt Brian Cook. The election was the first to be fought on the country's new electoral register, on which Chelmsford had 78,000 voters, an increase of 13,000 from 1935. Once again the Liberals and Labour stood aside and honoured the unwritten political truce. The election was held on 26 April 1945, as Allied armies rumbled into the heart of Germany and in the same week that Belsen was discovered. The *Essex Chronicle* thought the election was a muted affair, perhaps because people had been stunned 'by the week's revelations from the European chamber of horrors'.[38] Turnout was 69 per cent, which included the votes of many servicemen and women serving abroad and repatriated prisoners of war. Millington and the Commonwealth party mirrored Driberg's remarkable victory, polling 24,548 votes against Cook's 18,117, thus overturning a Conservative majority of over 16,000.

---

33   Quoted in the BA 4 July 1942.
34   MOA Directive reply 2802, 27 January 1942.
35   MOA Directive reply 2685, 27 January 1942.
36   ERO A12967, Papers of Norman Hidden, Box 1, Political Memories 1944–50.
37   ECS 19 January 1945; ERO A12967.
38   EC 4 May 1945.

This defeat stunned Chelmsford's Conservatives, who entered a period of soul-searching in order to regain the seat at the general election. They had little time for consideration. The war in Europe ended only twelve days after the by-election, parliament was dissolved on 15 June and the general election was on 5 July. Their candidate was Hubert Ashton of South Weald. His father was a former president of the Essex Agricultural Society and the son was a popular choice with farmers. His opponents were the sitting MP, Ernest Millington, and the Liberal Hilda Buckmaster, a serving officer in the Wrens. In reality, Chelmsford's Conservatives seemed to have learnt little. An internal party letter noted that 'You may have seen letters from me in the press emphasising the fact that the Conservatives do not seem to be able to appeal to the masses – which is no doubt a good thing, seeing the mentality of the masses.'[39] Another letter hoped that 'the electors of the Chelmsford Division return to sanity'.[40] However, there was no great confidence in the result. 'You can count on the gentry, farmers and middle classes,' wrote one local Tory, 'but the trouble now is the evacuees and war workers. It is mainly an agricultural and strongly Conservative constituency, so we must hope for the best.'[41] The party tried to fight the election on new ground, as the constituency political agent made clear:

> The key-note of the campaign was to demonstrate that Conservatism is not dead or dying, but alive and go-ahead, not reactionary but progressive, not representative of one class but of all classes. The aim was to go on the attack and keep on the attack. Above all I sought to disprove the claim that the Conservative Party was a party of old people … Our aim was to reach the young people and the waverers.[42]

In the end the Conservative party, despite clawing back some of the ground lost in April, just failed to retake the seat. Millington polled 27,309 votes against Ashton's 25,229, holding on by just 2,080 votes. Hilda Buckmaster polled 5,909. The result of the Maldon by-election three years earlier, at a grim time in the prosecution of the war, had been a protest vote against government ineptitude and the inadequacies of the old order. In contrast, Millington's victories reflected people's hopes for a new post-war society not wedded to past political allegiances but based on support for those who offered change for the better for the majority, not the few. In reality, the voters who elected both men into parliament were attempting a local transformation, which they hoped would become part of a nationwide change when a general election was held.

39   ERO D/Z 96/25, letter from C.P. Widdows, 8 June 1945.
40   ERO D/Z 96/25, letter, 6 June 1945.
41   ERO D/Z 96/25, letter from Fred Fane, 3 June 1945.
42   ERO D/Z 96/25, Conservative party papers re 1945 general election, notes on the campaign.

The end of the war allowed people to hope that plans for a world no longer troubled by war, plans that until then had been largely theoretical, would now be brought to fruition. The war, endured by all the people, had awakened a determination not to return to the bad old days of the 1930s. To this end British political sentiment had moved to the Left during the war, as exemplified by the by-elections at Maldon in 1942 and Chelmsford in 1945. E.R. Millington, a serving RAF officer, and the successful Commonwealth party candidate at Chelmsford, wrote that:

> I believe that we have reached the end of an economic age ... an age which cannot prevent unemployment; inadequate housing, malnutrition among the children; an age which has got out of the control of its builders and masters. We must organise all our strength and all our resources to remodel the shape of British society without patching up the worn-out fabric of an old economic structure.[43]

On the other hand, many in the Conservative party hoped that the electorate would restore the status quo of 1939. Henry Channon, the party's MP for Southend, spoke for many party faithful when he argued that:

> I believe that after the war there will be a boredom with controls which we shall have to shake off, and get rid of them as quickly as possible ... I think the country is getting fed up with talk about a Utopia after the war; there appears to be too many blue-prints about and not quite enough reliance upon English common sense. We should not make too many wild plans which will be disappointing to the planners and to the people.

Channon's wish to both scrap wartime controls in favour of 'common sense' and to reject 'blue-prints', 'wild plans' and utopias was of course coded language disguising a philosophy longing for a return to cut-throat competition, the maintenance of social divisions and the retention of economic inequality.

Those fervently hoping for a new social order were aware that political change was required to make this a reality. The general election of June 1945, the first for a decade, was the perfect opportunity to begin this process. In that election people demonstrated their determination to make a new start in post-war Britain in no uncertain terms. Nationwide, the Labour party swept to power with a huge majority and for the Conservatives in Essex the result was a disaster. Prior to the general election a redistribution of seats meant that there

---

43   EC 20 April 1945.

were now 26 constituencies in Essex instead of twenty. Labour won 21 of them, the Conservatives three (Woodford, Southend and Saffron Walden) and the Liberals one (Harwich), while the Commonwealth party retained Chelmsford. Tom Driberg retained his seat at Maldon with many votes to spare. Although he finally followed his conscience to its logical conclusion, joining the Labour party before the election, his vote still doubled to more than 22,000 and his majority increased by a quarter to almost 8,000.[44] It remained to be seen whether the Labour party, which so many people had pinned their hopes on, would be able to rebuild society on more egalitarian lines out of the wreckage of the most destructive war in human history.

The foremost reason why Tom Driberg captured the Maldon seat so emphatically was the existence of local popular discontent concerning the inept manner in which the war was being run, discontent which demanded change at the top. As the *Essex Chronicle* put it, 'The electors wanted someone new, who stood for something new, and they found him in Mr Driberg.'[45] But there was more to it than that. In particular, there was widespread mistrust of the Conservative party as a reactionary force at the heart of this ineptitude. The party was linked in people's minds with the disaster of the Great Depression and the humiliation of appeasement. No-one wanted a return to those days. Over and above this, government incompetence and the seemingly feeble performance of the British military compared unfavourably with the Soviet Union's titanic struggle with Nazism on the Eastern Front.

---

44   G. Caunt, *Essex in parliament* (Chelmsford, 1969), pp. 115–17.
45   EC 3 July 1942.

5

Second front

Heroic Russia

Let's have less nonsense for the friends of Joe,
We laud, we love him; but the nonsense − no.
In 1940 when we bore the brunt
We could have done, Boys, with a second front.
A Continent went down with a cataract,
But Russia did not think it right to act,
Not ready? No, but who shall call her wrong?
Far better not to strike till you are strong.[1]
     (Lt Herbert Maxwell-Scott, Army Welfare Officer, Saffron Walden)

Pre-war opinions about the Soviet Union had been thrown into confusion when Stalin signed the Nazi–Soviet Non-Aggression Pact in August 1939, which gave Hitler a free hand to deal with Poland. Eric Rudsdale wrote in his diary:

> It was in the papers today that the Germans have made a pact with Russia, who has quite calmly double-crossed the British military mission which is in that country. This has caused great excitement and anger, people feeling that England has been completely fooled.[2]

Stalin's action made war inevitable. His reputation fell even further when he exploited the pact to participate in a new partition of Poland. Having heard the news on the wireless, one Ilford resident felt that Russia deserved all that was coming to her. After that, to provide greater protection for Leningrad in a future war with Germany, Stalin occupied the Baltic states and then invaded Finland when she refused to cede territory. At the start of October the *Essex*

---

1   IWM 7200, papers of Lt H. F. Maxwell-Scott, Army Welfare Officer, Saffron Walden, 1939–44, probably February 1943.
2   ERO D/DU 888/22, journal, 22 August 1939.

County Telegraph asked whether Russia was 'Bear or Octopus?'.[3] In November the Bishop of Chelmsford, adroitly, did not condemn Stalin as he had Hitler. He merely debated whether or not Hitler's invasion of Poland had awakened the Soviet Union from its slumber. Perhaps with an eye to Stalin as a future ally against Hitler, he wrote rather presciently that 'it would be safe to forecast that a terrible war with Russia may prove the downfall of Germany'.[4]

The local Communist party branches in Essex toed the party line. Ken Saunders, a member of the Colchester branch, dismissed the war as 'a sordid imperialistic squabble' between Britain, France and Germany. Stalin had remained aloof from this, and his actions in Poland and the Baltic had been done to protect the working people of Russia.[5] When Stalin attacked Finland the Colchester branch had no sympathy for the Finns, who were condemned as 'only ruled by bankers and capitalists supported by various anti-Bolshevik countries'. Another speaker added complacently, 'When the Finnish workers are in power they will undoubtedly benefit from the Soviet influence in every way.'[6] M. Barnard had been a loyal local supporter of Communism throughout the previous decade. He was a prolific letter-writer in defence of Soviet actions and in 1939 he adopted the Communist line that Stalin's part in the partition of Poland was done not for territorial gain but to prevent further German advances. However, in his enthusiasm for Stalin's apparently altruistic actions, Barnard strained political credulity beyond breaking point. He claimed, 'Hitler has largely now to obey Stalin, and has had to practically allow Communism in Germany now Russia is going to be the predominating [sic] power in Europe.'[7]

Some of the clergy, fed on tales of Bolshevik persecution of Christians, were as appalled as they had been by Hitler's attack on Poland. In March 1940 the vicar of Emmanuel Church, Forest Gate, wrote in his service register 'Finland's Calvary when they surrendered'.[8] Even the *Essex Chronicle*, which measured its political judgements most carefully, noted that 'The Russian invasion of Finland is a thing unscrupulous even in these days, when want of scruple is common ....' Nevertheless, upon reflection the *Chronicle* was critical of the British and French governments for what it saw as their encouragement of Finnish resistance in the expectation that Anglo-French aid would be forthcoming, the same sort of encouragement that had led Poland to disaster.[9] The *Telegraph* found the invasion 'so revolting as to be almost unrealisable'.[10] Indeed, the invasion

3   ECT 7 October 1939.
4   CDC November 1939.
5   ECS 28 October 1939.
6   ECT 19 December 1939.
7   EC 29 September, 13 October 1939.
8   ERO D/P 592/1/52, Emmanuel Church, Forest Gate, register of services, 1938–47, 17 March 1940.
9   EC 8 December 1939, 29 March 1940.
10   ECT 2 December 1939.

was the end of the line for that faithful Soviet propagandist, M. Barnard, who condemned it as 'monstrous and infamous'. In his disillusionment he turned on Stalin with all the fury of someone who felt that he had been betrayed: 'Now one man has, with the abysmal folly which curses humanity, sacrificed it all when he had the opportunity of giving Europe a great moral lead.'[11]

Some people, however, were conscious of the irony of the British government's position, as Eric Rudsdale confided to his diary on New Year's Eve 1939:

> At the moment the Russians are pilloried in every paper for their attack on Finland, and there is great agitation for an expedition to help Finland. I suppose if the pact with Russia had been successfully brought off last July, we should be urged to send help to the Russians against the 'brave and gallant' Finns, who in that case would not have been brave or gallant at all. The amount of lies and hypocrisies now handed out to the public is simply staggering, and the public loves it.[12]

There the situation remained for almost two years. France was defeated and Britain was almost brought to her knees, and all the time Stalin remained neutral. Then, on 22 June 1941, Hitler attacked the Soviet Union and everything changed. The *Essex Chronicle* was left with egg on its face, as it had declared only two days before the invasion that 'there is no actual reason to suppose at present, that war between the two Powers is imminent'.[13] The *Essex County Standard*, however, was unsurprised by the turn of events: 'When Rogues Fall Out' headed its editorial a week later. 'Both have been aggressors and both have played a double game,' it noted. However, it was Russia which received its support. The *Standard* felt that

> the meanness, perfidy and brutality of the Nazi attack have compelled the unhesitating sympathy and the unqualified support and friendship of all who wish to rescue mankind from tyranny and the degradation of Nazism and lawless dictatorship.[14]

The Bishop of Chelmsford, who had more than once criticised the failure of smaller states to unite against Fascism, felt that in this case 'Judas was for once recognised' and Russia was prepared. He had always been an advocate of a Russian alliance, but in 1939 he felt that 'the mirage of appeasement and

---

11 EC 29 December 1940.
12 ERO D/DU 888/22, journal 31 December 1939.
13 EC 20 June 1941.
14 ECS 28 June 1941.

political prejudice still filled the sky', preventing such an eventuality.[15] The British Communist party naturally now supported the war, more from a desire to preserve the Soviet Union than a wish to bolster British capitalism.[16]

Of course, now that Stalin was an ally his earlier transgressions were conveniently explained away by those in responsible positions. The *Essex County Telegraph*, which viewed Hitler as the Anti-Christ and upheld a consistently Christian viewpoint in all its judgements, nevertheless adopted a thoroughly cynical approach towards Stalin:

> We did not like Stalin's operations, but we pointed out in this column that his actions carried with them no threat against Great Britain. If the Russian bear wished to play the octopus also and reach his arms around all the Baltic countries our safety would not be endangered, and no national ambitions we might have would be thwarted. Stalin threatened no-one, but he frustrated Hitler's plans.[17]

The *Burnham Advertiser* was also content to forget the past and merely commented that 'the two old friends are again united with the object of destroying the Nazi monster'. Stalin's brutal treatment of his own people was now interpreted as an exaggeration of interwar anti-Bolshevik propaganda.[18] The *Essex Chronicle* felt that, in England, antipathy to Bolshevism had blinded people to Soviet achievements, which it argued somewhat euphemistically had been the result of 'some very rough proceedings' and 'merciless discipline', and which had made the Russia of 1941 better able to withstand the German onslaught than that of 1914.[19] 'Most of us were the victims of the wild prejudice with which Russia was regarded in political circles,' noted the Bishop of Chelmsford.[20] In spite of their differences with Soviet policy some clergy were able to feel that Britain and the Soviet Union had common ideological aims. A large majority of the clergy in the Dunmow deanery signed a resolution supporting Russian resistance to 'the pagan forces of racial greed and tyranny'. The resolution included an optimistic commitment 'to reap the fruits of their and our united efforts in a social structure wherein liberty shall be a sure heritage of all people, and the rights of property shall give place to those of human personality'.[21]

Nevertheless, at this early stage in the Russo-German war there were still some who found it hard to shrug off the idea of Communism as loathsome,

---

15   CDC August 1941.
16   R. Mackay, *The test of war: inside Britain 1939–1945* (London, 1999), pp. 103–6.
17   ECT 5 July 1941.
18   BA 19 July 1941.
19   EC 8 August 1941.
20   CDC February 1942.
21   EC 19 September 1941.

subversive and dangerous. The Bishop of Chelmsford discovered this in August 1941, when he condemned the hypocrisy of the Fascist rulers of Italy, Spain and Vichy France by saying, 'Paradoxical though it may sound, it is more religious to repudiate openly all religion than to manipulate it in the fashion of these nominally Christian nations.' He continued, writing that 'I could shake hands with a non-praying Stalin but I should beg to be excused from doing so with a Petain, Darlan, Mussolini, or Weygand who can go happily to their Mass with dishonour and trickery in their hearts.'[22] His comments provoked a storm of protest and he admitted that about half of the letters he received relating to them were 'angry and abusive'. He remained unrepentant nevertheless, referring to the German attack on Russia as 'an unspeakable and unexpected blessing to our cause'. He even went on the offensive to further justify his previous comments:

> Russia is a country which is officially atheistic but which contains millions of Christians. England is a country which is officially Christian but which contains millions of virtual atheists. I much prefer England to Russia as a country to live in: but I would rather live in Russia than in Spain, Italy or Germany.[23]

The *Essex Chronicle* was completely in agreement with the Bishop, believing as it did that Russia 'was suffering a gross and unprovoked attack', and its leader, although an avowed atheist, was the holder of power ordained by God.[24]

Even as German armies advanced deeper into Russia there seemed to be some confidence that they would fail, just as Napoleon had done 130 years earlier. 'Germany will certainly break her teeth in this conflict, and a big step will have been taken towards the abyss which is gaping before her,' wrote the Bishop of Chelmsford.[25] The *Essex Chronicle* had also commented at the outset of the war in the east that 'such a tremendous space cannot be conquered and held down from Berlin, and even if the Russians could not maintain themselves in the field, the Germans would still find it a terribly exhausting war'.[26] During the next four years British admiration for the embattled Soviet Union and its people knew no bounds. The reasons for this are easy to identify – the immense suffering of the Russian people, the endurance and courage of the Red Army and the grateful awareness that Russia's prodigious sacrifices kept the German war machine away from Britain. There is no doubt that the change in attitude

---

22   CDC August 1941.
23   CDC September 1941.
24   EC 25 July 1941.
25   CDC August 1941.
26   EC 27 June 1941.

to the Soviet Union affected people from all backgrounds. In 1942 the *Essex County Standard* reviewed Colchester Repertory Company's production of *Distant Point*, by the Russian playwright Afinogenev. The *Standard* noted the taste for all things Russian and added that 'in all conscience the pendulum of public opinion on the subject has known a swing violent enough to dislocate any long-suffering instrument'.[27]

Fundraising for the gallant new ally, in the form of the 'Aid for Russia' campaign, was a regular feature of the war years in towns and villages. For example, Colchester's 'Aid for Russia' Flag Day in December 1941 raised £355.[28] Russian history became a popular topic in lectures, although the interpretation given was often highly selective. When Sir Bernard Pares, the eminent historian and expert on Russia, gave a talk in Colchester in the spring of 1942 he conveniently airbrushed out Stalin's tyranny and the sufferings of the Russian people during the industrial upheavals of the 1930s.[29] In that same year the Bishop of Chelmsford addressed a meeting organised by the Russia Today Society, an organisation formed in 1928 to foster better Anglo–Soviet relations. With some justification the Bishop said that 'If it had not been for the oceans of blood shed by the Russians there would be a million women in this country mourning their husbands or their sons.' He then went on to urge people to 'unlearn' everything they had been taught about Russia. 'We had been taught all wrong,' he lamented, 'and it was a very painful subject to enlarge upon, but if ever we were – to use a vulgarism – "led up the garden path" we were about Russia.' He responded to those who had professed themselves horrified at his support for a non-Christian country with the argument that, 'He would point out that religion was a national expression, and the study of history had taught him to be profoundly suspicious of any attempt to use religion as a political weapon.' At the same meeting Colchester's eminent female doctor Ruth Bensusan-Butt, who had visited Russia in 1932, agreed that religion was at a low ebb then, but that it was less the result of Bolshevism and rather 'attributable largely to the relics of a priest ridden Tsarist regime which kept the people back', a situation which was being eradicated by the growth of education.[30]

The height of the British people's Russo-mania came in the winter of 1942/3 with the great Russian victory at Stalingrad, which prompted this message to be sent from Essex:

> We the women workers of the Transport and General Workers Union in Colchester, send greetings to women engineering workers of

---

27   ECS 25 April 1942.
28   ECS 17 January 1942.
29   ECS 11 April 1942.
30   ECS 16 May 1942.

Stalingrad, and express our sincere admiration of your heroic resistance to the common Hitlerite enemy.[31]

The event more or less coincided with the 25th anniversary of the creation of the Red Army and in Colchester the Red Flag was hoisted from the Town Hall. 'How the old "diehards" must be squirming with fury,' wrote the amused Eric Rudsdale.[32] The *Southend Times*'s editorial on the anniversary was fulsome in its praise: 'Such history and you will not find more heroism, more granite endurance than we are witnessing today …. Today the lustre of that glory is deeper and more glorious. We are proud to salute the heroes of the Soviet Union.'[33]

During 1942 there had been a groundswell of opinion that the Soviet Union was bearing the brunt of the Nazi war machine and that the country's colossal sacrifices were not being matched by those of Britain and America. In particular, there was a growing demand for a Second Front, an invasion of Western Europe, in order to relieve the pressure on Russia. The difficulties in planning such an operation against strong enemy defences were apparent to discerning observers, but even the disaster at Dieppe in August 1942 did not dissuade the supporters of such a scheme. Naturally, the Communist party was a particularly strident advocate of the Second Front. Following the German attack on Russia it had quickly abandoned the concept of the conflict as an imperialist war and reinterpreted it as a war for the freedom of the working classes everywhere, particularly in the workers' paradise, Russia. In Colchester a branch meeting in February, under the banner of 'Victory in 1942', urged the Second Front alongside greater equality for India as an ally.[34] In August another Communist party meeting in Colchester was still adamant that victory in 1942 was possible. One speaker, Nancy McMillan, stated that 'There was not yet a feeling that we were in this war right up to our necks,' the implication being, of course, that the Russians were in just that predicament.[35] Even when the Second Front was eventually opened on D-Day on 6 June 1944 there was still an awareness that Russia's burden was far heavier. In October an advertisement for the 'Aid to Russia' flag-day carried the headline 'Russia Still Bleeds'.[36]

By 1944 the Red Army was driving German forces from Russian soil and entering Eastern Europe. With the defeat of Germany looking increasingly certain supporters of the Soviet Union now felt the need to calm a revival of fears of Communist expansion westwards. The Bishop of Chelmsford,

31   ECT 9 January 1943.
32   ERO D/DU 888/26/2, 23 February 1943.
33   ST 24 February 1943.
34   ECS 21 February 1942.
35   ECS 29 August 1942.
36   ECS 6 October 1944.

a confirmed Russophile even before the war began, had never at any time during the war been convinced that Stalin had any sinister designs on Europe. However, by 1941 even he had to perform mental acrobatics as he tried to explain that the world had nothing to fear from Communist expansionism:

> If a nation is happy and contented nothing is less likely than that it will go to war with its neighbours in order to elevate them to a similar state of happiness and contentment! Presumably Russia enjoys its present method of government. I should now find it impossible to believe that it would ever bother its head how other nations governed themselves much less engage in war to force them to adopt a similar constitution. Why on earth should it?[37]

Three years later his message remained the same:

> The bogey of a predatory Russia which was determined to absorb all its neighbours and to impose upon them, willy-nilly, her own form of government is now seen to be one of those night-mares which disturb the slumbers of very short-sighted and astigmatic partisans.[38]

However, he had always been realistic enough to see that the geopolitical situation in Eastern Europe could never be the same after the war. In 1941 he had predicted that the Soviet Union 'will demand a very big say in the re-adjustment of things in the Baltic and the Balkans'.[39] By 1944 he was writing that 'Few reasonable people can blame her if she seeks in some ways to secure herself against wanton attacks in the future.'[40]

The Polish government-in-exile's resistance to such ideas, which required her to cede land to the Soviet Union, brought severe criticism from the *Essex County Telegraph*:

> Stalin has shown a spirit of goodwill towards the Poles, which has, we fear, been sadly lacking on their part, … but which should be seen and understood by all in Western Europe as a good augury for the future and as making needless and groundless the fears of those few who yet show reluctance towards the Soviets.[41]

---

37 CDC August 1941.
38 CDC May 1944.
39 CDC December 1941.
40 CDC May 1944.
41 ECS 17 February 1945.

When, in late 1943, Colchester's MP Oswald Lewis resurrected criticism of the Soviet invasion of Finland he was lambasted in the press by left-wingers. J.B. Amos of Tendring asked whether or not it was wrong to criticise the Soviets, 'who were far-sighted enough to want their boundary line put back several miles from Leningrad'. He then went on to make the rather remarkable assertion that 'Certainly the Russians cared for Russia, but only because Russia is a democratic country.'[42] The revival of praise for the Soviet system, part of the leftward swing that the British people had made since 1942, reached its zenith as the war neared its end. A Cambridge University lecturer, speaking at Colchester, felt able to pass off such nonsense as the following as a critical appraisal of the state of Russia: 'Dr Gottlieb likened the USSR to a modern version of the Ark, [where] peoples of various nationalities and classes were gathered together, under the protection of the Soviet state.'[43]

English soil foreign sons

During the war the county was confronted by large numbers of foreigners in the form of Allied servicemen brought from the furthest reaches of the globe. Allied troops arrived in Essex early in the war. Some were exiles from countries conquered by the Nazis – Poles and Czechs, and later the Free French. The largest number, however, were troops from Commonwealth countries such as Australia, New Zealand, India and Canada, and these imperial forces were present in Essex by 1940. The journals of Eric Rudsdale suggest that to Colchester's residents these men brought with them a touch of the exotic. This was certainly the impression he got when he watched a large number of Australian troops march down the High Street singing 'Waltzing Matilda':

> They marched oddly, carrying their rifles as they pleased, looking like some strange army of bygone ages, as they straggled along the street, laughing and shouting, their great 'cowboy' hats looking stranger in the moonlight. There must be many thousands of them. Some say ten thousand … Big crowds lined the streets to see them go by. It was a most amazing sight.[44]

Even more remarkable to Rudsdale were the Indian soldiers in the town. In the autumn of 1941 he witnessed a

---

42   ECS 17 December 1943.
43   ECS 2 February 1945.
44   ERO D/DU 888/23, journal, 14 October 1940.

weirdly romantic sight in the High Street – a long file of Indians, leading horses up from the station, grey, brown and black, some of them obviously Mongolian. The men wore steel helmets, and carried carbines on their backs. The moon shone, making their faces shine as if they were oiled. Strange cries and words of command floated along the line. It was a most extraordinary sight, like a caravan coming into some far eastern city.[45]

On another occasion he watched two Indians knelt in prayer in the direction of Mecca. He commented that 'It is a strange sight to see Mahomedans [sic] praying on the Holly Trees lawn, but perhaps it is no more stranger than the fact that both Moslems and Hindus are enlisted to help England and "godless Russia" to "save Christianity".'[46] Most of these early arrivals from the Empire almost certainly ended up fighting with the Eighth Army in North Africa or in the Far East and during 1942–43 they were superseded by an influx of American servicemen.

America's pursuit of neutrality during the first two years of war had elicited mixed responses in Essex. An Ilford resident commented acerbically of the Americans that they were obsessed by money, but she was grateful that they were on the Allied side.[47] On the other hand, the diarist Ernest Edwards never lost his faith in Roosevelt: 'The President slays with his fine gift of oratory the few isolationists of the U.S.A and ridicules the idea that the great free people of America are immune from the terrors of the brutal Dictators…. Good, we are well pleased Mr. Roosevelt,' he wrote, after Roosevelt's speech promising all aid short of war.[48] Regarding what he saw as Roosevelt's support for Britain's democratic values, he wrote, '[w]e would add that it is the knowledge of his great country's moral support to our fight, which helps and aids us in the struggle which lays [sic] ahead.'[49]

By early 1942, two months after Pearl Harbor, there were only 4,058 American personnel in Britain. A year later this had risen to a quarter of a million, to over a million by January 1944, and to 1,671,000 on the eve of D-Day. The American servicemen who settled in East Anglia were part of the United States Army and the United States Army Air Force. By the spring of 1944 there were 45,833 American service personnel in Essex, less than in either Suffolk or Norfolk.[50] The American aircraft that flew from airfields in East Anglia were part of the Eighth Air Force, or the 'Mighty Eighth' as it became

45   ERO D/DU 888/24, journal, 31 October 1941.
46   ERO D/DU 888/24, journal, 17 December 1941.
47   MOA Directive Reply 2694, 3 March 1942.
48   ERO S 3150, Diary of Ernest Edwards, 11 June 1940.
49   ERO S 3150, Diary of Ernest Edwards, 25 October 1940.
50   R. Reynolds, *Rich relations: the American occupation of Britain 1942–45* (London, 1995), pp. 99, 103, 110–11.

known, which was created in January 1942.[51] By the end of 1943 there were 66 American air bases in the United Kingdom, including eighteen in Essex. The aircraft of Ninth Bomber Command, which flew from Essex airfields, all participated in the great American daylight bombing campaign that devastated German cities but proved so costly in both machines and men.

The first American servicemen to arrive in Essex were the engineers who came to build the airfields. The first of these was at Great Saling, where an Engineer Aviation Battalion of 800 men arrived in the summer of 1942. The main runway was finished in three months and it was officially opened in April 1943 amidst great ceremony, with six American generals in attendance. The airfield's name was changed from Great Saling to Andrews Field after the death of Lt Gen. Frank Andrews only nine days after the airfield was opened. He was at the time the overall Commander of American air forces in Europe.[52] The building of these airfields was a colossal undertaking. At Boreham, for instance, 130,000 tons of concrete and 50 miles of cable was laid.[53] All the hard core for the runways consisted of brick-rubble from bomb-damaged areas of London. When lorries from Earls Colne and White Colne stations unloaded the rubble the men often came across dead animals and even body parts from victims of the Blitz.[54]

The construction of American airfields often effected a radical change in the landscape which was not always appreciated by locals. At Boreham, American engineers felled 86 acres of Dukes Wood before starting work, and 94 acres of Mann Wood was cleared at Matching.[55] An American serviceman recalled building the airfield at Chipping Ongar during the winter of 1942/3, the wettest in living memory, as a far from pleasant experience: 'And down there we just worked constantly in mud, mostly up to our knees,' he said.

> There's not much that you can say that's good about being at an air force construction area because it is nothing but mud and sweat and dirty work. Concrete flying all over the place, lorries running up and down, runways which are partly built, cutting down trees and those they couldn't bulldoze they blew up.[56]

The mud in fact was a foot deep and it had to be scraped away by machines into great banks at the roadside.[57]

---

51 G. Smith, *Essex airfields in the Second World War* (Newbury, 1996), p. 28.
52 Smith, *Essex airfields*, pp. 48–9.
53 B. Jones, *Wings and wheels: the history of Boreham airfield* (London, n.d.), p. 10.
54 E. Willingham, *From construction to destruction: an authentic history of the Colne Valley and Halstead railway* (Halstead, 1989), p. 90.
55 Smith, *Essex airfields*, pp. 65, 180.
56 ERO SA 1/635/1 An American Soldier at Willingale airfield.
57 EC 25 May 1945.

American forces did not begin work on Birch, near Colchester, airfield until 1943, but almost two years earlier there was considerable opposition to plans to build an airfield there. Rudsdale was alarmed at the likely impact of airfields generally but he detested the opposition at Birch because they were quite willing to have the airfield built at another village, Tiptree. He attacked this selfishness by writing,

> The amenities will be interfered with, and, worst of all, Norfolk's Grove, the best covert for miles, will be uprooted! Therefore extinguishing the common rights on Tiptree Heath, and bullying the Air Ministry to establish a large aerodrome on the very edge of a populous village.[58]

A few months later he visited the construction work at Boxted and complained that 'it is heartbreaking to see the amount of damage that is being done'.[59] In 1943 he travelled with American officers around the Colchester area identifying sites for shooting butts. When he pointed out how their activities had already altered the landscape a Major Miller replied, 'Well, wouldn't you rather have us here than the Germans … we can't bother about the convenience of a few British farmers, you know.' Rudsdale noted that 'It was obvious from his manner that he had already had a good deal of criticism since he came to England.'[60] The damage done in Essex was part of a much larger national picture. The building of 450 new airfields took up 330,000 acres of woodland and farmland, and further land was requisitioned to build defensive measures against invasion, and to provide training grounds for the military. Yet in Essex this represented only 0.15 per cent of the county's land by 1944, and only 0.3 per cent of the county's agricultural area was requisitioned for airfields.[61]

The arrival of the Americans added another layer of colour and distinctiveness to the presence of foreign personnel. Ernest Armitage, a Chelmsford resident, speculated on the identity of one strange uniform in the town: 'Chinese Admiral, Stationmaster on the Canadian Pacific Railroad, Lock-keeper on the Manchester Ship Canal, Commissionaire at the Metro-Goldwyn Studios, Hollywood,' he wrote. 'For myself I think the wearer was just a Gas Inspector, or maybe an SS man. Who knows?'[62] American service personnel were scattered throughout the county at their airfields but they were particularly numerous in Chelmsford, Braintree and Colchester. Braintree had so many American air bases around it

---

58   ERO D/DU 888/24, journal, 24 November 1941.
59   ERO D/DU 888/25/2, journal, 18 August 1942.
60   ERO D/DU 888/26/3, journal, 29 April 1943.
61   W. Foot, 'The impact of the military on the agricultural landscape of England and Wales in the Second World War', in B. Short, C. Watkins and J. Martin, *The front line of freedom: British farming in the Second World War* (London, 2006), pp. 133–4, 136.
62   EC 11 September 1942.

that it was a favourite destination for their servicemen. By early 1943 it was being described as an American town, 'and her prominent citizens are acquiring a nasal twang to their accent'.[63] The evidence suggests that relations between the people of Essex and foreign servicemen were generally cordial, and in some cases very intimate. In January 1943 a senior American officer wrote to the County Welfare Officer, who had helped to oversee the reception of his men in Essex:

> This group of American officers and men that I commanded came into Essex last summer with some wonderment and concern as to how the countryside would react to us with the immense load we have placed upon your roads, your recreational facilities, and your hospitality. I can say that, without exception, everyone has been extraordinarily kind, friendly and hospitable.[64]

When the American Red Cross Club was opened in Chelmsford in 1943 Ott Romney, who was in charge of these clubs, told the Essex people present, 'You are a very old country; we are a new country. We sprang from you. There is a closeness between us that is particularly noticeable nowadays. It is a cordiality that must be capitalized.'[65]

Sergeant 'Al' Insley of New York confirmed this impression in a letter to his parents in which he described the hospitality of a Chelmsford family: 'They have been my best friends,' he wrote. 'It is what I call my other home in England. I spend almost all my passes there, also, they open their door to me and save my little bedroom with a nice soft bed, any time I care to stop there.'[66] In 1943 an *Essex Chronicle* journalist interviewed a number of American servicemen, of whom 80 per cent said they liked Chelmsford. 'We like your town, we like your people – they're swell – but there's nothing like home,' they enthused. They enjoyed dancing at the Corn Exchange and Shire Hall, although they found it hard to understand why the British went to bed so early, by which they meant midnight. As for local girls: 'They're great sports. No need to get bored here. They're sportier than the dames at home.' The journalist did not ask them to elaborate on the term 'sporty'. One sergeant had a list of the names and addresses of 23 local girls. However, they were less than enthusiastic about British humour, finding it rather slack in comparison with the quick-fire dialogue they were used to. 'Give us a slick show with pep in it,' they urged. 'Most of your shows are too slow.'[67]

---

63   EC 28 May 1943.
64   EC 22 January 1943.
65   EC 26 February 1943.
66   EC 30 April 1943.
67   EC 8 January 1943.

Figure 5.1. Children of Lindsell Primary School, near Dunmow, are given an Easter Day treat by American servicemen, probably from nearby Andrews Field air base. (Essex Record Office)

American servicemen were particularly popular with women and children. Children were the recipients of much generosity. For instance, at Christmas 1942 a Lt Whittaker of the American Army provided entertainment at the Shire Hall in Chelmsford, giving 780 chocolate bars to evacuees, to children whose fathers were in the Forces and to those who had been bombed out.[68] Such largesse was typical of the troops' relationship with children. At Matching parties were given to local children at Christmas and Easter and each company on the base adopted a 'Blitz Orphan'.[69] American servicemen who were 'overpaid, oversexed and over here' had the wherewithal to tempt British women, as they had much more ready cash than their British counterparts. They were able to offer drinks, food, chocolate, nylons and other supplies that British families who had been on rations since 1940 could only dream of. Pam Hobbs's sister Connie had an American friend who often brought supplies to supplement the family's diet. He provided ham, butter, vegetables, tea bags, eggs and fruit cake. He became a part of the family for eight months until he was posted abroad and killed at the Battle of the Bulge in 1944. He had obviously told his relations back home about his 'adopted' family, for it was his sister who wrote telling them of his death.[70]

68   EC 1 January 1943.
69   N. Collecott, *As we were: an Essex family during and after the Second World War* (Durham, 1993), p. 45.
70   P. Hobbs, *Don't forget to write: the true story of an evacuee and her family* (London, 2009), pp. 231–5.

In Chelmsford local women came to the rescue when it was decided to open an American Red Cross Club. A problem had arisen because American servicemen who missed their trucks back to base were left stranded in town. They packed into the YMCA, hotel accommodation was sold out and many men slept in the fields or even asked to be put in police cells.[71] As a result the American Army and Chelmsford Borough Council discussed creating a hostel and it was the American Red Cross who provided it. The hostel, which was sited in an unoccupied part of the Saracen's Head Hotel, had beds for 30 men and served daily meals for 300. It opened early in 1943, when an appeal was made for Chelmsford women to volunteer as hostesses. Within days 150 had volunteered, working four-hour shifts during the sixteen hours that it was open.[72] The closeness that existed between foreign servicemen and English women was not just limited to domestic hospitality. By the summer of 1944 wartime marriages in the Chelmsford district were averaging twelve to fifteen a week, with a large proportion of the grooms being American servicemen. The age of brides was much lower than before the war, between seventeen and 22 years, while grooms were aged between nineteen and 25.[73]

However, the 'special relationship' in Essex was certainly not all sweetness and light. Anglo-American marriages there may have been, but male–female relationships were not always as romantic or as wholesome. One correspondent referred to 'The Braintree Fishing Fleet',

> which in this case consists of a large number of the female sex, who descend on Braintree usually on a Wednesday (market day). The catch is usually American soldiers. They apparently do very well, are at their best between twelve and four o'clock and turn up week after week.[74]

Colin Ridgewell recalled that, as a boy in the Essex countryside, he and his friends often came across copulating couples, especially after the Americans arrived. On one occasion they were up a tree when an American soldier and a British servicewoman appeared and had sex almost directly beneath them.[75]

As with soldiers of any nationality, some Americans overstepped the boundary of what was deemed acceptable. Sex between consenting adults who were not married to each other was socially frowned upon but rife during the war. Other activities were definitely taboo. In 1943 two American soldiers were found guilty of sexual offences against a fourteen-year-old girl. They were

71   EC 11 September 1942.
72   EC 9, 16 October 1942, 19, 26 February 1943.
73   EC 1 September 1944.
74   EC 9 June 1944.
75   C. Ridgewell, *Looking better looking back* (London, 2004), p. 115.

sentenced to eighteen months' hard labour, dishonourably discharged from the army and deprived of American citizenship. The American authorities were clearly eager to impress on their British hosts that they considered such activity to be utterly unacceptable. This was despite the fact that the girl was considered to have consented to the act – she was put on probation for three years.[76] In 1944 another fourteen-year-old girl from Chelmsford who had already been remanded for seven days was remanded for a further fourteen. She was found wandering the streets and taken home. The constable who escorted her reported that he had

> found one American soldier hidden in a necessary [toilet] at the rear of the house. I asked him what he was doing there, and he said, 'I am waiting for my friend to come out so that I can go in.' I found other American soldiers at the premises and they said they were waiting to go into the house.

It is unclear how widespread this sort of prostitution was, but it may have been informal and opportunistic rather than organised.[77]

There were also other bones of contention. At Braintree the regular influx of Americans meant that pubs were crammed and locals were often unable to get in. Pubs were often drunk dry very quickly.[78] Colchester was full every night with Americans from the surrounding airbases. Eric Rudsdale was no admirer of the newcomers. He wrote of 'streets crammed with Americans, raucous voices, pushing, jostling, calling out to girls' and later added that there were streets 'full of Americans, wandering aimlessly, their jaws always moving'. On 4 July 1943 he saw '[b]ig crowds of Americans, English, ATS, sailors, rolling about the streets, nearly all drunk. Independence Day I suppose.'[79] To be fair Rudsdale despised troops of most nationalities, including the British. In 1940 he criticised Australians for 'their promiscuous urination in shop doorways'. On Christmas Eve 1941 he was particularly appalled at the scenes in the town, which involved Allied troops of all nationalities:

> The streets were packed with howling mobs of soldiers and ATS girls. Everyone saw drunken soldiers sprawled on the pavements, or reeling along, singing. Every public house was crowded, and by walls and in shop doorways soldiers were pissing. I have never seen the streets in such a state since the Australians were here – pools and trickles every

76   EC 6 August 1943.
77   EC 8 September 1944.
78   EC 28 August 1942.
79   ERO D/DU 888/26/4, journal, 22, 26 June, 4 July 1943.

few yards. Beer bottles, glasses, and mugs were lying in the gutters, and I all but fell over two glass tankards on the steps of the Playhouse as I came out. Army lorries were going slowly up the High Street, collecting those men who were quite incapable. The inert bodies were being heaved over tailboards, respirators and tin-helmets following with a metallic crash.[80]

Rudsdale was not the only one who found the presence of foreign troops unwelcome. He wrote in his journal in late 1941 that an acquaintance, Ida Hughes-Stanton, 'told me that there are now 65 Anglo-Polish babies in the Manningtree district, including a mother and a daughter who have one each'. He added that 'I don't believe it, but it's an amazing story. She suggested that the next lot of babies would be born with black beards and little turbans.'[81] When Scottish soldiers were paraded through the streets to a service in All Saints accompanied by bagpipes, one of Rudsdale's colleagues at the museum commented, 'What an outrage to let them make that hideous din on a Sunday.'[82]

Fraternisation with prisoners of war brought with it the risk of prosecution and social disgrace. Two Land Army girls at Great Bardfield were taken to court and fined for sending letters to Italian prisoners working in the fields nearby.[83] Such daily contacts were possible and were hard for the authorities to monitor. Joan Wright, a young farm worker from the Saffron Walden area, divided her enthusiasm evenly between the cinema and Italian prisoners of war, or ''Ities' as she called them in her diary, with whom she came into regular contact. The depth of her fraternisation was very risky indeed. Her diary included comments such as, 'Saw 'Ities – one walked to Market Farm with me – Corporello – had cigarette with Corporello', and 'Had [a] ring from Corporello'. The Italians worked in the area from January to early March 1943 before moving elsewhere, and not having contact with them was clearly painful. 'Still miss 'Ities', she wrote on 3 April. The Italians had obviously made quite an impression on her, for in the Memoranda section of her diary she wrote little pen pictures of some of them, revealing activities which would have got her into a great deal of trouble had they come to light:

Nicolas Cook, 29, very nice, kissed
Corpotelle very nice, kissed
Mike 25, corporal, Major, His hair grows in a peak on his forehead – jet

---

80   ERO D/DU 888/24, journal, 24 December 1941.
81   ERO D/DU 888/24, journal, 23 October 1941.
82   D/DU 888/24, journal, 19 January 1941.
83   EC 17 July 1942.

black, he is thin with his head inclined to poke forward – passionate
lover, very hot-blooded.
Bill 21, flirtish
John Stubes kissed
Had ring from Corpotelle and Nicolas

Joan's passion for the Italians does not seem to have been lessened by the
fact that she had a boyfriend through the later part of the war with whom she
had discussed marriage. In time Americans arrived in the area and she then
dated a number of them, writing 'Saw my Yankee' on 8 July 1944, although
even this too produced problems: 'Out with Yank until 11 – dad mad at me,'
she wrote on 10 July.[84]

Not everyone approved of the hospitality shown to Americans and some
reacted maliciously. One Chelmsford couple, Charles and Lilian Hayward,
were publicly insulted for providing bed and company to American troops.
Mrs Rosetta Bond and her sister of Little Bardfield befriended two young
American soldiers and entertained them at home. Some time after this Mrs
Bond's husband, who was serving in Burma, received three anonymous letters
alleging that she was having an affair with both men.[85] Other women took
the greater risk of associating with black American soldiers. One woman in
Brentwood was heard to utter in an unsubtly loud voice, 'just look at that girl
with that bloomin' n----r!'[86]

If the Americans were uncertain of their reception in Essex, local people
were equally anxious. Olive Foulds worked in the canteen at the Ridgewell
airbase. She later recalled, 'We went in with fear and trepidation. We heard
you can't do this and you can't do that when the Americans come but we
found that those we dealt with were very nice and pleasant.'[87] Sheila Kent
worked with the Americans at Saffron Walden as part of her duties. She and
local residents found it something of a culture shock. Most young girls had a
Hollywood view of their visitors but after meeting them many locals thought
them relaxed but slovenly. Accustomed as they were to the class-ridden nature
of the British Armed Forces, people were shocked at the absence of any marked
deference between American officers and men. Nevertheless, she thought that
the American presence did wake up the sleepy rural town of Saffron Walden.[88]

Americans struggled to understand what locals were saying and, according
to one RAF serviceman, they likened '[t]he Essex dialect … to certain southern

84   ERO A12799, Diaries of Joan Wright, Box 1, 1943-5, 16, 18, 25 January, 27 February, 1, 2 March, 3 April 1943.
85   EC 31 March, 12 May 1944.
86   EC 9 June 1944.
87   ERO SA 1/639/1 Olive Foulds.
88   ERO SA 1/625/1 Sheila Kent.

states of America'.[89] Americans were also irritated when they listened to the radio. 'Texas is [pronounced] Texas not Texahs', complained one serviceman, and the *Essex Chronicle* bemoaned the fact that 'these little things do much to arouse people's sense of derision'.[90] Even simple things could lead to confusion. Olive Foulds commented that, in the canteen at Ridgewell,

> We decided for a treat to give them a boiled egg. We put them in egg cups and gave them the bread with it. They looked at them as a bit mysterious. We said, 'What's wrong with them?' They said 'we've never had an egg sitting in a thing like this.' They were so used to having their eggs shelled and on a plate.[91]

The issue of American servicemen in Britain being subject to American rather than British law did irritate some people. The British Government, which had no wish to alienate its greatest ally, conceded the position by passing the United States of America (Visiting Forces) Act in August 1942. The application of this law produced one controversy in Essex. In March 1943 a 24-year-old American soldier, Private Charles Schaffer, who had previously had an unblemished record, was sentenced by an American military court to life imprisonment for raping a woman in Tiptree. Both the verdict and sentence caused an outcry in the village, with local church leaders urging a retrial because of the 'terrible sentence'. A campaign was organised to put pressure on the American authorities, spearheaded by Mrs Logan, the wife of the doctor who gave evidence at the trial. A petition was signed by several hundred Tiptree residents and there were rumours of new evidence that may be forthcoming. The campaign seemed to have an effect, for within two months Schaffer's sentence was reduced to just seven years, and two years later he was released from prison after the evidence was considered to have disproved the charge. Whether Schaffer's release was based on the original evidence or new material is unclear; nor was the role of the woman concerned ever discussed in detail in the public domain. The case did not receive the sort of national publicity accorded to that of Leroy Henry, a black American soldier who was sentenced to death for raping a white British woman and then acquitted.[92] Nevertheless, both demonstrated the willingness of British people to campaign against what they regarded as a miscarriage of justice as well as a willingness to challenge the 'special relationship' by taking on the American authorities.[93]

---

89   ERO SA 1/633/1 Cecil Swallow.
90   EC 1 January 1943.
91   ERO SA 1/639/1.
92   J. Gardiner, *Wartime: Britain 1939–1945* (London, 2004), pp. 605–6.
93   EC 12, 19 March, 14 May 1943, 15 June 1945.

In a similar manner, there was some disapproval of the importation of segregation by the Americans. Tom Driberg, Maldon's MP, spoke out against this in the Commons:

> It is not discrimination 'by the American forces' that I was protesting against; we could not presume to criticise what they do among themselves. What is disquieting is that, under pressure from them, our Government has acquiesced in the imposition of the colour bar in English public houses and other places, thus introducing for the first time in this country an infection of racial prejudice, from we have been comparatively free, and which may spread and persist. All I ask is that, if we refrain from attempting to change their attitude to colour, they should reciprocally respect ours. The colour bar simply doesn't happen to be a custom here, and they should be told so in a firm and friendly way.[94]

Driberg's comments fell on deaf ears in a parliament that was not prepared to risk the 'special relationship' over such an issue. Locally, too, he was criticised for stirring 'the muddy recesses of a dark and disagreeable pool'.[95]

Following the Normandy landings the German forces in France were driven eastwards and as a result during the autumn the Americans transferred their airfields from East Anglia to more forward positions on the continent. Units transferred from late July onwards, although American aircraft continued to operate at Boreham until the end of the war. Most army units of all nationalities had already left to participate in the invasion of Normandy and consequently the foreign military presence in Essex was much reduced. By the beginning of 1945 the number of American service personnel stood at just over 12,000, a reduction of 75 per cent in just eight months.[96]

The lull in the air war

The Blitz ended in the early summer of 1941 when the Luftwaffe moved many of its units east for the attack on the Soviet Union. Intensive air raids on Britain were now impossible to maintain and there was a significant reduction for three years, until the appearance of the V-1. The impact of this sustained lull was felt above all in Metropolitan Essex, as raids on the capital became rare. From 28 June 1941, when a few bombs were dropped on Chingford and Ilford, to 17 July 1942, when the Ford works was attacked, there were no air raids at all on the area. After the attack on Ford there was no raid until 17–18 January

94   BA 10 October 1942.
95   ECS 3 October 1942.
96   Reynolds, *Rich relations*, p. 397.

1943. Indeed, in 1943 raids amounted to less than one a month on average and only 76 people were killed.[97] The lull in raiding saw nervousness replaced by a feeling of relief. A Group 7 shelter survey in March 1942 showed that the use of public shelters had almost died out.[98]

After the great air raid and 'Fire of London' on 29/30 December 1940 fire-watching was introduced, although it was not made compulsory until August 1941, when those performing it became known as Fire Guards. The normal operational pattern was three people on duty during the blackout with sufficient reliefs to 'avoid the fatigue which would result from an undue number of persons being kept awake at night when no enemy attack is in progress'. When no raid was in progress firewatchers nevertheless 'should be awake, dressed and ready for duty'. Most people found the new responsibility onerous. Mrs L.M. Webb, who worked at the Romford Tuberculosis Dispensary during the day, acted as spokeswoman for those experiencing long working days followed by domestic duties and then Fire Guard responsibilities. An additional cause of resentment in Romford occurred in 1942 when the Ministry of Labour began 'directing' Fire Guards into other branches of Civil Defence. The organisation, which had grown over two years as a group of voluntary residential fire-watchers, felt that those with a good record of voluntary duty were the ones being redirected, 'with total disregard of the consequences on the homes of the inhabitants of the Borough'.[99] Single women aged twenty to 45 could be directed to their place of work or anywhere in their local authority where there was a shortage of fire guards; married women were limited to their neighbourhood. Only expectant mothers, those with children under fourteen and those working more than 55 hours a week were exempt from these duties.[100]

Raids on Extra Metropolitan Essex continued throughout this period, although they, too, were much reduced in intensity. Pamela Russell continued her nightly duties in her ARP post in Stubbers. On 1 July 1941 she wrote to her friend to say that 'mercifully the Hun has kept very quiet on the whole so that one does not spend an undue amount of the night telephoning'.[101] A new pattern to the raids, however, was an increase in opportunistic daylight attacks. These often occurred with little or no warning: aircraft appeared, dropped their bombs, rarely on key targets, and raids often consisted of aircraft strafing towns, villages, farms, harbours and railways. After the last heavy raid of 10/11 May 1941 the county experienced an average of just one raid per week during

---

97   Drawn from ERO C/W 2/3/2, Group 7 War Diary: Operational Report 1939–28 March 1945.
98   ERO C/W 2/13/2, Group 7 shelter surveys, 2 March 1942. There were only 1,584 occupants of shelters, two-thirds of these in West Ham.
99   ERO A12978, Papers of Alderman William Russell, Romford 1936–46, File 30, (Fire Guards). (Compulsory Enrolment Order, 1941).
100   R. Douglas Brown, *East Anglia 1942* (Lavenham, 1988), p. 104.
101   ERO D/DRu C5, Letters of Pamela Russell of Stubbers, 1939–44, letter, 1 July 1941.

the rest of the year. This fell to one a fortnight during 1942, although the rate increased slightly in 1943. With very few exceptions these raids were light, were only occasionally widespread and caused very little damage in comparison with those of 1940. Compared with those of the Blitz, casualties were slight. Between the summer of 1941 and the end of 1943 fewer than a hundred people were killed in air raids, and about 600 were seriously injured. On the whole these raids were apparently aimed at keeping the civilian population in a state of nervousness and demonstrating that the Luftwaffe could still raid at will. Places that were hit were of limited importance. For instance, coastal resorts and villages on the Tendring peninsula were strafed regularly and bombed.[102]

The Luftwaffe's attacks were not entirely random, however. During this period the two towns that received its closest attention were Chelmsford and Colchester. Both were on the main Great North Eastern Railway (GNER) railway line to Liverpool Street and both had factories churning out munitions and other essential war supplies – particularly Chelmsford, with its three great works, Marconi, Hoffmann and Crompton Parkinson, in the centre of the town. Up to the end of 1941 Colchester had got off quite lightly. Many bombs had fallen in the surrounding area and a few in the town itself, but there had been no serious damage. Then, in early 1942, in revenge for the RAF's bombing of medieval German towns such as Rostock and Lübeck, the Luftwaffe began attacking England's historic towns and cities – Bath, Norwich, Canterbury, York and Exeter. Colchester's status as a historic town led its residents to fear the worst, although it was not a target in these so-called 'Baedeker Raids'.[103] Eric Rudsdale, who had been exceptionally critical of Colchester Council's demolition of the town's old houses in the name of progress, responded to the apparent threat by writing that 'It certainly would be ironical, if after all these years of senseless destruction, leaving so few buildings still standing, if the Germans attacked the place as a town of British culture.'[104]

However, on 11 August 1942 a single German aircraft dropped four 500-pound bombs with tragic results. The bombs fell on Severalls Mental Hospital, on the northern outskirts of the town. The west block, which housed elderly female patients, suffered a direct hit. In total, 38 patients and two members of the nursing staff were killed and 23 others were injured. Civil Defence staff worked through the night and all the next day to recover the injured and the bodies.[105] It is hard to gauge the level of sympathy in the town towards the tragedy. In Eric Rudsdale's opinion:

102   Dates from ERO T/A 679/1 Daily Situation Reports by Essex County Constabulary HQ to Sub-divisions, 3 October 1940–30 April 1945.
103   A. Calder, *The people's war: Britain 1939–1945* (London, 1969), pp. 286–7.
104   ERO D/DU 888/25/1, journal, 28 April 1942.
105   ERO T/A 679/1.

GB 82 41 b
Nur für den Dienstgebrauch
Bild Nr. 446 L 020
Aufnahme vom 3. 10. 39

Chelmsford
Kugellagerfabrik (Hoffmann Manufacturing Ltd.)
· Länge (ostw. Greenw.): 0° 28′ 30″ Breite: 51° 44′ 20″
Mißweisung: — 10° 9′ (Mitte 1940) Zielhöhe über NN 30 m

Maßstab etwa 1 : 16 600

Genst. 5. Abt. Oktober 1940
Karte 1 : 100 000
GB/E 30

N

Figure 5.2. A German aerial reconnaissance photograph of the Hoffmann ball-bearing factory at Chelmsford, taken in 1940. (Essex Record Office)

There does not seem to be very much interest in the affair, which is perhaps not altogether surprising as Severalls is a little world of its own … holds some 3,000 lunatics and a vast army of people to look after them. The cost to the public of looking after these creatures is enormous, and it seems strange that all types of them, even cretins, are kept in luxury while honest, sane, people starve.

In a conversation Rudsdale had with a Mr Craig, 'a good chapel man', the latter said that 'if bombs had to fall at Severalls, they could not have fallen in a better place – all the victims were quite incapable'. That this was probably not the view of the families of the victims is indicated by a brief note sent to Rudsdale to explain why its writer was unable to come to work. It said simply, 'War Agricultural Committee. Colchester. Dear Sir, I am having two days off because of losing my dear young daughter killed in air raid Severalls Mental Hospital, Colchester. Essex. Mr C. Poole 227 Lexden Road.'[106]

Chelmsford, like Colchester, did not experience large-scale enemy air raids during the Blitz. Although bombs fell on the town they caused little damage and few casualties. The outlying districts around Chelmsford were the recipients of more enemy missiles than the town itself, although most of them fell on farmland. It was ironic, therefore, that on 21 May 1941, just ten days after the last raid of the Blitz, Chelmsford should suffer its first serious air attack of the war. A German aircraft dropped a single large high-explosive bomb on a residential district in the town. It demolished ten flats and damaged 160 houses, shops and municipal buildings. Casualties, however, were light – six people were killed and eight injured.[107] The town was then spared for more than a year until, on 19 July 1942, another solitary German plane, undetected in low cloud, launched a low-level attack on the town centre. Arriving at 6.15am, it dropped three bombs inside the Hoffmann works and one outside it. The damage to nearby residential property was severe, with more than 500 houses affected. Two houses and two flats were demolished, while casualties, once again, were light, with six dead and 32 hurt. Production at Hoffmann's was significantly disrupted, with the value of the firm's total output falling by a third in August, although it recovered very quickly.[108] On 19 October, in another daring daylight raid, Hoffmann's was targeted again by a solitary raider, once again obscured by low cloud and poor visibility. Six weeks' production, equivalent to the total output for two weeks of the country's ball bearings, was lost. Housing adjacent to the factory was badly hit once more, with seven houses demolished and fourteen so severely damaged as to be uninhabitable and in need of pulling

---

106 ERO D/DU 888/25/2, journal, 12 August 1942.
107 ERO T/A 679/1, 21 May 1941.
108 ERO T/A 679/1, 19 July 1942.

down. There were eight fatalities and 51 people injured. In neither of these two raids did the town's sirens sound and the raiders had disappeared before people realised what had happened.[109]

However, it was in the spring of 1943 that Chelmsford suffered its two worst raids by aircraft of the entire war. On 15 April the Luftwaffe launched a widespread raid on north and central Essex, but the Chelmsford district received special attention. During the attack, which lasted for an hour and a half, a parachute mine, high-explosive bombs and incendiaries, including phosphorous bombs and firepots,[110] were dropped on the town.[111] It was unfortunate that at the start of the attack a firepot put about 200 telephone lines out of action, including those of the Civil Defences, so that messengers had to be used instead. The communications breakdown meant that the fire services often arrived late to fires, which took a much firmer hold than they might otherwise have done. Rural fire brigades, which would have been called to give assistance, were left kicking their heels while Chelmsford burned. Casualties were incredibly light – just six people were injured – but the damage was severe. An unexploded bomb on the London and North Eastern Railway (LNER) line temporarily brought traffic to a halt. The cathedral was slightly damaged, a hotel and a suet factory were destroyed, several buildings at the prison were seriously damaged and the governor's house was destroyed. Several county council offices were seriously damaged. The parachute mine alone demolished twenty houses and damaged another 200. In all, almost 2,000 houses were either seriously or slightly damaged as a result of blast or fire. Fortunately, most of the bombs missed the three factories and many failed to explode.[112] Fifteen-year-old John Marriage commented in his diary,

> [m]any shops in town have lost their windows (we have not). They have been pumping water all day. They could not blow all clear as there was not much electricity. Telephones have been put up. Very little gas.... Evening part of it I looked for pieces of shells etc. and got some.[113]

The people of Chelmsford hardly had time to lick their wounds before an even heavier and more sustained raid took place only a month later, on 14 May. The attack took place in good visibility and a bright moon – 'the bomber's moon'. It was over extremely quickly, possibly within the space of about ten minutes, but its impact was severe and deadly, comprising the most damaging raid the

109 ERO T/A 679/1, 20 October 1942.
110 A firepot was a canister that contained several incendiaries; on impact the firepot broke open, releasing its load.
111 A. Begent, *Chelmsford at war: a chronology of the county town of Essex during the Second World War* (Chelmsford, 1996), pp. 175–7, 186: ERO T/A 679/1, 15 April 1943.
112 ERO T/A 679/1, 15, 17 April 1943.
113 ERO A11545, War diaries of J.E. Marriage, diary no. 9, 15 April 1943.

town experienced during the entire war.[114] According to Civil Defence records during those few minutes the Luftwaffe dropped five parachute mines, 44 high-explosive bombs, twelve firepots, a phosphorous bomb and an unknown number of incendiaries.[115] The impact of such a concentrated attack on the centre of a small country town was devastating. Casualties were inevitably much heavier than in the previous raids. In total 46 people were killed (including three RAF and one American Army servicemen), 121 were hospitalised and 105 slightly hurt. The three RAF personnel were killed when a bomb fell on a barrage balloon site that they were manning. A direct hit on the Home Guard Drill Hall ignited a large quantity of ammunition that was being stored there. The Eastern National bus garage was bombed and gutted, the Public Library was slightly damaged and the WVS offices were destroyed. There was extensive damage to the town market and the Territorial Army premises, and the YMCA and telephone stores were wrecked. The cathedral was again damaged, as was the shire hall and police station. Many shops and businesses were either damaged or destroyed. All three of the town's main factories were damaged, Marconi's seriously.[116]

In the same raid a high-explosive bomb and incendiaries damaged dozens of houses, gutted some farm buildings and damaged several historic buildings at Broomfield, a picturesque village just north of the town. John Marriage found that the technical school was shut, so he and his mother went into town to see the devastation.[117] The following morning Pat Lewis, who had just left school and was heading to work, got on a bus that had had all its windows blown in.[118] Tragically, at Boreham, to the east of the town, New Hall School was hit. The pupils had been evacuated some time before, but it was being used as a hospital for the elderly and several people were killed. Nearly a thousand people were made homeless by the raid. To ease the resulting accommodation problem the influx of war workers into the town was halted for two weeks. The change in the tempo of raids was very noticeable. Pamela Russell on 24 May wrote,

> The Hun has been rather attentive to us lately… six days on end which was rather fatiguing, what I call anti-personnel raids, as they appear to be planned chiefly in order to keep unhappy wardens out of their beds.[119]

This raid on Chelmsford was the Luftwaffe's last serious raid on Essex for several months. By the end of 1943 the county had experienced comparatively little

114 ERO D/DU 1307/1, Report of the Blitz Officer for the morning of 14 May 1943 (Chelmsford).
115 ERO T/A 679/1, 14 May 1943.
116 Begent, *Chelmsford at war*, pp. 190, 192: ERO T/A 679/1, 14 May 1943.
117 ERO A11545, 14 May 1943.
118 Author's notes of interviews with Mrs Pat Lewis, 24 May 2012.
119 ERO D/Ru C5, letter 24 May 1943.

enemy action for two and a half years. After becoming all too familiar with the siren's 'banshee wailing' during the Blitz, the sound of the siren seemed to be a thing of the past. It was now the turn of German cities to be pulverised and the Luftwaffe had its hands full defending its own territories. It was much too soon to be complacent, though.

Bombing Germany

The British people took great comfort in 1940 and 1941 from the fact that, although they had suffered military disasters in Europe, the RAF was bombing Germany. People in Essex and throughout the country believed or chose to believe that RAF raids on Germany were conducted on a higher moral plane than German attacks. Many people simply could not accept that British air raids were killing large numbers of German civilians.[120]

Prior to the Blitz the *Essex County Standard* thought that British air raids should be aimed at 'targets of military importance'.[121] Shortly after the Blitz had started the *Essex Chronicle* stated that people 'are incited to a fiercer spirit of resistance now that the realities of war are brought home to their very doors'. However, it was confident that the RAF was not involved in retaliatory raids but was bombing genuine military targets.[122] From 1942 onwards the writer S.L. Bensusan associated the spring and summer with the Anglo-American air armadas, recalling 'the drone of the giants of destruction' which passed overhead to bomb the continent. As he sat in his country home at night, trying to read but distracted by the noise, he could not help thinking of the fate of the bomber crews:

> What manner of man must be he who hears the defenders of this island passing overhead night after night, on their way to the sombre and terrible adventure from which only a part may return! This evening young men full of the joy of life, responsive to the call that takes them to the great bombers, passing into an immense loneliness under the moon and stars, in the knowledge that at any moment their huge weapon may be a molten mass falling through space to death – while somewhere at home, mothers, wives, and sweethearts are being very brave.

Bensusan was also keenly aware of the suffering of Britain's former allies as the air campaign intensified in preparation for D-Day. 'Nature has a double

---

120 Calder, *People's war*, pp. 490–4.
121 ECS 31 August 1940.
122 ECC 13 September 1940.

face,' he wrote. 'She could smile over England and lend that same light to aid destruction over Germany and poor helpless, distracted, occupied France.'[123] Others were able to take a more dispassionate view of the fate of the hapless French. On 26 January 1943 Colchester's MP, Oswald Lewis, spoke in the House of Commons calling for the destruction of French cities such as Lorient which housed U-boat bases. 'It may be true that the result would be a loss of many French lives,' he said, 'but it is in French interests that war should be made shorter. I urge that we take that means of shortening it.'[124] Denis Knowles of Colchester followed the air raids on Germany and made occasional entries in his diary. 'We lost 42 aircraft and the Germans eighteen fighters,' he wrote on 14 February 1942. 'We raided Berlin. Heaviest raid to date. Nine Bombers missing,' he added some time later. In late 1943 he noted that 'Berlin received heaviest raid of war on three nights last week. Total destruction in *Unter den Linden* and neighbourhood.'[125]

Understandably few people were inclined to voice their concerns for the suffering of the German people. The belief persisted that the Allies' air war was continuing to damage only Nazi war industries. In 1942 the 'Wings For Victory' campaign featured advertisements focusing on the clinical damage inflicted by the Allies. 'But there are still trains carrying munitions, tanks, oil, food for the Huns', read one such advertisement. 'We need many planes to stop them in their tracks.'[126] Equally, there was little sympathy for Italy's incomparable works of art when Rome was bombed in July 1943. The *Southend Times* commented:

> But what can it profit the world if monuments remain while the spirit which destroyed them has been destroyed? When Hitler burnt the books he sought to annihilate the free and adventurous mind which makes possible all great achievement. And today the world knows that the spirit which rose out of the ruins of London, of Warsaw, of Rotterdam, is a far more priceless asset than all Europe's monuments of stone.[127]

Clearly, for the *Southend Times* the possession of freedom was far more important than accusations of philistinism. The *Burnham Advertiser* also accepted that air raids were not an exact science and that tragedies would result, but it drew a clear comparison between allied methods and those of the Germans:

---

123 S.L. Bensusan, *Fireside papers* (London, 1946), pp. 47–8, 180–2.
124 ECS 30 January 1943.
125 ERO C 1397, Box 1 Diaries of Denis Knowles of Colchester 1939–45, 14 February 1942, 27 March, 28 November 1943.
126 ST 7 April 1943.
127 ST 4 August 1943.

In our raids on munitions factories, ship building yards, railways, etc., at such places as Rostock and Lübeck, we may occasionally have damaged ancient buildings, but wherever this has happened it has been by accident rather than design....There is a great difference, however, between this and a deliberately arranged programme to destroy historic old buildings of no military value. But it is a way the Huns and Vandals have always had.[128]

Not everyone felt able to give their moral support to the Allied air offensive, however. The clergyman who wrote the 'Puzzles for the Padre' column in the *Woodford Times* strongly disapproved of indiscriminate Allied bombing. He wrote:

What will a gallant English gentleman, let alone a Christian man, say when he is asked to go and tip out his devastating load on the small children and small houses of humble folk? God knows it is bad enough that some of the stuff aimed at general and vital military targets must miss its mark, and make an accidental but horrible shambles of women and kiddies. That is a side of things that the Air Force does not like to think about ... There are some things that man cannot do without losing his soul.'[129]

Neither was Eric Rudsdale enamoured of the Allied air war against Germany. 'There go the RAF to bomb more cathedrals,' he wrote on 5 April 1942.[130] He wrote of the losses on both sides: 'It is impossible to prevent oneself from wondering how many people at present asleep in Germany will never see the morning, and how many of the crews of those bombers are seeing England for the last time.'[131] Yet he felt unable to condemn the Nazis' Baedeker raids on Britain because at the same time the RAF was pounding German cities. As these raids were increased in frequency and ferocity gloom overtook him. In January 1943 he wrote,

Felt depressed by the news that the RAF had raided Berlin in daylight this morning. No doubt this will result in more unpleasant reprisals. We have now reached the stage when we can no longer claim we bomb 'military objectives'. This was a 'demonstration' for the people of Berlin. It is a silly, childish effort, of no military value whatsoever.[132]

---

128 BA 2 May 1942.
129 WT 18 October 1940.
130 ERO D/DU 888/25/1, journal, 5 April 1942.
131 ERO D/DU 888/25/2, journal, 28 July 1942.
132 ERO D/DU 888/26/1, journal, 30 January 1943.

Shortly afterwards he again lambasted the RAF's activities. 'But how can we rightly complain of our own sufferings at the hands of an enemy with whom we are at war,' he mused, 'when every day RAF planes are blasting the homes of Danes, Dutch, Belgians and French, killing innocent people who have no wish to be mixed up in the war at all?'[133]

Some Essex people had mixed feelings about the bombing campaign. When S.L. Bensusan reflected on the destruction caused by German raids, he wrote that they were 'scenes of the kind that few Englishmen could watch unmoved', even though, in his opinion, 'we are not good haters'. Sybil Olive of Chelmsford recalled:

> I must admit that I don't think that anyone was too concerned. I think I remember Dresden as being something that I was concerned about because I could see no point in that … in bombing a town that had no factories or whatever. Not that they didn't do the same thing of course. But it did strike me at the time as being a quite unnecessary loss of civilian life but in the main we were glad they were getting the same as we were getting, which is quite understandable.[134]

P.A. Anderson was less ambivalent: 'Everybody wants the raids on this country avenged. Bomb Berlin is the general cry'; later he added, 'As we did not hear them say "war" we will not hear their cry for peace.'[135] Ernest Edwards, the Southend diarist, commented in a similar vein:

> [w]e read that Krupps factory received direct hits from the RAF and that it is claimed that 400 workers were killed and 1,800 were injured. Any sorrow we might feel for this loss of life is deadened by the thoughts of Coventry, Birmingham and Southampton.[136]

These sentiments were not isolated ones. A survey of Londoners in early 1944 revealed not only that six out of ten gave complete support to British raids on Germany but that 75 per cent believed that the RAF was aiming exclusively at military targets.[137]

---

133   ERO D/DU 888/25/1, journal, 26, 27 April 1942; ERO D/DU 888/25/2, journal, 28 July 1942.
134   ERO SA 14/1458/1.
135   P.A. Anderson with J.N. Anderson, *Dangerous skies: war events and family life 1941* (Raydon, 2007), pp. 68–9, 235.
136   ERO S 3150, Edwards diary, 14 December 1940.
137   Calder, *People's war*, p. 491.

Towards the end

In December 1941 a new enemy, Japan, had inflicted a series of disastrous defeats on the British Empire. The *Essex County Telegraph* described the Japanese as 'a wily people, full of tricks and schemes, but always with an eye to the main chance'.[138] On 12 January 1942 Herbert Maxwell Scott wrote, 'Damn these Japs. They picked a good time to commence their operations and all my boyhood memories of The Yellow Peril come back. It will, I fear, be a long time before we fix them.'[139] In contrast, Eric Rudsdale, commenting from his anti-imperialist standpoint, saw little to mourn in these disasters and noted rather cynically that:

> No doubt they [the Japanese] are determined to clean the white races out of Asia for ever, and a good thing too. If the more primitive peoples of Asia are to be exploited, they might as well be exploited by people of their own colour and from their own continent.[140]

Three days later, as he reflected on these new developments in the war, he wrote, depressingly: 'So another chapter of misery and death begins.'[141] The *Chronicle* had warned its readers of Japan's threat to Malaya and Singapore since the spring of 1941.[142] 'It has been the most sensational week of the war,' it wrote in the days following the attack on Pearl Harbor.[143]

The Japanese attack provoked a range of responses in Essex. The Bishop of Chelmsford reflected that 'It may be that in some strange way all this will shorten the horror and bring peace nearer.'[144] It seems unlikely that many people were as optimistic. For instance, a week after the Japanese attack Rudsdale wrote, 'People becoming very depressed owing to the great successes of the Japanese in the Far East.'[145] The *Essex County Telegraph* tried to be positive:

> The entry into the war at this time [of Japan] will cause us all further losses, further anxieties, and further and harder work, but we would say at once that it should *not* have the effect of lengthening the war. On the contrary, after the first losses have been met and all our war plans and high strategy been overhauled and revised in the light of America's full entry into the conflict, the effect should be to *shorten* it.[146]

138 ECT 5 July 1941.
139 S. Maxwell Scott, *Pa's wartime letters and this & that* (2010), p. 103.
140 ERO D/DU 888/24, journal, 8 December 1941.
141 ERO D/DU 888/24, journal, 11 December 1941.
142 EC 2 May 1941.
143 EC 12 December 1941.
144 CDC January 1942.
145 ERO D/DU 888/24, journal, 15 December 1941.
146 ECT 13 December 1941.

The *Burnham Advertiser* accepted that Japan would prove to be 'a hardy foe'. Although it expressed confidence in the United States and in ultimate victory, it too warned that

> [i]t will not prove to be a walkover. Some hard fighting and cruel losses are inevitably ahead of us and we shall defeat the new enemy only if we put aside all sentimentality and face with sober realism the gravity and extent of the latest development in the war.[147]

Japan's entry into the war did not dampen the enthusiasm of those calling for a Second Front in Europe. Both the Bishop of Chelmsford and the *Chronicle* dismissed such calls as impractical. Some individuals had their own reasons for opposing such a premature action. Primrose Stewart of Brentwood had a husband in the army and she feared that he may be involved. For her the thought that some people, and by implication particularly the Communist party, were pressurising the government 'into over-hasty action is infuriating, partly as it comes largely from those who held as aloof as possible from the war until Russia was invaded'. She was equally scathing about the intervention of Chelmsford's female lathe-operators, who had urged a second front, 'who consider, doubtless from female intuition, that they know more about the military situation than the Prime Minister and the head of the Services'.[148]

Germany's invasion of the Soviet Union exposed the people of Essex to something of the horror of the Nazis' treatment of Russia's Jewish population. Following an official statement in the House of Commons about the organised murder of Russian Jews, the *Southend Times* condemned the Nazis in no uncertain terms: 'Such cold-blooded predetermined massacres of men, women and children by the thousands would make the most ruthless conquerors in history shudder with disgust. These are foul crimes of bestial murderers.'[149]

Given that the vast majority of European Jews were within Hitler's grasp there was little practical help that the government could provide, but some Essex residents called on the government to assist them. Captain Jack Macnamara, Chelmsford's MP, was critical of those who wrote to him, believing that the government could in some way help 'but are too pig-headed or idle to stir themselves to action. They may not quite say that, but they do imply it.'[150] H.J.D. Lemon of Colchester wrote to the *Essex County Standard* to say:

---

147 BA 13 December 1941.
148 BA 31 July 1942.
149 ST 20 January 1943.
150 EC 26 March 1943.

Hitler is now exterminating these six million hapless people in circumstances of hideous and unspeakable cruelty. Unless some plan of rescue is quickly devised, nothing can be more certain than that they will die a terrible death. If we and our Government make no attempt to help them, except by wholly ineffective denunciations and threats, we shall gravely compromise our claim to be the protagonists of mercy and justice.

He urged the United Nations to negotiate with Hitler for the release of Europe's Jews, who would be given temporary refuge in Allied or neutral countries before being admitted to Palestine by the British Government.[151] The Essex Federation of Women's Institutes urged the government to relax the immigration laws to allow the entry of all refugees, especially Jews. However, not everyone was happy about such a suggestion. One delegate stated, 'I am concerned about post-war effects. Our boys came back after the last war to sell flowers by the roadside while the Jews were getting the jobs our lads should have had.' Such comments, which would not have been out of place in post-1918 Germany, demonstrated that there were British people who also did not see Jewish people as British or as British citizens.[152]

Samuel Hurnard of Lexden, Colchester, complained of 'our nation's feeble policy towards the Jews'. He called on the government to scrap its 'barred door policy' in Palestine and instead implement the Balfour Declaration to prevent the British people being complicit in the extermination of the Jews.[153] Crawshay Frost of Goldhanger offered a variation on pre-war suggestions in Essex that Europe's Jews should be colonised in Madagascar. His plan was for the United States to admit one million Jews on condition that they worked in farming, not in the cities. In return, Australia would admit a million American negroes to live and work in tropical Australia, where the white race could not survive, while the Australian Government passed laws 'to keep temperate Australia for the white race'.[154]

After a year of disasters, particularly the fall of Singapore and Tobruk, 1942 ended on a high note, with Britain's first significant land victory of the war at El Alamein. 'This is the best news which has come to us since the war started,' wrote the *Essex Chronicle*. 'No-one, thinking of the many disappointments we have had, had dared to hope for anything so good.'[155] The *Burnham Advertiser* was even more triumphalist:

151 ECS 20 February 1943.
152 EC 2 April 1943.
153 ECS 6 March 1943.
154 EC 12 February 1943.
155 EC 6 November 1942.

Victory is in the air! By this I do not mean that the war will be over this year or within any fixable time. What I do mean is that the turn of the tide has come, and that the future war news, with perhaps occasional slight set-backs, will be such as to keep us in good spirits until we receive the joyful news that complete success has crowned our arms, and that we can proceed with the punishment of the knaves who have involved the world in the biggest crime in history.[156]

Like the *Advertiser*, the *Chronicle* urged its readers to remain realistic. 'It should not lead to wishful thinking; we must keep our balance; the advance towards final and complete triumph achieved in the last seven days may represent only one part in a hundred; but the part is ours.'[157] However, less than a year later, following victory in Africa, the invasion of Italy and the downfall of Mussolini, it was becoming harder to exercise restraint. Following Italy's surrender the *Essex County Standard* headlined its article with 'End of the War Brought Almost Within Sight'. The newspaper was now declaring that 'It may be confidently asserted that the doom of what remains of the Axis is assured.' It added 'This is only a matter of time, and it is not unduly optimistic to believe that the time is now not likely to be very considerably prolonged.'[158]

However, as Fascism abroad began to crumble, British Fascism once more became controversial. In November 1943 Herbert Morrison ordered the release of Oswald Mosley, the pre-war leader of the British Union of Fascists, after three comfortable years in prison. The decision was much resented and provoked an outcry. Colchester health workers sent an angry resolution to Churchill, stating:

That this … [workers' union] is alarmed at the increasing and continual release of Fascists from detention, and calls upon the Home Secretary to immediately re-intern Sir Oswald Mosley and those other Fascists who would threaten working class liberty in Britain.[159]

The Colchester branch of the AEU wrote to Morrison condemning Mosley's release as 'an outrage to the armed forces who are fighting Fascism, and also to those who have already died in the struggle'.[160] The Southend branch of the Communist party held a protest meeting. 'We Communists have no illusions

---

156 BA 14 November 1942.
157 EC 6 November 1942.
158 ECS 10 September 1943.
159 ECS 26 November 1943.
160 ECS 3 December 1943.

about Fascism,' it stated. 'It is the enemy of the human race and must be exterminated or the world drops into chaos.'[161]

After the disasters of the early years of the war, events in 1942 and 1943 coalesced to convince people in Essex, and throughout the country, that victory was assured in the long term. The fact that the Soviet Union had not succumbed to invasion and the Red Army was inflicting terrible losses on the Nazis buoyed spirits in Essex and stirred calls for a Second Front. The presence of American troops and the American Air Force in the county, the latter combining with the RAF in its relentless air offensive against German cities, finally eased concerns about invasion. These developments were crowned by the victories at El Alamein and Stalingrad in the winter of 1942/3 and by Italy's withdrawal from the war in July 1943. However, there was a general recognition that victory was a long way off.

---

161 ST 1 December 1943.

6

Carrying on

Wartime childhood

For children, evacuation and all that flowed from it left an impression that, in many cases, stayed with them throughout their lives. It is here that we must start. In early 1940 a Ministry of Health census of schoolchildren revealed that, nationally, 57 per cent of evacuees were still in the reception areas.[1] In Essex, which had received a fifth of all evacuees from London's 'danger areas', 61 per cent of them still remained – a total of 15,521 children.[2] By the time the Blitz began this figure had fallen slightly, but the horrors of heavy bombing led to a renewed exodus that peaked at 35,065 in January 1941.[3] These statistics are only part of the story. In fact evacuation was a multi-layered affair and consisted of much more than just London evacuees arriving, drifting home, and then returning during the Blitz. London evacuees who were sent to Essex coastal resorts were evacuated in June 1940 when invasion threatened, as were many of the resident population of schoolchildren from these towns. At the same time large numbers of children in Metropolitan Essex and in resorts such as Southend were not evacuated. The former experienced heavy bombing and disrupted education. However, the baleful effect of the war on learning was felt in most reception areas, too.

For some children, the journey to new homes was interminable. J. Norman, a second-year pupil at Colchester Royal Grammar School, wrote:

> Ipswich, Newmarket, Cambridge. Oh dear, nearly dark. I feel half dead! Bump! Stopped again. Out of the carriage windows our heads popped. Where's this? Iching? No, Hitchin! How many more miles? I don't know. Look out, we're going! That's funny, we're going backwards! There were many remarks. Oh dear, how much further? Look, there's

---

1   R. Titmuss, *Problems of social policy* (London, 1976), p. 139.
2   ECS 24 February 1940.
3   ERO T/A 679/1 Daily Situation Reports by Essex County Constabulary HQ to Sub-divisions, 3 October 1940–30 April 1945. For some reason that was not explained the police record ceased to record the number of evacuees after 21 October. Neither was it resumed in 1944–5, when there may have been a resumption of voluntary evacuation due to the doodlebug campaign.

a town; can you see it? Look over there. We are slowing down. Hold tight! Bump! Out of the window popped our heads. Porter, where's this? Wellingboro [sic]. How many more miles? Seven? Hurrah! Look out, we're off. Bump! No mistake, this is Kettering. Bump! Crash! Down came the luggage. B–r–r–r–r–r – it's cold. How ever long have we got to wait on the platform?[4]

Heather Nice was a seven-year-old girl from Lexden near Colchester, who was evacuated to Irthlingborough in Northamptonshire. She, too, found the journey irksome:

I still recall that awful long tiring journey, the train being pulled off into the sidings to let troop trains pass, having nothing to drink or eat – for we had eaten and drunk all that we were allowed to carry, the boredom and the discomfort, for the train was packed and airless, and the weather very hot.[5]

Boredom was preferable to utter misery. Some West Ham schoolchildren were destined for Somerset, 'but being provided by the railway company with a non-corridor train (no toilets) the needs of nature proved too strong and they had to be deposited at Wantage (in Oxfordshire)'.[6]

The arrival at a destination was rarely a joyful affair, as most evacuees were hungry, thirsty and extremely tired. Having finally reached Kettering Grammar School, one of Norman's peers described the food offered them as 'pieces of leather-like bread and margarine on plates before us, with some stale cheese, which looked as if it was made in Napoleon's time, and some wet biscuits'.[7] Arrival was followed by an ad hoc selection process, where local people chose the evacuees they wanted to be billeted on them. The nicest, cleanest children were picked first; dirty or unprepossessing ones, or more than two siblings, were often left to the last. At Goldhanger a thirteen-year-old London girl had arrived in a large party with her mother, sister and two brothers. Eventually her family was the only one left because it was not easy to billet such a large number of people and keep them together. It was the local policeman and his eldest daughter who finally took them in. 'Mother told us later that she had felt as if we were like cattle being looked over in a cattle market.' The girl added that 'such a vehemently distasteful impression was in no sense the fault of the decent country folk who generously opened their homes and their hitherto

4   CLSL *The Colcestrian*, December 1940.
5   Nice quoted in L. White (ed.), *Lexden in wartime: memories of local people, vol 2* (Colchester, 2008), p. 22.
6   M. Graham, *Oxfordshire at war* (Oxford, 1994), p. 31.
7   CLSL *The Colcestrian*, December 1940.

undisturbed lives to total strangers'.[8] When Doris Sime's party reached Lydney in Gloucestershire, refreshments were served, but only after a further hour had passed in which all the children were medically examined. Finally they reached the mining village of Bream and were taken to the Village Hall. What followed was truly appalling, if mercifully brief:

> We were greeted by a hall half full of villagers who wanted to do their bit for the war effort. The grab began – if they fancied the look of a child, then they grabbed. Brother and sister were separated and the crying was unbelievable.

It was only the timely intervention of the much-respected district nurse that put a stop to all this and imposed order on the proceedings. Aided by the squire's wife and local teachers, the billeting was then carried out in a less terrifying way.[9]

This insensitive treatment of evacuees tended to be the same throughout the reception areas. Throughout the country evacuees were blamed for bringing with them or causing a whole range of social problems, but the greatest cause of disharmony between newcomers and residents – however much the latter exaggerated the extent of the problem – was the issue of personal hygiene.[10] A young lad from Great Baddow was quite emphatic that villagers had been appalled by the habits and state of evacuees.[11] When evacuees arrived at Mersea Island in 1939, because of the extent of vermin, especially lice, their hosts took the evacuees' clothes and burned them, then bathed them and gave them new outfits.[12] Margery Allingham found evacuees who came to her village to be healthy but 'the habits of nearly all of them would have disgraced any two-months-old pup'.[13] At Stanway near Colchester some of the evacuees who were described as unclean had been patients of London County Council hospitals and suffered from scabies, impetigo and incontinence. The headteacher at Stanway School set up a clinic staffed by volunteers but the number of children who were admitted overwhelmed the facility and a Minor Ailments Hospital was eventually established at nearby Wakes Colne.[14]

At an official level the Assistant Medical Officer of Leyton, a borough that sent evacuees into the Essex countryside, recognised the truth in some of these stories. She noted that some families were a 'virulent source of infection'

---

8   Federation of Essex Women's Institutes, *Essex within living memory* (Newbury, 1995), p. 218.
9   M. Roberts and R. Roberts, *Under the flight path: home front diaries from south east Essex* (St Osyth, 1995), p. 42.
10   Titmuss, *Social policy*, pp. 114–27, outlines these various problems.
11   MOA Diarist 5205, 13 October 1939.
12   R. Bullen, 'A community at war: Mersea Island 1939–45', MA Thesis (Essex University, 2006), p. 22.
13   M. Allingham, *Oaken heart* (London, 1941), p. 137.
14   ECS 20, 27 January 1940.

to others and that the train journey in crowded carriages spread vermin to children who had never been infected before. Many middle-class parents brought their children home because of the spread of verminous conditions.[15] Problems remained throughout later evacuations. Because so many hospitals were damaged or destroyed in the Blitz it was difficult to carry out effective medical examinations of children. In consequence, Chelmsford's Public Health Department carried out inspections of evacuees as they arrived 'in fairness to householders in such areas … in order to prevent the spread of infectious diseases, and also to prevent the billeting out of persons who, for one reason or another, are not suitable or fit for billeting in private households'.[16]

In September 1939 well-off residents resisted being allocated evacuees and, across the country, it was often working-class families that stepped in to accommodate them. In the village of Broomfield, near Chelmsford, one woman asserted that villagers were disgusted that well-off residents had resisted billeting, preferring not to be inconvenienced. Such people, she alleged, metaphorically barricaded themselves behind their doors, hoping that they would not be chosen.[17] Even during the Blitz there was local resistance to evacuation, in this case of bombed-out, traumatised families. The local authorities around Epping sent a deputation to the Ministry of Health trying to fend off the evacuation of these families to their areas, their main objection being 'the considerable differences in social standards between Dockland inhabitants and the householders of these suburban areas'. The result was that the Minister 'did not think it practicable to insist too strongly upon the re-housing and billeting of evacuees on the spot, in view of the resistance which the authorities were putting up'. As a result, much of the rehousing and billeting occurred in Hertfordshire.[18]

Reception areas were often taken aback by both the unexpected numbers of evacuated people and the problems that they brought with them. On the other hand, the parents who sent their children away or who went with them found some unpleasant shocks in store for them, too. Parents were often anxious about what their children would find in their new homes. One mother from Southend was afraid that her boy would be billeted on people who might drink and curse.[19] Mothers and children who had led comfortable lives in suburban areas were shocked at the primitive conditions in rural cottages. Ten-year-old Wendy Barnard from Clacton arrived at a cottage at Wyre Forest near Kidderminster to find oil lamps instead of electricity, candles to light the way

15   SE 6 December 1940.
16   SE 19 July 1941.
17   MOA Diarist 5424, 7, 19 September 1939.
18   TNA CAB 102/726 Care of the homeless at West Ham after air attacks, 1942.
19   MOA TC5 5/2/C, Box 2, Evacuation material, east coast evacuation, 28 May 1940.

to bed, irons that had to be heated on the fire, cooking done on a range and a battery-powered wireless, the batteries of which had to be changed every week. Water was brought from a well outside the back door. As there was no plumbing, a tin bath hung on the wall outside the house.[20] Nearby, Hazel Fairhall, also from Clacton, experienced the outside privy, known locally as a 'two holer', for the first time. She and her evacuee companions took it in turns to cut up the *Radio Times* into squares before threading them with string and hanging them up as toilet paper.[21] Uprooted from everything that was familiar to them and as disdainful of country life as their hosts were of them, many parents left with their children very quickly. A 36-year-old married woman who had evacuated with her family from Romford to Scotland returned home, saying that it was too quiet and there was nothing to do in the evenings.[22] Mrs Marie Baines, a 48-year-old mother who had been evacuated with her children to Lindsell, a tiny village near the small town of Dunmow, said, when interviewed by an *Essex Chronicle* journalist:

> You mean you are longing to get back to South East London? To tell the truth, yes (trying not to appear ungrateful). I know it is healthier here, no strain, no rush – I know all that. I was pallid when I came here, look at me now. But I do miss my old surroundings – the streets, the traffic, the crowds, the noise, friends dropping in for the evening, you know, that sort of thing. I'm a born Londoner, and I love the place.[23]

In 1941 Ernest Stone, Vicar of Clavering and the local billeting officer, wrote:

> I wish I could say the efforts of the people of our villages were really appreciated. We know that our London evacuees don't want to come into the country, but we never asked them to come. We have all done our best for them but I doubt whether ten per cent of them are really grateful. Such cases of gross ingratitude that have come to my notice would almost make one despair of the future.

One evacuated mother said to him, 'it would kill me to stay here'.[24]

The relationship between hosts and evacuees, whether children or adults, was complex because people from widely different social backgrounds were

---

20   J. Collett (comp.), *There'll always be an England: the story of a group of World War Two evacuees, told in their own words of how they were torn from home, town and family to a life amongst strangers in an alien environment* (Stourport on Severn, 2006), p. 14.
21   Collett, *There'll always be an England*, p. 21.
22   MOA, TC5 5/1/H Box 1, Evacuation material, Romford, 1 November 1939.
23   EC 3 October 1941.
24   J. Cooper, *Clavering at war 1939–1945* (Clavering, 2012), pp. 16, 67.

being thrown together. At West Mersea an official report stated that, following the arrival of evacuees, there was a fortnight of 'acute tension' before both groups adapted to each other.[25] Things were not really as simple as this, however, for the local billeting tribunal met every fortnight to hear complaints from both sides. In all there were 92 complaints, which averaged out at about ten a month during the tribunal's existence.[26] A Mrs Weavers from West Ham wrote to the *Stratford Express* complaining of her daughter's experience in Somerset, which she described as a 'lousy hole':

> She had a long walk from school to the farm twice a day … and at lunchtime the woman was always out and left her dinner, which was comprised of paste sandwiches and cake, on a plate. Sheep and chickens were all in the kitchen, even at meal times. … The farmer, his wife and children, all swore. Never a hot meal. She wore out in three weeks six pairs of socks, two pairs of shoes, one pair of slippers. None were mended. The woman read her letters and was constantly accusing her of stealing the fruit.[27]

At Paglesham, sandwiched between the rivers Roach and Crouch, local girl Zillah Harris noted that

> one lad's landlady wants to get rid of him, wants his room! Says he is greedy, gave him salts and he was always wanting to stay in bed, which she wouldn't allow, though he had to later as he had a cold, which he gave to her children. If he goes out, she locks the door and he can't get in, if he goes for a walk and is late, he has no tea or supper.[28]

Peter and Wallace Stokes, from Clacton, also had a miserable experience in their first billet, in the village of Arley in Worcestershire. Their new foster mother treated them like unpaid servants, kept the money that their parents sent to them and encouraged her own two children to bully them. The food was very basic and the boys began to lose weight, becoming noticeably thin. Eventually they were moved to a new billet with a kindlier couple.[29]

Some older children who objected to being evacuated carried out a campaign of emotional blackmail to get their parents to bring them home. For example, Avis, who had been evacuated to Hatfield Peverel, had already

25 D.E. Johnson, *Exodus of children* (Clacton-on-sea, 1985), p. 23.
26 Bullen, 'Community at war', p. 23.
27 SE 19 July 1940.
28 Harris quoted in Roberts and Roberts, *Under the flight path*.
29 Collett, *There'll always be an England*, pp. 67–70.

written one letter home that day, before she penned another nine-page missive, of which this is but a small part:

> I know I shall go crazy if I don't come home now … Please Dad if you *love* me take me home. Be a *real* father to me, I want to come home. If you want to give me a birthday present, one that I want, you would take me home. If you had some fatherly love for me you would come tearing down here in the car and take me home at once. I think I have cried every day since I've been back thinking of you and Mum and home…. I know you are thinking it is safer here than at home but I don't care. All my hankies are wet through with crying but if you love me as you say you will read between the lines of this letter and say 'yes, I see she is unhappy, she must come home at once.'[30]

In West Ham rumours circulated that the borough's teachers and children had been separated in Treorchy in Wales, which caused alarm among parents. The *Stratford Express* played its part in defusing the situation by publishing many letters from children who said they were happy in their new surroundings.[31] Such were the fears that were generated about rural conditions that mayors and councillors from several boroughs in Metropolitan Essex visited reception areas to see conditions for themselves.[32] Occasionally a child's experience of evacuation was truly horrific. Ten-year-old Pam Hobbs was evacuated from Leigh-on-Sea to the Midlands in 1940. When a female evacuee from her school was sexually abused by the brother of a villager, the man was imprisoned. The story got in the papers and reflected badly on the village, whose inhabitants resented the adverse publicity and felt that it was no longer appropriate for the evacuees to remain. They were moved to a village twelve miles away and were forbidden from having any contact with their previous lodgings for the duration.[33]

Historians have tended to focus on the negative aspects of evacuation,[34] but not every child's experience was disastrous. When interviewed, ten-year-old Johnny Downes from Camden Town made it clear that he did not want to return home

---

30 ERO D/DU 935/26 Copy of a letter from a girl named Avis to her father, date uncertain.
31 SE 14, 21, 28 June 1940.
32 SE 3 January 1941.
33 P. Hobbs, *Don't forget to write: the true story of an evacuee and her family* (London, 2009), pp. 108–13.
34 For instance, J. Gardiner, *Wartime: Britain 1939–1945* (London, 2004), pp. 28–46; H.L. Smith, *Britain in the Second World War: a social history* (Manchester, 1996), pp. 41–2; R. Mackay, *The test of war: inside Britain 1939–1945* (London, 1999), pp. 124–5, 166–7; S. Hylton, *Their darkest hour: the hidden history of the home front 1939–1945* (Stroud, 2001), pp. 42–8.

Figure 6.1. Secondary school evacuees, probably from Tottenham High School in north London, enjoy a Maths lesson in their new surroundings at Hatfield Peverel, near Witham. (Essex Record Office)

> because there are more things to do in the country. During our holidays I helped to make hay. I never saw hay before the war. I love fowls, and ducks, and goats, and pigs. All I could keep in London was tame mice. I shall work on a farm all the time when I am old enough.

Did he miss anything?

> I did at first – the stalls in the streets, the penny bus ride to school, the policemen (when you are small they walk you across the street). But there are so many things here that we didn't have in London. I would rather be here. After school we play cricket in a field – not up against a wall.[35]

The feeling that evacuation opened up new rural idylls for urban children can be seen in the first wartime magazine produced by the pupils of Trinity County School, from Wood Green in North London, who were evacuated to Hatfield Peverel. One pupil wrote of the village:

---

35   EC 3 October 1941.

It is a place of peace; here, under wonderful blue skies, looking out over meadows and cornfields, or walking beneath majestic trees, centuries old, one feels that war is incredible. Yet it is war that has brought us here to this hospitable little village, with its kindly, welcoming people, who are doing and have done their best to make us feel so 'at home'.[36]

Another pupil, Joyce Garrett, wrote, 'Some of us were driven off in purring cars to secluded mansions, others trudged a simpler way to cottages and farms, but wherever we were sent our welcome was warm.'[37] In 1939 one vicar in rural Essex commented

Christmas has brought new friends this year ... the vicarage is full, serving the same high purpose of hospitality but with one difference. The welcome voices are so many children and that is a fine thing for our village and indeed a fine thing for them.[38]

Sometimes evacuees, who even at a comparatively young age fancied themselves more sophisticated than their rural hosts, gently mocked them in an affectionate manner. This poem 'The Evacuation of London', written by Doreen Drage and Eileen Jones, pupils of Tottenham High School that had been evacuated to Saffron Walden, makes this clear:

That in Saffron Walden there's a tribe
of Alien People that ascribe
the most outlandish ways and dress
On which their neighbours lay such stress,
Their children away to avoid invasion
Long time ago in a mighty band
From Tottenham Town to Walden land,
But why, they do not understand.[39]

In spite of the negative publicity that surrounded evacuation at the time it was not uncommon for evacuees to be received with great kindness. Mrs L.M. Trigg of Twickenham, near Clevedon in Somerset, sent this letter to the mother of Ronald and Patricia Webb, eleven- and ten-year-olds from Barking, who had been billeted on her:

---

36 ERO D/DU 935/2, Magazines of Trinity County School (Wood Green) at Hatfield Peverel 1939–41, No. 1, September 1939.
37 ERO D/DU 935/2, No. 3, Autumn term 1939.
38 ERO SA 1/455/1, BBC Radio Essex broadcast, Essex at War, 'Christmas Under Fire' (1989).
39 ERO D/DU 1712/1, Tottenham High School evacuation magazine, May 1940 (at Saffron Walden), pp. 35–6.

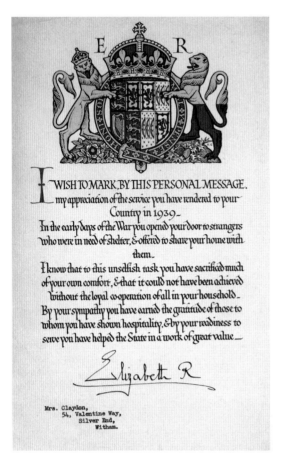

I WISH TO MARK, BY THIS PERSONAL MESSAGE, my appreciation of the service you have rendered to your Country in 1939.

In the early days of the War you opened your door to strangers who were in need of shelter, & offered to share your home with them.

I know that to this unselfish task you have sacrificed much of your own comfort, & that it could not have been achieved without the loyal co-operation of all in your household.

By your sympathy you have earned the gratitude of those to whom you have shown hospitality, & by your readiness to serve you have helped the State in a work of great value.

Elizabeth R

Mrs. Claydon,
54, Valentine Way,
Silver End,
Witham.

Figure 6.2. A certificate awarded to a Mrs Claydon of Silver End near Witham for taking in evacuees in 1939. (BRNTM 2010.237, Braintree District Museum Trust)

I have the pleasure of looking after your two children, Ronald and Patricia. I should like to assure you that they will have a good home and I shall do everything in my power to make their stay a happy one. I have a little boy who will be a little playmate for them. I am enclosing a snap taken last week of my mother, Michael and myself, hoping this will give you a feeling of confidence. Our garden is four acres and therefore they will be able to live out of doors. They are now playing in the garden. If the opportunity arises I shall be very pleased to welcome you here.[40]

Evacuation thus raised issues of social adjustment in reception areas but it also complicated the need to educate the nation's schoolchildren. All schools were closed in evacuation areas, even though many children stayed behind. They

---

40   ERO D/DU 1595/11 Evacuation material relating to Frederick and Michael Webb, letter, 5 September 1939.

remained shut even when air raids failed to materialise, to prevent evacuees from returning en masse. Even in neutral areas, where children were not evacuated, schools were closed. In both cases this was because schools were inadequately protected and were seen as extremely vulnerable, but it nevertheless created tensions between parents and local authorities. In Romford one trainee teacher said that at the beginning of the war she was constantly harassed by mothers wanting to know when schools would reopen, as their children had nothing to do.[41]

Once evacuation had been achieved the priority was to ensure that disruption to children's education was kept to a minimum, something not easy to achieve. In some cases evacuated schools were expected to use buildings that had not been designed for educational purposes. When the girls of Tottenham High School arrived at Saffron Walden there was no secondary school and it took several weeks before they were established in two separate houses – Freshwell House and Myddleton Place. The parish church was used for assemblies and the school was allowed to use the facilities of Saffron Walden Training College. It took time to transform the buildings to the semblance of a school. The headteacher wrote:

> [D]irt and cobwebs held their sway unassailed in Myddleton House and before there could be any thought of putting furniture into the rooms, everything had to be thoroughly cleaned, and every floor had to be scrubbed. While on their knees, scrubbing, many girls must have thought what a strange beginning to a school term we were having.

Desks, chairs, tables and books eventually arrived in removal vans. Writing materials were scarce. One girl wrote of

> that most coveted article – ink. We remembered, with pangs of remorse, those careless blots, of which we took little notice, and the many times we emerged from the form room with our fingers bathed in ink, never thinking that one day we should miss this luxury.[42]

The pupils from Wood Green had a similar experience at Hatfield Peverel, where there was also no secondary school. Fortunately only a third of the pupils, about 120, had come. It was a week before their new 'school' was ready at Hatfield Peverel Priory. The younger pupils occupied the building in the morning and the seniors in the afternoon. At first only two classrooms had tables and chairs but this was eventually put right. In Science individual practical

---

41   MOA TC5 5/1/H, 29 October 1939.
42   ERO D/DU 1712/1, pp. 4, 19–20, 25.

work was very difficult owing to the shortage of materials. Demonstration apparatus was stored in a packing case and carried to the room where the lesson was given. However, both staff and pupils made the best of it and the atmosphere became less formal. Male staff were attired in bright clothes and were not expected to wear gowns. Boys wore khaki and girls had dark, knitted, woollen jumpers. Barbara Taunt, a pupil, described this relaxed atmosphere:

> School is a very unorthodox place now. In one form room you may see a French lesson in progress. One boy out front holding up the blackboard, in another room a Maths lesson is proceeding with the board propped up on a cupboard or even on a chair. Such lessons as Art are much more interesting for visits are made to the old church close at hand, where the architecture studied in the classroom can be sketched from the actual building. Biology and Botany, too, are enjoyed to the full in the organised nature rambles.[43]

Younger pupils were more fortunate, as there was always an elementary school wherever evacuees were sent. Because rural schools were too small to absorb many newcomers on the whole a pattern of school-sharing was adopted, with local pupils and evacuees taught in the school building in the morning and afternoon respectively. Only when significant numbers of evacuees returned home during the Phoney War were schools able to teach both local children and remaining evacuees in the same classes. For instance, at Felsted Primary School Shift 'A' comprised the local pupils and 50 evacuees from Noel Park School in Wood Green; Shift 'B' was made up of 69 evacuees from Sybourn Junior School, Leyton, and 50 others from Noel Park. After a month of this arrangement the Noel Park pupils were transferred to the Congregational School Room. The village primary school retained its evacuation system until January 1940, when full-time education was resumed. Shortly afterwards the remaining Leyton evacuees, together with four of their teachers, were absorbed into the village school, with all its seven classes being a mixture of locals and evacuees.[44]

The education that was provided at first was often of an ad hoc nature. St John's Green Infants School in Colchester was closed when war broke out and education was provided in private houses, with groups receiving five hours' tuition a week. It was not until January 1940 that house groups were discontinued and the school reopened.[45] At West Thurrock Primary School two 'correspondence classes' were set up, followed by three house groups; these continued until the

43   ERO D/DU 935/2, October 1939, Summer term 1940, Summer term 1941.
44   ERO E/ML 181/4, Felsted CPS logbook, 1914–43, minutes, 16 September 1939, 22 January, 1, 7 February 1940.
45   ERO T/P 464/1–3, St John's Green CPS (Infants) logbook, minutes, 30 October, 10 November 1939, 10 January 1940.

school was reopened in February 1940.[46] In Southend the borough closed all its schools on the outbreak of war. It adopted a policy of dispersal, known as the Elementary Education Group Teaching Scheme, which used 801 private houses and 42 halls that had been placed at the borough's disposal by individuals and organisations. Groups of between ten and 30 children were taught in them. By December the borough authorised a resumption of full-time education for all junior and senior pupils, although this was delayed by the difficulty of providing shelters in damp areas. The education of infants continued to be a thorn in the borough's side. In February 1940 parental pressure led to infants being returned to school, although numbers were limited to one class per school, with teaching being done in the school hall. At the same time group teaching continued for parents who were reluctant to send their children to school. Following the evacuation of most of the borough's schoolchildren in June 1940 schools were closed again, many of them having been requisitioned by the military. It was not until 7 December that group teaching was resumed, with the proviso that parents accepted full responsibility for the safety of their children. Attendance was still voluntary, and just two hours of teaching was given per day.[47]

The war inevitably intruded into every aspect of children's education. Schools sometimes addressed the deaths of former pupils. In June 1941 one school logbook included the entry, 'the managers received with regret the news of the loss at sea of H. Hollington and W. Christmas [old students of Tilbury Lansdowne Road Council School].'[48] As in the Great War, the pupils' patriotism was exploited for the war effort. Southend High School for Boys, evacuated to Mansfield, had talks on 'The Home Front' and 'The Fifth Column'.[49] The senior boys at Felsted Primary school made fifteen revetment wattle hurdles as part of the anti-parachutist campaign.[50] Schools were exhorted to participate in the endless round of savings campaigns. In 1941 Hedley Walter School raised £4 11s for the Government's Overseas Tobacco Fund for servicemen abroad. Thanks to their effort this provided 4,550 cigarettes, enough for 910 men to get 50 each. That same year a school concert raised £5 for Clementine Churchill's 'Aid to Russia' Fund, and her handwritten letter of appreciation was proudly placed in the school logbook.[51]

The prospect of air raids was tackled energetically by headteachers. The head of the Mayflower Primary School in Harwich wrote: 'As war has unhappily broken out, school cannot be reopened until adequate protection for the children against

---

46   ERO T/P 426/8, West Thurrock CPS logbooks minutes, 20 November, 4 December 1939, 2 February 1940.
47   ERO D/BC 1/1/2/21 XX/1, Southend Borough Council, Education Committee minutes, 7 February, 1 May, 13, 26 October, 1 November, 8 December 1939, 14 March, 30 April, 3 December 1940.
48   ERO E/MM 1633/2 Tilbury and West Tilbury Council Schools, logbook, staff meeting, June 1941.
49   ERO D/BC 1/14/6/1 Southend High School for Boys, minutes, 1936–46, report, autumn term 1940.
50   ERO E/ML 181/4, 24 September 1940.
51   ERO T/P 421/11 Hedley Walter School, Brentwood, logbook, 28 May 1941, 5 January 1942.

air raids has been made.' A month later, as there was still no shelter, homework was given to those children who called at school and it was not until 7 December that the school was reopened.[52] Alerts and air raids were the most disruptive aspect of school life during 1940–41 and 1944–45 and the scale of this is hard for us to comprehend today. Alerts were more frequent than raids but schoolchildren took shelter whenever they sounded. For instance, the logbook of Moulsham Junior Girls School at Chelmsford reveals that between 16 September and 20 December 1940 the sirens sounded on 46 of the 90 days during that period, an average of one occurrence every other day. It was not as predictable as that, however, for on 4–8 November the alert sounded every day. From January 1941 to the end of the Blitz in May there were alerts on a further 29 days.[53] At Parsons Heath School in Colchester the children spent an hour and 40 minutes sheltering on 7 January 1941. On 21 January there were three alerts, resulting in a loss of two hours and three minutes from the timetable. By 7 March 15 alerts had affected almost eleven hours, the best part of a day and a half's education.[54]

Schools devised a variety of strategies for dealing with these enforced breaks. At Bocking children were assembled in corridors 'and passed the time in community singing until the all clear signal was given'.[55] At Radwinter children sheltered in the school lobby, where they too spent the time singing, although the headteacher noted 'not that much protection is obtained by so doing'.[56] Children at Bradfield were 'scattered as much as possible over the building' during an alert.[57] At Grays, close to the Thames, things were particularly bad in the early days of the Blitz. The headteacher recorded that

> the worst air raid of the week came today. It lasted from 9.30am to 2.10pm. Some of the older children did weaving (by choice). Others acted classroom plays and the younger children read their story books and played games. Fortunately we were able to provide light refreshments – milk, biscuits and barley sugar.[58]

Schools in some parts of Metropolitan Essex were very badly hit. At one time in West Ham only sixteen of its 60 schools were being used for educational purposes; the rest were damaged, destroyed or requisitioned by the civil and military authorities.[59]

---

52   ERO T/P 444/1–5 Mayflower CPS logbook, 4 September, 18 October, 7 December 1939.
53   ERO E/E 215/7/1 Moulsham Junior School logbook, various entries.
54   ERO T/P 461/2 Parson's Heath CPS, Colchester, logbook, 7 March 1941.
55   ERO T/P 361/2 Bocking Church Street CPS logbook, 17 October 1939.
56   ERO T/P 350/1/1 Radwinter Church of England PS, logbook, 21 August, 3 September 1940.
57   ERO T/P 384/2 Bradfield CPS logbook, 17 October 1939.
58   ERO T/P 439/3–4 St Thomas of Canterbury RCS, Grays Thurrock, logbooks 1926–1943, 13 September 1940.
59   E.D. Idle, *War over West Ham: a study of community adjustment* (London, 1943), pp. 89–90.

It was very difficult to maintain educational standards in such adverse circumstances. There is no formal evidence available with which to assess the children's mental reaction to alerts and raids, but they cannot have been conducive to studying. Disrupted sleeping patterns during the Blitz and the doodlebug period must have undermined effective learning for many children, as did absenteeism after heavy night raids. After the devastating raid on Chelmsford on 14 May 1943 the headteacher of Moulsham Junior School wrote, 'at two am this morning there was a heavy blitz on the town. In consequence, only 145 children present this morning out of 255'.[60] The logbook of Staples Road Infants School, Loughton, demonstrates the terrible impact the doodlebug campaign had on learning in the summer of 1944. On 30 June the logbook recorded that 'there were frequent warnings lasting the whole of the week. School work had to be abandoned so many times that there was very little work done'. On 3 July there was a simple notation that read 'In shelter all day'. Three days later the headteacher wrote, 'attendance very low owing to disturbance by raids'. On 25 July it must have been with some relief that he wrote, 'This is the first day that the children spent in school. There was no alert during the day.' Unfortunately, attendance plummeted the next morning after 'a very disturbed night'. As late as 31 August he noted that 'the siren sounded so frequently that the whole morning was spent going in and out of the shelters'.[61] This was the pattern of severe disruption that was repeated in schools all over the county during that dreadful summer.

The impact on pupils' learning can only be partially assessed and some of the evidence for this is anecdotal. By 1943 Doreen Idle reported that there were disastrous gaps in the education of elementary schoolchildren in West Ham. The children who should have started school at five years old but had not started until six or seven were the ones most affected. In one school of between 300 and 400 pupils she found that no child of seven could read. In nursery classes of four-year-olds only a minority could count and the concentration span of elementary school pupils in the borough was said generally to be poor.[62] During 1940–41 and 1944–45 school timetables were adhered to fitfully. The Moulsham Junior School logbook records that 'the timetable will be followed as far as possible but as the air raid siren sounds so frequently, routine work cannot be carried on. Teachers, however, do much oral work in the shelters.'[63] Some schools were anxious in case the influx of evacuees lowered the attainment of local pupils. The headteacher at Pebmarsh requested an additional teacher to cope with London evacuees, 'many of whom were

---

60   ERO E/E 215/7/1, 14 May 1943.
61   ERO T/P 369/2, Staples Road Infants School, Loughton, logbook, 30 June, 3, 5, 25, 26 July, 31 August 1944.
62   Idle, *War over West Ham*, p. 88.
63   ERO E/E 215/7/1, 2 September 1940.

very backward in their work'.[64] One infant teacher from Metropolitan Essex was appalled at the educational provision available to her evacuated pupils. There were 200 children of all ages and abilities in three rooms; there was no school hall, so they could only do PE outside on dry days; there were no desks or blackboards, so teaching had to be for the whole group – drawing, needlework, nature study or acting, which was hard with three teachers in the room at the same time. There was no staffroom and the teachers were forced instead to use the school bus at break times when it was not in use. In consequence she regarded evacuation as a complete failure, complaining that children still in evacuation areas were receiving little education while evacuees and those in reception areas were getting inadequate schooling.[65]

A major issue affecting the level of educational progress in reception areas was the number of times evacuees moved billets or schools, or both. The evidence suggests that most children moved billets at least once or twice.[66] This was often related to a change of schools as they grew older. Wendy Barnard was evacuated aged ten; when she passed her scholarship a year later she moved from the village school at Wyre Forest to join Clacton County High School, which had been evacuated to nearby Kidderminster, before everyone returned to Clacton in 1942. John Leffek, a Clacton boy, remembers being taught in Heightington village hall, near Bewdley, in Worcestershire. There were no teachers from Clacton and the class contained a large number of Birmingham evacuees. There seems to have been little formal education. As he could already read he read *Beano* and *Dandy* to groups of children. Brenda Manser had passed her scholarship in Romford, so, when her parents decided that the family should stay in Worcestershire, she too attended Clacton County High School.[67] Nevertheless, in spite of wartime adversities some schools did well. After 21 of the 31 eleven-year-old pupils in the school passed their scholarship to proceed to secondary education, the headteacher of St John's Green Primary School in Colchester commented that

> in view of the extremely unsettling conditions, constant changes of pupils and air raid interference, I consider that the results reflect great credit on the cooperative work of the staff. No special instruction is given, and no homework set; the exam is taken as part of the normal school routine.[68]

64   ERO T/P 364/5, Pebmarsh CEPS, logbook, 14 November 1940.
65   MOA Evacuation report, Box 1, TC5/1/D, Infant school teachers, 1939, 6 November 1939.
66   See, for instance, Collett, *There'll always be an England*, which focuses on the experiences of Clacton evacuees.
67   Collett, *There'll always be an England*, pp. 8, 15, 43, 48, 49, 69–70.
68   ERO T/P 464/1–3, 7 July 1940.

A study of wartime childhood would be incomplete without mentioning the children in Metropolitan Essex who were not evacuated. The evacuation of September 1939 was only partially successful. In West Ham, for instance, 5,800 were evacuated but thousands remained.[69] Barking schools were reopened because so many children had stayed behind and 1,837 attended. In 1940 attendance was made compulsory and 9,000 pupils were present. When the second evacuation from Barking occurred in June 1940 schools were closed for five days, but when they reopened there were still 6,000 pupils in attendance. It was not until the Blitz started that attendance fell, with only about 30 per cent of children at school. However, after raids ceased attendance recovered and exceeded previous totals.[70] In West Ham, two months after the devastating attacks of the early Blitz, the borough reopened 32 schools for children aged nine to fourteen on a part-time basis, and about 2,000 attended. Nine months later the number of enrolments had tripled.[71] In both places pressure was exerted by some parents to restart education.

The wartime experience of Essex children was as disparate as that of children from any other part of the country. Like adults, they shared the dangers of air attacks throughout the county, the social and economic dislocation of being bombed and the gruelling physical and emotional consequences of enemy action. Whether they remained at home or were evacuated, the war disrupted their childhood and education, and, for good or ill, influenced their development. For many children their most vivid memories were of evacuation. Some people believed that evacuation would raise an awareness of injustice and inequality in society among evacuees, their parents and their hosts. It certainly resulted in upper- and middle-class households being confronted with the results of urban deprivation, probably for the first time in their lives. However, one historian believes that '[o]n the contrary, the evacuation opened the eyes of the working class to the advantages of the few',[72] which was perhaps one reason why the political views of individuals had begun to swing to the left quite early in the war. One elementary school teacher from Essex felt that evacuation might have had positive benefits by revealing the dreadful conditions in which many evacuees had been brought up.[73] There were certainly fears in the evacuation areas about how children may have been changed by their experiences. One young Essex teacher felt that children who had been billeted in better houses than their own would be severely dissatisfied after the war and critical of everything their mother did.[74] There were concerns in Metropolitan Essex that

69   SE 21 June 1940, 21 November 1941.
70   SE 22 November 1940, 16 January 1942.
71   SE 29 November 1940, 18 July 1941.
72   T. Crosby, *The impact of civilian evacuation in the Second World War* (London, 1986), p. 10.
73   MOA Box TC5/1/D, Infant school teachers, report on evacuation from Walthamstow to St Albans area, 1939.
74   MOA Box TC5/1/D, Infant school teachers, report on evacuation from Walthamstow to St Albans area, 1939.

children would be so affected by their new environment that they would lose a fundamental part of their local identity:

> Just take our Norfolk children, for instance. Gone are the Cockney idioms and phrases that used to colour their speech so vividly. Unconsciously they have mimicked their country friends to such an extent that some parents will doubtless be somewhat puzzled to understand them when they return home. I foresee that the Tower of Babel, with its multiplicity of languages, will be as nothing compared to a re-assembled London school with its widely assorted dialects acquired as a result of the great evacuation scheme.[75]

Some felt that the limitations of wartime education, particularly in the early days of evacuation, when it was in some disorder, would have a permanent negative impact. One man, looking at adolescents who were receiving no schooling, commented that they were dole fodder. He added that they may as well have been born in an era when education was not compulsory.[76] Others felt that evacuation brought out the best in people. The headmistress of Tottenham High School, reflecting on its first nine months at Saffron Walden, wrote:

> On looking back, I feel a deep sense of gratitude that I was privileged to share the experiences of these last months with so splendid a body of companions. The spirit of comradeship which we had endeavoured to practise in our daily lives at school stood up to its severest test triumphantly.[77]

Chin up: leisure and entertainment

There had been a significant expansion in leisure pursuits during the inter-war years stimulated by a fall in working hours, an increase in real wages, decreased spending on drink, the advent of paid holidays and growing secularisation. Sports such as professional cricket, football and rugby league were watched by huge crowds. The most significant development of all involved a revolution in mass communications revolving around the cinema, wireless and literature.[78] Faced with such a wide range of leisure pursuits, this chapter will focus on examining only these mass forms of entertainment.

---

75   SE 18 July 1941.
76   MOA TC5 5/1/H, Box 1, Evacuation material, Romford 29 October 1939.
77   ERO D/DU 1712/1, p. 3.
78   A. Thorpe, *Britain in the 1930s* (Oxford, 1992), pp. 103–10.

In 1939 people's leisure activities resumed their usual tempo throughout the country, inconvenienced only by the blackout. Cinemas and theatres reopened and sporting fixtures that were not drastically affected by the conscription of young men continued. Only on the coast and rivers, where security concerns were paramount, were holidaymaking, sea fishing and boating brought to a premature end.

The wireless remained as indispensable in people's lives as it had been before the war. People found the anti-British propaganda of various British and German broadcasters known collectively as 'Lord Haw-Haw' irresistible. Ernest and Ethel Edwards referred to Haw-Haw as 'the German comic of Hamburg' and Ernest noted in his diary that 'as usual it is enough to make us laugh'. However, as Britain's situation became perilous they changed their tune. Referring to one of the British broadcasters, Ernest noted in April 1941, 'We hold in shame he who born in this country would sell his honour to the enemy for pieces of silver.'[79]

The BBC's news bulletins kept the nation abreast of the war with an immediacy that the newspapers could not match and for some people listening to them became essential. The writer Samuel Bensusan rarely seems to have missed one:

> The seven o'clock service might be permitted, you listen while dressing or about to dress, but if there had been a raid during the night you would not be told about it … The one o'clock could hardly be overlooked, seeing it brought the Cairo bulletin; and six o'clock might have an afternoon communique from Russia. At nine o'clock there would be a discourse by some expert. Midnight might be left out, because it often murders sleep and Admiralty generally chooses this service to regret to announce.[80]

The diaries of Ernest Edwards during the desperate early summer of 1940 demonstrate the importance of news bulletins in people's lives. On 10 May he and his wife Ethel heard of Chamberlain's resignation and the appointment of Churchill as prime minister. They listened to hear of the fall of Holland and on 17 May of the German breakthrough at Sedan. Two days later a brief hope of escape from disaster in France was given in Churchill's broadcast. 'It is with great eagerness that we listen to the Prime Minister's speech at nine pm,' wrote Ernest. 'Churchill tells us plainly of the grave times in which we live but we gain hope by our great trust which we unreservedly place in him.'[81]

---

79   ERO S 3150, Diary of Ernest Edwards, 26 January, 18 March 1940, 3 April 1941.
80   S.L. Bensusan, *Fireside papers* (London, 1946), p. 156.
81   ERO S 3150, 10, 15, 17, 19 May, 23 June 1940.

Figure 6.3. These pub regulars in the village of Springfield, near Chelmsford, listen to a radio broadcast about Churchill and Roosevelt's Atlantic Charter in 1941. (Imperial War Museum)

Millions avoided the war by tuning in to the escapism of light entertainment programmes such as 'It's That Man Again' (ITMA), featuring Tommy Handley, 'The Brains Trust', 'Music While You Work' and 'Forces' Favourites'. Not everyone found the radio all that necessary, though. Eric Rudsdale was irritated by the portable radio owned by his acquaintances, the Hoopers, writing, 'They carry this damn thing with them wherever they go, and insist on turning it on for every news bulletin.'[82] By the summer of 1941 D.W. Thomas, Vicar of St Michael, Kirby-le-Soken, felt that people had reached a 'zero-point' in 'listening in'. He wrote:

> [p]ersonally, I find once a day is enough for me. There is no doubt, due to the fact that there is much repetition, and this is also notable in other items, especially in the musical ones. The same tunes seemed to be played over and over again. Some time ago one felt that the sooner the 'Nightingale in Berkeley Square' was shot the better.[83]

82   ERO D/DU 888/25/2, 16 August 1942.
83   ERO D/P 169/28/19 St Michael, Kirby-le-Soken, newssheet, August 1941.

Other clergymen found less trivial reasons for despising the radio. The Revd Hartley Brook, vicar of Braintree, questioned the suitability of BBC programming. He complained, 'It has long seemed to me that the BBC, when choosing comedians, prefer uncouth illiterates, especially gentlemen from Lancashire.' He later decried 'the suggestiveness and crudity of much of the variety that is broadcast, particularly in the Forces'.[84]

Wartime radio also brought fleeting fame to a few Essex places, as the BBC went out of its way to emphasise that this was a war fought by ordinary people. In early 1940 a new series of programmes entitled 'Parish Magazine' was intended to show a cross-section of life in small rural towns. Halstead was one town chosen. An old soldier and an elderly darts player were featured, and Essex dialect was heard.[85] In late 1941 the famous band leader Henry Hall's programme 'Guest Night' was broadcast from Colchester, featuring the West End stars Lyle Evans and Eric Barker.[86] In 1943 the BBC visited Southend and broadcast a news bulletin about the town. It was shown at 6pm, and it was confidently expected to reach Southend servicemen in the Middle East.[87]

The daily newspapers also provided a great deal of information for the British people, and, within the limits of censorship, kept them well informed about the war. The Edwards in Southend often noted in their diary that they read 'about all manner of events in the war, both at home and abroad'. Ernest described their newspaper, The *Daily Mirror*, as 'this everyday necessity'.[88] They were intensely irritated when German air raids on London delayed the arrival of their daily paper, often by several hours. For instance, on the morning after 'Black Saturday' their paper did not arrive until 11.51am, at which point Ernest read of the previous night's 'gigantic raids' – news that confirmed what they had heard on the wireless on the nine o'clock bulletin.[89]

As the war progressed people spent a greater proportion of their incomes on entertainment. During the war food consumption fell and expenditure on clothing, household and luxury goods was drastically reduced. Motoring and holidaymaking were virtually impossible, and major sporting events had disappeared from the calendar. Over and above this everyone was exhorted to invest as much money as possible in war savings. Whatever spare cash was left was often spent on what remained of entertainments. The result was that spending on entertainments rose by about 120 per cent between 1938 and 1944.[90]

84 EC 9, 23 January 1942.
85 ECS 11 May 1940.
86 ECS 1 November 1941.
87 ST 28 July 1943.
88 ERO S 3150, 21 September 1940.
89 ERO S 3150, 8 September 1940.
90 A. Calder, *The people's war: Britain 1939–1945* (London, 1969), pp. 366–7.

The cinema retained its mesmerising hold over the British people during the war as the most popular form of wartime escapism. About 25 or 30 million people went to the pictures each week, many of them several times a week.[91] The diary of the farm girl Joan Wright for 1943 shows that she went to the cinema at nearby Saffron Walden at least once a fortnight. Much about the war seemed to pass her by, but as a dedicated film-goer she nevertheless found time to lament the death of a British cinema star on 3 June: 'Leslie Howard killed'.[92] Ethel and Ernest Edwards were regular cinema-goers even during the Blitz. They often went to the cinema and then stayed up all night on ARP duty.[93] The Chelmsford schoolboy John Marriage was a regular film-goer. His tastes were varied, including, in 1942–43, *Bambi*, *The Jungle Book*, *In Which We Serve*, *Tarzan's New York Adventure* and *Desert Victory*.[94]

In Essex the war produced a resumption of the interwar battle over Sunday cinemas. The battle had already been decided in 1932, when Sunday viewings were legalised, but the churches and some local authorities maintained a stubborn resistance against the desecration of the Sabbath. However, the war provided potent arguments for those seeking Sunday cinema. With first-class sport crippled and workers, now working longer shifts, in need of every scrap of leisure time, the opening of cinemas on Sundays seemed logical. Besides, in many towns where large numbers of servicemen and women were now based military commanders were anxious to provide additional leisure opportunities and the government supported this. Consequently, in 1940 local authorities such as Chelmsford and Colchester applied for the formal government permission that was still required. Resistance at Braintree was able to delay Sunday cinemas until 1943, but when the military there were refused permission to use a licensed cinema for Sunday showings army officers bypassed the system. They formed a 'Cinema Club' for the troops and used a requisitioned hall as a cinema. The men paid 3d a week and were allowed to bring two friends to a performance. The 'friends' were invariably young women from Braintree. The film was followed by an hour's dancing.[95] Local charities benefited from Sunday cinema: at Colchester the total raised from entry charges was £1,154 by the end of November 1941, of which five per cent went to the Cinematograph Fund, 50 per cent to the Essex County Hospital and fifteen per cent to the Colchester and District Nursing Association.[96]

The war saw no reversal in the pre-war domination of British cinemas by the American film industry. As British studios were hit by the conscription of

91   Mackay, *Test of war*, p. 186.
92   ERO A12799 Diaries of Joan Wright, Box 1, 1943–5. Leslie Howard was the British actor who played Ashley Wilkes in the great wartime film *Gone with the wind* (1939).
93   ERO S 3150, 7 November 1940.
94   ERO A11545 War diaries of J.E. Marriage, 1942–5.
95   EC 10 January 1941.
96   ECS 7 February 1942.

personnel and their studio space the production of British films fell from about 150 a year before the war to a third of this by 1941–42[97] and, between 1940 and the end of 1944, for every British film shown in Colchester there were five or six American films.[98] At first, comparatively few British films had war themes. Cinema chains and proprietors were keen to keep up morale by showing comedies and dramas and these were not overtaken by war films until 1943, when 45 per cent of showings were of this genre. During America's period of neutrality Hollywood was well aware of the American people's desire for isolationism and its output of war films was minuscule. Nevertheless, in 1941 local cinema audiences were able to see a growing number of American films that were anti-isolationist, or urged war preparedness, or were overtly anti-Fascist. Yet it was not until after Pearl Harbor that Hollywood stepped up its production of war films and (allowing for repeats) Colchester cinema audiences were subjected to about 500 showings of such films from 1940 to 1944. In 1940 only one film in every 70 British and American films was a war feature, but this proportion rose to one in nine by 1942 and one in four in 1943–44. Junella Chapelle, a young columnist on the *Essex Chronicle*, wrote, 'We are tired of war films, we can see the best films of the war on the news reels. And you, sirs, cannot compete with the real thing.' In concluding, she appealed instead for musicals, comedies and mysteries.[99] Francis Minde, the manager of the Ritz, Chelmsford, took her words to heart and announced that for November he had booked escapist films.[100] Chapelle's admiration of the 'real thing' was reflected in her comments on *Desert Victory*. The preliminary artillery bombardment at the battle of El Alamein left her stunned. 'Nothing I have ever seen filmed before can compare with these few minutes. I forgot for the moment the surrounding cinema, the thousand others sitting there with me, they forgot too. We were at El Alamein.'[101]

In spite of the difficulties it faced, the British film industry produced many classic films during the war which were immensely popular with the viewing public. In 1943 Noel Coward's smash hit *In Which We Serve* received official approbation locally when a preview at the Rivoli cinema was attended by councillors, clergy, officers from the nearby Shoebury garrison and Thames Naval Control, as well as naval ratings and other invited guests. 'It is no ordinary film entertainment,' noted the reviewer, 'but one that will grip the imagination and create a lasting impression on the audience by its stark realism, natural dialogue, profound patriotic appeal, and the characters who live their roles rather than act them.'[102] American films also got a favourable

---

97   Calder, *People's war*, p. 367.
98   Based on an analysis of all films shown in Colchester's five cinemas during that period.
99   EC 8 October 1943.
100 EC 22 October 1943.
101 EC 12 March 1943.
102 ST 6, 27 January 1943.

press. Over Christmas and New Year 1942–43 *Mrs Miniver* broke all records at the Tivoli, Southend. The reviewer was unsurprised, 'for the picture is rich in qualities which make a second and even a third visit as satisfactory as the first'. The reviewer added that 'it reveals, without any flights into the realms of heroics or villainies, the simple, modest heroism brought into being by a middle-class English family's reaction to the upheaval of 1939'. In September 1942 it was announced that the epic *Gone with the wind*, which had been showing in London for three years, was coming to Chelmsford. The town's cinema box offices were besieged by cinema-goers delighted by MGM's announcement that nothing would be cut from the film when it was shown in the provinces.[103] Twelve-year-old Patricia Clayden cycled from the Rodings on a Sunday to see the film.[104]

The reception of cinema output was not always positive, however. A Mass Observation survey from Chelmsford in 1942 that included films noted that *The Great Dictator* was the most discussed picture. Although many liked it others were disappointed because they felt that it was not funny.[105] Eric Rudsdale's distaste for propaganda meant that he was not impressed by the comments he heard of the film. In early 1941 he wrote:

> It has been greatly advertised as an 'exposure' showing the 'absurd' and 'ridiculous' aspects of Hitler … and the public were urged to see it almost as a patriotic duty. The fact that they did not may show that there are still a few slight signs of intelligence left. I would not dream of going to these stupid shows myself – for one thing, Hitler is certainly not funny, whatever else he may be.[106]

The constant perils of the war, even on the Home Front, led to a feeling that every moment was precious and was not to be wasted. This partly explains why millions took refuge from the terrible realities of war in the cinema. It also explains the hugely increased appetite for the finer things in life that led to a nationwide renaissance in the arts – what Sir Kenneth Clark, the director of the National Gallery, called 'an assertion of eternal values'.[107] Early in 1942 a Mass Observation respondent from Colchester wrote that there were many things that he wanted to do, although he accepted that he might not survive the war. In view of that possibility he wanted to get all he could out of life in terms of not simply physical pleasures but experiences that nurtured the soul.[108]

---

103   EC 11 September 1942.
104   Author's notes of interview with Patricia Clayden, 24 May 2012.
105   MOA TC66 66/3/F, Town and Country survey, Chelmsford, 1942.
106   ERO D/DU 888/25/1, 17 April 1941.
107   Quoted in Gardiner, *Wartime*, p. 468.
108   MOA directive reply 2685, January 1942.

Figure 6.4. 'Keep them laughing.' A scene from Colchester Repertory Company's production of Terence Rattigan's farce *French without tears* in 1940. (Essex Record Office)

This renaissance in the arts included the theatre. Before the war there were comparatively few facilities for larger drama groups in Essex. Chelmsford had neither a theatre nor a repertory company, although an Arts Theatre Company spent much of the war campaigning for such a venue. Colchester had 'The Rep', but it too lacked a purpose-made theatre for its performances. The Colchester Rep nevertheless flourished, and during the Phoney War its audiences were maintained, with a total attendance of 72,000 people.[109] The disappearance of many of the company's experienced men provided an opportunity for younger men to fill the breach, and during the 1944 season it had the largest number of players in its history, with ten actors and seven actresses.[110] During the war the company tapped into the popular desire for escapism and made comedy the mainstay of its wartime seasons. At least seven out of every ten of its productions were comedies, often the works of well-respected dramatists such as J.B. Priestley, Noel Coward and George Bernard Shaw. More varied aspects of its repertoire included a season of London productions in 1940 and annual performances of Shakespeare. Like many repertory companies, Colchester's worked for the Entertainment National Service Association (ENSA) entertaining the troops and every summer it toured military establishments.[111]

Art, too, increased in popularity. The Braintree-born artist Edward Bawden and his friend, the equally renowned artist Eric Ravilious, who had settled at Castle Hedingham in the 1930s, both became war artists. Ravilious, a

109 EC 11 May 1940.
110 EC 11 April 1942, 1 September 1944.
111 EC 18 April, 25 July 1942, 24 September 1943.

brilliant watercolourist, pottery decorator and wood engraver, was assigned to the Admiralty and painted warships, submarines and dockyards, and even accompanied a Royal Navy warship on the dangerous route to the Arctic and Norway in 1940. He was one of Britain's greatest war artists and his painting of the aircraft carrier HMS *Glorious*, only a short time before its destruction by the German battlecruisers *Scharnhorst* and *Gneisenau* in June 1940, was one of the finest paintings of the war. Ravilious' work was cut short when he was lost on an air–sea rescue mission off Iceland in 1942, aged just 39.[112] In the same year the work of both artists (Ravilious's posthumously) was displayed in Chelmsford Library. His bold use of form and colour had already established him as an artist able to capture the idea of Englishness between the wars, but his work was not universally appreciated by locals. One letter to the *Essex Chronicle* that claimed to represent the tastes of ordinary people condemned the exhibition as 'trumpery pictures', 'petty crudeness' and 'an insult to art and the public intelligence alike'. A letter sent in by J.K. Popham of Great Leighs was headed 'Chelmsford encourages Mad Art'.[113] These views were not supported by the greater number of letters which came in in defence of the exhibition, however. In 1941 a group of relatively unknown Essex artists, including Frank Emanuel, Walter Bayes and H.E. du Plessis, attracted nothing but praise when they exhibited some of their works depicting local landscapes in the National Gallery as part of an exhibition on the changing face of Britain.[114]

The cinema, the theatre and what remained of sport were not to everyone's taste. However, other organised leisure activities declined and going away for holidays became a virtual impossibility. In addition, many people faced hours of enforced residence in air-raid shelters. An Ilford resident admitted to having gone out almost every night before the war, but now her amusements ended with the nightly raid. Before the war she rarely went to bed before 11 o' clock but during the war she was asleep by 9.30pm[115] She now hardly ever listened to the radio, as they did not have one in their shelter, but she read a great deal. More books were read in the 1930s than in any previous decade thanks to the publication of cheap books by Penguin and the Left Book Club. By 1939 libraries in the UK issued 247 million books, tripling the number issued fifteen years earlier.[116] However, during the war books were harder to obtain because publishers had their supply of paper cut to 40 per cent of their pre-war amount. Despite this, there was an increase in book buying because hundreds of libraries were blitzed and stocks had been destroyed.

---

112   A. Kelly, 'Eric Ravilious: the art of war', *History Today* (June 2010), pp. 42–7.
113   EC 13, 20 November 1942.
114   CLSL *Essex Review*, vol. 50, 1941,October, pp. 2–6.
115   MOA directive reply 1396, 8 October 1940.
116   Thorpe, *Britain in the 1930s*, p. 109.

The county's library service held up well under the twin threats of air raids and local authority cost-cutting. At Colchester the town's new library was commandeered as the town's Food Control Committee's offices even before it had opened to the public. Consequently the library spent the war in cramped conditions on East Stockwell Street. Thanks to temporary alterations, which involved using half the Reading Room as the lending library, the library was much used during the war. Initially it was still able to accommodate 1,000, but the blackout, shorter working hours and the smaller room halved this to 500.[117] The number of books borrowed rose steadily, from 18,000 a month in 1939–40 to more than 30,000 a month for the rest of the war, in spite of a 50 per cent cut in expenditure during 1940/41.[118]

At Chelmsford librarians found that there was a significant increase in the number of people using the library for longer periods owing to the blackout.[119] The library issued 310,000 books during 1942 and the number of people reading had increased by half since pre-war days, amounting to 40 per cent of the town's population by 1943.[120] During 1941–42 the library service in devastated West Ham was actually extended, not reduced. Branches were opened in parts of the borough that were distant from the central library: one, for example, in a shop in Forest Gate. It was anticipated that it would issue 300 books a day, but instead gave out 700. Fines for overdue books were cancelled for both adults and children. A brand new library section was begun for children aged five to eight years. Books were sent regularly to schools, ARP depots and shelters. On one occasion 1,000 Penguin books were sent to the borough's four biggest shelters possessing adequate lighting. The borough's evacuees were provided with books, too: in November 1939 some 4,700 were sent to Bridgewater and Taunton in Somerset, where many West Ham children had been sent.[121]

John Marriage, who was fifteen years old in 1943, loved western books, or, as he wrote, 'cowboys'.[122] Mrs Milford Tweedy, who ran a mobile library serving troops in isolated areas, found that men preferred Wild West and detective stories, which seems plausible, as these genres also featured high in cinema listings. The most popular books were *The Saint* and *Sapper* series and books by Edgar Wallace. Mrs Milford Tweedy admitted that the demands of more serious readers were hard to meet. Soldiers who borrowed from Colchester Library had particularly highbrow tastes. Books on philosophy and psychology were in great demand, as were classical literature and modern poetry. The reference

---

117 CBC Public Library Committee annual report, 1939–40.
118 CBC minutes, 14 October 1940, 10 May, 7 June 1943, 10 January, 11 April 1944.
119 ChBC minute 8 January 1940.
120 EC 27 March 1942, 8 January 1943.
121 Idle, *War over West Ham*, pp. 85–6.
122 ERO A11545, 11, 18, 19 December 1942, 1 January 1943.

library, especially its art section, was in constant use by troops.[123] On the other hand, one of its librarians said that 'officer cadets incline to the academic, while other ranks more frequently study technical works'.[124] A Leigh-on-Sea resident explained how a friend of his took a parcel of books to wounded soldiers thinking that novels would be welcomed above all, but in fact books of travel, history, poetry and religion were all welcome.[125]

Other more cerebral activities were severely curtailed by the war. The *Essex Review*, the journal devoted to antiquarian matters, continued to publish its annual volumes, even commemorating its fiftieth anniversary in 1941. Occasional visits were made to its spiritual home, Colchester, as on 20 August 1941, when members visited the churches of St Peter and St Martin. Nevertheless, by 1945 it was struggling to carry on because of rising costs.[126] The Southend and District Antiquarian and Historical Society resumed its meetings in January 1945, when a new programme was outlined. In view of petrol restrictions it was decided that excursions would only be to places on bus routes in the immediate vicinity of the town.[127] The Essex Archaeological Society continued to function, although it noted that its activities 'had been necessarily curtailed, and excursions have had to be postponed'. Its visit to Sudbury in Suffolk in September 1945 was its first outing since July 1939. It, too, managed occasional visits around Colchester and assisted in the countywide scheme to achieve a photographic record of churches. However, the war made it hard to attract new members and, as existing members died or moved, numbers fell from 622 in 1940 to 535 by 1943.[128] Colchester had been the setting for exciting archaeological discoveries in the 1930s, especially in the Sheepen area, but excavations were brought to a halt by the war.[129] The digging of air-raid shelters provided some small compensation by revealing items of interest.[130]

As with art, music of every sort was greatly appreciated during the war. In 1942 a Chelmsford resident commented that people had become increasingly appreciative of serious and uplifting music, whereas in his opinion dance music had declined in popularity.[131] This view was supported by a Colchester resident who felt that life could be cut short at any moment and who, thus, longed to hear music of a less ephemeral nature.[132] As in general the availability of entertainment

---

123 ECS 12 September 1942.
124 ECS 15 June 1940.
125 MOA Directive Reply 2677, May 1942.
126 *Essex Review*, vol. 50, January 1941, pp. 1–2, October, pp. 245–6; 1945, January, p. 43.
127 *Essex Review*, vol. 54, January 1945, pp. 44, 87.
128 *Transactions of the Essex Archaeological Society*, vol. 23, New Series, 1942–5, pp. 381–3, 388–90, 391–4; 1944–9, vol. 24, New Series, pp. 189–93, 203.
129 P. Crummy, *In search of Colchester's past* (Colchester, 1981), pp. 15–16.
130 Eric Rudsdale recorded several of these potentially interesting finds, for instance, on 27 September 1939: ERO D/DU 888/22.
131 MOA Directive Reply 2802, 27 January 1942.
132 MOA Directive Reply, 2685, January 1942.

had declined in wartime, and as people had increased earnings at their disposal, they often tried out classical music. For those with serious musical tastes there was no shortage in the county, as it was visited by world-famous performers. In 1942 the renowned English pianist Irene Scharrer performed at two venues in Colchester. The second of these was a Chopin recital at the Cooperative Hall before a large and appreciative audience.[133] Colchester was also entertained by Lev Pouishnoff, a Ukrainian émigré who at the time was the leading exponent of Chopin. He played at the Regal to a packed house.[134] Clifford Curzon, the English pianist renowned for his interpretations of Mozart and Schubert, performed Brahms, Haydn and Schumann at Colchester, Brentwood and Chelmsford.[135] Not all wartime musical tastes were elevated, however. In Chelmsford a Rhythm Club was established in 1939 to cater for jazz fans. Its attendances were said to be poor and musicians were hard to come by. After starting in a pub it was kept alive for a couple of years in private houses before it folded in 1941, but was re-formed in the following year with more than 30 regulars.[136]

Dancing maintained its immense pre-war popularity and dance halls were packed throughout the war, even during air raids. Dances were held at the Corn Exchange in Chelmsford, where precautions were taken to ensure that only bona fide adults took part. Civilian and military police checked identity cards and turned away anyone who had none.[137] Such was the demand for dancing in the town that when in early 1944 the authorities handed over the Corn Exchange to the military as a social club, ending dancing there, a 700-strong petition was organised to protest.[138] Eric Rudsdale described a dance on the lawn of the Holly Trees near the Castle:

> The lawn was crowded with a swaying mass of girls and men moving slowly to the jigging senseless tunes, blared out by a microphone fixed to Holly Tree House … could see Agnes L…, the former waitress, dancing with her sister, the blonde beauty from the fire brigade with a soldier, a tall, stately blonde with a Canadian …, and a very beautiful ATS girl with a soldier … Many girls not more than thirteen or fourteen years old were dancing with soldiers.[139]

The war also resulted in the first visit of the internationally renowned dance company the *Ballet Rambert* to the county in 1944, performing *Les Sylphides*

---

133   ECS 28 March, 11 April 1942.
134   ECS 12 September 1942.
135   ECS 23 May 1942.
136   EC 3 April 1942.
137   EC 25 September 1942.
138   EC 14 April 1944.
139   ERO D/DU 888/25/2, journal, 25 July 1942.

and other pieces in Colchester.[140] More popular tastes were also very much in evidence during the war, as foreign servicemen brought their own styles of dancing with them. There were regular performances of Polish folk dancing by Polish troops[141] and at least one performance of Russian folk dancing.[142]

Factories were often entertained by performers during lunch hours, although the quality was variable. Sybil Olive said, '[s]ometimes you got quite good people, well-known people came, most of the time it was rubbish, but we enjoyed it, it made a break.'[143]

Across the nation alcohol maintained its importance during the war in the lives of millions, and the public house remained a key source of social activity. New patrons, in the form of adults relocated by evacuation, replaced those called up, and in some areas, certainly in Colchester, Braintree and Chelmsford, British and foreign servicemen and women packed out pubs, to the discomfiture of locals. Beer continued to be produced in large quantities throughout the war, and consumption rose by a quarter as wages increased.[144] In spite of this all parts of the county experienced a beer shortage at one time or another. There was a general shortage in the first week of July 1941, when Essex pubs showed 'no beer' signs. On Romford market day some publicans used the extra hour of trading they were allowed, but others closed early as their stocks had gone.[145] In the first weekend of May 1944 such a crisis struck Colchester:

> Never have so few pubs been called upon to serve so many as last weekend. Never indeed has the shortage of beer been so acute in Colchester. On Sunday we had the unprecedented sight of queues lined up waiting for a pint – and those few houses who opened were quickly sold out.... While a few old sweats took it badly, the majority went without, without even a grumble.[146]

By the autumn of 1944, with signs of victory at hand, some magistrates were allowing hotels to extend their licensing hours for dances and social evenings, but this was regarded as a hollow gesture by tipplers, who were aware that continuing beer shortages meant that eight out of every ten pubs were closed at night.[147] Pubs sometimes reflected the more democratic tone of the new age. In 1941 the army requested that rooms be set aside in pubs in Brentwood

---

140 ECS 12 May 1944.
141 ECS 16 May 1942.
142 ECS 21 July 1944.
143 ERO SA 24/1457/1 Sybil Olive.
144 Gardiner, *Wartime*, p. 170.
145 BA 5 July 1941.
146 ECS 5 May 1944.
147 ECS 25 August 1944.

and Billericay so that officers could avoid fraternising with their men, but the publican at the White Hart rejected the request out of hand:

> There is no distinction made in this house. Why should there be anyway? All our servicemen, whether officers or tommies, are tackling the same job, making the same sacrifices, and deserve when off duty the same consideration from civilians.[148]

The general pre-war tendency towards sobriety in the county continued, assisted by weaker beer, strictly enforced closing hours, longer working hours and the proliferation of daytime and night-time duties in civil defence and the Home Guard. By early 1940 at Mistley only one person had been proceeded against for drunkenness since the war began and, similarly, in the Lexden and Winstree licensing area only one case of drunkenness was prosecuted during the first three years of the war.[149]

National travel restrictions on the railways, the abolition of the basic petrol allowance in 1942 and the imposition of the coastal exclusion zone made holiday travel almost impossible. The Whitsuntide holiday of 1940, when 20,000 visitors arrived at Southend by train, was the last busy weekend at Essex's seaside resorts for three years.[150] Whitsuntide and August Bank Holidays became tame affairs. The *Essex County Standard* thought that most people were in gardens or allotments at Whitsuntide in 1941, although cinemas were full.[151] Nevertheless, there were always some who ignored the coastal ban. In July 1941 Southend magistrates heard the first cases against 'holidaymakers' who had arrived at Benfleet. Several were summonsed, although on that particular weekend so many arrived that the local police had been unable to put them straight back on the train.[152] To enable people to feel that some form of holiday experience had been made available to them the government promoted the concept of 'holidays-at-home', which consisted of various entertainments organised by local authorities. These began in 1941, in July or August, the time when many people would have taken their annual holiday. To minimise disruption, the holidays of factories engaged on war production were staggered.[153]

The improving war situation led the government to lift the coastal ban at times during 1943–44 and this prompted a rush to the seaside. In 1943 Clacton experienced its busiest Easter since 1940 and Whit Monday saw the

---

148 EC 14 November 1941.
149 ECS 24 February 1940, 14 February 1942.
150 SD 16 May 1940.
151 ECS 7 June 1941.
152 BA 12 July 1941.
153 EC 20 June 1941.

largest crowds of the war.[154] Southend was inundated as Londoners flooded in. The *Southend Times* interviewed one woman who had brought her three children on three successive days and planned to do so on a fourth. The London Midland Railway (LMR) tried to give priority to members of the Forces and war workers, and only a limited number of tickets were on sale from London to Southend. Many day trippers thus made the trip by buying tickets to Pitsea, East Horndon and other stations en route, staying on the train to Southend and paying the excess fare when they arrived.[155] Although many of them brought their own food there were large queues at local cafes and many residents were unable to get a meal.[156] Parts of the beach were opened, but with unmarked hazards still in place people ventured on it at their own risk. It was not until 1944, well after D-Day, that the army permitted more general access to beaches.[157] The August Bank Holiday of 1943 produced another torrent of visitors, although by now the town was experiencing regular visitations each weekend. The upsurge in visitors meant that 1943 was the first year of the war that Southend had experienced anything like a summer 'season'. Such were the numbers involved that the *Southend Times* campaigned to allow only residents to be served in Southend's restaurants.[158] Clacton and Walton took longer to recover, however. An *Essex Chronicle* reporter saw the green shoots of recovery there in July 1944, with guest houses reopened and visitors in evidence. Eleven leading hotels were advertising accommodation, parts of the beach were available to the public, three cinemas were open and there was dancing. Staff shortages limited what was possible, however: for instance, the proprietor of the Shakespeare Hotel at Clacton was doing all the cooking in his establishment. Unfortunately, with few shops open there was little to buy and prices were high.[159]

The wartime coastal ban, which was imposed in 1940 when invasion loomed, was lifted at Easter 1943 for a while, allowing seaside visits to be resumed, then re-imposed after a few months in order to facilitate movements of military traffic as D-Day neared, and was finally removed on 25 August 1944. A journalist described how Southend was then swamped:

> In the Southend district ... scenes in the town and on the sea-front were reminiscent of peace-time bank holidays, the usual good humour typical of the holiday spirit of the tripper prevailed ... crowds, many of whom cheerfully stood in the compartments, packed in the proverbial

154 BA 30 April, 18 June 1943.
155 ST 14 July 1943.
156 ST 16 June 1943.
157 ECS 18 August 1944.
158 ST 21 July, 4 August 1943.
159 EC 28 July 1944.

'sardine' tradition on both the outward and inward journey. For the great majority the available beaches were the immediate objective, and some who came earlier in the weekend and found accommodation impossible at short notice, were nevertheless enthusiastic after sleeping in the open.[160]

The general leisure activities that had occupied many people before the war continued unabated. Many of these were activities enjoyed by older people, or by those who, because of their war work, were still in the county. The new British Restaurants, offering plain food at affordable prices, provided a social opportunity for their customers. One person from Leigh-on-Sea found that they were a popular venue for many lonely people.[161] Many horticultural shows were abandoned for the duration but those that survived were given an unexpected stimulus by the 'Dig For Victory' campaign and the increased emphasis on the use of allotments and gardens. For instance, the Mile End Horticultural Show, near Colchester, was held every year from 1940. In 1943 the show had 500 entries.[162] Most churches kept various social activities alive, and bowling and darts clubs and leagues operated throughout the war. In 1940 the Essex Bowling Association re-formed its competitions to minimise transport costs. Nevertheless, with reduced numbers as a result of evacuation, subscriptions were more than halved.[163]

Villages, no matter how small, usually maintained a very varied social life in spite of wartime restrictions. Tiptree, for example, was able to sustain an amateur dramatic society and put on a chrysanthemum show. Its Women's Institute met regularly and all sorts of activities centred around the Anglican and Baptist church, such as the Bible Society and whist drives.[164] Throughout the county activities which, before the war, had been purely social or local fundraising affairs were now devoted to raising money for the war effort. For instance, every village organised social events such as bazaars, flower shows and whist drives to raise money for the relentless round of national savings drives such as Warship Week, or for Aid to Russia. A ploughing match at Great Bentley was held in aid of the Agricultural Red Cross.[165]

Just as during the First World War, the new conflict brought an end to professional football, a sport which was enormously popular with a large proportion of the population. The English Football League closed down and the FA Cup was abandoned after 1941. The government ordered that only

---

160   ST 30 August 1944.
161   MOA Directive Reply 2677, January 1942.
162   ECS 6 August 1943.
163   EC 2 February 1940.
164   ECS 8 March 1941.
165   ECS 1, 15 March 1941, 27 August 1943.

friendly matches were to be played, with a 50-mile travel limit, and crowds restricted to a maximum of 15,000. As well-known professional teams lost players to conscription, the scratch teams which they fielded led to shock results such as Chelmsford City beating Spurs. In 1940 the Football League decided to carry on with a North and South group of teams, but without professionalism, trophies or medals. There were to be no points awarded for wins or draws, and League tables were to be compiled on goal average. West Ham United, Essex's premier professional team, finished runners-up in the Southern group in both 1939/40 and 1940/41, although Southend United performed poorly in both seasons.[166] The Southern League followed government instructions and arranged friendly fixtures with police approval.[167]

Colchester United had ended the 1938/9 season as Southern League champions but struggled to keep going from the outset of war. All work at the club was halted, all loose property was packed away and the players' contracts were suspended.[168] Having opted out of the new Southern League the club's directors decided to play friendly games, but they were not well attended.[169] Consequently, in mid-January 1940 the directors suspended all playing for the season.[170] By April they were considering an appeal to gain relief from rent and rates.[171] The Supporters' Club, which had done much to assist the club financially, closed down in June, by which time the club had made a loss of £870.[172] Although the Layer Road ground was derated and the rent halved to £67 a year, the latter was only met because some directors paid it out of their own pockets. The ground itself was commandeered by the ARP and Auxiliary Fire Service (AFS) in 1941 and much damage was inflicted on it in the next few years.[173]

Chelmsford City's season in 1939/40 was very successful but, in common with most clubs, it was unable to organise a second wartime season. Draconian travel restrictions made away games almost impossible and the invasion fears and the Blitz during 1940/41 were not conducive to organised sport. Chelmsford City therefore closed for the duration, although the ground was used by Southend United, with some Chelmsford players turning out for them. Southend, however, proved to be unreliable tenants, playing 36 games but paying only £50 in rent.[174] Southend United survived longer than its Essex neighbours. The Football Association (FA) set up regional leagues to minimise

166   J. Rollins, *Soccer at war 1939–45* (London, 1985), pp. 15, 221–2.
167   ECS 23 September 1939.
168   ECS 16 September 1939; ECT 21 October 1939.
169   ECS 14 October 1939.
170   ECS 6, 20 January 1940.
171   ECS 6 April 1940.
172   ECS 26 October 1940.
173   ECS 5 November 1943.
174   S. Garner, *Wheel 'em in: the official history of Chelmsford City Football Club* (Rainham, 2001), p. 11.

travel and Southend were placed in the Southern Section A, which included Arsenal and Spurs. However, the standards of the matches were a shadow of pre-war days, with gaps in professional teams filled with local amateurs. Southend's Roots Hall ground was also commandeered by the army as an Officers' Training School and was not returned until 1944. An attempt was made to persuade West Ham to ground-share with them, but the latter team declined.[175] Eventually, in October 1941, the club also folded for the duration. It disbanded still owing £310 in rent to Chelmsford City, with a debt of over £6,000, and faced the possibility of having to seek re-election to the Football League when the war ended.[176] West Ham, as a well-established professional league club, was able to keep going through the war. The club ensured that its players were given an equal chance to play and the pool of players was rotated at the expense of maintaining a settled side.[177]

During the war the FA broke with tradition and gave permission for friendly games on Sundays, although they were not of a league form and no gate money was taken. The rule forbidding Sunday league football was also relaxed in the case of works teams that were unable to play on any other day; they were permitted to play other works teams and teams that did not contain men of military age. The survival of football after the start of the Blitz was assisted by the authorities' allowing games (and other open-air sporting activities) to continue providing that there was an efficient spotter system in place. Games could continue after an alert was sounded until the alarm was given by the spotter the moment that enemy aircraft were seen.[178]

In spite of the many difficulties local football leagues survived in the county throughout the war. A Southend Borough Combination existed, as did a Brentwood and District League.[179] In 1939 the leading amateur clubs in south Essex formed the South Essex Combination, although it was abandoned a few weeks into the 1940/41 season.[180] At Colchester a Junior Combination was formed in 1940 which eventually consisted of two divisions totalling 22 teams. They included five works teams, two military teams and three Civil Defence teams.[181] Rowhedge FC, who were the league champions in 1942, typified the age profile of these civilian teams. The average age was nineteen and the youngest player was fifteen. Because of travel restrictions each player had to cycle several miles to each away game, play the match and then cycle home. As

175 Rollins, *Soccer at war*, p. 27.
176 P. Mason, *Southend United: the official history of the Blues* (Harefield, 1993), pp. 36–9; BA 24 August 1940, 30 August 1941; SD 13 August, 10 September 1941.
177 Rollins, *Soccer at war*, pp. 112–13.
178 ECT 14 December 1940.
179 ECT 27 October, 17 November 1939.
180 Rollins, *Soccer at war*, pp. 205–7.
181 ECS 18 April 1942.

none of the men were well off the club was financed by the directors of the Rowhedge Shipyard.[182]

Essex County Cricket Club had experienced difficult years during the interwar period, facing recurrent financial crises and poor performances on the pitch. It was therefore ironic that in the late 1930s the club's playing fortunes began to improve; it might have been a force in the county championship had the war not intervened. County cricket was abandoned for the duration in 1939 and, with the club secretary called up (eventually ending up in a Japanese Prisoner of War (POW) camp in Singapore), it was left to a war emergency committee to sustain the club's fortunes. One-day matches were organised against local clubs on county grounds and the club's professionals were kept on at the rate of £1 a game with expenses. In 1940 six fixtures were arranged against four schools and teams from Ilford and Chelmsford. The club's grounds were little affected by enemy action, but four players were killed, including two in RAF service and two in air raids (one as a warden). In spite of the lack of games – and, therefore, gate receipts – the continued payment by club members of their subscriptions kept the club afloat and between 1941 and 1944 it made small profits of between £292 and £350.[183]

Like football, cricket was affected at all levels. Colchester and East Essex cricket club decided to carry on even though more than twenty of its players had been called up.[184] Wivenhoe and Great Baddow cricket teams both made a virtue of a necessity and decided not to run a second eleven, while Romford opted to play games only against local teams.[185] Unlike football, however, cricket (and golf) did attract some controversy for playing on the Sabbath. In July 1942 a two-day cricket festival in which many county players were involved was arranged in Castle Park, Colchester, by the military authorities. The mayor gave the tournament his blessing as part of the stay-at-home summer entertainments. At the same time a Sunday golf tournament was organised. There was criticism in the press by some residents, who argued that 'the Sabbath is vitally linked with the answers to our prayers for the Divine intervention that will bring an end to the horrors of war, and a spiritual awakening to the whole world'.[186] The Colchester Free Church Federation Council protested that the event 'distracts from that which fundamentally concerns man as a spiritual being and, furthermore, throws unnecessary burdens of labour on many'.[187] The protests were given short shrift by an unsympathetic borough council. It argued that the game was of some significance because ten English internationals and one

182 ECS 30 May 1942.
183 D. Lemmon and M. Marshall, *Essex County Cricket Club: the official history* (London, 1987), pp. 202–3, 205–7.
184 ECS 6 April 1940.
185 ECS 9 March 1940; EC 2, 16 February 1940.
186 EC 25 July 1942.
187 EC 1 August 1942.

from New Zealand were involved. It lauded cricket as a clean game that was a release for munitions workers from their monotonous jobs in these 'abnormal times'.[188]

All other sports and pastimes were subject to the same restrictions and resultant problems as football and cricket. The Essex Hounds opted to carry on, although, with many of its members on active service, doing vital war work or occupied in Civil Defence duties, its hunts were reduced to two a week.[189] Golf, too, was affected: the county-wide Mullis Trophy competition was cancelled at the outset and many other competitions were abandoned.[190] The Belfairs golf course in Leigh-on-Sea lost half its holes to the army for anti-aircraft emplacements.[191] Orsett Golf Club lost much of its land to two military camps and the club was left playing just four to nine holes. During the invasion scares of 1940–41 wires were stretched across parts of the course to deter gliders and it was not until the autumn of 1944 that the course was derequisitioned.[192] Chelmsford Golf Club adopted a set of war rules that were similar to those used elsewhere. Members were encouraged to collect all bomb and shell splinters to prevent damage to the club's mowers; during an air raid players were allowed to take shelter without being penalised; if the ball was moved by a bomb explosion it was to be returned as near as possible to the correct spot; and if a ball was destroyed a new ball should not be repositioned further forward. All members of the Forces were regarded as honorary members for the duration and American troops could play for a nominal fee.[193] The war also brought baseball to Essex, in the shape of Canadian and American troops. In late 1943 the first ever baseball match played at Southend took place in front of a large crowd. The two teams, 'Keller's Killers' and 'The Gypsies', were American. The *Southend Times* commented that 'the event, comparatively obscure in itself, might well be taken as a microcosm of that firmly founded understanding which, as the result of a close object, has more closely bound two great nations of the earth'.[194]

The possibility of enemy naval action had an immediate impact on coastal leisure activities, just as it did on sea fishing. In early 1940 the Colne Yacht Club, hit by a loss of members and the subsequent drop in subscriptions, decided that, although events would continue, there would be no prizes awarded because of the cost.[195] At about the same time, others, such as the Stour Sailing Club

---

188   EC 8 August 1942.
189   EC 22 September 1940.
190   EC 30 September 1939.
191   J. Williams, *Leigh-On-Sea: a history* (Andover, 2002), p. 115
192   D. Hamilton, *Orsett Golf Club 1899–1999* (2000), pp. 36–7.
193   K. Warden and M. Williams, *Chelmsford Golf Club 1893–1993* (Chelmsford, 1993), pp. 54–5.
194   ST 27 October 1943.
195   ECS 9 March 1940.

at Manningtree, also decided to carry on.[196] Even small-scale activities were affected. As soon as war broke out all owners of boats with outboard motors were asked not to use them on rivers in case the noise obscured any air-raid warning or all-clear; the authorities were also afraid that they may panic people into believing that Germans were landing.[197] By the summer of 1940 such considerations were academic as the government-imposed coastal restriction zone effectively prevented owners from even getting to their boats, let alone using them. They were left idle until 1945.[198]

The war inevitably affected people's leisure pursuits and impinged upon all forms of entertainment, but not in the catastrophic way predicted before the war, when aerial bombing was thought capable of destroying civilisation itself. Sporting events played by young men before large crowds, such as football and county cricket, were limited by conscription, travel restrictions, war work and Civil Defence duties, and the leagues they had thrived in dwindled to small-scale localised affairs. Coastal pastimes such as boating and fishing, as well as holidaymaking, vanished for much or all of the war. Nevertheless, pre-war pursuits that could be carried on indoors or in shelters, such as reading and whist drives, and sports played by those too young or too old for conscription, or by war workers, carried on as usual. Gardening continued as both a pastime and an essential part of the 'Dig For Victory' campaign. A thirst for art, drama and music flourished in the uncertain atmosphere of the times. Social activities were maintained in every town and village, although they were very often subordinated to the war effort, becoming fundraising events for some wartime cause or other. In this aspect of wartime life leisure and entertainment were characterised by both continuity and change, but not even the direst of circumstances could bring them to a standstill.

---

196   ECT 13 April 1940.
197   BA 9 September 1939.
198   J. Wise, *The story of the Blackwater Sailing Club* (Maldon, 1999), p. 72.

7

Criminals, conchies and clergymen

The seedier side of life

People adapted their choice of entertainment and leisure activities to wartime circumstances. In the same way, individuals chose whether to behave lawfully or to exploit these conditions by circumventing or breaking some restrictions, thus making life more tolerable. More crimes were committed during the war than at any time since 1918. Nationally between 1939 and 1945 the number of reported crimes per year rose by 60 per cent from 300,000 to almost half a million.[1] In Essex the number of indictable offences rose from 6,730 in 1939 to 13,107 by 1945, an increase of about 90 per cent.[2] However, non-serious crime declined owing to the huge reduction in both motoring offences, as the use of private motoring was drastically reduced, and drunkenness. In fact, the main reason for the increase in overall levels of crime was the introduction of new types of laws to break. The Emergency Powers (Defence) Bill, passed in August 1939 and renewed annually throughout the war, set aside all existing laws and laid down huge numbers of new ones which were designed to safeguard the security of the realm. Unfortunately the blackout and a 25 per cent reduction in the country's police force made it easier for many crimes to be committed.[3]

Criminal prosecutions in the county followed the national pattern of the war. In the first few months, even though air raids did not materialise, great emphasis was placed on strict observance of the blackout. At Southend 147 people were prosecuted in the first four months of the war for showing light from house windows. During 1940 there were 343 prosecutions, and the figures failed to fall below 200 in the last two years of the war.[4] After the fall of France, when the authorities were concerned at the possibility of both invasion and air raids, magistrates became less tolerant of blackout offences, especially in coastal areas. For instance, Walker Sergeant of Brightlingsea was imprisoned for a

---

1   J. Gardiner, *Wartime: Britain 1939–1945* (London, 2004), pp. 588–9; D. Thomas, *An underworld at war: spivs, deserters, racketeers and civilians in the Second World War* (London, 2003), p. 16.
2   ERO C/DX/1/1/5–9, Chief Constable of Essex annual reports, 1938–41, 1944–5.
3   S. Hylton, *Their darkest hour: the hidden history of the home front 1939–1945* (Stroud, 2001), pp. 186–7.
4   ERO D/BC 1/7/5/4, Southend Chief Constable's annual reports, 1939–45.

month for frequent infringements of the blackout.[5] Nevertheless, many people maintained a lax attitude and there were 300,000 prosecutions nationally for blackout infringements in 1940.[6]

The government was eager to maintain a united front against the threat of enemy action and was anxious to stamp out defeatist talk in case it undermined the nation's morale. Throughout the country this led to a spate of court appearances by individuals who were thought to have made such utterances. The authorities were especially vigilant after the fall of France, when people feared that defeatists and fifth columnists might assist invading German troops.[7] Allan Shippey, a well-known Colchester stationer with pacifist beliefs, was accused of making a statement 'liable to spread despondency or alarm'. It was alleged that he had said that when the Germans invaded the government would flee to Ireland or Canada. The charges were not proved, although the judge remarked that Shippey's comment was 'foolish and very indiscreet'. Similar charges were made against Frank Cadman from Lexden, although these too were dropped. Both men were known to have anti-war, pacifism sentiments, Cadman being a Quaker, and their prosecutions were thought by some to have been politically motivated.[8] However, the prosecution of 30-year-old Phyllis Bateman, a Post Office clerk from Clacton and a former BUF member, was on more solid ground. She was detained by soldiers after saying to them,

> Why have you allowed yourselves to be led into a war which is of no concern of yours? Why don't you get together and revolt? I have heard Mosley speak and I think he is a fine man. I admire his policy, and we should not have gone to war. Germany is more superior in force and arms to us, and I think it is useless to continue the war. Thousands will be slaughtered for nothing. We ought to ask for peace terms now and save the slaughter.[9]

People were also prosecuted for actions that would have seemed inoffensive in peacetime. One man was fined £5 for not handing over stray pigeons to the authorities.[10] These had to be examined in case they carried messages from the enemy or even from fifth columnists. Unofficial photography of wartime features was illegal. George Valance was fined £1 for photographing a bomb crater on his own property.[11] In September 1940, as the Blitz began, the bodies

---

5   ECT 20 July 1940.
6   Gardiner, *Wartime*, p. 589.
7   Hylton, *Darkest hour*, pp. 184–5.
8   ECS 20 July 1940, ECT 20 July 1940.
9   ECT 27 July 1940.
10   ECT 25 January 1941.
11   ECT 10 August 1940.

of dead German airmen were found throughout Essex. In the first prosecution of its kind, three men from Sampford and Bardfield were fined £3 each for removing articles from one such body, namely a ring, cufflinks and a pistol.[12] Ernest Edwards, the Southend ARP warden and diarist, was first on the scene when a Heinkel bomber was brought down in the town. Although surrounded by the burned and mangled bodies of the crew, he 'managed to get a few souvenirs including the glove of one of the crew'.[13] He got away with it because he was not seen.

Just as in the Great War, much emphasis was placed on ensuring that the people who were fighting the war on the Home Front were kept supplied with the necessities of life. Rationing was introduced and a whole host of regulations was put in place to ensure that people were not cheated by unscrupulous traders and shopkeepers. Consequently, the courts were full of traders who broke the new regulations. Large firms were not immune from legal action; in early 1942 Stratford magistrates imposed a record £16,000 fine on a Leytonstone firm for purchase tax and quota frauds involving the sale of more goods than was allowed.[14] Less severe was the fine given to Paxman and Davey, Colchester's premier engineering firm, whose canteen manager was found guilty of failing to keep an accurate record of meals and hot drinks, an offence in which the firm colluded. The court believed that the firm's failure was designed to cover up the fact that it obtained over 2,200 lbs of goods more than it was allowed.[15]

Many shopkeepers and smaller businesses were just as willing to break the rules and some carried out their frauds with barefaced effrontery.[16] Lilian Caroen, who ran a café in Chelmsford, sent grossly inflated figures to the Food Office to obtain more rationed goods than she was entitled to. Over a period of four months she claimed to have taken £5,856 in cash, whereas her real takings had been £700. She was sent to prison for four months.[17] Claude Wilson, the licensee of the Golden Fleece in Chelmsford, was fined £81 for falsifying statements to obtain rationed food in amounts that he was not entitled to. When food inspectors searched his hotel they discovered two cupboards containing rationed and unrationed food, including a hundredweight each of tea and margarine, two quarters of butter, 156 lbs of jam, 14 lbs of marmalade, four hundredweight of various types of sugar and quantities of lentils, flour and tinned food, constituting a veritable Aladdin's Cave of hoarded goods. He claimed that he had bought the food at his previous establishment in Harrow

---

12   ECS 21 September 1940.
13   ERO S3150, 31 August 1940.
14   SE 6 February 1942.
15   ECT 9 January 1943.
16   Hylton, *Darkest hour*, pp. 196–7.
17   EC 16 July 1943.

before rationing began, but the court dismissed this claim.[18] Wartime rationing regulations were so complex that people were prosecuted for an astonishingly wide range of offences. To ensure that there were no epidemics of animal disease, and also to limit profiteering, slaughtering could be carried out only in authorised places. In 1941 three men from Colchester were fined £50, £40 and £16 respectively for contravening this regulation.[19] The importance of domestic crop production was such that magistrates showed little leniency towards farmers who allowed their animals, usually cattle, to stray onto arable land.[20] Misuse of valuable feeding stuffs was also a serious offence. Constance Pelly of Ingatestone was fined the large sum of £30 for feeding oatmeal to chickens when it was illegal to use it as animal food.[21]

Large numbers of ordinary people were prepared to make false declarations in order to obtain more rationed goods than they were entitled to. In December 1942 three Colchester residents were fined £5 each for making false declarations to obtain free milk. Only those with an average weekly wage of £3 10s qualified for free milk, and these people earned £4. At the Colchester Police Court it was said regarding the witnessing of forms of declaration for milk that the reliability of some 2,000 forms were regarded as dubious.[22] Cases of looting were comparatively rare outside Metropolitan Essex, mainly because the intensive air-raids that offered these opportunities were not as great. After the heavy raid on Chelmsford in April 1943 Henry Hodgson, a painter, was imprisoned for receiving looted goods. Edward Perry, another Chelmsford resident, was jailed for a year for looting after the same raid. His offence was considered to be particularly heinous because he abused his position on the Special Repair Service that patched up bombed buildings in the town.[23] In 1942 the use of private cars was prohibited, but some individuals still tried to evade the regulation. Joseph Wells, a Chelmsford doctor, was fined £35 for misusing his legitimate petrol allowance when he twice drove to his golf club and back.[24] Even large reputable concerns lapsed in this respect. The South Essex Waterworks Company was fined £145 for colluding in its employees using company cars in an unauthorised manner.[25]

The introduction of rationing, combined with the activities of both criminals and opportunists, created a black market in almost all types of goods. While there were plenty of unscrupulous individuals there were also huge

18   EC 31 July 1942.
19   ECT 14 June 1941.
20   ECT 24 May 1941.
21   EC 24 September 1943.
22   ECT 22 December 1942.
23   EC 28 May, 11 June 1943.
24   EC 4 December 1942.
25   EC 16 April 1943.

numbers of people who, while striving patriotically to win the war, did not hesitate to evade any regulations if they proved inconvenient, particularly if family members wanted certain items. There is no way of assessing the size of the black market but evidence in the form of anecdotes and from police and magistrate's courts suggests that most people resorted to it either occasionally or on a regular basis. Elsie Shingler, a young working woman from Leyton, recalled that

> a lot of people used to run out (of food) especially if they had families, but if you had a bit of money and you knew people you could use the black market. It was under the counter straight from the shopkeeper. It didn't do no harm [sic] but it was all illegal. We'd get it in the little places.[26]

Black market dealing occurred throughout the county but it was particularly focused on its markets, and the epicentre of such activity was Romford market. Here black market goods were displayed and sold openly and without subtlety. Rationing coupons were not used in these transactions. Romford market's notoriety led to questions in parliament and protests by legitimate traders and the borough council. Plain clothes police officers and government inspectors scoured the market but black marketeers warned their associates by use of a tick-tack system. One trader, Benny Ralton, complained that 'the whole trouble has been caused by a small clique who come down from East London every now and then with no scruples about honest trading, and hop back home again as soon as they have got rid of their stuff'.[27]

Theft and the black market were connected by a sort of criminal umbilical cord. The theft and selling on of clothing and petrol coupons and food ration books was widespread. Three Colchester women were convicted of selling clothing coupons in October 1944.[28] The demand for clothing coupons made them extremely valuable and the black market in such items was fed by audacious thefts, such as the one at Walthamstow in 1942, in which thousands were stolen.[29] In a theft on an even larger scale, 100,000 complete ration books worth £500,000 were stolen at Romford in 1944.[30] One Colchester newsagent was taken to court for receiving more than 16,000 cigarettes that had been stolen from the garrison by soldiers.[31] This was only the tip of the iceberg in a garrison town such as Colchester, where the theft of military property by servicemen was

---

26   J. Steele (ed.), *A working class war: tales from two families* (London, 1995), p. 18.
27   EC 3 April 1942, ECS 31 January 1942.
28   ECT 3 October 1944.
29   SE 6 March 1942.
30   Thomas, *Underworld at war*, p. 160.
31   ECT 20 January 1945.

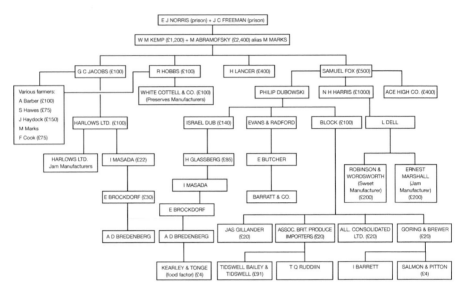

Figure 7.1. Diagram produced by the Essex Police to outline the wide range of businesses and individuals who were prosecuted as a result of investigations of the theft of a huge amount of molasses from Holehaven Wharf in 1941 by an organised gang from Canvey Island.

commonplace. Food, bedding, blankets and petrol were sold on to shopkeepers, friends and anyone with the cash to buy whatever was on offer. On one occasion two men were caught filling vehicles with 48 gallons of army petrol at the back of the Essex Arms in Colchester. The man found guilty of receiving was jailed for three months.[32] The Food Executive Officer of Barking was imprisoned for three years for writing illegal permits to grocers allowing them to obtain ten times their sugar allocation. The grocers were also imprisoned or fined.[33] The scale of individuals' and businesses' involvement in the distribution of stolen goods was made clear by the police investigation that followed the theft of 232 tons of molasses from a warehouse in Holehaven. The criminals sold it at £3 a ton, although it was later changing hands for up to £49 a ton.[34]

Even reputable firms were up to their necks in the theft of government property. The manager of Weddel's, a Colchester wholesale meat dealer, was found guilty of stealing two tons of army meat valued at £300[35] and sentenced to three years in prison, one year for each of three offences. Five men were given various sentences for receiving, but the court's greatest opprobrium – a sentence of fifteen months' imprisonment – was heaped on a sixth receiver, a

32 ECT 5 April 1941.
33 Thomas, *Underworld at war*, pp. 140–1.
34 ST 22 October 1941, 21 January 1942.
35 ECT 12 April 1941.

butcher who at the time had been the secretary and group organiser for the meat distribution of local butchers. The Recorder commented that

> when the country is fighting for its life and food problems are of the highest importance, you chose to make money by buying Government property which I am satisfied you knew was stolen. In my view you have put forward an impudent defence. You have gone into the witness box and given a thoroughly false and perjured story.[36]

The mass evacuation of Clacton's and Southend's civilians in 1940 also left thousands of empty properties that in the blackout were a thieves' paradise. Not surprisingly, between 1941 and 1945 house- and shop-breaking offences in Southend rose by more than 300 per cent.[37] Once the ban on the use of private cars was introduced in 1942 the theft of bicycles reached epidemic proportions in some areas. During 1944 1,555 bicycles were stolen in the Essex County Constabulary area.[38]

The war led not only to rising levels of crime but also, apparently, to a decline in the nation's moral standards[39] fuelled by circumstances such as the absence of fathers on active service, the employment of women and teenage girls on war work, the arrival of servicemen from overseas – particularly Americans – and a moral panic about increasing levels of criminality among young people. Ernest Bryant of Brightlingsea condemned the 'present wholesale most callous greed of the people – their frivolity and insolence, stealing, racketeering, empty-headed amusements and unbridled sexual promiscuity'.[40] R.B. Bertin, vicar of Leyton, bemoaned the sale of 'vile and suggestive' literature in the area, and the *Stratford Express* focused on foreign books. 'The covers of these books,' it noted,

> are invariably devoted to a picture of a seductive looking female, displayed in garish colour, designed with the sole object of catching the eye and capturing the interest of those who apparently have nothing better to do than to waste their time and money upon such rubbish.[41]

One of the main social indicators used to support the theory of a national moral decline was the incidence of venereal disease. Between 1930 and 1939 there were between 1,500 and 2,000 new cases each year in Essex. Southend's Medical Officer of Health reported that in 1938 his department was dealing with 749

---

36   ECT 26 April 1941.
37   ERO D/BC 1/7/5/4.
38   ERO C/DX/1/1/8, EC 27 October, 1 December 1944.
39   Hylton, *Darkest hour*, pp. 148–50.
40   ECS 28 April 1944.
41   SE 1 May 1942.

cases.[42] During the war there was an exponential increase in Essex, with the number of new cases rising from 1,048 a year in 1940 to 2,732 in 1945. The county's Medical Officer believed that the large rise in cases at the end of the war was caused by returning soldiers who had been infected abroad, and who in some cases had not completed their course of treatment before returning home. Such was the concern at the prevalence of venereal disease that when the documentary film *Social Enemy Number One*, which dealt with the phenomenon, was shown at the Regal, Colchester, in 1943, the *Essex County Telegraph* took a party of local notables to see it and assessed their response. The Mayoress, an assortment of clerics, the matron of the hostel for women and girls, a female probation officer and representatives of the ATS, welfare and medical staff were all present. The party preferred the documentary to an American film on venereal disease that had been shown earlier, but all agreed that both films underplayed both parental responsibility in sexual matters and the prevailing ignorance of the topic.[43]

The war did create circumstances that could be exploited by people of both sexes who were prepared to challenge existing sexual mores. Nevertheless, social unease about declining standards of sexual morality almost invariably pointed to women and young girls as being at the root of this phenomenon, partly because they were often left to face the consequences of sexual activity and partly because they were regarded as the victims of predatory males. On the other hand, the age-old beliefs that 'boys will be boys' and that they needed to sow their 'wild oats' still prevailed. Where boys were concerned the law and society seemed less concerned with moral danger than with their contribution to rising crime. A study of the records of the Southend Juvenile Court from 1939 to 1942 reveals that boys were involved in a total of 828 detected crimes.[44] Of these, 345 (42 per cent) were thefts and 223 (27 per cent) were breaking and entering. The latter crime was made easier by the blackout and the large number of shops left empty by evacuation. Fifty-three per cent of all theft was committed by boys of thirteen and under; the same age group committed 62 per cent of all breaking and entering offences. In both cases boys as young as eight were brought before the court.[45]

When the Chelmsford Diocesan Welfare Association pointed to an 'enormous' need for moral welfare work in 1943, it focused entirely on 'vulnerable' women – citing as examples the lonely young woman whose husband was serving abroad, 'and [who] in that loneliness finds companionship with another man'; 'the young girl of fourteen who loses her head because for the first time she has

42   ERO Essex Medical Officer of Health annual reports 1930–9; ERO D/BC 1/6/1/37, Southend Medical Officer of Health, annual report 1938.
43   ECT 22 June 1943.
44   Undertaken by the author.
45   ERO D/BC 1/1/13/2/12–15, Southend Juvenile Court Registers, 1942–45.

a pay envelope containing 30s or more'; the woman who marries after a brief courtship and discovers after her husband goes off in the armed forces 'that she did not care enough'. It was teenage girls, not boys, who were brought to the courts because they were considered to be in moral danger (in other words, they were likely to be in danger of, or actually involved in, sexual activity) and in need of care. When Miss M.G. Bird, a probation officer attached to Stratford court, produced her annual report in 1941, she seemed to support this interpretation:

> In the latter months of 1940 when home life, and to some extent, working life became interrupted by raids, many young girls, chafing under restricted liberty (real or imaginary) within their homes, disappeared. They felt safe from pursuit by harassed mothers, who were too fearful to venture forth in the gunfire or who had to look after young children at home. Such girls rarely bothered to find lodgings but spent the night in public shelters, often behaving in such a way as to result in complaints being made. They had no place to keep their clothing, nor of washing them, and as for a bath, that was an unpleasant experience from which, by the fortunes of war they were mercifully spared. Consequently, when these girls were at last found … they were pictures of bedraggled, deplorably unsavoury womanhood.[46]

The authorities were often appalled at the way some young girls challenged what were seen as traditional patterns of behaviour. A fourteen-year-old Colchester girl was taken to court for associating with soldiers. The court implied that there must have been a sexual side to these associations when it was said that she had arrived in school wearing slacks and cosmetics and was smoking and coming home late at night.[47]

The lure of the uniform was undoubtedly irresistible to some young (and older) women, and the main reason why young girls were considered to be in moral danger was the fact that they were beyond the control of their parents and associated with soldiers. For instance, in 1941 two thirteen-year-old girls in Colchester who frequented pubs and were seen with soldiers were taken into care.[48] One eighteen-year-old young woman was prosecuted for travelling without a train ticket, but she was also described as a 'border-line mental defective', 'man-mad', and a danger to herself.[49] A similar line was taken with two girls, aged eighteen and nineteen, who seem to have worked as prostitutes in a Colchester brothel. Both girls had had a child, they associated with soldiers

---

46   SE 24 January 1941.
47   ECT 13 July 1943.
48   ECT 11 January 1941.
49   ECT 8 March 1941.

and 'also coloured troops' and they slept in shelters with soldiers. They were said to have 'disgraced their womanhood' and a thorough medical and mental report was ordered before sentencing.[50] However, it was not just teenage girls who were seen as endangering the moral fabric of the nation, but a certain type of older woman, too. In the case described above the Colchester woman brothel-keeper was only twenty years old and had previously been jailed for a similar offence. Nancy Pullen, a 23-year-old Wivenhoe woman, had already been convicted of child cruelty and abandonment when she was convicted of living off immoral earnings. In June 1942 she was found on the garrison 'lying on the grass on the Abbey Field, surrounded by a dozen soldiers'. That same evening she was discovered with another half a dozen soldiers and 'on June 15th she was found with a soldier, wrapped in a blanket'. When a fourteen-year-old boy was convicted of assaulting younger children the case revealed a catalogue of neglect by the three mothers of the children. They, too, did not conform to the traditional pattern of respectable motherhood. One had seven children, three of them illegitimate, and all three women 'often took men into their houses'. The court declared that the children were in moral danger, and some were placed in foster homes, with the court recommending that they should never be returned to their mothers.[51] The consumption of alcohol by girls and young women was regarded as a major factor in their delinquent behaviour. At the Brewster sessions at Saffron Walden publicans were criticised for serving teenage girls, and the practice of 'treating' – girls being bought drinks by men – was condemned as abhorrent. The town's police complained of constantly having to take sixteen-year-old girls home dead drunk.[52]

In 1943 the Essex Federation of Women's Institutes was addressed by Dr Youll of the county medical staff. Explaining why the focus was on girls rather than boys, she said, 'I think it is the girl or young woman who sets the standard of any religion.' She added, '[Y]ou must tell the girls the frightful risks they are running if they persist in a certain type of life.' Those present responded by reiterating their desire for women police, a no treating order, a curfew for young girls similar to the one introduced at Bath, which covered girls under fifteen years old, and a programme of education by welfare workers. At the diocesan conference that year the Bishop of Chelmsford suggested an 8pm curfew for all girls under the age of eighteen. He also urged the imposition of legal restraints on serving alcohol to young people, especially girls.[53] The Diocesan Moral Welfare Association provided advice and shelter for unmarried mothers from all backgrounds, as well as working to prevent young girls and

50   ECT 16 November 1943.
51   ECT 28 September 1943.
52   EC 20 March 1944.
53   EC 8, 22 October 1943.

women away from home from being exploited. Up to the end of 1944 about 6,000 women and girls (not all of them unmarried mothers) and children had been helped, with about half of them having stayed in one of the five diocesan hostels, some of them for up to six months.[54]

The prevailing concerns about sexual immorality during the war stretched further than just to young girls. Early in the war one person overheard a conversation involving a Chelmsford councillor bemoaning the number of women in the town who were being 'ruined' by men who had little to think about but sex.[55] In 1942 Mass Observation carried out a Town and Country Survey of Chelmsford that included observations on how sexual attitudes had been affected by the war.[56] It noted that traditional forms of sexual behaviour had survived, although there was less restraint and more freedom. In the same way, there was more talk about sex by men, and by girls, too, because the latter were working alongside men where there used to be all men. The survey concluded that total war rendered morality of secondary importance and that as society was out of normal gear so morality suffered. It gave examples of a more casual approach to sex, commenting that couples indulged in forms of sexual activity in cinemas and dances halls, standing in shop doorways, beside walls and in lonely paths and places. In summer, when the blackout did not provide cover, couples were said to seek out areas of tall grass. At about the same time as this report was being written a twelve-year-old Braintree boy was birched for an offence against a younger girl. A Mrs L. Killick of Chelmsford, who described this as 'a savage and brutalising punishment', clearly saw a causal link between childhood conduct and overt displays of sexual behaviour by adults. She wrote to the *Essex Chronicle* to say

> I would suggest that before this magistrate passes any more of these sentences he should visit the parks, and highways and byways where our children play, and see them littered with canoodling couples who do not make the slightest attempt to keep their love-making private.[57]

Eric Rudsdale was appalled at the way in which every aspect of sex was publicised or seemed to be available in a casual manner. In 1941 he wrote

> I note that even that little shop in Crouch Street … which used to be a sweet shop when I was at school, and has been empty for some time, has now opened as a 'sex shop'. A large board outside says 'Madame

54   ERO D/CAc 12/1/22, 24, Chelmsford Diocesan Moral Welfare Association, annual report, 1943, 1945.
55   R. Douglas Brown, *East Anglia 1940* (Lavenham, 1981), p. 19.
56   MOA TC66 66/3/F Town and Country survey, Chelmsford, 1942.
57   EC 18 September 1942.

Lady Herbalist; advice free to Ladies, consult at once', and on the door 'Rubber Goods Supplied'. I think that previously only about two places in the town sold 'french letters' and 'pessaries'. Certainly nothing quite as blatant as this has ever appeared before. The window contains boxes of 'female pills', sheaths etc.

In his opinion 'the amount of sexual perversion which goes on among troops and civilians alike is enormous'. In public lavatories he frequently saw things written on the walls offering homosexual assignations. The language used was of the crudest type.[58] At the entrance to another lavatory he discovered, written in pencil, the words 'All Military Personnel: Pros given here. U.S. Army'.[59] On one occasion he heard two Canadian soldiers trying to gain access to the castle for a sexual encounter.[60]

It is impossible to quantify the amount of casual, opportunistic prostitution in wartime Essex, but it was likely to have been as widespread as it was throughout the rest of the country.[61] The number of cases brought before the courts was very small and on the whole they suggested that the women exploiting the new circumstances were running brothels on a small scale from private houses or rented accommodation. Eric Rudsdale bemoaned the transportation of young girls, some aged fifteen or sixteen, into American army camps in army trucks nicknamed 'passion wagons'. He alleged that local opinion was outraged by such activities, especially as in other circumstances these girls would have been arrested as prostitutes.[62] Later he wrote, 'the amount of casual and professional prostitution in this town is simply staggering'.[63] In 1944 the Colchester police were stopping every woman in the town and checking ID cards. Any women found to be from London were of course entering a prohibited area, but they were also suspected of being prostitutes. Consequently, local women found being asked to show their ID cards insulting. Rudsdale was in a café when he heard one woman say that she had refused to show hers: '… and I told him, if you speak to me like that, I'll tell my mother. I'm a very good girl, I am, I don't go about with Yanks.'[64]

A notorious case of this sort occurred in Chelmsford in 1944 when Madge Gooley, a Londoner, arrived in the town. Police were always on hand to turn away visitors who had no permit to be in the prohibited area and she returned home without leaving the station. Sometime later in London she was arrested, brought back before the Chelmsford bench and sentenced to one month's

---

58   ERO D/DU 888/24, journal, 6 May 1941.
59   ERO D/DU 888/26/4, journal, 11 June 1943.
60   ERO D/DU 88/24, journal, 6 June 1941.
61   Hylton, *Darkest hour*, pp. 146–8.
62   ERO D/DU 888/26/5, journal, 7 August 1943.
63   ERO D/DU 888/27/2, journal, 9 March 1944.
64   ERO D/DU 888/27/4, journal, 13 July 1944.

imprisonment, the maximum sentence available, for entering a prohibited area. The *Essex Chronicle* felt that she had been imprisoned because she was or had been a prostitute rather than for violating the prohibited area, and that a miscarriage of justice had been committed. Letters poured in from individuals and organisations supporting her and criticising what one described as 'local Bumbles, dressed in a little brief authority'. Samuel Looker of Billericay condemned the court's action, asserting that 'it is not a court of morals'. The Maldon Communist party lent its voice to the protest and the National Council for Civil Liberties contacted the Home Secretary, Herbert Morrison. He refused to intervene and Madge Gooley had to serve her full sentence.[65]

The new wartime conventions that some people chose to adopt could create difficulties. When a young woman wrote to the *Essex Chronicle* to say that she would dance only with servicemen, not civilians, the chairman of the local British Legion who wrote in her defence said,

> It never occurred to me that any civilian would take anything but a back seat in times like these. Nothing but fighting will win this war and all other efforts are subsidiary to this. The man who wields the sword is of far more importance than the man who makes the sword.[66]

Other letters, however, attacked the young woman's stance. One Chelmsford woman wrote of those women befriending servicemen:

> Most of them appear to be either soured spinsters like the Ilford Land Army, or gold-digging sluts who prey on Servicemen looking for companionship. Several Americans have told me how these brats have cleaned them out of all their cigarettes and a week's pay in a single evening. British servicemen are safe from these women because their week's pay wouldn't last an hour.[67]

Another social phenomenon that was regarded as indicating moral decline in wartime was the increase in bigamy, committed by both service personnel and civilians, both men and women. In February 1942, of the thirteen cases at the Essex Assizes eleven involved bigamy. Apart from the obvious benefits of acquiring a new partner, some individuals used the opportunity to obtain a government separation allowance if the marriage involved service personnel who went abroad. Not all bigamous servicemen ended up with stiff prison sentences. Mr Justice Singleton pointed out that the judges

---

65   EC 25 August, 1, 15 September 1944.
66   EC 9 June 1944.
67   EC 2 June 1944.

realise and they are often so reminded, that an able-bodied man is of more use in the Navy or Army than he is in prison, and yet they have to remember that if such offences are passed over lightly, that fact in itself may encourage other people to think lightly of the crime, and may lead to a further increase in it. It is indeed surprising to find that men who would not stoop to obtaining money or goods by false pretences sometimes think little of obtaining a woman or young girl by such means.[68]

Nevertheless, the sentences for servicemen who committed bigamy, usually a few months in prison, were light when compared with that meted out to Madge Gooley.

Dissenters and their critics

Just as in the First World War, the government was prepared to accommodate those with a conscientious objection to performing any form of military service or work that promoted the war effort. The National Services (Armed Forces) Act of 1 September 1939 required all men aged eighteen to 41 to register and be placed on the Military Service Register and be liable for call-up. Anyone who objected to having his name put on the register could apply for it to be put on the Register of conscientious objectors instead and was called before a local tribunal to plead his case.[69] In the Great War there had been 16,000 conscientious objectors in the years 1916–18, following the introduction of conscription. By the end of the Second World War the total was 59,192, just 1.2 per cent of the five million men called up;[70] the much larger number is partly explained by the fact that conscription was in place throughout the war, which lasted two years longer than its predecessor.

Young men who were not in the forces were often treated with suspicion and regarded as shirkers. One serving soldier, who returned to Essex on leave in the winter of 1939/40, was deeply distressed by what he saw:

It seemed that all the best tables in the restaurants and the best seats in the theatres were filled, not by men in the fighting forces but by young men in civilian clothes, while the brave lads, whose leave is so short, had to take a back seat or stand in a queue.[71]

68 EC journal, 13 February 1942.
69 R. Mackay, *The test of war: inside Britain 1939–1945* (London, 1999), p. 106.
70 Hylton, *Darkest hour*, p. 85.
71 EFJ March 1940.

Some of the comments that were made about conscientious objectors were scarcely more measured than they had been a generation earlier. One letter to the press signed 'Loyalist' asserted that 'A man who will not fight for his country does not deserve to live in it.'[72] N.R. Bowler of Mile End, Colchester, described conscientious objectors as 'cowardly opportunists' who should be compelled to wear 'some type of badge with a suitable monogram displayed prominently'.[73] The National Services Act had not attempted to define the concept of conscientious objection, preferring to leave it to the discretion and sense of justice of the tribunals. However, the editor of the *Burnham Advertiser* could see no possible argument to justify men taking up such a position:

> The conflict in which we are engaged is essentially a battle between good and evil … If the present war was being fought by us for the purposes of aggrandisement in any way, one could understand the position of 'conscientious objection'. But the reverse is the case; we are fighting, so that people, ourselves and all other nations, may live in freedom, having the liberty to profess our own faith and to express our own opinion. All conscientious able-bodied men should therefore be prepared to fight to the uttermost on the side of right and not stand idly by profiting by the bravery and self-sacrifice of others.[74]

Young people were also acutely aware of the dilemma facing these men. Mary Hellen, a sixth-former from Tottenham transplanted to Saffron Walden with her school, wrote of the terrible dilemma facing some conscientious objectors:

> England expects …
> How often has he heard those words of old,
> And vainly sought to turn his thoughts away
> From war, and what his duty then would be.
> He is a coward, weakling – yes, he knows,
> And yet he cannot overcome his dread
> Of killing fellow-men, and being killed.
> Why must he face the horrors all for nought?
> If men must fight, why was he born a man?
> He hopes to gain exemption, yet he knows,
> With tortured conscience grappling with his fears,
> That England still expects.[75]

---

72 ECS 17 February 1940.
73 ECS 2 March 1940.
74 BA 1 June 1940.
75 ERO D/DU 1712/1 Tottenham High School evacuation magazine, May 1940 (at Saffron Walden).

Organisations such as the Peace Pledge Union provided advice to conscientious objectors to allow them to prepare for their appearance before the tribunals. This is why N.R. Bowler's letter attacked them for their 'carefully tutored and rehearsed views' – but, in view of what was occurring in Germany at the time, his suggestion that they be compelled to wear an identifying badge was inappropriate, to say the least.[76]

Some parishes were prepared to provide assistance. The Revd W. Sydney Smith of Billericay was known to be sympathetic to conscientious objectors. A letter to him on 11 October 1939 urged him to do all he could to help pacifists 'who may soon be suffering here too'. The writer Freda Book asked him to get in touch 'with the young men who are feeling isolated in their faith, and to give them moral support or practical explanation of the regulations against the time when they come before tribunals'. Billericay had an active branch of both the Fellowship of Reconciliation and the Peace Pledge Union, and a joint letter from these groups to the Revd M.N. Lake of Laindon noted that 'There may be in your congregations people who feel unable to take part in this war – young men who, whether because they are earnestly endeavouring to live Christian lives, or for whatever reason, refuse to take life.'[77]

Although conscientious objectors were unpopular, public disapproval of them was relatively muted during the Phoney War, when Britain seemed in no danger of attack. When the Liberal *Essex County Telegraph* printed a statement of the Fellowship of Reconciliation's beliefs, Leonard Read of Langham praised the *Telegraph* for including views 'with which you and the bulk of the country disagree, even abominate!'. He went on to say that 'It is, I say, encouraging, in the welter of insanity, panic, camouflage of truth, centralised regimenting of yeomen masses, and misinformation, to see a paper – would it were a national daily! – that is not afraid to print such comment.'[78] However, this is not to say that disapproval did not flare up during this period. Although press coverage of the proceedings of tribunals was far less comprehensive than in the Great War, the proceedings of the East Anglian Tribunal were reported in brief terms. For some even this was too much. R. Newton of Rayleigh objected on the grounds that they advertised the 'weak, wishy-washy, namby-pamby plaints', and 'feeble wailings and specious nonsense' of conscientious objectors.[79] On the other hand, the Revd L.C. Blower, Rector of Chignal St James and Mashbury, wanted reporting to continue because the men concerned 'were a danger to their country, and should rightly be held up to public scorn'.[80]

---

76 ECS 2 March 1940.
77 ERO D/P 516/29/3A Billericay St Mary Magdalene PCC, loose papers 1939, minutes of the Billericay PCC, 1931–41, letters 11 October 1939.
78 ECC 20 October 1939; ECT 24 October 1939.
79 ECC 29 December 1939.
80 ECC 5 January 1940.

Local councils found themselves in the front line of debate because some of their employees were conscientious objectors. This presented them with a dilemma, in that these men were being paid from public funds that also financed the war. Others feared that they might be promoted into the positions previously held by servicemen. This often caused acute divisions of opinion in council chambers whenever the matter came up for discussion. In February 1940 Colchester Borough Council appointed a conscientious objector named Alan Cooper in the Treasurer's Department. There was immediate opposition to the appointment, both within and outside of the council, because Cooper had replaced a man who had just left to join up. An attempt to dismiss him and readvertise the job was narrowly defeated. In the debate one councillor condemned all conscientious objectors:

> They would sit in a comfortable chair, reading books on how to evade national service and would study leaflets issued by certain 'Stop-the-war' societies who were attempting to 'mass-produce' Conscientious Objectors: they were content to sleep at night undisturbed by the fact that other men at sea braving the terrible perils of the mines, etc, in order that food might be provided. Their motto was 'Let others sacrifice all. We will sacrifice nothing.'[81]

Comments such as this appalled some people, even if they did not necessarily approve of conscientious objectors. J. Andrews, a Colchester resident, wrote condemning what he described as 'the heresy hunt' in the council chamber.[82]

However, the sudden collapse of France in the summer of 1940 focused the spotlight more harshly on pacifists. Support for the Peace Pledge Union fell away and even the staunchest of its well-known supporters announced their support for the war.[83] Public awareness that pro-German collaborators had assisted the German armies in the Low Countries meant that there was widespread concern about fifth columnists. Conscientious objectors, who had hitherto been viewed as rather distasteful shirkers, although not pro-Nazis, now became a potential fifth column, with their refusal to fight and their anti-war propaganda having the potential to sap Britain's morale. The fact that Britain's very survival seemed to hang in the balance only served to accentuate the public's alienation from conscientious objectors. Consequently, during 1940 and 1941 further steps were taken against them over and above the ongoing work of tribunals.

In July 1940 the issue was raised once more in the council chamber at Colchester. By now the council employed three men in addition to Cooper who

---

81   ECC 10 February, 9 March 1940.
82   ECC 30 March 1940.
83   Such as Bertrand Russell, A.M. Joad and the author A.A. Milne; Mackay, *Test of war*, p. 108.

were conscientious objectors. A fierce debate ensued around the motion 'it being imperative that the nation as a whole should rise as one man to resist invasion, the council pledges itself not to employ any man who refuses to take up arms for our national defence'. Councillor Wright said that 'I don't like to have to pay rates to support a Conscientious Objector or anybody not willing to protect our own native soil.' Others were adamant that they regarded the motion as the antithesis of the British concepts of fair play and justice. Alderman Alec Blaxill felt that the war was being fought 'for the sanctity of treaties'. The government had laid down a legal basis for conscientious objection and yet the council was seeking to ignore it. 'We have entered into a contract,' he argued, 'and now we seek to break it simply because we are appealed to from panic and fear. We are asked to vote because we are asked to be afraid. That is what it amounts to. Well, let us have a little more "guts".' Another who was present, Alderman Smith, asserted that 'It is against the rights of the individual, and we are persecuting these people.' The motion was watered down into a less belligerent form, but it was still passed by just one vote and the four men were dismissed.[84]

In January 1940 the Southend branch of the National Association of Local Government Officers voted to take steps to protect any of its members from being penalised by Southend Town Council once they registered as conscientious objectors. On 7 June rumours reached the branch that the council planned to sack them. The branch sent a letter of protest to the council, noting that the decision was 'entirely at variance with the principle of freedom of individual conscience for which this country stands'. However, only two members of the branch actually resigned in protest over the council's action.[85] Sometimes, however, such decisions were more subtle, and a little less sweeping, but no less devastating to the men affected: Clacton UDC avoided sacking such men by placing them on leave of absence for the duration of the war without salary or wages.[86] Essex County Council also decided that any of its employees who were required to perform alternative work by a tribunal would be granted leave of absence without pay 'if any other suitable applicant is available'. A simultaneous attempt to sack all conscientious objectors was lost by 39 votes to 22.[87] These actions were unsurprising. By July 1940 almost 140 local authorities nationally had sacked or suspended conscientious objectors, and only thirteen had ruled against dismissing them.[88]

As in the Great War, most conscientious objectors appealed on religious grounds. Members of the Plymouth Brethren, the Church of New Jerusalem

84   ECS 6 July 1940.
85   ERO D/DS 116/5 NALGO, Southend branch minutes, 24 January, 14 June 1940.
86   ECT 6 July 1940.
87   ECS 11 January 1941.
88   A. Calder, *The people's war: Britain 1939–1945* (London, 1969), p. 496.

and Seventh Day Adventists, as well as members of mainstream churches, all appeared before tribunals.[89] At the same time men from all sorts of occupations were present. Not all men based their appeal on religious grounds, though. Harry Shingler of Stratford was 24 when war broke out. He had been politicised by eight years of unemployment in the 1930s. He detested capitalism but dismissed Russian communism as 'state capitalism'. In his opinion it was a war over trade in which workers everywhere were exploited. He refused to serve in the Forces and was sent to jail. After being cooped up in his cell for seventeen hours a day he was eventually released when he agreed to do demolition work on bomb-damaged houses.[90]

Some conscientious objectors tried to distance themselves physically from the war and established colonies where they worked together on the land. Seven of these men who had been registered for agricultural work took up residence at a farm at Further Ford End, in Clavering, in 1940. They were part of an organisation called the War Resisters International and they renamed the place Lansbury Gate Farm, after the renowned pre-war pacifist and anti-war campaigner George Lansbury. They worked 50 acres, clearing the run-down estate, and in their first year produced large amounts of produce. A booklet they wrote emphasised that 'it is no mere spirit of non-cooperation and unhelpfulness that we withhold our support from the national effort'; rather, they claimed to be trying to promote brotherhood in a civilisation facing collapse. 'The task so urgently facing mankind today is the integration of society,' they asserted; '[T]his is our aim, to make our experience in communal living an offering to the new society.' The Saffron Walden Advisory Committee of the EWAC had little sympathy for the War Resisters. In 1941 it alleged that 'much of their labour is useless', and they were threatened with military service unless their work improved. The Advisory Committee also felt that seven men was excessive for only 50 acres and that only four were needed. The inadequate state of their farming was again criticised in January 1942, although the colony may still have been in existence at the end of that year.[91]

The experiences of Stanley Compton of Lexden, Colchester, may not have been typical of the difficulties facing conscientious objectors, largely because his own character aggravated his situation.[92] Compton was 32 years old when war broke out. He was asked to report for interview and, subsequently, stated that he '[o]pened Bible, pointed to St John 8, 14, revert back to v12. Yet a second point, St John 9, 34–41. Ch. 10, ch. 12, 12–50.' The biblical verses he used, which dealt with Christ confronting those who judged him, seemed

89   ECS 18 November 1939, 16 March 1940.
90   J. Steele (ed.), *A working class war: tales from two families* (London, 1995), pp. 3–6.
91   J. Cooper, *Clavering at war 1939–1945* (Clavering, 2012), pp. 94–5.
92   His papers are found in ERO D/DU 1190/1.

Figure 7.2. Conscientious objectors undergoing training with farm machinery in Essex. (Imperial War Museum)

deliberately chosen to challenge the interviewers. Compton was a combative man who did not shrink from alienating people. Prior to his case being heard at the Cambridge Tribunal he wrote a letter addressed to 'The Casuists of Cambridge'. This title was intended to convey his contempt for those on the tribunal by implying that they were men skilled in using words to achieve their ends, even if those ends flew in the face of justice. He described the form which he had to complete as 'subtly worded, which makes it a subterfuge and so much waste paper'. He stated that he would perform only civilian duties or care for people 'incapacitated in or by non-combatant duties'. It was the main part of his letter, however, that showed how little he cared about the tribunal:

> You must excuse my seeming rudeness as the knowledge that God has given unto me has put my mind above *your world's* petty affairs and opinions, therefore I washed my hands of *your world* long ago. God consecrated me into his Army of Christian Soldiers in my youth,

when I vowed allegiance to *The King of Kings*, the last and only King with, and by Divine Right. Could a worldly soldier, at one and the same time, serve openly, two worldly Kings or nations at war with each other? Even less can a Christian Soldier serve his God and yours (Mammon), that being so makes it impossible for me to recognise your National Service (Armed Forces) Act.[93]

Compton was granted the status of a conscientious objector and in 1942 he was working on a farm in the Writtle area. His manner remained abrasive, whatever provocations he faced. He had also had a period of ill-health that had hampered his ability to work effectively. He wrote a letter to E.W. Godfrey, the District Officer of the EWAC, which was not designed to calm troubled waters. He stated that it was his Christian duty to expose and end the behaviour he had witnessed, which hindered the effort 'to succour humanity', and he refused to work any longer for his foreman. He continued:

With this in mind I hereby give notice that my conscience will not allow me to work under unjust incompetent nincompoops, who have the audacity to assume authority, and in their self-righteous pride give themselves the title of 'superiors', yet have not the courage of their convictions. Their incompetence in resorting to slander and general insulting behaviour (thereby forfeiting the title of superiors) has resulted in my recovery being retarded and undermined my health.[94]

Godfrey replied in an unhelpful letter that showed no real sympathy for Compton's situation:

You are, I believe, a Conscientious Objector and have been directed … to work the regular hours as laid down by the Ministry of Labour. There can, therefore, be no question of you working a less number of hours as required in your letter. Mr Ellis is the foreman in charge of your gang and has been engaged in that capacity for some considerable time. I have complete confidence in him and his abilities and you will continue to work under him.

In two final paragraphs Godfrey betrayed his contempt for Compton and towards conscientious objectors in general:

---

93   ERO D/DU 1190/1, letter from Compton to 'The Casuists of Cambridge', 14 August 1940.
94   ERO D/DU 1190/1, Letter, Compton to E.W. Godfrey, 14 March 1942.

I suggest that the best way for you to 'succour humanity' is to work hard, the full number of hours required and so help feed the people of this island who might otherwise starve. In this way you may also help to defeat the enemy and so retain in power a form of government which has recognised your views but expects some effort on your part in return. I assure you that, should the enemy be successful against us, no such indulgent attitude would be shown to you.[95]

Others had an easier time than Compton. A Mr Batsford was in his thirties when he went before a tribunal, not because he was a pacifist but because, as he said later, 'I object to any government interference with the individual's belief.' In 1939 he worked on the land at Epping Forest. He wrote that 'I had next to me someone who fought in the Boer War when he was sixteen and on the other side I had a person who fought in the 14–18 War. One day I found a Nazi flag. I said I'm as much against them as against this government.' He added:

Nobody offered me a white feather … when I was on the land in the Epping area there was 140 of us … Plenty of people worked with us who were not conscientious objectors. We seemed to be all in it together. I mean we was all getting subject to the bombing during the Blitz.[96]

The churches at war: 'laying aside all malice'[97]

In 1939 Gerald Rendell, Vicar of Dedham, took the Church of England to task for failing to ignite popular support for what he regarded as a crusade to preserve civilisation:

In these distressful days, few symptoms are more disquieting than the coldness of righteous indignation and the tameness of spiritual reactions against atrocities so brutal in execution, and extensive in scale, as any that defaces the pages of history.[98]

However, on the whole Rendell's call for the Church to generate war fever was not heeded by his fellow clergy. As one historian puts it, 'It was more sombre, calm, resolute, and much less gung-ho and naïve.'[99] The Bishop of

95   ERO D/DU 1190/1, letter, E.W. Godfrey to Compton, 23 March 1942.
96   ERO SA 9/494/1 Mr Batsford.
97   1 Peter 2:1
98   ECS 11 November 1939. His letter was originally written to the *Guardian*.
99   C.G. Brown, *Religion and society in twentieth-century Britain* (London, 2006), p. 163.

Barking preached, 'In our sermons the less we say about the war the better.' He continued: 'The clergy are not as a rule competent to pronounce on the course of the war as the journalists of the day, and people read quite enough about the war in their newspapers.'[100] The Bishop of Chelmsford agreed. 'People do not go to church to hear "hymns of hate" and denunciations of Hitler,' he wrote at the start of the war. 'I believe that this not only does no good but it does real harm.' He added that soldiers 'do not appreciate inflammatory sermons from those who will run no such risk'.[101] These approaches were wise. Civilians and servicemen were more questioning than their fathers in 1914, and their approach to war was sometimes one in which religion had little part. Many clergymen urged their parishioners not to be overwhelmed by hatred for the enemy. When the Vicar of South Benfleet spoke of the Church's duty in war, he mentioned the need for it to continue to provide consolation and opportunities for prayer, including 'for the victory of peace and goodwill in the hearts of all men, and to prove to all that hatred of one's fellows shall have no place among Christian people'.[102]

Nevertheless, such sentiments did not prevent clergymen from supporting the war. Just as in 1914, it was interpreted by many as a battle against tyranny. The Bishop of Colchester asserted that Britain was fighting against 'arrogant and diabolical forces'.[103] T.H. Curling, Vicar of Halstead St Andrews, defended Britain's role in the war in words that could have been written in 1914:

> We Christians can face the war with confidence. The cause is right and just and we believe we are entrusted by God with the glorious stewardship of protecting the weak. We know that our nation has no other intention towards Germany but to rid her of mad intolerance and oppression and to make possible a new Germany which will enrich the common treasure of mankind with her scholarship, art and religious thought.[104]

Supporting the war was sometimes done regretfully. The vicar of St Mary-at-the-Wall in Colchester wrote, 'But it is sadly true that evil can only sometimes be cast out by force; and to rid Europe of all the oppression and injustice that Hitlerism stands for … is a cause worth fighting for.'[105] The Bishop of Chelmsford believed that Nazi crimes were sufficient to justify resistance. He condemned the desire for personal revenge but added that 'it would be equally

---

100 EC 26 April 1940.
101 CDC November 1939.
102 ERO D/P 300/29/3, South Benfleet PCC special meeting, 16 September 1939.
103 ECS 27 April 1940.
104 ERO D/P 96/28/45 Halstead St Andrew, parish magazine, October 1939.
105 ERO D/P 246/28/40 St Mary-at-the-Wall, Colchester, parish magazine, October 1939.

wrong for a Christian Society to stand passively apart from the systematic outraging of the decencies of life and the violation of all it understood to be just and good by ruthless and evil people'. He believed that this would amount to 'complicity in wickedness'.[106] Later, as the war was nearing its end, he also criticised those who preached that the enemy must be forgiven if it meant letting them off scot-free. For him the idea of failing to punish such sinners was 'amoral sentimentalism and is definitely unrighteous'.[107]

Some saw the conflict as a consequence of sinfulness since the last war. Charles Thomas, of the Elim Pentecostal Church in Chelmsford, argued that developments such as women wearing men's clothes were a manifestation of such sins. 'Surely shorts and shirts, or beach pyjamas or walking the promenade in bathing slips, must also be an abomination unto the Lord,' he asserted. 'The fact is that within the last three decades we have given ourselves over to the world, the flesh and the devil. The devil is now paying his wages.'[108] Essex Baptist churches sent out 'A Letter to Parents: What About Your Children and their Future?'. It stated that 'our children cannot remain truly free unless this land of ours becomes more truly Christian'. It continued, 'It will be nothing less than a tragedy if our British youth are allowed to lapse into that very paganism against which we are struggling to the point of sacrifice.'[109] T.M. Shepherd, the president of the Essex Baptist Association, commented, 'It is a tragedy to see the force of enemy explosives blowing our church fabric to smithereens, but it has been a greater tragedy that many of those churches have become "White Elephants", discarded by our generation.'[110] The Bishop of Chelmsford focused on the country's official and personal failures:

> When we look back on the last ten years we see the weak leadership of many of our statesmen; we see the absence of principle in the government of our country ... What was said then? Oh for pity's sake let us have a comfortable and peaceable life.... Give peace in our time, O Lord ... That was the cry.[111]

The failure of the war to 'purify' the national character meant that churches continued to campaign against moral laxity. 'What of people who not only tolerate nudity and "strip-tease" on the stage, but who apparently enjoy it? They would hardly bother about staging such "turns" if they were not paying propositions,' wrote Leonard Stokes, the Vicar of St Alban, Westcliff, adding:

---

106 CDC February 1942.
107 CDC October 1944.
108 EC 20 September 1940.
109 ERO D/NB 2/3, Essex Baptist Association minute, 10 May 1940.
110 ERO D/NB 2/27, Essex Baptist Association handbooks, president's address in the 1941 association handbook.
111 CDC August 1940.

'What of "bottle parties" and football pools? What of a country where the clergy are expected to sign government forms for the unmarried mother?'[112] The churches battled ineffectually against the opening of Sunday cinemas.[113] The Bishop of Chelmsford described himself as a Puritan, arguing that 'the Puritan contribution is responsible for the iron in our blood and our backbone of steel',[114] and he bemoaned the disappearance of the Christian Sabbath. However, he regarded the idea that Britain was a Christian country as a delusion and questioned whether the minority should seek to impose its will on the majority. He could not bring himself, therefore, to oppose Sunday cinemas for troops in areas where there were few recreational facilities, provided it was only for the duration. Nevertheless, 'the steady destruction of general Sunday observance is so prominent, that I regard it as deplorable in *every* way'.[115] Neither did he oppose the government's decision to make Good Friday a normal working day. The Romford Rural Deanery was so disturbed by this general situation that it passed a resolution stating that:

> In view of this country's claim to be fighting for the preservation of Christian principles, this Conference regards with profound apprehension the increasing encroachment upon the sanctity of Sunday, and urges that immediate action be taken to endorse the principle that the public Worship of God is of supreme National importance, and that everyone should be given the opportunity to attend Public Worship every Sunday.[116]

The Church of England was acutely aware that if it was to reach out to the nation in time of war it had to undergo the same sort of spiritual revival that it was urging upon the nation. A lay observer accused it of suffering from inertia, however:

> Our churches are drifting along in the old sweet way, so completely wrapped in complacency and self-satisfaction as to be dead from the neck upwards.... Surely it is time someone should give them a thump on the back to awaken them to a sense of their possibilities and responsibilities.[117]

The Bishop of Chelmsford was not unmindful of such complaints. Following the collapse of France he wrote:

112 ERO D/P 535/28/34, St Alban, Westcliff, parish magazine, May 1940.
113 See Chapter 6 of this work.
114 CDC March 1943.
115 CDC May, November 1941.
116 CDC May 1941.
117 ECS 3 September 1943.

So you only began to pray for peace when you looked like getting hurt yourself? You had no particular interest in those other people, but you expect God to rush to protect the British Empire when it is in trouble? Not a very noble idea of prayer![118]

In 1943, at a meeting of the Rochford and Canewdon Rural Deanery, the Revd W.C. Norris, a diocesan missioner, urged a reawakening of the Church, beginning in its parishes. The Church needed to preach fundamentals, reaching 'the lapsed, the Indifferent, the Antagonistic, and in part the young mothers so many of whom are ignorant of the Christian faith'.[119]

Identifying the need for renewal was easier than carrying it out, particularly in wartime. In 1940 Cardinal Hinsley, the Roman Catholic Archbishop of Westminster, founded 'The Sword of the Spirit', a crusade 'of prayer, study, and action for the restoration of a Christian order of justice and peace'. Father John Heenan, the Essex-born future cardinal, who was then parish priest at Manor Park, advised Cardinal Hinsley on this spiritual crusade. Anglican clergy and Free Church ministers also supported it, but the Catholic hierarchy refused permission for Catholics to participate in Anglican services and any spirit of cooperation faded after Hinsley's death in 1943.[120] The situation was not helped by the fundamental theological chasm separating the two churches, nor by the Bishop of Chelmsford's unremitting criticism of the papacy throughout the war. The Church of England addressed the need for spiritual and social renewal with its 'Religion and Life Weeks', which were designed to convince people that a new world order was needed – an order based not on the shallow foundations of materialism but on religion. The Colchester Religion and Life Week, the first to be held in the eastern part of the diocese, went ahead in September 1943. The arrangements were made by an executive committee of Anglican and Free Church leaders who had spent the previous year in active cooperation.[121] Other efforts were made throughout Essex to make use of the war to foster a greater sense of unity between the Free Churches and Anglicans. In 1941 the Young People's Fellowship of St Botolph, Colchester, arranged a series of talks between the two denominations in order to learn more of the viewpoint of other Christian churches and to understand both the essential unity shared by them and 'whether unity, without uniformity, is possible or desirable'. One of the speakers, the Revd J.C. Compton of Eld Lane Baptist Church, spoke on the question of a United Christian Front. He stated that the

118   ECS August 1940.
119   ERO D/E 8/11, Rochford and Canewdon Rural Deanery minute, 26 July 1943.
120   Quoted in Calder, People's war, p. 482; S.M. Foster, A history of the Diocese of Brentwood 1917–1992 (Brentwood, 1994), p. 78.
121   ECS 9 July, 13 August 1943; CDC October 1943.

Baptist position was 'unity without uniformity, and that our unity lies in our common faith in Christ, and in the Christian way of life'. In his view, if the two churches were to come closer they needed to cultivate admiration for the best features of all churches, recognising the unity that already existed and seeking both greater fellowship in worship and prayer and more cooperation in the struggle to improve society.[122]

To combat what he saw as the prevailing ignorance of the Christian faith in society, an ignorance that had existed before the war, the Bishop of Chelmsford produced a booklet entitled *The Catechism of the Creed*. He issued a copy to all clergy in the diocese and instructed them to use it with everyone, especially children and Confirmation candidates. In fact, his 'Catechism' enjoyed a much wider success. It was made available to Anglican clergy throughout the country and sold out within three days; within weeks, 27 bishops had permitted its use in their dioceses. To further strengthen his diocesan clergy's ability to teach the Christian faith the Bishop of Chelmsford required all junior clergy (those in Orders for less than three years) to attend a summer school of instruction in Sunday School and youth training.[123] He also attempted to reawaken interest in Anglican services, beginning by deriding the idea of 'bright and attractive services with breezy little talks' from the clergy as a 'complete delusion' because they demonstrated a complete ignorance of the true meaning of worship, which was not simply a form of entertainment.[124]

Early in the war the need for diocesan economy almost led to the termination of the job of Martin Shaw, the diocesan director of music. Shaw was an immensely gifted composer and hymn writer, and a man who had done much to raise the standard of choral singing in parish churches in the diocese. Fortunately the £200 required for his salary was donated by a gentleman who also offered to raise the money required in future years.[125] Shaw travelled the diocese continuing to uphold musical traditions and to work for the survival of church choirs through music that was both artistic and popular, and he encouraged congregations to participate. In late 1942 he was part of a group of Anglicans who held an experimental school at Pleshey aimed at addressing the neglect of the aesthetic in church services and, like their seventeenth- and nineteenth-century predecessors, at stimulating a new interest in the beauty of holiness.[126] Later Shaw organised a 'Conference on Worship and the Arts'. In a discussion on 'The Voices of the Clergy' he emphasised the importance of elocution if clergy were to reach their congregations.[127]

---

122 ECT 2 September, 14 October 1941.
123 CDC February, March 1943.
124 CDC April 1942.
125 CDC April, June 1940.
126 CDC November 1941, August 1942.
127 CDC December 1944.

There were those who felt that if the Anglican Church was to provide effective leadership during the war it must also address the urgent social and political issues that were being debated throughout the country. In this it was led by William Temple, archbishop of Canterbury, and Cyril Garbett, archbishop of York. Temple's book *Christianity and the Social Order* advocated family allowances, improved pay, paid holidays and better housing.[128] The Anglican hierarchy in Essex supported the need for social change and reform. Both the bishops of Chelmsford and Barking were acutely aware of how the Blitz had challenged traditional attitudes and created an atmosphere which was conducive to change. As the Blitz began, the Bishop of Chelmsford wrote that 'The rich man equally with the penniless tramp is in the firing line.' Later he told people that 'We have all acquired a new standard of values which may be expressed by saying that *people are more important than property*.'[129] His episcopal colleague at Barking wrote, 'In a single moment one land-mine might give the necessary impulse to improvement which the better elements in the community had been powerless to impart during years of perhaps half-hearted agitation.'[130]

The campaign to put the churches at the forefront of the debate about social and economic reform was launched early in the war. Four days before Christmas 1940 a letter appeared in *The Times* signed by Hinsley, Cosmo Lang, the Archbishop of Canterbury, William Temple, then the Archbishop of York, and the Moderator of the Free Church Federal Council. They urged the adoption of five standards necessary for the organisation of society. These were the abolition of extreme inequality in wealth, equal educational opportunities, the safeguarding of the family, the restoration of the sense of a divine vocation to daily work and the use of the planet's resources for the benefit of the whole human race. This was presented as a theological basis for the social, political, economic and international reconstruction of the post-war world. In January 1941 a great gathering of Anglican clergy and laity met at Malvern to consider 'the ordering of the new society that is quite evidently emerging'. These developments took root in fertile soil in the diocese. In the spring of 1941 the Bishop of Chelmsford received a letter from four incumbents who had been discussing the five standards in the context of the post-war reconstruction of the Church. The letter suggested a national system of Christian education, staffed by teachers 'qualified by conviction and ability', as the only way to maintain a 'Christian Social Order'. It urged the Church to proclaim

> without fear for the temporal status or private position, that the
> Christian Gospel demands that outward and visible expression should

---

128   Calder, *People's war*, p. 485.
129   CDC August 1942.
130   CDC October 1940, June 1941.

be given in the international and social order to the inward and spiritual truths of the Fatherhood of God and the brotherhood of man.

Finally they urged supporting parliamentary candidates who pledged to support these principles.[131] In accordance with their wishes the Bishop held a diocesan conference to discuss the Church's current and post-war problems. Nevertheless, he emphasised that, in his opinion, optimistic talk about the nature of the post-war world was 'moonshine' unless it was accompanied by the creation of a new social structure built on a Christian foundation. Legislation in areas such as education, carried out by 'jerry-building reformers', would be unavailing unless it had a Christian basis. This was a view from which he never wavered.[132]

The clergy recognised that for the Church to flourish it had to concentrate on the young, particularly as it was proving difficult to hold on to them after the age of about thirteen. Even in the dark days of the war the Bishop of Chelmsford was urging the immediate overhaul of the education system to create a better post-war world. He called for the Church to ensure that the Christian position percolated throughout whatever new education system was created.[133] For him the war had finally ended the 'absurd' belief in human progress under the benevolent influence of education and science. He felt that man had no intrinsic power of self-improvement, arguing that 'he is a dangerous and cruel animal and is liable to drop to a lower level than any other animal'. His plan for a diocesan conference in 1942 to discuss post-war reconstruction was partly influenced by his fear that the war may make young people even more 'inaccessible'. He was therefore pleased with the provision for religious instruction in schools in the 1944 Education Act. Anglican schools were free to teach their own doctrines and the government provided financial aid for the reconditioning of Anglican schools to a maximum of 50 per cent. This was a reasonable concession to the Established Church, but it was much resented by the Free Churches and Roman Catholics, who were struggling under the same economic difficulties during the war as the Anglican Church.[134]

The loss of young adult members of congregations to the armed forces and the evacuations of 1939–40 affected the membership of churches of all denominations. Churches in the evacuation areas were particularly affected by falling attendances, although the phenomenon was not unusual in neutral or reception areas. In the spring of 1940 the Bishop of Barking sent a questionnaire to his parish clergy. Of the 83 replies, 49 showed that attendances had been maintained, seven showed an increase, and 33 showed a decline. In 62 cases

131 ECT 11 July 1941.
132 CDC July 1942.
133 CDC September 1941.
134 CDC December 1943.

the number of communicants had also been maintained, in fourteen there had been an increase, and in seventeen numbers had fallen.[135] The war also made an immediate impression on the number of confirmations in the diocese; in the last four months of 1939 only 200 people were confirmed instead of the usual figure of about 2,000. The explanation was the evacuation of huge numbers of young people from Metropolitan Essex.[136] All churches were affected. By the end of 1940 St Mary Magdalene at Colchester had lost its Parochial Churh Council (PCC) secretary, one of its choristers, all its Rover Scouts, many members of its Young Men's Social Club and a number of the older ones of the Young People's Fellowship to the armed forces.[137] The Essex Baptist Association bemoaned the fact that in 1941–42 more than half of its churches had no baptisms.[138]

The age and gender profile of some churches was revealed in early 1942 by an *Essex Chronicle* survey of four in Chelmsford. In both the Anglican cathedral and the London Road congregational church the average age of the congregation was said to be about 55, and two-thirds were women. The High Street Methodist Church had an average age of 45, and it was 35–40 at London Road Roman Catholic Church.[139] Elsewhere the picture was similar: at Little Waltham parish church the congregation consisted of six women to every man.[140] Ninety per cent of the congregation at St Michael and All Angels at Westcliff was female, and to maintain a functioning PCC, seven of the twelve members were also women.[141]Although women had been present on PCCs since they began in 1920, it was unusual that they were in a majority. The trend for churches to have a majority of female worshippers had been developing before 1939 and the war simply exacerbated this tendency. By early 1940 the Bishop of Chelmsford was mourning the loss of male choristers, especially as some choirs, which before the war had been made up entirely of males, simply disappeared for the duration.[142] Some churches, such as Emmanuel (Forest Gate) and Holy Trinity (Southchurch), found that females were prepared to fill the gap and form a choir. In the latter church the female choir continued to expand even after the male choir was re-formed.[143] At St John the Baptist (Southend) a choir of males and females was created in 1941 and augmented by twenty boys in the following year.[144]

---

135 EC 26 April 1940.
136 CDC March 1940. The churches and parishes of Metropolitan Essex were referred to by the Diocese of Chelmsford as 'London Over The Border'.
137 ECS 1 February 1941.
138 ERO D/NB 2/27, handbook 1941–2.
139 EC 20 March 1942. No information is provided as to the methodology used in the compilation of these surveys. It is assumed that they are impressionistic rather than sociological.
140 EC 10 April 1942.
141 ERO D/P 557/28/7, St Michael and All Angels, Westcliff news bulletin, February 1942.
142 CDC May 1940.
143 ERO D/P 592/29/4, Emmanuel Church, Forest Gate, PCC minute, 13 April 1944; ERO D/P 120/8/8 Holy Trinity, Southchurch, PCC minute, 9 April 1942.
144 ERO D/P 534/29/2, St John the Baptist, Southend, PCC minute, 29 May 1942.

After 1942 government orders concerning travel had the side effect of further damaging church attendances. For example, the loss of early morning Sunday bus services prevented worshippers from travelling to churches whose form of worship attracted people from a wide area, such as St Peter's, Colchester.[145] Roman Catholics to the north of Colchester who normally travelled by bus to worship at St James the Less, the town's main Catholic church, met instead at the Dog and Pheasant pub in West Bergholt.[146] The Essex Congregational Union expressed relief that none of its congregations had been dispersed, but the numbers attending many of its churches had been reduced as women, especially, were engaged in essential war work and often worked on Sundays. Changes in service times due to the blackout often meant that evening congregations were smaller than in pre-war days.[147]

The churches which were most affected by the dual problems of evacuation and conscription, particularly the former, were those of the seaside resorts of Clacton, Frinton, Walton and Southend. Some members of local churches did remain behind, but in most cases congregations were reduced to a fraction of pre-1940 numbers. For instance, St Paul, Clacton lost 75 per cent of its communicants by the second half of 1940,[148] and St Saviour, Westcliff had lost 90 per cent.[149] At least all the congregational ministers from Essex coastal towns were able to find temporary pastorates.[150] When the minister of the London Road congregational church in Chelmsford retired through ill health they were urged to appoint Herbert Stock from Clacton, whose congregation had collapsed, and within a fortnight they did so.[151] The Leigh-on-Sea Baptist church suffered badly. 'Not in ones but in scores its members intimated intention to hive off,' wrote John Pritchard, the pastor, 'in most instances without registering their new abode.' He noted that 'The exit had exceeded all imagination and affected all churches.' The remaining members of the congregation wanted Pritchard to stay but finally 'acceded to his release', although not all the church's work was suspended at once. Within a short time Pritchard was in Monmouth; the secretary and treasurer had already evacuated themselves to Kent.[152] Percy Norris, the Rector of Trinity Church, Southend, who had ministered to the parish for sixteen years, had intended to resign but stayed on after war broke out. However, when virtually all the congregation left in June 1940 he too departed.[153]

---

145   ECS 30 April 1943.
146   ECS 23 January 1943.
147   ECT 24 March 1941.
148   ERO D/P 570/1/27 St Paul, Clacton, extrapolated from register of services.
149   ERO D/P 576/1/16 St Saviour, Westcliff, extrapolated from register of services.
150   ERO D/NC 11/1 Essex Congregational Union, Chelmsford District minute, 23 September 1940.
151   ERO D/NC 22/11 London Road Congregational Baptist Church, Chelmsford, minutes, 23 July, 6 August 1940.
152   ERO D/NB 11/5/84 Leigh-on-Sea Baptist Church, The Outlook, August 1940.
153   ERO S 3294 Box 1, Trinity Church, Southend, parish magazine, July 1940.

Former members of Essex church congregations were scattered across the length and breadth of the country. By January 1941 John Muir Elliott, the Vicar of St Michael and All Angels, Westcliff, had received letters from former members of his congregation who were now residing in the United States, Scotland, north Wales, London and 22 other English counties; people who had only moved as far away as Leigh-on-Sea also wrote.[154] Elliott was more fortunate than H.A. Robins, Vicar of St Erkenwald, Southend, who was saddened that it had not been possible to trace many of those on the church's electoral roll.[155] Local Baptist ministers held a conference and a central Baptist church for the borough was mooted, but the general chaos and uncertainty that summer made it impossible to formulate any definite plans.[156]

Everywhere churches were experiencing the problems of evacuation, rising costs of living and falling incomes. Churches of all denominations inevitably suffered financially from evacuation and the call-up of men and women. The loss of much of the regular income from weekly collections was a particularly severe blow and, again, it was seaside resorts that suffered most. The average monthly collections at St Saviour, Westcliff, fell by about 84 per cent between August 1939 and the second half of 1940, which was hardly surprising considering the loss of the greater part of its congregation. It is not surprising that in 1943 Emmanuel Church, Forest Gate requested that nominees to the PCC should have been PCC members in the past or possess 'business experience'.[157] Churches had no choice but to economise. Only a fortnight after war began the PCC at St Peter, Upton Cross compensated for its reduced income by slashing £132 a year from clergy stipends and other salaries.[158] The PCC at St Saviour, Westcliff suspended offertories for any purposes outside the parish and, as a temporary measure, cut the salaries of the vicar and organist. When the Vicar, J.L. Featherstone, was called up as an army chaplain five months later he exhorted the PCC as he left to undertake 'the most stringent economy in expenditure'.[159] The pre-war plans that some Anglican parishes had of engaging an assistant priest were now put off indefinitely, as at Emmanuel Church, which blamed the 'prevailing conditions' for its decision. This was a sensible step as by 1942 the church's pew rents, which had brought in £300 a year before the war and had formed part of the vicar's stipend, had greatly decreased, so that the PCC granted him £50 a year to make up for some of the deficiency.[160]

154 ERO D/P 557/28/6 news bulletin, January 1941.
155 ERO D/P 539/8/2 St Erkenwald, Southend, PCC minute, 28 March 1944.
156 ERO D/NB 2/3 Essex Baptist Association minute, 16 June 1940.
157 ERO D/P 592/29/4 APCM minute, 29 April 1943.
158 ERO D/P 593/29/5 St Peter, Upton Cross, PCC minute, 19 September 1939.
159 ERO D/P 576/29/4 St Saviour, Westcliff, PCC minutes, 16 September 1939, 29 January 1940.
160 ERO D/P 592/29/4 PCC minute, 4 September 1939, APCM minute, 9 April 1942.

The largest of the expenses faced by Anglican parishes was their share of the Quota, the annual sum of money which was expected from them to finance the running of the diocese. The Diocesan Board of Finance froze the Quota at the pre-war total of £14,500 in anticipation of financial problems. In spite of the financial strains of war the sums contributed by individual parishes reflected their continuing commitment to the Church. Between 1939 and 1944 the percentage of the Quota collected from parishes was never less than 86.3 per cent, and in four of these years it was over 90 per cent.[161] The sums raised varied from parish to parish, and deanery to deanery, as they had done before the war. There was a very early recognition that some metropolitan parishes that were heavily bombed in 1940 were unlikely to contribute anything to the Quota. On the whole, though, most parishes considered meeting their share of it as a priority. In 1943, out of 534 parishes in the diocese, only about one in six paid less than their share or nothing.[162] Astonishingly, in 1943 and 1944 the West Ham deanery, which had suffered appallingly from enemy action, sent in 96.8 per cent and 98.36 per cent of its quota, which was set at £1,163.[163] There were mild protests by a handful of parishes of the West Ham Deanery in 1940 but the total remained unchanged; the reason given was that if exceptions were made for a few they would have to be made for all.[164] The PCC at St John the Baptist, Southend, irritated at having to meet its allocation of £100, a figure based on the number of communicants from several years ago, resolved to pay only £50 a year as a protest.[165] Even those who felt unable to contribute their share of the quota apologised for their shortcomings. The PCC of St Saviour, Westcliff, faced with a large overdraft and other wartime problems, sent only £5 of its £102 quota in 1941, together with an explanation.[166] All Saints, Southend pleaded 'sheer poverty' as the reason for its being unable to pay anything.[167]

Churches continued to rely on well-established methods to raise money. A churchwarden at St Michael and All Angels appealed for people to contribute to Easter Offerings, which customarily had gone to the vicar and in the past had amounted to 'quite an appreciable part of his income'.[168] Gift Days, when members of the congregation, parishioners and even passers-by donated money, were used by many parishes to supplement both clergy stipends and church income. For instance, at Emmanuel Church the Gift Day brought in £130 in 1942, £176 in 1943 and £190 in 1944.[169] The Vicar of St John's, Chelmsford,

---

161 Abstracted from the CDC 1939–44.
162 CDC April 1944.
163 CDC March 1944; ERO D/E 9/5, West Ham Ruridecanal minute, 30 July 1940.
164 ERO D/E 9/5, 30 July 1940.
165 ERO D/P 534/29/2, PCC minute, 5 February 1944.
166 ERO D/P 576/29/4, PCC minute, 27 November 1941.
167 ERO D/P 537/8/1 All Saints, Southend, APCM minute, 22 February 1940.
168 ERO D/P 557/28/6, news bulletin, March 1941.
169 ERO D/P 592/29/4, PCC minutes, 19 October 1942, 10 October 1943, 22 October 1944.

W.S. Brown, sat in a tent in front of the church for fourteen hours on 7 July 1944 and collected £206.[170] Prior to the war attempts had been made to persuade congregations to commit a definite sum of money each week in free-will offering schemes to enable churches to undertake some financial planning based on a predictable income. These had not been an unqualified success, but during the war such attempts continued. For instance, at St Michael, Kirby-le-Soken the scheme was certainly in operation throughout 1941 in spite of a reduced congregation and as people began to return the amount committed was increased from about £8 in the first quarter of the year to £14 in the third quarter.[171] At Emmanuel Church, Forest Gate about 30 to 40 per cent of those on the electoral roll were part of a free will-offering scheme in 1942.[172] Wartime restrictions and inconveniences hampered the social activities that often formed an important part of church fundraising. In 1940 the newly arrived curate-in-charge at St Saviour, Westcliff came up with an extraordinary idea. He decided to cancel the annual summer bazaar and organise an 'imaginary bazaar' instead. With all hell breaking loose across the Channel, people came to the church hall and donated what they would have spent at the bazaar to the 'imaginary stall' of their choice. The event was a success and raised £62.[173]

Churches were sometimes thankful for external assistance. The finances of St Erkenwald, Southend were rescued in 1941 when an anonymous donor gave a gift of £100.[174] A member of the congregation of Epping congregational church paid the £9 needed for corrugated iron sheets required as a blackout.[175] Some members of the congregation who had moved elsewhere continued to send regular financial contributions. John Muir Elliott appealed for evacuee members of the congregation to donate half their usual weekly contribution to the church and the other half to the church they were now attending, although he added, 'I very much like to hear from you, whether you send any contribution or not.' His news bulletin, which was sent to those who had given him their new addresses, stressed that the church was in desperate straits. A churchwarden, the verger, the organist, the PCC secretary and the magazine secretary had all left. With only seven PCC members left it could not hold an official meeting, and there was no choir. Sunday collections had fallen from the usual £18 to £2–3 and he did not expect to pay the Quota.[176] His heartfelt appeal reaped rewards and he admitted that what was being sent had enabled the church to avoid going without 'necessaries'. In the second half of 1940,

---

170 EC 14 July 1944.
171 ERO D/P 169/28/19 St Michael, Kirby-le-Soken, news sheet, May, November 1941.
172 ERO D/P 592/29/4, APCM minute, 9 April 1942, PCC minutes 18 October 1942, 21 June 1945.
173 ERO D/P 576/29/4, PCC minutes, 16 May, 2 July 1940.
174 ERO D/P 539/8/2, PCC minute, 12 March 1941.
175 ERO D/NC 26/18 Epping Congregational Church, deacons' minutes, 11, 18 August 1940.
176 ERO D/P 557/28/5, news bulletin, August 1940.

while weekly collections totalled £87 donations from those who had left came to £112, and in 1941 this continued to be the case.[177] The parish just about paid its way in 1941 but the next year it had to resort to a special grant of £75 from the Ecclesiastical Commissioners towards the vicar's stipend, reducing the parochial obligation to £200. The diocese stepped in to assist other churches that were unable to find a way out of their financial difficulties. All Saints Church, Southend was heavily in debt before the war and had already been bailed out by the diocese, which in 1939 extended a loan of £250 and granted an additional loan to install a new heating system. This new loan fell through when war broke out but the diocese did take over the £500 owed to the bank. In 1942 it again came to the rescue, with two interest-free loans.[178] Some churches received an unexpected income when their halls were requisitioned by the authorities. Emmanuel Church Hall was taken over as an ARP post and the PCC negotiated an annual rental of £45.[179]

The government was anxious to encourage the protection of the nation's Anglican ecclesiastical heritage, particularly after the frightful damage wrought by the Blitz. A government scheme exempted Anglicans from having to insure their churches, vicarages and parish halls, which it undertook to repair if damaged. For the vast majority of Anglican churches insuring them would have been prohibitive, primarily because of their ancient and irreplaceable nature. However, insurance of the contents, which in many cases had never been done before, was now made compulsory. This involved insuring all the objects found in buildings used for the act of worship – the organ, bells, pulpit, pews, hymn books, crucifixes, church plate and so on. The cost was high – 10s per £100. The scheme was made retrospective, from September 1940, so that churches damaged since the start of the Blitz would not be at a disadvantage. The insurance scheme was a parish responsibility and it placed a heavy burden on the already stretched finances of individual churches. Most did not have a fund of money lying idle in banks and they had to rely on their congregations and parishioners, as well as the products of economies. The PCC of St Michael, Kirby-le-Soken decided that it was impossible to insure all the church's possessions at their full value because they could not pay the premium, so they set an insurance limit of £1,000, allocated between the organ (£500), the bells (£375) and other goods (£125).[180] Other parishes were more ambitious. St Saviour, Westcliff insured its church contents for £3,000 and those of the church hall for £350. The Free Churches also had to insure both their properties and contents, but without

---

177   ERO D/P 557/28/6, news bulletin, April, July 1941.
178   ERO D/P 537/29/1 All Saints, Southend, PCC minutes, 20 April, 11 May, 10 August, 1 October 1939, 9 March 1941, 21 July 1942.
179   ERO D/P 592/29/4, PCC minute, 4 December 1939.
180   ERO D/P 169/28/19, newssheet, June, August 1941.

government assistance. Epping congregational church insured itself with two different congregational insurance companies, which covered its church, hall, cottage and house.[181] For those Anglican churches that suffered air-raid damage a Diocesan Reorganisation Committee equipped with statutory powers to deal with such matters was established in 1941. In the next two years it dealt with 382 claims and received from the government's War Damage Commission £23,142 in whole or partial settlement of them.[182]

The Bishop of Chelmsford maintained a fervent pastoral role throughout the war. He trod a fine line between supporting the war and urging people to forsake vengeance and opposed indiscriminate bombing by both sides. He sought to illuminate the twists and turns of the war for his congregations, but always from a prayerful viewpoint. He never wavered from his pre-war anti-Fascism and hoped that the Soviet Union, under the stress of war, might become a Christian nation again, freed from the bonds of Stalin's totalitarianism.[183] In October 1940 he issued a pastoral letter outlining what he saw as the essence of the Church's contribution to the war: 'to keep the will of God clear before the nation; to deepen faith in Him; to cheer the anxious, the broken-hearted and the bereaved with the assurance that Christ's message to the world is true'.[184]

Essential to the success of this mission was the need to preserve Christian values at the heart of society. As already noted, to preserve a future Christian society the Bishop supported R.A. Butler's 1944 Education Act, which retained the role of the Church of England in the state education system.[185] When the government created its Service of Youth mission to try to provide meaningful activity for young people the bishop urged that religious principles should not be shouldered out by a secularist emphasis on physical training and 'the building of character'. He supported a full-blooded committed Christianity rather than an easy-going approach, which he despised. He had no time for those who preached that the British people were united in morality even though they had drifted from public worship, and he described the popular idea that everyone was a Christian at heart as 'sentimental eyewash'.[186] He was scathing of anything which he felt damaged the church's work and teaching. For example, he condemned the *Songs of Praise* hymn book, which was widely used, because it gave a 'weak and reduced view of certain doctrines of paramount importance', namely the doctrines of the Cross and Advent. A few of its hymns 'strike me as twaddle', he wrote.[187]

---

181 ERO D/NC 11/1, deacons' minute, 18 May 1941.
182 CDC August 1941, September 1943.
183 M. Fox, *Chelmsford Diocese – the first 100 years* (Chelmsford, 2013).
184 CDC October 1940.
185 CDC May 1944.
186 CDC, March 1942.
187 CDC, September 1940.

By the end of the war more than 10 per cent of the clergy in the diocese of Chelmsford had become chaplains to the armed forces. Some of these were conscripted, but many had ignored the exemption offered by the government to those candidates for ordination who had been accepted before war broke out. In 1941 the number of 'reserved' candidates was considered sufficient to meet about 75 per cent of peacetime requirements, but within two years the situation was less optimistic. Of nineteen candidates in training in 1939, ten had volunteered for the armed forces. Of the eight chosen in 1940/41 four were called up. There were hopes that four candidates may be ordained in 1944, but after that the 'normal supply' of ordinands from the Church's 'usual sources' dried up. The exodus of clergy was still a significant loss for the diocese, especially as about half of all clergy were over the age of 50 and an increasing number of clergy were retiring. The war had also not eased the Church's difficulties in attempting to find incumbents for villages with a small population and an inadequate endowment.[188]

The physical destruction inflicted on the infrastructure of Essex's churches was immense. Fourteen Anglican churches, ten parsonages, twelve schools and five halls were demolished and required rebuilding. In total, 665 buildings were damaged, including 321 churches, 176 parsonages, 62 schools and 23 other buildings.[189] On the other hand, the war brought unexpected benefits. The future Cardinal Heenan's Catholic parish in Manor Park consisted of two churches whose congregations worshipped separately and hardly knew one another. The war united these Catholics and, indeed, according to Heenan, the whole community of Manor Park.[190]

Even before the war the Bishop of Chelmsford had launched an appeal for £300,000, to be raised over seven years for the needs of the diocese, but now a new one would clearly be required. Church buildings needed to be repaired and rebuilt; given the need to meet the requirements of the 1944 Education Act many of its schools needed reconditioning and extending, while new ones were needed; and several hundred clergy and lay workers would need to be trained if the Church in Essex was to be revitalised. Government grants would fall far short of what was required to assist in reconstruction, and post-war town planning would create new housing areas requiring churches. The appeal was expecting a great deal of people considering the upheavals of war and the anticipated austere demands of post-war society. The previous diocesan appeal, ending in 1936, had raised £264,000, twenty per cent of which had come from just two or three wealthy donors. The Congregational Union, finding itself in the same situation, appealed for £500,000 for the reconstruction of

---

188 CDC, September 1943, January 1941, August 1943, January 1945.
189 ECS 16 March 1945.
190 Foster, *Diocese of Brentwood*, pp. 75–6.

its churches. In the Chelmsford area every church contributed, so that by September 1943 they had raised over 80 per cent of the £4,213 promised.[191]

In reality the churches were well aware of the uphill struggle they faced in the post-war world. In 1944 the Bishop of Chelmsford wrote a book entitled *The Christian in the World of Tomorrow*. Although it was a devotional book he included sections on post-war problems. His appraisal was not an optimistic one, because he could see no evidence that Christianity would be allowed to exercise any substantial influence over the decisions that would shape the new world.[192] In the last days of the war a visiting clergyman spoke at a church conference in West Ham on the theme of 'The Church's Witness in the Post War World'. He warned of a national sense of tiredness that would underlie everyone's actions and thoughts, and added that:

> Life will not alter at the cessation of hostilities, as situations will be far too greatly involved to do so immediately and some people will suffer disappointment in various ways. There will be a sense of frustration which will have to be met and dealt with, so this war will mean women as well as men returning to a civilian life, who will all need guidance in their new start in life.

However, in the speaker's opinion the Christian faith had a great opportunity to provide guidance to those who needed it. 'God treats persons as persons and not as things,' he argued, 'and this must be our attitude towards those looking for guidance from the Church.'

The British people slogged their way through the war with a weary, dogged determination. But the notion that they were united behind the government in all matters and dedicated to making any sacrifice necessary in the furtherance of victory has long been exploded as a myth generated during the war and sustained afterwards. In Essex, as everywhere else, there were many people who exploited the war to their own advantage, whether by breaking the new government wartime regulations or by committing criminal acts. The extent of people's participation in such activity is unknown from a statistical standpoint, but is likely to have been very widespread. Individuals also took advantage of wartime circumstances to engage in illicit sexual activities that prompted an alarmist debate about the nation's moral decline, a debate propelled by anxieties about young people's promiscuity, especially that of girls, the rise in cases of bigamy and the increase in venereal disease. Conscientious objectors challenged the general support for the war that existed in the population by standing aside

191 ERO D/NC 11/1, minute, 20 September 1943.
192 CDC April 1944.

from it, whether for religious or political reasons, and, in consequence, many were regarded as a potential fifth column. Essex churches, on the other hand, adopted the same sort of supportive attitude towards the war as it had in 1914–18. To most clergy the war was a righteous one, fought to overthrow a regime steeped in the corruption of dictatorship, intolerance and racism.

8

Doodlebugs, rockets and victory

Never again

Essex churches formed just one part of the growing consensus that a post-war Britain could not return to the days of social inequality, poverty, overcrowding and unemployment. This desire for social change was typified by just one incident. On 26 April 1941 Ernest Edwards recorded the funeral of eight ARP men, killed in West Ham during the great raid of five days earlier. The funeral procession was three-quarters of a mile long, the eight coffins carried in ARP ambulances laden with flowers. The Revd W.W. Paton, the borough's inspirational ARP Controller, said over the open grave, 'At this the altar of remembrance, let us be resolved that, as our comrades lived and died, that the common people who made the traditions for which we fight shall have a new and better life.'[1] Here, early in the war, long before the prospect of victory, was the idea that the people's sacrifice must result in them inheriting a better world.

During 1940 the country was too engaged in its struggle for survival to pay much attention to the opportunities that might be offered by a world once more at peace. But, after the entry of the Soviet Union and America into the war in 1941 opened up the possibility of victory, people allowed themselves the luxury of thinking about the future. These thoughts were not universally positive. The *Southend Times* warned against both 'post-war defeatism, focussing too much on the problems of a new world order,' and the idea that 'an earthly paradise' would be created out of victory.[2] The pessimistic Thomas Wisbey of West Bergholt feared that

> [t]he rich man will still suffer from a disease which makes him try to double his riches and also makes him forget his fellow humans who have very little … the poor man will also be suffering from the disease which makes him envious of all who are better off than he.[3]

1   ERO S3150, Edwards diary, 26 April 1941.
2   ST 22 January 1941.
3   ST 20 January 1940.

Nevertheless, by 1942, when people were musing on the future, they were generally in a positive frame of mind. Above all they were determined to eradicate the unequal features of society that had disfigured the country in order to ensure that they were not cheated out of the fruits of victory, as they felt they had been in 1918.[4] The focus of most people was on the elimination of poverty and the retention of the full employment that the war had brought. There must be no return to the misery of mass unemployment. Living conditions had to be improved by the demolition of slums and the building of new houses. Above all, education must be made accessible to all and used to promote social mobility. Public opinion in Britain had taken a decisive shift to the Left, away from those who were seen as responsible for the inter-war debacle. Articulating these feelings in 1942, Tom Driberg, Maldon's Independent MP, said,

> I hope that after this war when we do get back to peace, and when reasonable conditions of living are established, there will be a much wider distribution of the good things of life and a much more securely guaranteed standard of living for all our people.[5]

Although Churchill's wartime government was a coalition including members of the Labour party, and the prime minister himself had breathed new life into the nation in the dark days of 1940, many working people did not trust the Conservatives. The scars of the 1930s were, for many, too deep to be erased by a war. Moreover, the military disasters of 1939–42 were widely ascribed to a combination of incompetent leadership and the inadequacies of vested interests. People were dissatisfied with the way the war was being run and this was accompanied by a nagging suspicion that a post-war Tory government, whose members had failed to adapt to the demands of war, would merely seek to put the clock back and restore the bad old days. Another reason to turn from a past tainted by capitalist excess and Depression was the fact that the achievements of Britain's civilian and military leaders compared unfavourably with those of the leaders of the Soviet Union.[6]

There was a belief that the war had blurred class distinctions, which raised hopes for a more egalitarian new world. The Essex and Suffolk Brotherhood, a free-thinking religious organisation, asserted that for a stable future there must be 'a clear social and moral purpose – a certain moral ideal which would produce social unity amongst all classes'.[7] Stanley Tiquet's experience of ARP

---

4   D. Kynaston, *Austerity Britain 1945–51* (London, 2007), p. 21.
5   ECS 28 November 1942.
6   A. Calder, *The people's war: Britain 1939–1945* (London, 1969), pp. 17–18.
7   ECS 23 May 1942.

work in Wanstead and Woodford demonstrated this sense of wartime unity. He commented that:

> We had men and women working and living together in the same crowded and unsuitable premises: paid and unpaid workers were side by side on the same job: people who talked different kinds of English, and had different personal and educational standards, and quite different sorts of good manners were herded together.... In spite of these apparent difficulties, none of those whom we really valued, senior or junior, ever left us or let us down badly; and a sense of team spirit and communal loyalty, absent at first and quite a novelty to many of them, was very soon powerfully felt.[8]

Norman Hidden, a local Communist party member, spoke of wartime unity, but

> not of a forced or an artificial kind like the present coalition, but a free and equal working together of parties, groups and individuals with similar ideas and principles wherever their general aims and methods converged; that is to say, in planning along the lines of their conscience and highest beliefs for a new and better Britain, a new and better world.[9]

The first practical result of the idea that the lives of British people had to be improved was the Beveridge Report. Sir William Beveridge was a distinguished administrator who had seen poverty at first hand in the East End. In 1942 his report outlined proposals for a comprehensive post-war system of social security by attacking 'the five giant evils' of want, disease, ignorance, squalor and idleness. It was a sensation and eventually more than 630,000 copies of the abridged version were sold.[10] A Mass Observation survey the day after the report was published revealed that 88 per cent of people wanted the report implemented.[11] The government's lukewarm response to the report provided ammunition to those who feared that a Conservative-led post-war administration would not tackle social inequalities and evils. Tom Driberg, a proponent of the new spirit that was abroad, argued that when it came to progressive reforms 'the well-meaning ones (progressive Tories) would be quashed by the hard-fisted ones'.[12] In six by-elections held around the time of the Beveridge debate in parliament the

8   S. Tiquet, *It happened here: the story of civil defence in Wanstead and Woodford 1939–45* (Wanstead, 1947), p. 156.
9   ECS 9 June 1944.
10   Kynaston, *Austerity Britain*, p. 21.
11   J. Gardiner, *Wartime: Britain 1939–1945* (London, 2004), p. 582.
12   EC 7 July 1944.

Conservative vote fell each time, as concerns about the report's future coalesced with the discontent caused by military setbacks in Africa and Asia.[13]

Education was another key issue that people rightly regarded as being in need of radical reform. In the pre-war system education ceased for most children at fourteen and only a tiny, socially privileged elite received a secondary education and then went on to university, thereby ensuring for themselves the better paid jobs and higher social status. Public opinion and most enlightened politicians were agreed that this socially divisive system had to be changed. H.H. Reid, Headmaster of St Helena School, Colchester, went a step further and argued that hope of avoiding future wars lay with 'the education and re-education of the peoples of the world'. In his view the status of education had to be raised and greater awareness generated of its benefits, both domestically and internationally.[14] Thanks to the work of R.A. Butler, MP for Saffron Walden and President of the Board of Education, the Education Act of 1944 was passed.

The Act organised education in three progressive stages: primary, secondary and further education, the first two controlled by local authorities. The school-leaving age was raised to fifteen. Prior to this age secondary education was divided between grammar schools and 'modern' schools, with their emphasis on technical education, with entrance to each determined by an examination at the age of eleven (the '11-plus'). The act actually retained many of the existing inequalities in the education system but it was seen, nevertheless, as a great achievement. The historian Angus Calder described it as 'the most impressive ever passed in the field of British education'.[15]

A Council meeting of Essex Women's Institutes praised Butler's assertion that, in future, young men and women 'shall win their dignity in their own way, and not have it created for them by birth or by false values'.[16] The Church of England was pleased that church schools retained a place in the national educational structure and that a daily act of worship was now compulsory in all schools, but its ultimate aim of establishing a Christ-centred educational system was never a realistic possibility. Some Essex boroughs – Chelmsford, Colchester, Maldon, Saffron Walden and Harwich – had their own reason for regretting the new system, as they were included in the 169 local authorities that lost their powers over education in April 1945, which were then transferred to the county council. They were considered too small to wield the greatly enhanced powers that were handed down from on high. The boroughs of Barking, Dagenham, Ilford, Leyton, Romford and Walthamstow retained their powers as 'excepted

---

13   EC pp. 583–4.
14   ECS 28 July 1944.
15   Calder, *People's war*, p. 544.
16   ECS 8 October 1943.

Figure 8.1. 'Homes Fit For Heroes.' Prefabs at Dagenham as a solution to the housing shortage at the end of the war. (Barking & Dagenham Archive and Local Studies Centre)

districts' to make their own educational schemes, but the new act partitioned the rest of the county into five divisions.

By 1943, as victory looked increasingly likely, the country became preoccupied with the pressing issue of post-war housing.[17] Bombing, especially in Metropolitan Essex, had destroyed large numbers of homes and rendered tens of thousands of other homes uninhabitable. Many pre-war houses that were already of a poor standard deteriorated because there were neither the materials nor the labour to maintain them. Slum clearance schemes had been carried out before the war, but they were now even more urgent. West Ham Town Council had established a Post-War Reconstruction Committee, which would be the means 'of undoing much that was wrong in laying out the district, and of providing houses instead of hovels, homes rather than hide-outs for its future citizens', as early as 1941. The council was aware of the irony that a fresh start in housing had been made possible 'by a ruthless enemy who had not the slightest intention of conferring benefits upon their victims'.[18] The town's Trades Council, however, feared what it called a 'patchwork' reconstruction

17   Kynaston, *Austerity Britain*, p. 20.
18   SE 26 September 1941.

and singled out 'landlordism' as a past evil to be avoided when new housing was constructed.[19]

With government encouragement, local authorities began identifying and purchasing building sites and calculating what was required for the first year after the war. Chelmsford Town Council's Housing Committee recommended three sites, on which 32 flats and 92 houses could be built.[20] In 1941 the town's population had grown so much as a result of its industrial importance that, in common with other industrial centres, firms were banned from accepting any more contracts unless they involved only a handful of workers.[21] Hoping to steal a march on its neighbours, a deputation from the council went to the Ministry of Health in July 1943, pleading for an immediate start to building in view of Chelmsford's acute housing need. Their request was rejected.[22] Nevertheless, local authorities large and small focused on their post-war housing needs. Lexden and Winstree RDC identified five building sites for a modest 38 houses.[23] West Mersea UDC had two sites in mind for just eight houses.[24] Colchester Borough Council recommended building almost 400 houses, but felt that even 1,000 would be inadequate to meet the housing needs of that first post-war year. In addition, they were dismayed that the number of houses identified for demolition by the Medical Officer would outstrip the modest house building scheme being advocated, resulting in an upsurge of homelessness or overcrowding.[25]

One solution to the likely shortage of materials was the use of prefabricated houses or 'prefabs'. In March 1944 Churchill broadcast that the government was preparing to construct up to half a million 'Portal' houses, named after the minister of works, Lord Portal, although by 1949 fewer than a third of that number had been built.[26] Tendring RDC was anxious for an allocation because they realised that by using them they could keep pace with the area's housing needs. It had found itself in an awkward position because in 1944 both its medical officer and the *Essex County Standard* carried out surveys of housing in the rural district around Colchester. The surveys revealed how much of the district's rural housing was akin to slums, how the problem of overcrowding was of serious proportions and how its inter-war housing programme had been inadequate.

Colchester, even though it had not been subjected to serious bombing and housing losses, faced serious problems because no houses had been built during

19   SE 6 March 1942.
20   ChBC minute, 4 May 1943.
21   Calder, *People's war*, p. 317.
22   ChBC minutes, 1 June, 6 July 1943.
23   ECS 28 May 1943.
24   ECS 8 October 1943.
25   ECS 21 January, 4 February 1944.
26   Kynaston, *Austerity Britain*, p. 102.

259

wartime. There were 285 names on Colchester Council's housing waiting list but it was estimated that more than 300 homes were required just to house the aged.[27] The council felt unable to rely on prefabs alone and, although it earmarked sites for 150 of them, and actually applied for 500, by early 1944 it had also commandeered disused aerodrome huts as temporary housing. One councillor expressed his concern that it would create 'slumdom', but the council pressed on with its experiment. Huts were converted and fitted with baths, lighting, heating and reasonably sized rooms. The experiment was based on the council's acceptance of the fact that the town would face a shortage of accommodation for the foreseeable future.[28] The council's action was a rather desperate, if practical, measure in the face of intense need. At Boreham, near Chelmsford, homeless people took over the empty Nissen huts left by the Americans and squatted there for several years.[29] Nationally, a loosely defined organisation called the Vigilantes set out to seize unoccupied houses for the homeless families of ex-servicemen and workers. The movement reached Southend, where a provisional committee was established. It called on the Borough Council to ask the government to grant it full powers to requisition all empty houses and rent them at reasonable prices to the homeless. It called for local authorities to be allowed to control all house-building aided by government subsidies to the exclusion of private builders, who, it was felt, would not build houses within the range of ordinary people. The Vigilantes actually occupied one house in Southend, transferring to it several servicemen's wives who had all been living in just one room. How far this movement progressed is beyond the scope of this book.[30]

Planning for housing needs was part of a wider agenda concerning the post-war reconstruction and reshaping of Britain's towns and cities. Southend Borough Council was already looking beyond a simple bricks and mortar approach and in 1942 it appointed a committee to plan the town 'as a residential, health and holiday resort', with an additional brief to consider attracting industrial undertakings.[31] Colchester Borough's Town Planning Assistant H.A. Kenn produced his own personal plan for the redevelopment of the town centre, which included the creation of a High Street 80 feet wide and streets 60 feet wide elsewhere. His proposals included providing scenic views of the castle and the Roman walls.[32] As similar plans had done in the 1930s, these ideas, which inevitably meant large-scale demolition of old but not necessarily decrepit housing in the name of municipal progress, caused some controversy. There were rallying cries to preserve what was left of Colchester's dwindling

27   ECS 26 May, 16 June 1944.
28   ECS 14 April 1944.
29   B. Jones and J. Frankland, *Boreham: a history of the racing circuit* (Romford, 1999), p. 5.
30   ST 18, 25 July 1945.
31   ST 24 June 1942.
32   ECS 3 December 1943.

Figure 8.2. Female wardens Kath Stewart and Jane Pomfret digging out a phosphorus incendiary bomb in the Waltham Holy Cross area of Group 7. (Waltham Abbey Historical Society)

historic buildings, already ransacked by the town council in the inter-war years. The Essex Archaeological Society, following the lead of the Council for British Archaeology, was anxious to ensure that the claims of Colchester's historic past were not ignored in any post-war planning.[33] For some Essex communities post-war planning took an unwelcome turn in 1944, when the eminent town planner Sir Patrick Abercrombie produced his Greater London Plan. Its aim was to move large numbers of Londoners out of the ravaged capital into small towns and villages which were to become 'satellite' towns. Braintree and Halstead were to absorb 30,000 people, and satellite towns were to be created at Margaretting (30,000), Ongar (30,000) and Harlow (60,000).[34] Being swamped by Londoners was an uninviting prospect for these small communities, although eventually only Harlow was developed as the country's first 'New Town'.

Back to the shelters

After the Blitz German air attacks on Essex, and indeed on the whole of London and south-east England, became much less frequent. Between mid-May 1941 and early 1944 there were only about twenty raids on Metropolitan Essex.

---

33   ECS 3 November 1944.
34   EC 15 December 1944.

However, in early 1944 two factors served to dispel the hope that air raids were a thing of the past.

Firstly, there was a brief return of German raiding in January and February 1944. This was much lighter than in 1940/41 but still comprised the most severe attacks for three years.[35] These sporadic attacks covered the whole of the county. Colchester received its most severe raid of the war on 23 February, when a German aircraft dropped canisters containing an estimated 1,400 incendiaries and eight oil bombs. Minor damage was widespread throughout the town, but immense damage was caused in the shopping centre around St Botolph's church, where huge fires broke out. Factories, shops, stores and a hotel were destroyed and 113 buildings damaged. The fires were so intense that it was said they could be seen from Bury St Edmunds, 25 miles away in Suffolk.[36]

Secondly, there were growing fears that the opening of the Second Front might produce German retaliation. The government was aware of a new German weapon by early 1943 and rumours about it were circulating quite widely by late 1943.[37] The *Chronicle* informed its readers of one such rumour, which stated that the Germans had offered not to use this 'terrible secret weapon' providing the Allies moderated their bombing campaign. The paper treated such an offer with contempt:

> Fools there may be among us … but, even in our own parliament, we hardly think there can be such crass stupidity as would believe that, if the Germans do possess these terrible new weapons, any mere bargain or promise would prevent them from using them to the utmost in their desire for revenge.[38]

Fears about renewed German air raids, which were expected once the Second Front was launched, led to a renewal of the agitation of 1940 in rural areas. At Little Waltham, for instance, the Chelmsford air-raid siren could not be heard but the use of whistles, which was the standard method of alerting the villagers, was actually forbidden between 6am and 10pm. At Runwell, which had tried to get shelters back in 1940, one woman condemned the classification of rural areas as places of limited risk, writing angrily that: 'It is all very well to draw lines on a map and say "This side is safe." German pilots respect neither lines nor boundaries. We are not yellow. Most of us were in the London blitz. So think of the kids and give us some measure of safety.'[39]

---

35   Angus Calder referred to this brief period as 'the little blitz': *People's war*, p. 555.
36   H. Benham, *Essex at war* (Colchester, 1946), pp. 59–60.
37   N. Longmate, *Hitler's rockets: the story of the V2s* (Barnsley, 2009), pp. 63–79.
38   EC 4 December 1943.
39   EC 25 February 1944.

It was perhaps fortunate that most of the county's residents did not know exactly what the enemy was planning. German scientists had been working on new aerial weapons throughout the war and during 1943 British Intelligence became aware of these developments. It was discovered that the Germans were experimenting with a long-range missile containing a powerful warhead. The War Cabinet appointed a special committee to investigate these revelations, and it eventually discovered that the Germans were in fact working on not one but two new weapons, named *Vergeltungswaffe Eins* (Revenge Weapon Number One), or V–1 for short, and *Vergeltungswaffe Zwei*, or V–2.

The code-name for the investigation of these new weapons was 'Crossbow'.[40] By the late autumn of 1943 much detail had been acquired on the new weapons and was being disseminated throughout the London Civil Defence Region, which of course included the relevant authorities in Group 7 in Metropolitan Essex. Clearly, as the target for these new weapons would almost certainly be London, Essex would once more be in the firing line. On 12 November 1943 an operational circular entitled *Shelling of London* was circulated. Neither aircraft nor airborne missiles were specifically mentioned, although the circular noted that 'It is believed that the enemy is preparing to shell London.' The menace represented by this new weapon was made clear:

> It seems possible that each shell may be materially bigger than any bomb yet dropped by the enemy and that the attack may be very intense – possibly up to six shells an hour – for a comparatively short period, say about a week. The enemy may, however, spread the period by reducing the intensity.[41]

The weapon involved was said to be far larger than anything used up to that point. The circular speculated that the damage inflicted might be ferocious, perhaps affecting an area of 800 acres. Within 60 acres of the site of an explosion all buildings could be so badly damaged as to require demolition, and in the next 180 acres the blast might render all houses uninhabitable. It was estimated that the assault could be continuous, with no focus to it, and might occur throughout the whole region. It seemed clear that, as in the Blitz, local Civil Defence arrangements would be stretched to the limit. Home Guard Battalions were given special training in light rescue techniques to assist during these attacks, and thirteen Home Guard Battalions were allocated throughout Group 7. By January 1944 local authorities were also instructed to begin requisitioning properties to house residents who might be rendered homeless in these new

---

40   In December 1943 this replaced the earlier code-name, 'Bodyline': Longmate, *Hitler's rockets*, p. 123.
41   ERO C/W 2/11/19, Preparations for Operation Crossbow, January 1943–August 1944. London Civil Defence Region operational circular, *Shelling of London*, 12 November 1943.

attacks, although the orders advised that it was not in the public interest for people to know why this was happening. The government feared widespread panic and a disorderly evacuation from the capital if the news leaked out.[42] It was not, in fact, until 22 February 1944, when Churchill spoke in the Commons and mentioned these new weapons as 'pilotless aircraft' and 'rockets', that they entered public knowledge.[43]

However, at the same time a conference of leading Civil Defence officers was told that the situation regarding these new weapons had changed in the preceding few weeks. They were informed that 'It is thought more probable than in November that a new threat of some kind exists but the probable consequences of it seem to be less formidable.'[44] They were told that it was more important to focus on the threat posed by pilotless aircraft, although no large-scale attack was anticipated before the end of February at the earliest. The meeting concluded with the salutary warning that the current appreciation of the situation was 'highly speculative'.[45] Once again an optimistic approach was the order of the day:

> There is no reason at present to expect attack, whether by new or old weapons, on a heavier scale, or with heavier individual missiles, than has been experienced hitherto. It is thought that any new weapon would probably be inaccurate, and that concentrated attack on a small scale target would not be possible.[46]

By the early summer of 1944 these new weapons had still not appeared but it was believed that they were being held in readiness for the imminent Allied invasion of Europe. As a result Civil Defence personnel whose services had been dispensed with during the lull of 1942–44 were recalled to full-time active service.[47]

The palpable feeling of tension that gripped Essex and, indeed, the whole country in the weeks before D-Day became even more acute once the Normandy landings were under way. However, D-Day was actually followed by another week of unexpected calm, with no German retaliatory attacks materialising. Then, on 13 June, the storm broke as the Germans launched their first V-1s. Ten were launched and three crashed on English soil, but only one reached its target – the capital – crashing on a railway bridge on the main

42   ERO C/W 2/11/19, Crossbow preparations.
43   Longmate, *Hitler's rockets*, p. 126.
44   ERO C/W 2/11/19, Conference of Group Co-ordinating Officers and ARP Controllers, 13 January 1944.
45   ERO C/W 2/11/19, Conference of Group Co-ordinating Officers and ARP Controllers, 13 January 1944.
46   ERO C/W 2/11/19, London Civil Defence Region memorandum, 4 April 1944.
47   ERO A12978 Papers of Alderman William Russell, Romford 1936–46. File 46 (Appeals that have been heard). Only three of these appeals failed.

Liverpool Street to Colchester line at Stepney. Six people were killed. The government authorised a news blackout of the incident but rumours spread rapidly that a German aircraft had crashed. It was soon clear that this was anything but a traditional aircraft or a solitary incident. The first raid quickly escalated into a continuous assault. V–1s came over in hundreds: 647 within three days of the first one. It was clearly ludicrous to maintain official silence about the situation, as countless numbers of people on the V–1s' flight paths had seen them and recognised that they were a new type of weapon. On 16 June Herbert Morrison broadcast to the nation and spoke of this new weapon, which he described as 'pilotless planes'. Shortly afterwards the government ordered that in official records they should be referred to as 'flying bombs' or 'Fly' for short.[48] However, because the V–1s went into a very steep descent once their fuel was expended they were also popularly known as 'divers', which is how Eric Rudsdale referred to them in his journal. Most people, however, called them 'buzz–bombs' or 'doodlebugs' because of the pulsating noise that their engines made and because of their elongated shape.

The first sighting of a V–1 over Essex was reported to Group 7 HQ by Civil Defence observers on 14 June. The description said:

[A] strange object, looking like an aeroplane, but with a flaming exhaust, was seen streaking and roaring across the sky, approaching London from the direction of the Thames Estuary. Many who saw it thought it was another German plane on fire and roaring to its destruction. The object fell and exploded in a neighbouring Group. The 'flying bomb' had arrived, and on the following night Group was to receive its first attack from the new missile.[49]

The first V–1 to land in Essex did so on 16 June at Baker's Hall Farm, Bures Hamlet, on the Essex–Suffolk border. The farmhouse, about 50 yards away from the blast, was badly damaged and other houses further away suffered slight damage. There were no casualties.[50] The first to land in Metropolitan Essex fell in Dagenham that same day. It caused minor damage and, as at Bures, there were no casualties. However, 47 minutes later a V–1 exploded in Ilford, this time causing substantially more damage. Overhead telephone wires and electricity cables were wrecked, about 200 houses were seriously damaged and another 500 houses and shops were slightly damaged. Four people were injured, two of

---

48   However, the Essex police record of V–1 attacks persisted in referring to them in 1944–45 as 'pilotless aircraft' or PACs: ERO T/A 679/1 Daily Situation Reports by Essex County Constabulary HQ to Sub-divisions, 3 October 1940–30 April 1945.
49   ERO C/W 2/3/2, Group 7 Operational report.
50   Benham, Essex at war, p. 68.

Figure 8.3. The devastating impact of the blast of a V-1 on a Great Eastern locomotive at Stratford. (Newham Heritage & Archives)

them seriously. Within just over two hours of the V-1 exploding at Dagenham, two more hit the town, the first one damaging the Ford factory, the second exploding in the grounds of the Rush Green Hospital, demolishing two wards and seriously damaging the rest of the hospital. Eight people died and thirteen others were injured. By the end of that first day of the offensive, four more V-1s fell at East and West Ham, Barking and Walthamstow. Six more people were left dead and 138 were injured. That same day 24 V-1s also crashed down on Extra-Metropolitan Essex, the majority on the south of the county.[51]

Between the arrival of the first V-1s and Morrison's broadcast three days later rumours travelled far and fast. On that day Eric Rudsdale and a colleague on the WAC heard 'what seemed to be the scream of a falling plane and a heavy thud'. His colleague commented that it must be one of the long-expected 'rocket planes'.[52] It was in fact the V-1 exploding at Bures. The authorities and civil defence workers soon established the pattern of V-1 attacks. Their course and distance (about 140 miles) were preset and after reaching this the engine cut out and the missile crashed to the ground. They flew at about 2,500 feet, so there was a pause of a few seconds before the V-1 finished its steep dive and

---

51   ERO C/W 2/3/2, 16 June 1944; ERO T/A 679/1, 16 June 1944.
52   ERO D/DU 888/27/3, journal, 16 June 1944.

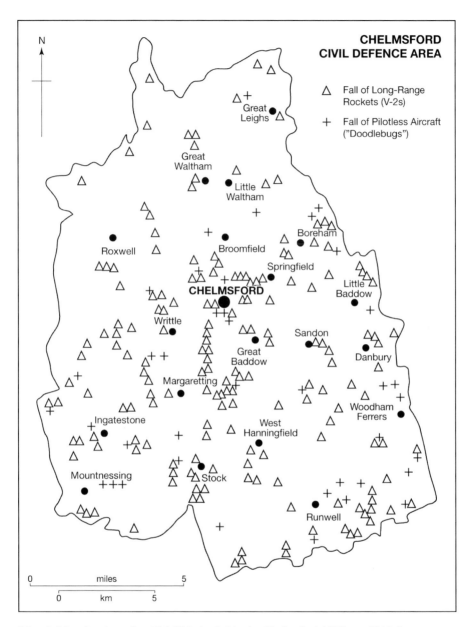

Map 4. Map showing where V-1/V-2s landed in the Chelmsford ARP area 1944–5.

hit the ground. A Romford Civil Defence memorandum in August 1944 noted that the V-1 had no ability to take evasive action, that it possessed a definite course, that it could be easily recognised both day and night from its unique sound, and that by the cutting out of its engine it gave warning of its fall and explosion. The time between the sounding of the alert and the explosion was often very short, however, because of the V-1's speed – 340 miles per hour. Incidents, the memorandum noted, were usually single ones, rather than the multiple high-explosive bombing of the Blitz. Fortunately the explosions rarely caused fires. Unfortunately, they were characterised by a very large blast effect which caused significant problems for those attempting to effect first-aid repairs on the large number of damaged houses and for 'general welfare services'.[53]

Soon 100 to 150 V-1s a day were hurtling towards London, despatched from various launch sites from Normandy to the Pas de Calais. Many did not complete the journey to their target, London, crashing instead on Essex towns and villages and on the Essex metropolitan suburbs. Evelyn Jessie Grubb and her family saw their first doodlebug on 16 June: 'Had first raid by pilotless plane last night,' she wrote in her diary. 'We saw the thing with flames coming out of the back.' Three months later she was still writing in the same vein: 'Alerts all day and night. Thumps when the bombs fall. Very wearying.'[54] Eric Rudsdale spent much time at an Observer Corps post at Boxted and on 18 July he counted sixteen 'divers' plotted on the board simultaneously.

The monotonous regularity of attacks by V-1s is recorded perfectly in the diaries of Denis Knowles, who lived at Oliver's Orchard on the outskirts of Colchester. His first mention of them was on 15 June 1944, when he wrote dispassionately, 'Raids started by pilotless aircraft.' After that he referred to them frequently for the next four months. On 29 June he recorded sardonically, 'A cold windy beastly month with Doodle Bugs to cheer us up.' On 5 September he witnessed a spectacular sight: 'About eight Doodle Bugs over at about eight a.m. I saw one and one exploded just as I got out of the door. Saw third chased by fighters. It was flying very low.'[55]

The V-1 bombardment was at its most intense during the summer of 1944. Of the 312 missiles that hit Metropolitan Essex, 297 landed in June, July and August, after which the number of incidents dwindled away to almost nothing. In the rest of the county 251 V-1s landed in June and August, while another 157 crashed down from September to December.[56] In terms of V-1 incidents, Essex was the fourth-worst-affected area after Kent (1,442), the London region

---

53 ERO A12978 File 72 'Flying Bombs', 'General characteristics of Fly attacks, August 1944'.
54 Diary of Evelyn Jessie Grubb, 16 June, 22 September 1944.
55 ERO C 1397, Diaries of Denis Knowles of Colchester 1939–45.
56 Figures for Metropolitan Essex from ERO C/W 2/3/2; figures for the rest of the county from ERO T/A 679/1.

Figure 8.4. A frequent occurrence in the summer of 1944, unusually captured on camera. The smoke from a crashed V-1 in Sewardstone, near Waltham Abbey, on 28 June. Like many of its kind, it landed in a rural landscape. (Waltham Abbey Historical Society)

(2,420)[57] and Sussex (886). As the Allied armies advanced they overran the V-1 sites in France, which were then moved further north, from where V-1s were fired from mobile launchers. This explains why V-1s launched after this time tended to land along coastal areas of Essex rather than inland and further west. During September two-thirds of all V-1s landed away from the coast, in central Essex and beyond. However, during October and November some 80 per cent landed in north Essex and along the coastal fringe.

The authorities were correct in assuming that the V-1 could not be aimed at individual targets with any degree of accuracy. That, of course, was not its purpose. The V-1 campaign was designed to terrorise the population of the London area and to break their spirit. Its greatest asset was its haphazardness. It could strike anywhere – even after the engine cut out it was extremely difficult to be sure where it would fall – and it caused great destruction and inevitable loss of life.

Just over 6,000 people in London and the surrounding counties were killed by the V-1s. In Metropolitan Essex 504 died, and ten times that number were injured. The number of casualties was much lower in the rest of the county, with just 75 deaths and 1,277 injured. Consequently, the death-rate in Essex

---

57   The 312 V-1s that landed in Metropolitan Essex were actually included in the total for the London region.

amounted to about ten per cent of the total. As in the Blitz, densely populated Metropolitan Essex suffered a far higher number of casualties even though fewer V-1s landed there than elsewhere in Essex. However, the V-1 did not inflict anywhere near as many casualties as the Blitz. For instance, only one person was killed in Chigwell compared to 78 during the raids of 1940–44. Almost nine times as many people in West Ham were killed by conventional bombing during these earlier periods than by the V-1s, and five times as many in Dagenham, East Ham and Ilford. Of course, the intensity of the V-1 campaign lasted only three months, whereas the Blitz occurred over eight months. The blast effect of V-1s was horrendous but they came down intermittently, singly, and were spread over a wide area. Even in Metropolitan Essex one in six V-1s landed in marshes, the Thames, the sea, farmland, wooded areas, golf courses or on open ground. In the rest of the county almost five out of every ten missiles expended themselves in this way. Even more significant is the fact that only one-third of V-1 incidents in the metropolitan area resulted in fatalities, and elsewhere in Essex there were fatalities in only 28 out of 402 incidents, with three-quarters of incidents resulting in no casualties at all.[58]

However, this is not to belittle the horror of the V-1s or the ordeal of the people who had to endure them. Such was the force of the blast that even V1s which did not land directly on residential areas could still cause significant damage. On 5 July one exploded on allotments in Ilford, demolishing three houses, seriously damaging 250 and causing slight damage to 450 others. One person was killed and 36 injured. Some 175 houses were damaged in Chingford on 1 July when a V-1 exploded in a reservoir.[59] When they did land in residential areas the results were often devastating. An incident in Leyton was responsible for the largest number of people killed in Essex in a V-1 attack; the missile landed at 6.05pm, demolishing ten houses and a crowded trolleybus. Thirty-six people were killed, 24 were seriously injured and 23 others had to be patched up.[60] In spite of their explosive punch, V-1s rarely demolished more than a comparatively small number of houses, often between five and twenty. However, other homes were often seriously damaged and required extensive first-aid repair work to make them habitable again. When almost 2,000 houses were damaged in East Ham by a V-1 on 26 June it caused such an acute accommodation problem that troops and the National Fire Service were brought in to assist with furniture removals.[61] The extremely large number of houses listed as damaged by V-1 blasts were usually further from the explosion

58   These statistics are based on the author's analysis of the information concerning the fall of V-1s found in ERO C/W 2/3/2 and ERO T/A 679/1.
59   Chingford Borough Council, *Chingford at war 1939–45* (Chingford, 1946), p. 133.
60   ERO C/W 2/3/2, 27 July 1944.
61   ERO C/W 2/3/2, 26 June 1944.

and often suffered superficial harm, consisting of blown-in windows or tiles blown off roofs. Although there was no telling when or where the next V-1 would land, the Civil Defence services were at least able to operate without bombs raining down at the same time, as had been the case during the Blitz. As aircraft were not being used it was now possible to use searchlights at night to assist in rescue operations and this was done many times in Metropolitan Essex.

The doodlebug campaign led to an exodus of some people from the capital and Metropolitan Essex, but not on the scale of the Blitz. Provided that they had a certificate from their own local authority classifying them as refugees and the permission of the county or borough constabulary, they were allowed to move. A large number arrived in Colchester and 360 were housed in the Lexden and Winstree area. At Brightlingsea about 200 arrived, although this fell by a quarter by the end of September.[62] The arrival of the V-1 gave a new edge to the fears of rural residents, as they were denied Morrison shelters, which were delivered only to so-called 'prescribed areas'. The Communist party branch at Clacton and Tendring, which covered a largely rural area, organised a petition demanding free Morrison shelters for everyone.[63] At Marks Tey a Mrs G.H. Grubb organised a petition protesting at the lack of a siren. A total of 900 of the village's 1,500 adults signed it. Elizabeth Grubb of Marks Tey wrote, 'The point is not so much that a siren should be installed as the deplorable fact that officialdom and bureaucracy can prevail over the rights of the ordinary civilian.' In the face of official obduracy, local efforts were made to overcome the problem. The Chief Warden of Chelmsford Central District experimented with a new warning system against V-1s. During attacks by aircraft it had been possible to reach rural areas on bicycles using whistles and bells for the all-clear. However, V-1s arrived in rural areas before alerts were sounded, so on 27 July a new rural V-1 warning system was put into operation, based on an improvement of telephone warnings. Each urban warden's post 'adopted' a rural post and a message was relayed as soon as a warning was given. It was anticipated that the message could be transmitted within three minutes of the siren ending.[64]

The arrival of doodlebugs also provoked renewed protests in urban areas. In Chelmsford, four months after the town council had given in to pressure to build new surface shelters, nothing had been done because of a lack of steel. By October, with no prospect of obtaining any materials, the Ministry of Home Security advised the council to cancel its contracts. Pressure on the council was sustained. The town's branch of the AEU demanded an improvement to Chelmsford's warning system by including during alerts 'Imminent Danger Warnings' to cover the whole borough instead of just the area of the three main factories. At the time

62   ECS 4 August, 22 September 1944.
63   ECS 6 October 1944.
64   EC 28 July 1944.

the town was covered by a hotch-potch of systems that provided a rapid warning to factories, banks, post offices, the county hall and the *Essex Chronicle* offices. Significantly, schools had no such system. Shortly afterwards it was announced that klaxon warnings were to be installed in Chelmsford and other Essex towns, following their introduction in London. In October 1944 the government conceded the issue of free Morrison shelters in the Chelmsford district, but only for those earning below £9 a week and with two or three children, a slightly more generous concession than that for free Anderson shelters.[65]

Doodlebugs were still hurtling across the late summer skies of Essex when the Germans unleashed the V-2. One of the reasons the Germans developed the V-2 was its ability to operate over greater distances than the V-1. The missile carried a warhead of more than 2,000 pounds, slightly larger than the V-1. However, its real advantage over its predecessor was its speed and trajectory. It flew at about 3,600 miles per hour, over four times the speed of sound, travelled at an altitude of 55 miles and, unlike the V-1, it did not betray itself with any sound until it nose-dived to earth with a terrific roaring sound and exploded at a speed of almost 2,000 miles per hour. This was the first, and for many the last, fatal intimation of the arrival of the missile. The RAF and all ground defences were impotent in the face of this new weapon.

The first V-2 to hit London landed at Chiswick at 7pm on 8 September. A few seconds later a second came down in Parnham Wood, near the Essex hamlet of Great Parndon, quite close to Epping. Only two cottages half a mile away were slightly damaged, suffering broken windows. Nevertheless, the sound of the explosion was like nothing heard before. Official interest in the first Essex V-2 was extremely high and the wooded site was much visited. The Parnham Wood crater was small, although it had caused considerable blast damage to surrounding trees, but the authorities concluded that the impact of the V-2 was no greater than a V-1 landing in a similar place. Local residents were not able to provide any meaningful information, although the incident was classified as a suspected 'rocket bomb'.[66] The government again imposed a news blackout on what was a new weapon of enormous magnitude, and encouraged rumours that people were in fact hearing the sound of gas mains exploding.[67] No-one was fooled by this ludicrously implausible explanation.

Enquiries were soon arriving at Group 7's HQ from outlying local authorities 'who had heard heavy and apparently unaccountable explosions' whose origin and position they were unable to verify. In fact, local authorities soon received details confirming the arrival of this new weapon. In official circles it was referred to as a long-range rocket with the code-name 'Big Ben'.

---

65   EC 27 October 1944.
66   Chingford Borough Council, *Chingford at war*, p. 138.
67   Longmate, *Hitler's rockets*, p. 182.

Metropolitan Essex did not have to wait long for the new weapon to arrive, for on 12 September one landed in Dagenham. There were no fatalities, but 85 people were injured.[68] However, on 14 September one landed in the centre of Walthamstow, killing seven people, injuring 54 and demolishing or badly damaging 52 houses. Ross Wyld, the ARP Controller of Walthamstow, blamed the government's reluctance to publicise the dangers of the V-2s for the deaths in his borough. He also pointed to a comment by the minister of health that the second battle of London was 'won but not over'. In his opinion this 'fatuous optimism' resulted in the return of large numbers of evacuees and encouraged people to sleep in their homes instead of in shelters.[69]

Something of the chaos and horror caused by a V-2 landing is conveyed in this description by a serving sailor, who had returned home to Farnan Avenue, Walthamstow, because his ship, HMS *Leeds*, was undergoing boiler-cleaning. He recalled that on 14 September

> I woke in the early hours of the morning to a terrific explosion … I attempted to go to sleep again when my parents insisted I should get up because the road was on fire. I quickly dressed and walked between the ruins of the houses adjacent to my own home. There were large piles of rubble by the side of the road and the gas main was burning furiously. I was one of the first in the road and there were … cries from the debris … we uncovered the head and shoulders of a New Zealander training with the Royal navy … We were unable to remove him … as a slate penetrated his side between his ribs … At this point the rescue team arrived and we left him to them. I next recall seeing an elderly man still in his bed on the remains of an upper floor in a room with only one wall standing. As we went to reach him he cried out that there were younger members of his family in the wreckage … We were able to trace their position by their cries and clear the way to a mother and daughter who were together in bed and trapped by heavy timbers across their legs … I recall one woman being dead in the branches of a tree, her chow dog being dead at the base of it.[70]

These weapons tested people's endurance to the limit. A nineteen-year-old woman from Walthamstow said,

> When going about your daily chores you were rocked out of your skin by the sound of these explosions just coming from nowhere …

68   ERO C/W 2/3/2, 12 September 1944.
69   Quoted in Longmate, *Hitler's rockets*, p. 173.
70   Quoted in Longmate, *Hitler's rockets*, p. 174.

Figure 8.5. Highbridge Street, Waltham Holy Cross, after a V-2 landed on the evening of 7 February 1945. In the foreground, the crater, 75 feet in diameter and about 40 feet deep, has filled with water from burst pipes. (Waltham Abbey Historical Society)

> These really did shake our morale and … had they continued … a large proportion of the population would have lost their sang-froid.[71]

The V-2s were launched from Holland, in areas that were not overrun by the Allies until 1945, so that the area east of London was very much in the front line. As a result 378 V-2s landed in Essex outside the metropolitan area. This meant that, outside the London region (517 V-2s), Essex was hit by the greatest number of rockets, six times as many as Kent and ten times as many as Hertfordshire, the other two most damaged counties.[72] To add a further perspective, one in every three rockets reaching England landed in Essex. There was an important psychological difference between the V-1 and V-2. V-1s could be seen and, as the campaign went on, more and more were shot down and failed to reach their target; in addition, even after the engine cut out there was a moment's warning before it crashed down. In contrast, there was no defence against the V-2. Jeanette Roberts, who worked in Chelmsford at this time, was aware of this when she recalled that,

---

71   Quoted in Longmate, *Hitler's rockets*, p. 227.
72   Longmate, *Hitler's rockets*, p. 385.

Figure 8.6. Wardens enter through a window of the wrecked house shown in Fig. 8.5 in an attempt to rescue a Mrs K. Peck, who later died of her injuries. (Waltham Abbey Historical Society)

> To me, all the other bombing had been horrific, because you never knew when there was going to be bombing, or who was going to be affected … but that was straightforward bombing. Those were bombs which were coming down, then you heard the explosion, if it wasn't right on top of you, you knew you were alright. But with the V–2s it was different … With the V–2s you had the crash before the sound.[73]

The V–2s were concentrated overwhelmingly to the south and west, with only about ten per cent falling north of Chelmsford, although this ensured that the whole county was affected. Once again the very rural nature of much of Essex prevented the sort of large-scale loss of life and physical destruction that was experienced by those areas nearer to London. The hundred or so V–2s that landed in rural Essex killed just 39 people, fewer than two people per rocket. Some 106 people were seriously injured and 432 slightly hurt. As with the V–1, most V–2 incidents resulted in either very few casualties or none at all. The most serious incident occurred in Chelmsford in the early hours of the morning of 19 December 1944, when a V–2 registered a direct hit on the Hoffmann factory

---

73   ERO SA 24/1460/1 Jeanette Roberts.

in the middle of the night shift. Only fifteen minutes earlier workers had been singing Christmas carols accompanied by the Salvation Army band. The place was devastated and the horror intensified when oil barrels caught fire. People were killed in their beds in houses adjacent to the factory. In all, 39 people were killed and 33 seriously hurt. Strangely enough, on the east coast people could actually see these deadly weapons being launched. 'You could see the rocket trails coming up from the other side. Five minutes later you heard the explosion and saw the black column of smoke,' recalled a Clacton man.[74] However, the advent of the V-2 removed a long-standing rural grievance, the absence of sirens. Now no one, town resident or cottage dweller, heard anything until it was too late.

The general picture was very different in Metropolitan Essex. Its urban environment was once more thriving, as persistent air raids had fizzled out, large numbers of people who had left London had returned and government pronouncements about enemy action had been complacent, and the enormous blast effect of the V-2 meant that many more people would be crushed, buried or trapped by collapsing buildings. Finally, the missile's lack of warning often caught people out of doors in larger numbers, thereby increasing the number of casualties. In fact, in Metropolitan Essex the number of casualties from V-2 attacks was almost a third higher than those of the V-1, and the actual figures dwarf those of the rest of the county. In all, 648 people were killed, 2,142 were seriously injured and 4,935 slightly injured. The scale of the attack on this region was light compared with both the Blitz and in some ways with the V-1 campaign, when many missiles crashed down each day, day after day. With the V-2s there was an average of one rocket every other day, and most days when there was an attack it was by just one rocket. Almost 40 per cent of all the missiles in the London Civil Defence Region landed in Metropolitan Essex, and Ilford, hit 35 times, suffered more times than any other part of London. With 117 dead and 465 serious casualties, only Deptford suffered more.

Evelyn Jessie Grubb's diary records one tragedy among hundreds in Metropolitan Essex, one that occurred only about two months before the end of the war. She wrote:

Poor dear Mr Hughes was killed last night in Fairholme Avenue. Rocket fell right by their dining room garden door. All in the house were killed. Blown to pieces. I can't believe it yet. Bert went round and was very upset. Started being sick and couldn't stop. Mr Hughes came so often on Sunday and sang to us – his lovely voice – Mr Watson sang duets – he always said as it got late, 'Ah, well, 'tis time I wasn't here.' He

---

74   Longmate, *Hitler's rockets*, p. 243.

won't be here ever again.[75]

One Essex resident's thoughts about the V-weapons extended to a poem which contained the lines:

> That twisted mess, the German mind,
> Perverted, vicious, dull and blind.[76]

Nevertheless, as weapons designed to generate terror among Britain's civilian population and inflict catastrophic damage on London, Germany's pilotless aircraft were a complete failure. The people of London and the Home Counties, including Essex, who had endured the Blitz, coped equally well with the horror of the V-1 and V-2. The authorities recognised this early on, despite fears, as in 1940, of widespread panic. The *Essex Chronicle* surveyed the early damage caused by these weapons and was delighted that German accounts of their effectiveness were grossly exaggerated. It commented,

> The Germans have been treated to very lurid stories of what these robot planes have done, and that is the chief value they have been to the enemy so far. Dr Goebbels' account of their performances reads like a chapter of one of Jules Verne's romances or a tale conjured up in the imagination of Edgar Allan Poe.[77]

Victory

By the spring of 1944 preparations for the Second Front were gathering pace, and could be seen everywhere in Essex and in every county along the south coast. It was alleged that houses were being shaken night after night by the tremendous Allied raids on northern France. The scale of the preparations was impossible to hide and weekly references were made in the press to the local preliminaries for 'the great assault on Germany'.[78] In the Thames off Southend hundreds of ships were at anchor in readiness for the invasion – tankers, store ships, Liberty ships, colliers, water carriers, troop transports, tank landing ships, hospital ships, repair ships and warships.[79] During April, invasion ships were also gathering at Harwich and the port's minesweeping fleet covered a thousand miles a week keeping sea routes clear.[80]

---

75   Diary of Evelyn Jessie Grubb, 21 February 1945.
76   EC 7 July 1944.
77   EC 16 June 1944.
78   BT 29 January 1944.
79   ERO T/Z 222/1, Thames Naval Control papers, Lt-Commander L. Baird, 'They Sailed the Ships', n.d.
80   R. Douglas Brown, *East Anglia 1944* (Lavenham, 1992), p. 62.

Residents in many parts of Essex, along with others in East Anglia, were among those who witnessed the very beginning of the opening of the Second Front. Charles Benham noted that on 6 June people,

> accustomed as they had become to the nightly passing of air armadas in the pre-invasion weeks, were roused from their sleep on Monday night, aware that something exceptional was literally in the air. Fleets of fighters swept low over roof-tops and glider trains could be seen in the night sky.[81]

The noise was deafening and for those living alongside main roads there was the added cacophony of passing convoys carrying troops and supplies. Many people stayed up all night, huddled against the cold, staring up at the sky. Wireless sets were turned on and everyone waited anxiously for the news they had longed to hear for four long years.

Eric Rudsdale wrote in his journal later that same day:

> Woke soon after three to a tremendous roar, and looked out to see the whole sky filled with planes, all carrying their navigation lights, dropping red and green flares in every direction. Just before four the Boxted 'drome lights came on, and all the Thunderbolts took off in pairs, in a series of shattering roars, coming up over the house and flashing away to the South West. The sky was just a mass of gleaming lights of all colours, and the house trembled with the vibration of thousands of engines.... Have never known the Americans to take off before dawn, so guessed this must be something big, and was not surprised to hear on the eight o'clock news that there had been heavy raids on Calais and Dunkirk.[82]

His historical conscience kicked in at this point and he added with alarm, 'Where is the [Bayeux] Tapestry?'[83] Evelyn Jessie Grubb and her daughter Pat watched the same aerial panorama over Metropolitan Essex. 'Invasion of Europe began this morning,' Evelyn wrote in her diary. 'The sky darkened with the never ending stream of planes. I'll never forget it. They just came and came roaring up over the trees. All in line like soldiers. We sat on the lawn and had a kind of front seat for the show.'[84] An Essex resident who was a young boy at the time later recalled:

---

81   Benham, *Essex at war*, p. 62.
82   ERO D/DU 888/27/3, journal, 6 June 1944.
83   ERO D/DU 888/27/3, journal, 6 June 1944.
84   Diary of Evelyn Jessie Grubb, 6 June 1944.

Strange thing about the invasion day every street in Southend and Leigh was absolutely full of soldiers. They had all sorts of lorries, they were towing guns and all sorts of vehicles. And then out to sea from this beach you couldn't see Kent at all because the whole of the estuary was absolutely full of cargo boats. Never seen a sight like it…. It was absolutely jam-packed. We woke up in the morning and I thought I'd go down and have another look at all them boats and every one had gone. Every single one, the whole Thames had emptied out.[85]

The following morning there were crowds in Colchester reading 'Invasion Communiqué Number One' in the windows of the *Essex County Standard*'s offices. Three days later the newspaper told the story under the headline 'How D-Day Dawned in Essex'.[86] The *Essex County Telegraph* purred gleefully, 'First the German and then the Jap. In that order they'll take the Rap.'[87] With victory in sight the newspaper was also prepared to give Stalin the benefit of the doubt as his armies stood and watched while the Nazis crushed the Warsaw Uprising:

No doubt Stalin's sympathies also are exercised by the knowledge of their plight, but he, more than any, must be the judge as to whether the actual relief of that city at this stage would entail a departure from plans and undue sacrifice and delay in other directions.[88]

Indeed, the paper continued its support for Stalin with unabated ardour as his armies advanced westwards. It commented that some people

are unwilling to learn that this Bolshevik bogey, like all other bogeys, is a figment of the imagination and has no real basis in fact. The Russia of today has no real desire to force revolutions upon other countries, adjacent to her or further away.[89]

Two months later people in Essex were able to witness at first-hand a second air armada flying to the airborne operation at Arnhem. Huge numbers of aircraft passed overhead, flying so low that it was possible to see the towing ropes and harnesses of the gliders very clearly. The glider fleet took over 90 minutes to pass: first American Douglas Dakota aircraft, then four-engined Stirlings and large numbers of Lancaster bombers followed by gliders. The first of the towing

---

85   ERO SA 1/455/1, BBC Radio Essex broadcast, Essex at War, 'Christmas Under Fire' (1989).
86   ECS 9 June 1944.
87   ECT 15 July 1944.
88   ECT 12 September 1944.
89   ECT 17 February 1945.

planes returned 90 minutes later and once more the sky was full of aircraft.[90] The failure of Arnhem and the German offensive in the Battle of the Bulge left some people crestfallen. One young woman wrote that 'Apart from the tragedy of Arnhem, we have had no reverses. I think the fact is that after a rich diet of spectacular advances and glittering victories, the plain fare of frontier-slogging and stiff local encounters seems almost unpalatable.'[91] However, these reverses were not sufficient to dampen the spirits of the *Telegraph*, which referred to the Battle of the Bulge as 'the dying beast's last struggle'.[92] In 1945, as Allied armies entered Germany, the full horrors of Nazi rule were revealed. An Essex officer who reached Belsen sent a letter to the *Chronicle*:

> It is without exception, the most ghastly sight that any of us has ever seen. You walk down the roads, and bodies are lying everywhere. You cannot tell who is alive and who is dead. The dead are piled up in many places, and many must have been dead for a week or more. Open any door of any hut, and the bodies, mostly naked, are lying everywhere. The German guards are being made to collect them, but it will take a long time. Most have died of starvation, and many are dying of typhus…. No words of mine, or anyone else's, can ever tell the horror of that camp. I watched men and women stumble over the heaps of corpses and just lay down and die…. All the German people are now completely obsequious and ready to help, but one cannot help thinking what they would have done to us had the positions been reversed.[93]

The *Essex County Telegraph* was appalled at these discoveries:

> All the terror tales of the Spanish Inquisition fade into insignificance before the ugly truth of the torture chambers of modern, scientific, Nazi Germany. The sickening horrors which have been revealed are worse than the imagination can grasp, but, much as one may hate and deplore the necessity, it is essential for the future peace of the world that these things should be placed on record and kept before the consciousness of the world, 'Lest We Forget'.[94]

Pam Hobbs's 22-year-old sister Connie was in Europe at the end of the war and her nursing unit was taken to Belsen, having first being warned that they

---

90   ECT 22 September 1944.
91   MOA, diarist 5358, 1 October 1944.
92   ECT 26 December 1944.
93   EC 27 April 1945.
94   ECT 21 April 1945.

would see terrible scenes there. She cared for some of the victims and later brought home a small photograph album of the camp taken by an American news photographer.[95] Lilian Impey of Myland Hall, Colchester, led a Friends' Relief Service team that left for the continent in March. After working in Belgium for several weeks the team was rushed to Belsen after the camp was discovered, where Impey and her colleagues worked to help survivors.[96]

Calls for the guilty to be brought to account had been heard for some time. Days after D-Day the *Billericay Times* stated, 'We stand pledged to liberate Europe. We also stand pledged to bring to judgement the men who, by their own acts, have drawn a dark curtain of barbarism over European civilisation.' The Nazis were condemned as people who had

> raised dishonesty, lying and peculation to the status of political principles. They have elevated murder, violence and pillage to the level of ethics. They have debased art and prostituted science. They have blackened men's souls and broken their bodies.

On the other hand, the paper affirmed that Britain's cause was

> the love of men for their children, for their women, their homes, their customs, and their rights. It is the assertion of men who regard no human as their master, and no fellow creature as their slaves. It is the inexorable, onward, upward drive of the beings whom God created in his own image.[97]

Gerald Debnam of Braintree was unforgiving. He hoped that Hitler would be captured so that his execution could be deferred for a year, during which time he should be put in a large cage and exhibited in all the large towns of the Allied countries. After this, '[t]he final trial and execution [was] to be in public and in aid of charity'.[98] Vengeance was also in the air at a meeting of Southend Borough Council. One councillor moved a motion that the Council 'expresses its abhorrence at the sadistic atrocities committed against political prisoners in the name of the German people' and that it should resolve not to buy German goods for a decade. The councillor concerned buttressed his motion with the statement that 'I am strongly of the opinion that the only good Germans one should trust are those who have entered the Kingdom of Heaven.' An amendment was moved rejecting the boycott of German goods but instead the

---

95   P. Hobbs, *Don't forget to write: the true story of an evacuee and her family* (London, 2009), pp. 314–15.
96   ECS 18 May 1945.
97   BT 10, 17 June 1944.
98   EC 27 April 1945.

Figure 8.7. The Führer awaits his fate. An effigy of Adolf Hitler sits on top of the VE Day bonfire built on the skid pan at Essex Police HQ in Chelmsford. (Essex Police Museum)

Council agreed not to enter any contract with anyone of German or Austrian nationality or with any firm whose capital was held by more than one-third of persons of German or Austrian descent.[99]

In spite of the hideous revelations that the end of the war in Europe brought, there was an outpouring of pride at what had been achieved. The *Southend Times* felt that this victory eclipsed all others in the past. 'This is a victory greater than all the victories of history,' it asserted, 'greater than all the triumphs of Alexander and Julius Caesar, of Saladin and Genghis Khan, and Napoleon and Wellington. No battle honours inscribed on our centuries-old colours can compare with this.'[100]

In common with the rest of the country, there were spontaneous celebrations all over the county on Victory in Europe (VE) Day. One girl recalled that

> the majority of celebrations that particular night was [sic] going on round the corner in Rectory Road. We went up there. And just everybody was hugging and kissing and singing and dancing "Knees Up Mother Brown" ... in a great big circle. It was absolutely marvellous.

99   ST 23 May 1945.
100   ST 16 May 1945.

Figure 8.8. Götterdämmerung. A model of a German aircraft crashes into the blazing bonfire, finishing off the Führer's effigy at Chelmsford. (Essex Police Museum)

Another participant commented that

> You go to a party now and it's another party … but that party, it was phenomenal. Pubs were open and you didn't pay for beer. You went in and grabbed a pint and the old barman was pulling as fast as he could and people were out in the streets singing and dancing … it's something you'll never see again … it was just as though you'd sat on an electric wire.[101]

On VE Day in Chelmsford High Street 'factory girls, shop assistants, typists, linked arms with Service men and women. American soldiers and Polish airmen showed us how they can celebrate a big occasion.' The celebrations were halted only temporarily at three in the afternoon to listen to Churchill's victory speech. At dusk a huge illuminated V-sign was placed on the Corn Exchange, together with fancy lights, spotlights and floodlights across Tindal

101 ERO SA 1/455/1.

283

Figure 8.9. Witham's VE Day parade marches through the streets of the town. The WVS is followed by a group of nurses, and then the area's wardens. (BRNTM NEG 4240, Braintree District Museum Trust)

Square. The dancing crowds, packed into the central area, grew larger and denser. 'Everybody was in it now,' wrote a *Chronicle* journalist:

> There are no lookers-on, except from the high up windows. You simply couldn't stand still. You had to dance, or shuffle, or wriggle this way or that way, just as the multitude swayed. The sombre Judge Tindal was never so outraged. One soldier managed to perch himself high on the Judge's head, an airman sat on his knees, and several more held on precariously at varying angles.[102]

The King's speech produced another brief hush before the celebrations continued into the early hours. On the skid-pan at police headquarters in the town a bonfire had been built and topped by an effigy of Hitler in uniform giving the Nazi salute. Later, a small-scale wooden model of a German aircraft was shown crashing into the Führer, and the bonfire was lit.

---

102 EC 11 May 1945.

At Colchester the response was apparently more muted. There was more of a feeling of thanksgiving for deliverance from the horrors of war, especially as many men were either still fighting the Japanese or were prisoners of war in the Far East. An *Essex County Standard* journalist out on the street on 8 May wrote, 'Instead of mafficking[103] the mood appeared to be one of chastened thankfulness by the townspeople, who for years had been in constant anxiety about husbands, sons, brothers and even sisters.' Nevertheless, the joy of victory could not be repressed indefinitely. Flags and bunting appeared, the High Street was crowded, church bells rang and victory music was played by military bands. That night the High Street was still packed with people, making it virtually impassable. 'Car drivers who stupidly tried to force their way through the throngs,' wrote the *Standard* journalist,

> had to run the gauntlet – soldiers, sailors, Canadians in hospital blue and ATS hoisted themselves on the running boards, on the bonnets, and even on the roofs. In trying to press their way through the crowds, many a car was lost to sight with a dozen men and women clinging to it.

Searchlights blazed away all over town. Bonfires were lit in streets and impromptu parties were held. Effigies of Hitler were burnt in Mill Road and Whaley Road. Soon prisoners of war began to arrive home. 25-year-old Cpl George Maddock, who had been taken prisoner at Dunkirk and spent five years in captivity, arrived back at Victor Road, where he lived, to find a victory tea party going on.[104] S. Welham, a fifth-form pupil at Colchester County High School for Girls, wrote a poem commemorating the event:

> Flags and bunting waving, streets all looking gay;
> Laughing, singing, cheering, for this is V.E. DAY.
> Bands and crowds parading, lights on everywhere;
> The day we've all been waiting for; 'Victory in the air.'
> The Nazi hordes have fallen, to Freedom's final thrust,
> And now the world is free again, from brutal force and lust;
> No more to hear the sirens wail, or bombers overhead,
> No more to lose our homesteads, no more to live in dread.[105]

---

103 The word 'mafficking' was used to describe the national celebrations following the relief of the siege of the town of Mafeking by British forces in the Boer War in May 1900. Since then the word had come to mean any form of exceptional celebration.
104 ECS 18 May 1945.
105 Colchester County High School for Girls, school magazine, 1944–45.

However, some individuals felt unable to share in these celebrations. The mother of a serving soldier wrote to him to say:

> I have not joined in this because to my idea the war is not over, it is over for us, we can lay our heads down in peace but while we are making merry there are still boys being wounded and killed. But we should thank God there is no more shelters … but when the Japs are finished I will have a proper VE Day.[106]

The end of the war in the Pacific was greeted with relief rather than with the wild enthusiasm of VE Day, although Helen Forrester recalls one rather lawless incident at Southend:

> Someone arrived with chairs and threw them on the bonfire to keep it going. People were breaking into the flats above the shops which had been left empty during the war apart from the furniture. Police were present but did nothing for fear of a full scale riot breaking out. Furniture was being thrown out of windows and breaking on the ground. A lot of the furniture looked very nice, but it was burned on the fires.[107]

However, the manner of the war's ending – the use of the atomic bomb – proved as controversial in Essex as it did elsewhere,[108] and people very quickly adopted profoundly different viewpoints concerning its use. Young John Marriage recorded the event in a matter-of-fact manner in his diary: 'We invent an atomic bomb, the first one was dropped on a Japanese city today.' Two days later he added, '60 per cent of Hiroshima has been destroyed say the Japs.'[109] The Bishop of Chelmsford speculated that 'It may be that the employment of this weapon hastened the end of the war with Japan,' but that 'nevertheless the minds of many people are profoundly disturbed.' As he continued it became evident that this new weapon was an affront to his own idealism:

> The effect of this abomination has been described in the press in lurid language…. The bomb we are told, was able to obliterate everything and every person in a large city of several square miles. It is quite idle to pretend in view of this claim that only military objectives and war workers were aimed at. The use of this missile beyond question wiped out scores of thousands of young children and women who were no

106 IWM 5265, letter from Dagenham, 8 May 1945.
107 ERO T/Z 454/1 Eyewitness account of VJ Day evening at Southend by Helen Forrester.
108 Calder, *People's war*, p. 586.
109 ERO A11545 War diaries of J.E. Marriage, 6, 8 August 1945.

more a legitimate target than are the people who read these words. It is quite impossible, with any consistency, to defend this kind of warfare. When the flying bombs and rockets were falling upon us we charged the Germans with the indiscriminate slaughter of non-combatants. That is precisely what the Allied Nations have done to a degree a hundred times greater than did the Nazis.[110]

The *Essex County Standard* was in full agreement with the Bishop. Although it felt that it was absurd to let the war drag on, it too felt that Britain had no right to protest at the Blitz and then approve of the bomb:

> The attempt to assume this moral superiority was in fact the real offence, not the use of the bomb. We dirtied our hands, rightly, necessarily, in a good cause and with a redeeming reluctance, six years, not six weeks ago, and perhaps it would have been better had we all faced the fact more squarely.[111]

After comparing this new weapon with the Blitz it concluded that 'By such comparisons can one dimly realise the power for good or ill which has been unleashed in the world this week.'[112]

In contrast, the *Essex County Telegraph* was an emphatic supporter of the bomb:

> The use of the atomic bomb was justified a thousand times over, and the proof of this is in the fact that through its use Japan was brought down long before this would have been possible in any other way, and that thereby thousands of lives were saved.... Indeed, we would go further, and let there be given to the Japanese emperor and his nation a definite assurance that any treachery or trickery on their part would bring swift retribution upon them in the form of yet another dose of the same medicine.[113]

Not all Essex people approved of the atomic bomb and the views of two residents were more in tune with those of the Bishop of Chelmsford than of the *Telegraph*. Sybil Olive approved of the bombing of Germany but she felt that

---

110 CDC September 1945.
111 ECS 24 August 1945.
112 ECS 10 August 1945.
113 ECT 25 August 1945.

Hiroshima is a different kettle of fish. That absolutely horrified me because that was completely unnecessary. The war was over to all intents and purposes and Japan were really ready to give in. You didn't see much about it in the paper but being politically active … it was pretty obvious that they were ready to give in and then they did this horrible thing.[114]

Jeanette Roberts was even more censorious:

Dreadful. I thought that really was. Although we'd gone through all the things that had happened, there hadn't been anything as dreadful as an atomic bomb. And for me I thought we had reached the lowest possible level to do that to our fellow human beings. Although they were Japanese, although it was said afterwards it shortened the war, I thought it really was the last straw.[115]

---

114 ERO SA 14/1458/1 Sybil Olive.
115 ERO SA 24/1460/1.

Bibliography

Primary sources

Essex Record Office

A5903 Papers of H.F. Bernard, relating to Harwich Civil Defence

A8071 Maldon Constituency Labour Party materials 1918–68

A11545 War diaries of J.E. Marriage, Box 4, diary no. 8 (1942), diary no. 9 (1943), diary no. 12 (1944–5)

A12402 Box 1, Billericay UDC minutes 1940–41

A12799 Diaries of Joan Wright, Box 1, 1943–5

A12967 Papers of Norman Hidden, Box 1, Political Memories 1944–50

A12978 Papers of Alderman William Russell, Romford 1936–46, File 3 (Urgent Defence Works), File 8 (Parish invasion schemes), File 11 (Civil Defence matters), File 14 (ARP Schemes for Industrial Schemes), File 19 (Public Shelters), File 30 (Fire Guards. Compulsory Enrolment Order, 1941), File 46 (Appeals that have been heard), File 67 (Parish Invasion Committees), File 72 (Flying Bombs)

C 1397 Box 1, Diaries of Denis Knowles of Colchester 1939–45

C 1412 Essex Home Guard, Battalion Orders, 1941–December 1944

C/DX/1/1/4–9 Chief Constable of Essex annual reports, 1938–41, 1944–5

C/W 1/2/10A Group 7 Air Raid message, 7 September 1940

C/W 1/3/10 Extra-Metropolitan Essex: County Chronological Files, 6–10 September 1940

C/W 1/4/2 Extra-Metropolitan Essex: County Commentaries, 1 September–1 October 1940

C/W 1/5/11 Group 7 Situation reports, 27 July–29 September 1940

C/W 1/6/1 Operational Summaries, Extra-Metropolitan Essex, October 1940–December 1943

C/W 2/1/10A Group 7 raid messages, 7–8 September 1940

C/W 2/3/2 Group 7 War Diary: Operational Report 1939–45

C/W 2/4/1 Group 7 general file

C/W 2/11/9 Invasion Defence Papers 1941–3

C/W 2/11/19 Papers relating to preparations for Operation Crossbow 1943–4

C/W 2/13/1 Group 7 shelter surveys, 1 January–1 December 1941

C/W 2/13/2 Group 7 shelter surveys, 2 March 1942

C/W 2/15/1 Group 7 repair of war damage, December 1940–December 1941

C/W 4/8 Uncontrolled evacuation camps at Epping Forest

D/B 3/5/36 Maldon Town Council minutes 1939–41

D/B 4M1/1 Harwich Borough Council minutes 1936–45

D/B 7 Hm 3/3/13 Chelmsford Borough Council, Civil Defence memorandum, 29 November 1942

D/B 7 Hm 3/3/18 Chelmsford Borough Council, Schools ARP Scheme, 1938–41

D/B 7 M2/22/2 Chelmsford Borough Council, Special committee, Domestic Air Raid Shelters, 1938-45

D/BC 1/1/2/21 XX/1 Southend Borough Council, Education Committee minutes, 1939

D/BC 1/1/13/12-15 Southend Juvenile Court Registers, 1942-45

D/BC 1/6/1/37 Southend Medical Officer of Health, annual report 1938

D/BC 1/7/5/4 Southend Chief Constable's annual reports, 1939–45

D/BC 1/14/6/1 Minutes, Southend High School for Boys, 1936–46

D/CAc 12/1/20–24 Chelmsford Diocesan Moral Welfare Association, annual reports 1941–5

D/DBg 80/30 Letter, James Hough, Brentwood School, 25 November 1940

D/DRu C5 Letters of Pamela Russell of Stubbers, 1939–44

D/DS 116/5 National and Local Government Officers' Association (NALGO), Southend branch minutes, 1939–43

D/DS 270/8 Southend Borough Council, Evacuation of Civil Population, 27 June 1940

D/DS 505/1/20 typescript, 'If Invasion Comes', no author, 1942

D/DU 746/22/1, 4 Essex War Agricultural Committee, compulsory cultivation orders 1941

D/DU 746/22/4 Essex War Agricultural Committee, compulsory cultivation orders 1942

D/DU 888/20 1938 Journal of Eric Rudsdale

D/DU 888/22 1939 Journal of Eric Rudsdale

D/DU 888/23 1940 Journal of Eric Rudsdale

D/DU 888/24 1941 Journal of Eric Rudsdale

D/DU 888/25 1942 Journal of Eric Rudsdale, 1–3

D/DU 888/26 1943 Journal of Eric Rudsdale, 1–6

D/DU 888/27 1944 Journal of Eric Rudsdale, 1–5

D/DU 935/2 Magazines of Trinity County School (Wood Green) at Hatfield Peverel 1939–41

D/DU 935/26 Copy of a letter from a girl named Avis to her father, date uncertain

D/DU 1190/1 Papers of Stanley Compton, Conscientious Objector

D/DU 1307/1 Report of the Blitz Officer for the morning of 14 May 1943 (Chelmsford)

D/DU 1595/11 Evacuation material relating to Frederick and Michael Webb

D/DU 1712/1 Tottenham High School evacuation magazine, May 1940 (at Saffron Walden)

D/E 8/11 Rochford and Canewdon Rural Deanery minutes, 1939–45

D/E 9/5 West Ham Ruridecanal minutes, 1936–48

D/F 271/1/WMS/5 Papers of Westcliff-on-Sea Motor Services

D/F 271/2/7 Westcliff-on-Sea Motor Services, correspondence

D/F 271/2/38 Southend Transport Proposed Coordination of Services

D/NB 2/3 Essex Baptist Association minutes, 1939–40

D/NB 2/27 Essex Baptist Association minutes, 1939–45

D/NB 11/5/84 Leigh-on-Sea Baptist Church, *The Outlook*, 1939–40

D/NC 11/1 Essex Congregational Union, Chelmsford District minutes, 1934–66

D/NC 22/11 London Road Congregational Baptist Church, Chelmsford, Meetings, 1932–43

D/NC 26/18 Epping Congregational Church, deacon's minutes, 1935–51

D/P 96/28/45 Halstead St Andrew, parish magazines, 1939–41

D/P 120/8/8 Holy Trinity, Southchurch, PCC minutes, 1922–69

D/P 169/28/19 St Michael, Kirby-le-Soken, newssheet, 1941

D/P 183/1/28 St Mary, Prittlewell, register of services, 1938–41

D/P 246/28/40 St Mary-at-the-Wall, Colchester, parish magazines, 1937–40

D/P 284/1/32 St Clement, Southend, register of services

D/P 300/29/3 South Benfleet PCC minutes, 1933–49

D/P 452/4 West Mersea CPS log book

D/P 516/29/3A Billericay St Mary Magdalene PCC, loose papers, 1939

D/P 534/1/36 St John the Baptist, Southend, register of services

D/P 534/29/2 St John the Baptist, Southend, PCC minutes, 1925–51

D/P 535/28/34 St Alban, Westcliff, parish magazines, 1940–41

D/P 537/8/1 All Saints, Southend, APCM minutes, 1928–45

D/P 537/29/1 All Saints, Southend, PCC minutes, 1922–54

D/P 538/1/12 St Andrew, Westcliff, register of services

D/P 539/1/17 St Erkenwald, Southend, register of services

D/P 539/8/2 St Erkenwald, Southend, PCC minutes, 1914–46

D/P 545/1/23 St James, Clacton, register of services

D/P 557/28/4–7 St Michael and All Angels, Westcliff, Parish news bulletins 1939–41

D/P 570/1/27 St Paul, Clacton, register of services

D/P 576/1/16 St Saviour, Westcliff, register of services

D/P 576/29/4 St Saviour, Westcliff, PCC minutes, 1932–45

D/P 592/1/52 Emmanuel Church, Forest Gate, register of services, 1938–47

D/P 592/29/4 Emmanuel Church, Forest Gate, PCC minutes, 1939–45

D/P 593/1/29 St Peter, Upton Cross, register of services, 1936–43

D/P 593/29/5 St Peter, Upton Cross, PCC minutes, 1939–45

D/P 641/28/1/15 St Michael, Gidea Park, parish magazines, 1940

D/UCi 1/1/18 Canvey Island Invasion Committee minutes, 1942

D/UCt M1/39 Clacton Urban District Council Evacuation Scheme, 1939

D/Z 12/1 Danbury Invasion Committee minutes

D/Z 96/25 Papers of Chelmsford Conservative party re the 1945 general election

D/Z 187/2/19 Maldon and Heybridge Cooperative Management Committee minutes, 1939–44

E/E 215/7/1 Moulsham Junior School logbook

E/ML 181/4 Felsted CPS logbook, 1914–43

E/MM 1633/2 Tilbury and West Tilbury Council School, manager's minutes

S 3150 Diary of Ernest Edwards, 1940–41

S 3294 Box 1 Trinity Church, Southend, parish magazines, 1938–40

T/A 524/4 Harlow parish council minutes, 1928–44

T/A 679/1 Daily Situation Reports by Essex County Constabulary HQ to Sub-divisions, 3 October 1940–30 April 1945

T/B 416/1 Letter, Lucy Weald to her daughter, 3 September 1939, re evacuation at Chelmsford

T/B 536/1–2 Secret wartime notebooks of Capt W.K. Seabrook, Group Commander, 202 Battalion, underground auxiliary Home Guard unit 1940–44

T/P 218/6 Newspaper cuttings relating to air raids on Woodford, 1940

T/P 350/1/1 Radwinter Church of England PS logbook

T/P 361/2 Bocking Church Street CPS logbook, 1936–45

T/P 364/5 Pebmarsh CEPS, logbook

T/P 369/2 Staples Road Infants School, Loughton, logbook

T/P 384/2 Bradfield CPS logbook

T/P 417/4–5 Layer de la Haye Church of England CPS, logbooks, 1923–78

T/P 421/11 Hedley Walter School, Brentwood, logbook

T/P 426/8–9 West Thurrock CPS logbooks

T/P 439/3–4 St Thomas of Canterbury RCS, logbooks, 1926–43

T/P 444/1–5 Mayflower CPS, Harwich, logbook

T/P 457/11 Colne High School, Brightlingsea, 1937–42

T/P 461/2 Parson's Heath CPS, Colchester, logbook

T/P 464/1–3 St John's Green CPS logbooks, 1938–59

T/P 542/1 Memories of evacuation by pupils of Woodford Green Preparatory school, 1939–40

TS 315 A. Joscelyne, 'Dunkirk Recollections', 1980

T/Z 222/1 Thames Naval Control papers

T/Z 453/1 Essay by T. McEnespie

Local government records

Chelmsford Borough Council minutes 1939–45

Essex County Council minutes 1939–45

Essex Medical Officer of Health annual reports, 1930–39

Sound archive (interviews carried out by Essex Record Office)

SA 1/455/1 BBC Radio Essex broadcast, Essex at War, 'Christmas Under Fire' 1989

SA 1/625/1 Sheila Kent

SA 1/633/1 Cecil Swallow

SA 1/635/1 An American Soldier at Willingale airfield

SA 1/639/1 Olive Foulds

SA 8/965/1 Ethel Dyer

SA 9/449/1 Jenny Hammond

SA 9/494/1 Mr Batsford

SA 14/1458/1 Sybil Olive

SA 15/704/1 Philip Bartlett

SA 16/760/1 Woolf Jacobs

SA 24/763/1 Caroline Evans

SA 24/1319/1 The Adams family, Epping

SA 24/1454/1 Doris Martin

SA 24/1455/1 Ivy Saggers (née Kelly)

SA 24/1457/1 Sybil Olive

SA 1/1458/1 Sybil Olive

SA 24/1459/1 Jeanette Roberts

SA 24/1460/1 Jeanette Roberts

Imperial War Museum Department of Documents

Private Papers

1031 Moyra Charlton

1237 J.L. Stevens
3957 T.H. Pointer
4833 F.W. Hurd
7200 Lt H.F. Maxwell-Scott
Miscellaneous Papers
3149 Letter from Audrey Fieldhouse to Sgt Pilot L.A. Fieldhouse, 20 September 1940
5265 Letters to R. Griffin

The National Archives
CAB 102/726 Care of the homeless at West Ham after air attacks, 1942
HLG 52/1511 West Ham financial difficulties and government grants 1941–5
HO 199/58 German aircraft crashed at Clacton, 30 April 1940
HO 271/721 Leyton Borough Public Shelter, West Ham and Leyton Tunnels, reports and
    correspondence
WO 189/2141 'Report on Air conditions in the Leytonstone–West Ham Shelter Tunnel:
    investigation carried out on the night of 8–9 April 1941'

Mass Observation Archive, University of Sussex
Directive Replies (numbers relate to the Essex residents who replied to Mass Observation
    questionnaires that were referred to as directives)
1396
2316
2481
2566
2677
2685
2694
2802
Diaries (numbers relate to Essex residents who kept diaries for Mass Observation during the war)
5010
5042
5054
5205
5340
5358
5370
5414
5416
5424
Topic Collections (contain information on various aspects of the Home Front in Essex)
TC1 1/3/H Housing 1938–48, Becontree and Dagenham, 1941–2
TC5 5/1/D Box 1, Infant school teachers, 1939
TC5 5/1/H Box 1, Evacuation material, Romford, 1939
TC5 5/2/C Box 2, Evacuation material, east coast evacuation, 1940

TC23 23/8/Q Air Raid material, Clacton, 1940
TC23 23/10/M Air Raid material, Romford, 1940
TC66 66/3/F Town and Country survey, Chelmsford, 1942
TC46 By-Elections 1937–47, Box 4, 46/4/A-E, West Ham, Silvertown, 1940

University of Essex
Margery Allingham Papers, Box 21

Unpublished material
Author's notes of interviews with Pat Lewis and Patricia Clayden, 24 May 2012
Diary of Evelyn Jessie Grubb, 1939–40, 1944–5, in the possession of Mrs Pat Lewis of
  Chelmsford
Forrester, H., Eyewitness account of VJ Day evening at Southend, in ERO T/Z454/1
Green, P., A Penny for Biscuits, in ERO T/Z 451/1
Letter by Joyce Nightingale in the possession of Mabel Jervis of Chelmsford

Colchester Local Studies Library
Chelmsford Diocesan Chronicle, 1939–45
The Colcestrian (magazine of Colchester Royal Grammar School), December 1940, July 1941
Colchester Borough Council minutes 1939–45
Essex Farmers' Journal, 1939–45
Essex Review, vol. 50, 1941, vol52, 1943, vol 53, 1944, vol. 54, 1945
Transactions of the Essex Archaeological Society, 1942–5, vol. 23; 1944–9, vol 24

Colchester County High School for Girls
School magazines

Newspapers
Chelmsford Library: *Essex Chronicle* 1939–45
Colchester Library: *Essex County Standard* 1939–45; *Essex County Telegraph* 1939–45
Essex Record Office: *Billericay Times* 1939–40, 1944; *Burnham Advertiser* 1939–42; *Southend
  Times* 1943
Southend Library: *Southend Standard* 1940; *Southend Times* 1941–42, 1945
Stratford Local Studies Library: *Stratford Express* 1939–42

Secondary sources
Addison, P. and Craig, J. (eds), *Listening to Britain: home intelligence reports on Britain's finest hour,
  May to September 1940* (London, 2010).
Alexander, I., *Maid in West Ham: my formative years 1924–48* (Winchester, 2001).
Allingham, M., *The oaken heart* (London, 1941).
Anderson, P.A. with Anderson, J.N., *Dangerous skies: war events and family life 1941* (Raydon, 2007).
Baker, W.J., *A history of the Marconi Company* (London, 1970).
Begent, A., *Chelmsford at war: a chronology of the county town of Essex during the Second World War
  1939–45* (Chelmsford, 1996).

Benham, H., *Essex at war* (Colchester, 1946).

Bensusan, S.L., *Fireside papers* (London, 1946).

Blake, D.J., *Window vision* (Braintree, n.d.).

Blaker, G., *War in West Ham*, Newham Story, <http://www.newhamstory.com/node/2498>, accessed 31 October 2014.

Brown, C.G., *Religion and society in twentieth-century Britain* (London, 2006).

Brown, P., *The fighting branch: the Wivenhoe to Brightlingsea railway line 1866–1964* (Romford, 1975).

Budds, D., *Wix at war* (2002).

Burrows, V.E., *The tramways of Southend* (Southend, 1965).

Butler, N., *The story of Wivenhoe* (Wivenhoe, 1989).

Calder, A., *The people's war: Britain 1939–1945* (London, 1969).

Calder, A., *The myth of the Blitz* (London, 1991).

Calder, R., *The lesson of London* (London, 1941).

Carter, E.J., *The diary of an air raid warden 1939–45*, 2nd edn (Loughton, 2009).

Caunt, G., *Essex in parliament* (Chelmsford, 1969).

Chamberlain, E.R., *Life in wartime Britain* (London, 1972).

Chingford Borough Council, *Chingford at war 1939–45* (Chingford, 1946).

Clacton VCH Group, *Clacton at war 1939–45* (2003).

Clarke, G., 'The Women's Land Army and its recruits 1938–50', in B. Short, C. Watkins and J. Martin, *The front line of freedom: British farming in the Second World War* (London, 2006).

Clifford, P.R., *Venture in faith: the story of the West Ham Central Mission* (London, 1950).

Colchester County High School magazine, 1944–45.

Coleman, D.C., *Courtaulds: an economic and social history: vol. iii, crisis and challenge 1940–66* (London, 1980).

Collecott, N., *As we were: an Essex family during and after the Second World War* (Durham, 1993).

Collett, J. (comp.), *There'll always be an England: the story of a group of World War Two evacuees, told in their own words of how they were torn from home, town and family, to a life amongst strangers in an alien environment* (Stourport-on-Severn, 2006).

Cone, P.J., *Harwich and Dovercourt in the twentieth century* (Harwich, 2004).

Cooper, J., *Clavering at war 1939–1945* (Clavering, 2012).

Crosby, T., *The impact of civilian evacuation in the Second World War* (London, 1986).

Crummy, P., *In search of Colchester's past* (Colchester, 1981).

Demarne, C., *The London Blitz: a fireman's tale* (London, 1980).

Dewey, P., 'The supply of tractors', in B. Short, C. Watkins and J. Martin, *The front line of freedom: British farming in the Second World War* (London, 2006).

Douglas Brown, R., *East Anglia 1940* (Lavenham, 1981).

Douglas Brown, R., *East Anglia 1942* (Lavenham, 1988).

Douglas Brown, R., *East Anglia 1943* (Lavenham, 1990).

Douglas Brown, R., *East Anglia 1944* (Lavenham, 1992).

Driberg, T., *Ruling passions* (London, 1977).

Driberg, T., Reporting on BBC World at War, episode 15, *Homefires: Britain 1940–44* (1974).

Essex County Council, *A report of the ARP committee on the organisation and administration of the civil defence services with a brief account of the operations in which they were engaged 1939–45* (Chelmsford, 1947).

Everitt, B., *Moore's: the story of Moore brothers, Kelvedon, Essex: passenger carrying through five generations* (author, 1998).

Federation of Essex Womens' Institutes, *Essex within living memory* (Newbury, 1995).

Finch, P., *Voluntary hospitals of Southend-On-Sea 1887–1948* (Southend, 1948).

Finch, P., *Warmen courageous: the story of the Essex Home Guard* (Southend, 1951).

Foot, W., 'The impact of the military on the agricultural landscape of England and Wales in the Second World War', in B. Short, C. Watkins and J. Martin (eds), *The front line of freedom: British farming in the Second World War* (London, 2006).

Foster, S.M., *A history of the Diocese of Brentwood 1917–1992* (Brentwood, 1994).

Fox, M., *Chelmsford Diocese – the first 100 years* (Chelmsford, 2013).

Foynes, J., *Under the white ensign: Brightlingsea and the sea war 1939–45* (author, 1993).

Gardiner, J., *Wartime: Britain 1939–1945* (London, 2004).

Gardiner, J., *The Blitz: the British under attack* (London, 2010).

Garner, S., *Wheel 'em in: the official history of Chelmsford City Football Club* (Rainham, 2001).

Gavin, Sir W., *Ninety years of family farming: the story of Lord Rayleigh's and Strutt and Parker Farms* (London, 1967).

Geere, M., *Reminiscences of a Land Girl in Witham* (Witham, 1987).

Gillies, M., *Waiting for Hitler: voices from Britain on the brink of invasion* (London, 2006).

Godwin, G., *Marconi 1939–1945: a war record* (London, 1946).

Goodale, A.P., *Southchurch: the history of a parish* (Southend, n.d.).

Graham, M., *Oxfordshire at war* (Oxford, 1994).

Green, P., *A penny for biscuits*, in ERO T/Z 451/1.

Gregg, J., *The shelter of the tubes: tube sheltering in wartime London* (London, 2001).

Hamilton, D., *Orsett Golf Club 1899–1999* (2000).

Harrison, T., *Living through the Blitz* (London, 1976).

Herbert, A.P., *The battle of the Thames: The war story of Southend pier* (London, 1947).

HMSO, *Front line 1940–41: the official story of the civil defence of Britain* (London, 1942).

Hobbs, P., *Don't forget to write: the true story of an evacuee and her family* (London, 2009).

Hoodless, W.A., *Air raid: a diary and stories from the Essex Blitz* (Stroud, 2008).

Hylton, S., *Their darkest hour: the hidden history of the home front 1939–1945* (Stroud, 2001).

Idle, E.D., *War over West Ham: a study of community adjustment* (London, 1943).

Jacobs, N., *The sunshine coast: bygone Clacton, Walton, Frinton and District* (Lowestoft, 1986).

Johnson, D.E., *Exodus of children* (Clacton-on-Sea, 1985).

Jones, B., *Wings and wheels: the history of Boreham airfield* (London, n.d.).

Jones, B. and Frankland, J., *Boreham: a history of the racing circuit* (Romford, 1999).

Jones, H., *British civilians in the front line: air raids, productivity and wartime culture 1939–45* (Manchester, 2006).

Joscelyne, A.W., 'Dunkirk Recollections', in ERO T/S 315 (1980).

Kaye, B., *The company we kept* (London, 1986).

Kelly, A., 'Eric Ravilious: The art of war', *History Today* (June 2010), pp. 42–7.

Kennell, R., *The story of Holland-On-Sea during the Second World War* (author, 2003).

Kynaston, D., *Austerity Britain 1945–51* (London, 2007).

Lemmon, D., and Marshall, M., *Essex County Cricket Club: the official history* (London, 1987).

Lombardelli, C., *Branch lines to Braintree* (Colchester, 1980).

Longmate, N., *Hitler's rockets: the story of the V2s* (Barnsley, 2009).

Lyle, O., *The Plaistow story* (London, 1960).

Mackay, R., *The test of war: inside Britain 1939–1945* (London, 1999).

MacKenzie, S.P., *The Home Guard: a military and political history* (Oxford, 1995).

Maldon Labour Party, 'Maldon Constituency Labour Party: The First Fifty Years 1918–68', in ERO A8071, Maldon Constituency Labour Party papers (1968).

Martin, J., 'The structural transformation of British agriculture: the resurgence of progressive, high-input arable farming', in B. Short, C. Watkins and J. Martin (eds), *The front line of freedom: British farming in the Second World War* (London, 2006).

Mason, P., *Southend United: the official history of the Blues* (Harefield, 1993).

Maxwell Scott, S., *Pa's wartime letters and this & that* (2010).

Momme, A., *Chronicles of a marauder bomber armorer* (Norristown, PA, 2010).

Murray, K.A., *A history of the Second World War: agriculture* (HMSO, 1955).

Nicholson, V., *Millions like us: women's lives in war and peace 1939–49* (London, 2011).

O' Brien, T., *History of the Second World War: civil defence* (London, 1955).

Owen, G., *Writtle: a village of distinction* (1993).

Paye, P., *Bishop Stortford, Dunmow & Braintree branch* (Usk, 1981).

Paye, P., *The Saffron Walden branch* (Oxford, 1981).

Ramsey, W.G., *The East End then and now* (London, 1997).

Reeve, J., *Wickford memories* (Hullbridge, 2005).

Reynolds, R., *Rich relations: the American occupation of Britain 1942–45* (London, 1995).

Reynolds, R. and Catton, J., *Thurrock goes to war* (Wickford, 1997).

Richards, G., *Ordeal in Romford* (Romford, 1945).

Riddiford, W., Dagenham ARP Diary, <http://www.lbbd.gov.uk/MuseumsAndHeritage/ BlitzBlog/Documents/BlitzBlogAugust1940.pdf >, accessed 30 October 2014.

Ridgewell, C., *Looking better looking back* (London, 2004).

Roberts, M. and Roberts, R., *Under the flight path: home front diaries from south east Essex* (St Osyth, 1995).

Rollins, J., *Soccer at war 1939–45* (London, 1985).

Rusiecki, P., *The impact of catastrophe: the people of Essex and the First World War (1914–1920)* (Chelmsford, 2008).

Sadler, R., *Sunshine and showers: one hundred years in the life of an Essex farming family* (Chelmsford, 1998).

Saunders, H.St.G., *For d at war* (London, n.d.).

Sheridan, D., *Wartime women: a mass-observation anthology: the experiences of women at war* (London, 1990).

Short, B., 'The dispossession of farmers in England and Wales during and after the Second World War', in B. Short, C. Watkins and J. Martin (eds), *The front line of freedom: British farming in the Second World War* (London, 2006).

Short, B., Watkins, C., Foot, W. and Kinsman, P., *The National Farm Survey: state surveillance and the countryside in England and Wales in the Second World War* (London, 2000).

Short, B., Watkins, C. and Martin, J. (eds), *The front line of freedom: British farming in the Second World War* (London, 2006).

Short, B., Watkins, C. and Martin, J. , 'The front line of freedom: State-led agricultural revolution in Britain 1939–45', in B. Short, C. Watkins and J. Martin (eds), *The front line of freedom: British farming in the Second World War* (London, 2006).

Smith, G., *Essex airfields in the Second World War* (Newbury, 1996).

Smith, H.L., *Britain in the Second World War: a social history* (Manchester, 1996).

Smith, V.T.C., *Coalhouse Fort and the artillery defences at East Tilbury: a history and guide* (Southend, 1985).

Stait, B., *Silver end: the war years* (author, 1995).

Stansky, P., *The first day of the Blitz* (Yale, CT, 2007).

Steele, J. (ed.), *A working class war: tales from two families* (London, 1995).

Summerfield, P. and Peniston-Bird, C., *Contesting home defence: men, women and the Home Guard in the Second World War* (Manchester, 2007).

Swindale, D.L., *Branch lines to Maldon* (Colchester, 1977).

Thomas, D., *An underworld at war: spivs, deserters, racketeers and civilians in World War Two* (London, 2003).

Thompson, R.J., *Battle over Essex* (Chelmsford, 1946).

Thornton, C. (ed.), *The Victoria history of the county of Essex, vol. xi, Clacton, Walton and Frinton: north-east seaside resorts* (London, 2012).

Thorpe, A., *Britain in the 1930s* (Oxford, 1992).

Tiquet, S., *It happened here: the story of civil defence in Wanstead and Woodford 1939–45* (Wanstead, 1947).

Titmuss, R., *Problems of social policy* (London, 1976).

Turner, E.S., *The phoney war on the home front* (London, 1961).

Wallace, M., *Nothing to lose, a world to win: a history of the Chelmsford and District Trades Union Council* (Chelmsford, 1979).

Warburton, S., *Chingford at war 1939–45: a record of the civil defence and allied services and incidents which occurred in the borough* (Chingford, 1946).

Warden, K. and Williams, M., *Chelmsford Golf Club 1893–1993* (Chelmsford, 1993).

Watt, P., *Hitler v Havering 1939–45* (Romford, 1996).

Wentworth Day, J., *Farming adventure: a thousand miles through England on a horse* (London, 1943).

Wentworth Day, J., *Harvest adventure: on farms and sea marshes, of birds, old manors and men* (London, 1946).

Wheen, F., *Tom Driberg: his life and indiscretions* (London, 1990).

White, L. (ed.), *Lexden in wartime: memories of local people, vol 2* (Colchester, 2008).

Wilkinson, J., 'Women at war: the provision of childcare in Second World War Chelmsford', *Essex Journal*, (autumn 2007), pp. 38–44.

Williams, J., *Leigh-On-Sea: a history* (Andover, 2002).

Willingham, E., *From construction to destruction: an authentic history of the Colne Valley and Halstead railway* (Halstead, 1989).

Wise, J., *The story of the Blackwater Sailing Club* (Maldon, 1999).

Wormell, P., *Essex farming 1900–2000* (Colchester, 1999).

Zweiniger-Bargielowski, I., *Austerity in Britain: rationing, controls and consumption 1939–1955* (Oxford, 2000).

Unpublished papers

Bloomfield, D., 'Bloomfield transport 1927–49' (unpublished manuscript, 2012).

Bullen, R., 'A community at war: Mersea Island 1939–45', MA thesis (Essex University, 2006).

Elcoat, G., 'Invasion preparations on the Essex Coast 1940–1', in ERO Box Z11B. (1960)

Innes, M.R., 'Chelmsford: a geographical and historical survey to 1951', unpublished typescript (1951).

Waddy, K., 'What were women's experiences at Davey and Paxman and Company during World War Two, and what impact did the presence of women workers have on the firm?', BA dissertation (Essex University, 2008).

Index

Abberton reservoir, Colchester, mined 23–4

Abercrombie, Sir Patrick, post-war
    development 261

Alcohol consumption 206–7

Althorne 100

Air fields
    Birch 153
    Boreham 152
    Boxted 153
    Chipping Ongar 152
    Great Saling (Andrews Field) 152
    Matching 152
    Ridgewell 160

Air raids, 35–63, 161–7, 261–62
    casualties and damage 46, 60, 61–3, 162,
    267–8, 273–4

Air-raid shelters 35–8, 40, 49–53, 269–70
    Anderson shelters 47–9, 54, 60
    deep shelters 49, 56
    shelter protests 47, 57, 271
    shelter surveys, Group 7 47, 49, 162
    tube shelters 49–52
    Allied air raids, on Germany 167–71
    see also Rocket weapons, German

Allingham, Margery, crime writer 3, 4, 9, 17,
    18, 26
    manuscript, hiding of 27
    'Black Saturday' 56

Anglo-American Oil Works Purfleet 45

Appeasement 1–3

Archaeology 204

Arnhem, aerial armada 279–80

Art 201–2

Atlas Ironworks 128

Atom bombs, use of 286–8

Barking 31, 35, 43, 49, 59, 60, 73
    black market 220
    Council war bonuses 73
    education 193
    evacuees 185–6
    'kitchen front' 104
    salvage of railings 87
    shopkeepers 76

Basildon 111

Battle of Britain 38, 39

Beach Divisions 66–7

Beckton Gasworks, East Ham 42, 44

Becontree 46

Belgium, surrender of 19

Belsen, concentration camp 138, 280–81

Benfleet 207

Beveridge report 5, 256

Bigamy 227–8

Billericay 56, 207, 230

Birch 107

Bishop of Chelmsford, see Henry Wilson

Blackout 15–16, 215–6

Black market 218–9, 220

Black Notley 29

'Black Saturday' 41–7, 56, 62, 196

Bloomfield Transport 86

Boggis, Father Jack, secretary of Driberg's
    election campaign 134

Boreham 67, 152, 167, 260

Borlase-Matthews, R., Independent
    candidate, Maldon by-election 128,
    130–1

Boxted 65, 153, 268, 278

Bradwell-on-Sea 15, 129

Braintree 54, 71, 81, 85, 86, 99

Abercrombie plan 261
American troops 153, 156, 157
cinema 198
farm repossessions 123
leisure 206
Maldon by-election 128, 133–4, 136
Brentwood 33, 54, 85, 87, 206
Brightlingsea 13, 16, 72, 78–9, 271
Broomfield 167, 180
Bures 86, 107, 265, 266
Burnham 12, 37, 76, 88, 128, 136
Butler, R. A. B., Conservative MP for Saffron
 Walden 116, 250, 257

Calder, Ritchie, left-wing political activist
 and journalist 5, 61–2
Canvey Island 65, 85
Chadwell Heath 15, 46
Chamberlain, Neville, Prime Minister 1, 2, 8,
 9, 10, 18
Channon, Henry, Conservative MP for
 Southend 140
Chelmsford 4, 6, 13, 16, 25, 28
 air raids 54, 61, 163, 164, 165–8
 American troops 153, 154, 155–6
 bus services 84, 85, 100
 by-election 1945 138–40
 cinema 198–200
 evacuation 13–14, 180
 factories 71, 81, 90
 food queue 104
 football 210
 general election 1945 139–41
 housing 258–9
 leisure 201, 202, 203, 204, 205
 petrol rationing 84
 VE Day 282–4, 282, 283
 V-1 and V-2 rockets 267, 271
Chigwell 35, 270
Chingford 35, 45, 161
Chipping Ongar 152
Church of England 16–17, 143, 236–53
Churches
 All Saints, Southend 247, 249

Emmanuel, Forest Gate 16, 19, 244, 246,
 247, 248
 finances 248
Epping Congregational Church 250
High Street Methodist Church,
 Chelmsford 244
Holy Trinity, Southchurch 244
Leigh-on-Sea Baptist 245
London Road Congregational Church,
 Chelmsford 244
London Road RC Church 244
St Erkenwald, Southend 246, 248
St James the Less Roman Catholic,
 Colchester 245
St John, Chelmsford 247
St John the Baptist, Southend 244, 247
St Michael, Kirby-le-Soken 248, 249
St Michael and All Angels, Westcliff 243,
 244, 246, 247
St Peter, Colchester 245
St Peter, Upton Cross 61, 246
St Paul, Clacton 245
St Saviour, Westcliff 245, 246, 247, 248, 249
Trinity Church, Southend 245
Churchill, Winston, Prime Minister 18, 20,
 31, 40, 130–3, 264
Cinema 198–200
Civil Defence 4–5, 35–6, 40, 42, 43, 48, 53, 56
 ARP men, funeral of 254
 female wardens 91, 162, 167, 259
 fire guards 162
 preparations for German rockets 262–3,
 271
 'spotter' systems, watching for enemy
 aircraft 77
Clacton 12, 21, 23, 25, 28, 29
 air raids 54
 beach divisions 66–7
 churches 245
 evacuees 180–1, 182
 local rates 88
 minelayer crash 37, 38
 crime 221
 shopkeepers 78

Clavering 6, 181, 233
Clayton, Hollis, Chairman of Essex NFU 116, 117
Coalhouse Fort, East Tilbury 23
Coastal defence system, Essex as part of 22–3, *23*,
Coastal ban, lifted 207–8
Coastal industries 78–9
Colchester 10–15, 25, 28, 70
    air raids 165, 262
    American troops 153, 157
    black market 219
    bus services 84, 103
    Daniell's, brewers 77
    Equitable Building Society 77
    evacuation 178
    farm repossessions 123
    football 210
    housing 258–60
    leisure 196–205
    local rates 88
    oyster industry 78
    post-war planning 259, 261
    repertory company 146–7, *201*
    shopkeepers 75–6
    VE Day 285
    war bonuses 73, 103
    war factories 81–91
    war savings 71–2
    WVS 108
Collier Row 54
Commonwealth party 130, 138, 140, 141
Compton, Stanley, conscientious objector 233–6
Conscientious objectors 15, 110, 115, 228–36, *234*, 251
    see also Compton, Stanley
Conscription 15
Coryton 39
Cost of living, rise of 72–3
Courtauld silk factories, Braintree and Coggleshall 81, 128
Cricket 212–14

Crime 215–22
    see also Black market
Crittall company, Silver End 81, 82, 83, 92, 128
Crompton-Parkinson, Chelmsford 83, 163
Crowther clothing company, Colchester 91

D-Day 264, 277–9, 281
Dagenham 35, *40*, 43, 46, *48*, 59
    Ford company 41, 70, 82, 91, 111
    prefabs 258
    V-1 rockets 265, 266, 270
    V-2 rockets 273
    war savings 72
    war survey 74–5
Danbury 13, 65, 100
Dancing 205–6
Davey and Paxman, engineering company, Colchester 81, 82, 103
Defeatist talk 25–6, 216
Dovercourt 14, 56
Driberg, Tom, Independent MP for Maldon 6, 99, 129–41, *129*, 161
    post-war hopes 255–6
Dunkirk, evacuation from 18, 19–20, 22, 25
'Dunkirk spirit' 21
Dunmow 86, 116, 145, 181

Earls Colne 128
East Ham 12, 31, 35, 44, 46, 47, 73
    local government arrangements after the Blitz 58
    local rates 89
    salvage 86–7
    V-1 raids 270
    war bonuses 73, 103
Education, of children in wartime 186–94
Education Act, 1944 243, 250, 251, 257–8
Edwards, Ernest, diarist 4, 18, 151, 171, 195, 197, 198, 217, 254
El Alamein, battle of 174–6
Epping 12, 59, 180
Epping Forest 46, 236

Essex County Council 27, 46, 47, 73, 88, 101, 103, 115, 232
    conscientious objectors, dismissal of 232
Essex Record Office 4, 5, 28
Evacuation of schoolchildren 11–14, 16, 28–31, 177–82
    reception areas, conditions in 177–85
    social problems of 178–9
'Extra Metropolitan Essex' 35, 53–7

Fambridge 100
Farming
    Essex War Agricultural Committee (EWAC) 110–16, 120–25
    Essex county farm survey 120–1
    Essex Farmers' and Country People's Association 123–4
    farm labourers 114–17
    farm repossessions 120–4
    ploughing-up campaign 111–12
    vermin, campaign against 112–13, *112*
Farms
    Baker's Hall Farm, Bures 265
    Barnston Hall, Dunmow 122
    Bower Hall Farm, Mersea Island *96*, 121–2
    Holmwood Farm, Colchester 121
    One Tree Hill, Laindon 111
    St Mary's, Great Bentley 121
    Thorrington Hall 121
Fascists 26, 175
Fashion, women's 105–7
Feering 72
Felsted 13, 114, 188
Finchingfield 128
Finland, Soviet invasion of 142–4, 150
Fire-watching 59, 162
Football 209–14
Ford company, Dagenham 6, 41, 59, 70, 82, 83
    air raids 161
    women employees 91
Fordham 65
Foreign troops, in Essex 150–61
France, fall of 20–1
Frinton 72, 78, 88, 245

Galleywood 106
General election of 1945 139–41
'Gilman's Dare Devils' *43*, 43
Goldhanger 174
Golf 212, 213
Gooley, Madge, prostitute 226–7
Graf Spee 14
Grays 8, 26, 83
Great Baddow 101
Great Bardfield 57, 158, 217
Great Canfield 21
Great Leighs 67
Great Parndon 272
Great Yeldham 70
Group 7 (Outer London ARP Area) 35, *36*, 39–41, *261*, 263, 265, 272

Haldane, Professor H. B. S., and deep shelters 49–50
Halstead 54, 70, 81, 86, 197, 261
Harlow 16, 54, 125, 261
Hatfield Peverel 67, 100, 182–5, *183*, 187–8
Harwich 23, 28, 35, 38, 54, 55–6, 80
    D-Day 277
    general election of 1945, Liberals retain 141
    local rates 88
    railway 86
Hoffmann company, Chelmsford 71, 81, 91–2, 163, *164*, 165
Holehaven 220, *220*
Holidays 207–8
Holland-on-Sea 10, 66–7
Home Guard (also Local Defence Volunteers) 6, 27, 31–4, *32*, 66–70, *68*, *70*
    See also League of Frontiersmen, Beach Divisions
Horticultural shows 209
Hornchurch 49, 54, 56, 61
Housing, post-war 258–61
    see also prefabs
Hunt, Reuben, Conservative party candidate, Maldon by-election 128, 130–1, 132–3, 134, 136

Idle, Doreen, left-wing political activist and
    journalist 5, 57–8
Ilford 35, 40, 270
Industrial relations 83–4, 103
Ingatestone 54
Invasion, concerns about 18, 22–5, 33–4, 64–6
    see also Signposts, removal of

Japan, entry into the war 172–3
Jaywick 66
Jews, European, Nazi treatment of 173–4

Kelvedon 72, 85
Kelvedon Hatch 54
'Kitchen front' 104–5
Knowles, Denis, diarist, Colchester 169, 268

Laindon 111
Lambourne 107
Layer Breton 107
Leigh-on-Sea 21, 26, 30, 183, 209
Leisure 194–214
    See also Alcohol, Archaeology, Art,
    Baseball, Cinema, Cricket, Dancing,
    Football, Golf,
    Holidays, Horticultural shows, Hunting,
    Music, Newspapers, Reading, Sailing,
    Theatre,
    Wireless
Lewis, Oswald, Conservative MP for
    Colchester 124, 150, 169
Leyton 12–13, 35, 40, 50–3, 59, 108–9
    evacuation 179–80
    V-1 raids 270
Leytonstone 15, 52, 217
Lexden, Colchester 61, 178
Lexden and Winstree Rural District Council
    97, 121, 259, 271
Lindsell 155, 181
Little Bardfield 159
Little Horkesley 54
Little Waltham 244, 262
Local Defence Volunteers (LDV) see also
    Home Guard

Macnamara, Jack, Conservative MP for
    Chelmsford until 1944 2, 138, 173
Maldon 13, 32, 54, 59, 76, 84, 86
    bus conductresses, threatened strike by
    103
    by-election 1942 127–38
    farm repossessions, meetings concerned
    with 124
    general election 1945 141
Maldon and Heybridge Cooperative Society
    76–7
Manningtree 158, 214
Marconi company, Chelmsford 6, 71, 80,
    82–3, 92, 100
    air raids, hit by 163
Margaretting, 261
Marks Tey 271
Marriage, John, diarist, Chelmsford 166, 167,
    198, 203, 286
Matching 152, 155
Mayland 54
Mersea Island 23, 23, 96, 123, 179, 182
Metropolitan Essex, Essex adjacent to
    Greater London 12–13
    see also Group 7
Millington, Ernest, Independent MP for
    Chelmsford 138–9, 140
Minelaying, off Essex coast by Germans 15
Morality, decline of 221–8, 238–9
    See also bigamy, Gooley, Madge,
    prostitution, venereal disease
Munich agreement 1, 2, 12
Music 205–6, 214

Nazeing 54, 94
Nazi-Soviet Non-Aggression Pact 142
Newspapers 77–8, 197
Norway, German invasion of 18
Nurseries, war 100–2 see also Women-at-War
    Committee

Ongar 54, 261
Osea Island 80, 86

Paglesham 182
Parachutists, German 26–7
Parkeston 80, 86
Paton, W. W., clergymen and political activist 59, 61, 254
Pebmarsh 86, *96*
Peldon 117, 122–4
Phoney War 14–18, 31
Plaistow 42, 46, 91
Poland, German invasion of 2, 3, 12
Post-war planning 255–61
    See also Housing, Abercrombie, Sir Patrick
Prefabs 259–60, *258*
Priestley, J. B., dramatist and broadcaster 20, 130, 133
Prisoners of war, Italian 110, 158
Prostitution 157, 222–3, 226–8
    see also Gooley, Madge
Purfleet 45

Rationing 74–6, 84, 119, 217–8
Rayleigh 8, 26, 32
Reading 202–4
Ridsdale, C. H., Bishop of Colchester 17, 237
Rochford 13
Rocket weapons, German
    V-1 rockets 161, 263–72, *266, 269*
    V-2 rockets 263, 272–7, *273, 274, 275*
Romford 4, 14, 25, 33, 47, 54
    air raids 54, 55, 56, 61, 162–3
    black market 219
    'conductorettes' 100
    education 187
    invasion committee 65–6
    leisure 206, 212
    V-1 rockets 268
    see also Collier Row
Rowhedge 79, 80, 212
Rudsdale, Eric, diarist 4, 10, 16, 18, 19, 20
    air raids, on Colchester 163, 165
    Allied bombing of Germany, disapproval of 170
    farming official, work as 121–2, 124

foreign troops, dislike of 150–1, 153, 157–8
    Japan, entry into war 172–3
    Land Army girls, disapproval of 97–8
    sex, comments on widespread availability in Colchester 225–6
    Soviet Union, view of 142, 144, 148
    V-1 rockets, personal experience of 265, 266
Ruggles-Brise, Sir Edward, Conservative MP for Maldon until 1942 32, 127–8
Runwell 262

Sadler, Ralph, Executive Officer of EWAC 110, 120, 122, 124
Saffron Walden 11, 13, 27, 29, 85, 105
    American troops 159
    evacuees 185, 187, 194
    farm labourers' wages 116
    farm repossessions 120
    general election 1945 141
    Italian prisoners of war 158
    'treating', young girls and alcohol 224
Sailing 213
Salvage 86–7, 108
Sayers, Dorothy L., Essex crime writer 134
Schools
    Bocking Primary 190
    Bradfield Primary 190
    Brentwood School 38
    Clacton County High School 192
    Colchester County High School for Girls 104, 285
    Colchester Royal Grammar School 177–8
    Gainsborough Road School, East Ham 44
    Hedley Walter School, Brentwood 189
    Lansdowne Road Council School, Tilbury 189
    Layer de la Haye Primary 12
    Lindsell Primary *155*
    Mayflower Primary, Harwich 189–90
    Moulsham Junior Girls, Chelmsford 190, 191

New Hall, Boreham 167
Parsons Heath, Colchester 190
Pebmarsh Primary 191–2
Radwinter Primary 190
Romford Girls' School 3
St Angela Roman Catholic *13*
St John's Green Infants, Colchester 13, 188, 192
St Thomas of Canterbury RC School, Grays 190
Southend High School for Boys 189
South Hallsville 46, *55*, 61–2
Staples Road Infants, Loughton 191
Sybourn Junior School, Leyton 188
Tottenham High School 11, *184*, 187, 194, 229
Trinity County School, Wood Green 184
Victoria Girls and Infants', Chelmsford 38
West Mersea County Primary 12
West Thurrock Primary 188
Second Front 148, 173, 262, 277–8
Sewardstone *267*
Shaw, George Bernard, political activist 133
Shellhaven 39
Shoeburyness 22, *39*
Shopkeepers 74–5, 78
    see also Maldon and Heybridge Cooperative Society
Signposts, removal of *24, 25*
Silvertown, West Ham 41–2, 44, 45, 127
Silver End 67, 81, 92, 128, 136, *186*
Soviet Union 141, 144
Southend 20, 21, 28–9, 30, 78, 84–5
    churches 244–5
    cinema 200
    crime 215, 221–2
    D-Day 277, 279
    education 189
    football 210–11
    general election 141
    holidaymakers 207–8
    housing 260

local rates 88–9
    tramways 85
Southminster 76, 94
South Ockenden 95
Spens, Sir Will, Regional Commissioner for Eastern England 35, 58, 64
Springfield *196*
Stalin, Josef, Soviet dictator 142, 143–5
Stalingrad, Soviet victory 147–8, 176
Stansted Mountfitchet 54
Stratford 41, 44, 50, *266*
Sudetenland, 1–3

Takeley Street 8
Tate and Lyle factory, Plaistow 46, 91
Teachers, women 90, 98, 103
Tendring 99
Tendring coast 54
Terling 67
Thameshaven 39
Theatre 201
Thompson, John Ockleford, Mayor of Chelmsford 61
Thurrock 27
Tilbury 39–40, 100, 125
Tiptree 67, 153, 160
Tobruk, German capture of *135*, 136
Tolleshunt D'Arcy 4, 9, 56
Tolleshunt Knights 54
Transport 84–6, 100, 103
'Trekkers' (refugees from air raids) 45

Upminster 11, 97

Venereal disease 221–2
VE Day (Victory in Europe Day) 282–6, *280, 282, 283, 284*
VJ Day (Victory Over Japan) 286
    See also Atom bombs, use of
V-1 rockets, *see* Rocket Weapons, German
V-2 rockets, *see* Rocket Weapons, German

Walthamstow 35, 40, 49, 59, 64, 219
    V-2 raids 273–4

Waltham Abbey 97

Waltham Holy Cross 35, *90, 261,274, 275*

Walton 66, 72, 78, 88, 245

Wanstead 13, 35, 66, 256

War, declaration of in 1939 8–10

War bonuses 73, 103

War savings 71–2

Wentworth Day, James, agricultural
commentator 117, 123–4

Westcliff-on-Sea 8, 84

West Bergholt 245

West Ham 5, 9, 12, 13, 25, 30–1
   'Black Saturday' 41–7
    churches 247
    education 190, 191, 193
    evacuation 178, 182, 183, 193
    football 211
    Group 7, part of 35
    housing 258–9
    invasion committee 66
    leisure 202
    local government problems after the
    Blitz 57–9
    local rates 89–90
    V-1 and V-2 rockets 270
    see also Silvertown, Plaistow, South
    Hallsville School

West Mersea, *see* Mersea Island

White Colne 86

Wickham Bishops 63, 67

Wilson, Henry, Bishop of Chelmsford 20, 31,
143, 144, 145–6, 147
   atom bomb, view on use of 286–7
   curfew on young girls 224
   Japan, opinion on entry into war 173
   national failings, as factors in early
   defeats 238, 240
   pastoral role 250–2
   social change, and the Church 243
   Soviet Union, views on 148–9
   Sunday observance, decline of 239
   war fever, disapproves of 237–8

Wilson, Stanley, county councillor 27, 57,
73–4

Wireless 195–7, *196*

Witham 54, 86, 94, 128, 136, *284*

Wivenhoe 79, *79*, 108, 212

Wix 23

Women, in factories 91–3, 100–1

Women-at-War Committee 101–2

Women's Auxiliary Police Force 99

Women's fashion 105–6

Women's Institute 107–8, 173, 255

Women's Land Army 6, 82, 90, 93–8, *96*, 103, 110

Women's Voluntary Service (WVS) 102,
108–9, 166

Women wardens *261, 90*

Woodford 13, 35, 141, 256

Woodford Wells *68*

Writtle 71, 235

EP

Essex Publications is a new imprint of University of Hertfordshire Press created to publish important scholarly studies on the historic county of Essex. Produced in collaboration with an editorial panel of experienced Essex historians, the series will reflect the long and complex history of Essex in volumes that cover both a chronologically long timespan and a wide variety of themes, including social, economic, cultural, environmental, architectural and military history. Books in the series will include individual monographs, collected studies and conference proceedings. They may encompass material on the whole county of Essex or on specific areas or places, but the content and analysis will always address topics of wider historical interest and debate. For more details, please see www.herts.ac.uk/uhpress.